Following the Drum

FOLLOWING THE DRUM

The Lives of Army Wives
and Daughters, Past and Present

Annabel Venning

headline

First published in 2005
by HEADLINE BOOK PUBLISHING

10 9 8 7 6 5 4 3 2 1

Cataloguing in Publication Data is available from the British Library

ISBN 0 7553 1258 9

Typeset in Bembo by Palimpsest Book Production Ltd,
Polmont, Stirlingshire

Printed and bound in Great Britain by Clays Ltd, St Ives plc

Headline's policy is to use papers that are natural, renewable and
recyclable products and made from wood grown in sustainable
forests. The logging and manufacturing processes are expected to
conform to the environmental regulations of the country of origin.

Text design by Ben Cracknell Studios

HEADLINE BOOK PUBLISHING
A division of Hodder Headline
338 Euston Road
London NW1 3BH

www.headline.co.uk
www.hodderheadline.com

For Guy

Contents

Acknowledgements

Following the Drum has, more than many books, been a collaborative effort. It could not have been written without the assistance and co-operation of a large number of people, who have kindly given up their time, lent their expertise and shared their memories.

First, I am hugely grateful to all the army wives, past and present, who bravely agreed to be interviewed. The more of them I spoke to, the more impressed I became by the challenges that they faced and the qualities that enabled them to cope. I have acknowledged all my interviewees in the bibliography, but I would particularly like to thank the late Cecilia Ross-Hurst and her family, who allowed me to interview her even when she was very ill. Although she does not appear in the book by name, she – and others who are not directly quoted – provided invaluable background. All the interviewees put up with my relentless and often irritating questions with unruffled good humour, many of them at busy or difficult times in their lives. Numerous army wives around Warminster in Wiltshire have also kindly allowed me to infiltrate their coffee mornings, pick their brains at toddlers' groups and interrogate them about their lives.

A number of people kindly gave me access to their private family papers: Mrs Philippa Szymusik gave me permission to use the memoirs of her mother, Barbara Egerton; Colonel and Mrs Peter Wade allowed me to use the papers of Molly Wade (née Ellis) and extended their generous hospitality; Richard Viner; the Man family; Mr and Mrs David Atkin-Berry; Miss Ann Birch; Mrs Betty Bootland; Mr Gerald Delaney.

If Army wives are the unsung heroines of British military history, then regimental museums and their curators and archivists are the unrecognized treasure troves of British social history. When I began this project one of my first tasks was to write to every regimental museum and archive in the country. I was impressed by the alacrity with which they responded and the mine of fascinating information that they were ready to put at my disposal. Among the many who helped me I am particularly grateful to the following: Major Hugo White and the staff of Duke of Cornwall's Light Infantry Museum; Rebecca Cheney at the Royal Engineers Museum; Colonel David Eliot at the Somerset Military Museum; Major Gerald Davies at the Gurkha Museum; WW Smith at the Gordon Highlanders Museum; John Lowles at the Worcestershire Regiment Museum; Lieutenant Colonel Roger Binks at the Royal Scots Dragoon Guards Museum; Lieutenant Colonel A Cumming, Regimental Headquarters, the Highlanders; Major Derek Gilliam at the Royal Electrical and Mechanical Engineers Museum of Technology; Paul Evans at Firepower! The Royal Artillery Museum; Peter Donelly at the King's Own Royal Regiment Museum; Peter Crocker at Amgueddfa, The Royal Welch Fusiliers Regimental Museum; Roger Chapman at the Green Howards Museum; Amanda Moreno at the Royal Irish Fusiliers Museum; Lieutenant Colonel John Darroch at the Royal Hampshire Regiment Museum; George Fraser at the Durham Light Infantry Museum; Ian Hook at the Essex Regiment Museum; Ian Maine at Aldershot Military Museum & Rushmoor Local History Gallery; Malcolm Sunter at the Fusiliers Museum of Northumberland; Captain J O'Grady at the Fusiliers Museum Lancashire; Royal Scots Regimental Museum; Royal Regiment of Fusiliers (Northumberland) Museum; Royal Leicestershire Regiment Museum; Museum of The Royal Hospital Chelsea; Museum of the Queen's Own Highlanders, Inverness; The Sherwood Foresters Museum; The Queen's Own Royal West Kent Regiment Museum; The Queen's Lancashire Regiment Museum; The Military Museum of Devon and Dorset; The Princess of Wales's Royal Regiment and Queen's Regiment Museum; Northamptonshire Regiment Museum; Museum of the Manchester Regiment; Castle and Regimental Museum, Monmouth; Newarke Houses Museum; Regimental Museum, 1st the Queen's Dragoon Guards; Jenny Rose Miller of Nairn Museum

I am also grateful to the following organisations and individuals who have helped me with research, contacts, information and other assistance: the staff of the British Library, the archive of the Centre of South Asian Studies at the University of Cambridge, the National Army Museum, the SSAFA archive and the consistently helpful librarians at Warminster library; the Army Families Federation (AFF); Burma Star Association; Far East Prisoners of War & Internees Fund; National Federation of Far Eastern POW Clubs & Associations; Children and Families of the Far East Prisoners of War (COFEPOW); the Victoria Cross Society; General Sir Michael Walker GCB CMG CBE ADC, Chief of the Defence Staff; Sue Bonney, former editor of AFF Journal; Colonel Peter Knox of the Crimean War Research Society; Colonel and Mrs Peter Andrews; Vanessa Andreae; James Holland; Colonel Les Wilson; Liz Rowlinson; the late Lynda Lee-Potter; John and Sybil Venning; Julia Weston; Glen and Mary-Jane Ogden.

Although my bibliography lists the sources I have consulted, I would like to acknowledge the particular debts I owe to the following works: Richard Holmes' *Redcoat: the British Soldier in the Age of Horse and Musket,* which not only brilliantly conveys the flavour of the era but pointed me towards many diaries and other sources which have been invaluable; Correlli Barnett's *Britain and Her Army* for the background against which my stories take place; Myna Trustram's *Women of the Regiment,* which helped to corroborate and explain information I found in pamphlets and other primary sources; David Bevan's *Standfast,* on whose superb narration of the sinking of the *Birkenhead* I lent for my retelling of that event; EEP Tisdall's *Mrs Duberly's Campaigns,* which proved the ideal companion to her own journals, and on which I drew for her letters; Jane Robinson's *Angels of Albion* for her account of the siege of Cawnpore, including Amy Horne's narrative; Piers Compton's *Colonel's Lady and Camp Follower.* I have also consulted two other histories of army wives, Veronica Bamfield's *On the Strength* and Noel St John William's *Judy O'Grady and the Colonel's Lady.*

I am very grateful to my publishers, Headline: to Heather Holden-Brown who first took up the idea with enthusiasm; Juliana Foster who became my editor and devoted her considerable energy and skill to improving it; Christine King, my copy-editor, whose remarkable ability to prune and remodel made it very much more readable; and to Val Hudson, Cathie Arrington, Rebecca Purtell and the sales and marketing teams whose support has been invaluable.

I am also deeply thankful that I was able to call upon the expertise of Colonel Sir William Mahon Bt. He guided me through the minefield of regimental nomenclature and military terminology and history, as well as setting me right on many other matters. Any remaining errors or omissions are my responsibility and will be corrected for the paperback edition.

I am indebted to Tif Loehnis, my agent, and her team at Janklow and Nesbit, who displayed faith and enthusiasm and supported me throughout this project.

None of this would have been possible without my family. First, my late grandmother, Beryl Walker, whose own memoir, *Following the Drum,* was the inspiration behind this book; my parents, Richard and Venetia Venning and my parents-in-law Martin and Angela Walters who have helped with research, contacts, advice and support; my sister, Belinda Venning, whose hospitality was vital to my research trips; my son, William, who has had to put up with a frequently preoccupied mother for the first two years of his life; Paula Wood (who is honorary family); baby Alice, whose gestation period has coincided with the writing of this book; and my husband, Guy Walters, to whom it is dedicated, and without whose unfailing encouragement and support it would have remained a pipe dream.

Introduction

India: August 1947. In the hill station of Simla, a lone British woman walks purposefully through the bazaar, disregarding all the warnings of the police, in order to buy fresh fruit and vegetables for her six-month-old baby and young twins. She is knowingly taking a huge risk, for Simla – like almost all of India – is in turmoil. With independence from British rule, the country has been partitioned into mainly Hindu India and the new Muslim state of Pakistan. But in an atmosphere of panic and suspicion, sectarian violence has broken out on a massive scale and brought about a nationwide bloodbath, in which hundreds of thousands of people are being slaughtered. The young British woman and her children are awaiting evacuation, staying in a hotel. At night, their bedroom is filled with Muslim servants, hiding from Hindu and Sikh killing mobs. Eventually the family is evacuated out of Simla and across India under armed guard, and boards a ship for Malaya, where the woman is reunited with her husband.

The young woman was my maternal grandmother, Beryl Walker. When I first came across her brief account of the final days of British India, entitled *Following the Drum*, I was struck by the resourcefulness and courage she must have needed to bring three small children safely through this chaotic, frightening episode, with her husband thousands of miles away. I began to wonder how many other women had, by virtue of their husbands' military careers, undergone similarly dramatic experiences and witnessed other seminal points in Britain's history as they followed the drums of their husbands' regiments around the world. While the soldiers travelled across oceans, marched over mountains and plains to garrison the outposts of Empire and defend Britain's interests across the globe, what of their wives and families?

Through my own family, I knew that army wives often spent much of their lives exiled from Britain and long periods apart from their husbands. They had to be strong, practical and resilient. My great-grandmother, Lucy Venning, began married life in the hills of Burma. During her husband's frequent absences, she spent her time writing him letters, collecting botanical specimens and looking after her four children. My paternal grand-mother (her daughter-in-law), married in India and also spent much of her time alone while her husband fought on the North West Frontier. Like many of the women I would come to know through their memoirs and journals, she found that life as a 'wife of' could sometimes be tough. One of her most testing moments was when she gave birth in Kashmir, Northern India, only for her newborn son to be struck down with dysentery. The baby (my father) survived, but many infants did not – garrison cemeteries in India and beyond are full of the gravestones of army children, testimony to the price paid by army families in the defence of the British Empire.

My mother too had her share of travels, first as an army daughter then as a wife, moving house on an almost annual basis from Hong Kong to Brunei, Germany to England, and back again. As a child I revelled in the excitement of stepping off the plane at the start of school holidays to discover a new home. Finding snakes under the bed or a scorpion on the breakfast table, and being allowed to fire a machine gun, made life as a 'barrack rat' an adventure. But as I grew older it dawned on me that for my mother, and for other wives, the instability of such an existence, the frequent separations from husband and children, the constant presence of packing boxes in the hall, could be challenging and at times difficult, and that tensions often existed between family life and the requirements placed on soldiers by the army.

My interest awakened, I began to look beyond my family's experience and to research the lives of other army wives. The more I read, the more intrigued I became as I discovered that many of these women had led lives that were often every bit as peripatetic, hard and dangerous as those of the men they followed. Today, families usually remain at home when the army goes to war, to watch, wait and hope; I was surprised to learn that in former times the lines between family and regimental life were much more blurred. While most women were left behind when the soldiers marched off to war, a small number went with them to perform such vital tasks as washing, nursing and cooking for the men. They also shared in many of their hardships. When the army marched through snowy mountain passes or icy streams, behind the orderly columns of men came the women, riding on baggage carts if they were lucky, but often on foot, many of them carrying children on their backs. Sometimes, like the men, their feet were bare and their stomachs ached with hunger. Those who had to give birth by the roadside had no alternative but to gather up their babies and hurry on. Some women actually went on to the battlefield itself, to tend their wounded husbands, or to search for their corpses after the battle was over. Others were caught up in the excitement of the moment and wanted to be part of the battle. A few even disguised themselves as men and fought as soldiers until their identity was revealed.

My research began with published journals and memoirs written, or related, by army wives themselves. But many women who were involved in some of the most dramatic episodes possessed neither the inclination nor the ability to record their experiences; fortunately, some of their stories are recorded in regimental histories and by the soldiers or officers who encountered them. Women's presence is evident too in official military records, from the standing orders published by the commanding officer of every regiment laying down the rules and standards of behaviour expected of the men and their families, to the records kept of courts martial. Despite the passage of years, even centuries, these stories – of husbands and wives, parents and children, relationships coming under strain amid the pressures of war or living abroad in a close-knit community – spring from the page with all the immediacy of a contemporary newspaper report or television drama.

As well as researching historical records, I wanted to build up a picture of modern army wives. I talked to many of them (and the odd husband), and was struck by the fact that while in most ways modern army spouses are immeasurably better off than their eighteenth- or nineteenth-century counterparts, they have to face many of the same challenges. They still need to be resilient and resourceful to cope with circumstances that few of their civilian contemporaries encounter. As well as raising children and running households while their husbands are away for long periods, they increasingly have to face the prospect of waving their husbands off to fight in some of the world's most notorious trouble-spots, from which every incident and casualty is reported within hours by the media. Again and again I was impressed by their stoicism: whenever I asked how they had dealt with the anxieties and pressures, the phrase that I heard repeatedly was, 'You just get on with it.'

Not all women have coped heroically, of course. Alongside the angels of mercy who risked their lives to go to the rescue of wounded men, loyal wives who stuck like barnacles to their husbands' sides through every hardship and disaster, and Samaritans who rallied round to help their fellow wives in times of need, there were women who put self-preservation before compassion – flirts and adulteresses, and drunkards whose love of liquor overcame whatever good intentions they may have had of doing their duty to their husbands and the army.

Although women have followed armies of whatever nationality for as long as men have fought – in the capacity of wives, mistresses, prostitutes, providers of food and drink and in many other guises – I have focused on the British army and taken as my starting point the 1660s. It was in 1661 that the newly restored Charles II signed a Royal Warrant authorising the creation of a 'Standing Army', and some of the oldest regiments in the British army can trace their service to the British Crown back to that date. So although the modern British army was not 'born' in 1661, the year marks an important stage in its evolution. It was in the 1660s too that the Moroccan port of Tangier came into English possession, brought by Charles's wife Catherine of Braganza as part of the marriage settlement. A garrison was established there to secure it, and it was not long before the troops' wives and children followed the drum to join them.

The stories I have chosen range from those days in the 1660s to the present day, from the battlefields of Europe and America to the Japanese internment camps of the Second World War and the ongoing conflict in Iraq. To bring out the similarities and contrasts in the lives of army wives through the ages, I have arranged the book by theme rather than chrono-logically or geographically. So I look at how women met their men in the first place, their courtship and early days of marriage, followed by their experience of travelling across the globe, or being forced to stay at home and in many cases endure a poverty-stricken existence. Whatever the circumstances, army wives have had to make a home for their families and look after their children – even if this has often meant enduring long separations from them. Living with the army has also meant observing the duties, rules and codes of behaviour (both written and unwritten) expected not only of its soldiers, but of their wives and children too. Failure to conform has sometimes had a heavy price. But as well as duty there are the pleasures of travel, romance and a vibrant social life – which might come to a shuddering halt when conflict erupted and women and children, as much as men, could be under siege, held captive – or in flight from that fate – or find themselves in the line of fire. Finally, there is the spectre that sets women who marry soldiers apart from their civilian sisters: the heightened prospect of sudden widowhood, when for them the drum beats no more.

Inevitably there is some overlap in these themes, just as in the lives of the women themselves the boundaries were frequently blurred. Women whose primary function was to make a home for their husbands and families could suddenly find themselves forced to perform very different roles as their lives were turned upside-down by war or revolt. In contrast to their men, they constantly had to combine domestic duties with the imperatives of the moment, nursing babies through the night and then taking their turn on watch duty in a siege, or marching all day and then being ready with refreshments for their weary husbands.

In recent years, women have been able to follow the drum as professional soldiers rather than in the supporting role of wives and daughters. Considerable as their achievements are, they are not included here: this book is about women who found themselves catapulted into extraordinary circumstances because of their relationship to the soldiers they followed, rather than through choosing a military career themselves.

Those professional women soldiers still give rise to controversy in some quarters, their full role in the military hotly debated. In earlier years, the subject of women's presence with the army, not as soldiers but as followers, was every bit as contentious.

I

Marriage and the Military

But you, my dear girl, how can I bear your being deprived of
the comforts and station in society which my wife had a right
to expect? My dearest girl in barracks; the wife of a soldier
in a marching regiment; subject to all sorts of annoyance
and privation! It makes me miserable.

> George Osborne to his fiancée Amelia, before
> his regiment left for the Waterloo campaign,
> in William Thackeray's *Vanity Fair*

From the seventeenth to the nineteenth centuries (and before), it was
common for women to accompany the soldiers of European armies
– though the practice was always controversial. Those who opposed it argued
that women were parasites and encumbrances on an army; those in favour
argued just as strongly that they were useful appendages. In 1683 the military authority Sir James Turner broached the subject in his classic history
of warfare, *Pallas Armata, Military Essayes of the Ancient Grecian, Roman and
Modern Art of War*. Turner, a Scotsman who himself served in several different armies on the continent and in the British Isles, represented the viewpoint that women, if they were morally upright and decent creatures, might
bring a civilising influence to bear upon the men as well as being of practical use: 'As a woman was created to be a helpmate to man, so women are
great helpers to armies, to their husbands, especially those of the lower
conditions.' He therefore advocated tolerating their presence in small

numbers. Not only did women, he pointed out, 'provide, buy and dress their husbands meat when their husbands are on duty, or newly come from it, they bring in fewel for fire, and wash their linens, and in such manner of employments a Souldiers wife may be helpful to her husband and her self'.

Such sentiments are echoed today by the current Chief of the Defence Staff, General Sir Michael Walker. He is keen to quash any notion that wives and families are not welcomed. Around 50 per cent of today's soldiers are married and this, he insists, is a benefit for the army – wives exerting a moderating influence on their husbands – and should be treated as such.

In former times, the army authorities would often have disagreed vehemently, seeing women as simply a drain on scarce resources, a distraction from the business of soldiéring, even an incitement to vice. In the seventeenth century, the armies of German states were attended by wives, and other women, in such numbers that 'Hureweibles' – described by Turner as 'Rulers or Marshalls of the Whores' – had to be placed in command of them. By the time of the Peninsular War in the early nineteenth century, an infuriated French general complained that Napoleon's invading army in Spain resembled 'a walking bordello'. For many commanders the mere absence of women was not enough – they preferred their soldiers free from matrimony in the first place, and sought to limit it by regulation, persuasion and punishment, although legally they could not actually prevent them marrying. James Wolfe, who became a general and the hero of Quebec in 1759, was himself a bachelor (although he was engaged at the time of his death). As a commanding officer, he constantly tried to impress upon his soldiers the incompatibility of marital and martial life. His subordinate officers were ordered to 'discourage Matrimony amongst the men as much as possible, the Service suffers bye the Multitude of Women already in the Regiment'.

Wolfe and others of his persuasion were helped in their mission by the infamous reputation of the 'rapacious and licentious soldiery', as the eighteenth-century political theorist Edmund Burke memorably described it, which made many parents anxious to protect their precious daughters from such debased creatures. Numerous plays and ballads attested to the faithlessness and profligacy of soldiers, and the inadvisability of becoming involved with them. Their popular image as heartless seducers was immortalised in such characters as the rakish Captain Wickham in Jane Austen's *Pride and Prejudice* and the duplicitous Sergeant Troy in Thomas Hardy's *Far from the Madding Crowd*.

Prejudice against soldiers was exemplified by a polemic published in the

London journal *Spy* in 1700. A soldier, it concluded, 'is generally beloved by two sorts of Companion, in whores and lice; for both these Vermin are great admirers of a Scarlet Coat'. By allying herself with such a reviled character, a soldier's bride subjected herself to such perceptions. On the brighter side, when the army rode high in public esteem, usually in the wake of great victories or when the security of the country seemed to be at risk, the families of soldiers sometimes benefited from the outbreaks of patriotism and sympathy for soldiers that ensued. A poem popular among the rank and file of the seventeenth to nineteenth centuries bitterly mocked this attitude:

> *When war is proclaimed and the dangers nigh*
> *'God and our soldiers' is the people's cry.*
> *But when peace is proclaimed and all things righted,*
> *God is forgot and the soldier slighted.*

And slighted too were his wife and children. Even today, when they are officially 'welcome' in the army itself, soldiers' wives and families are still seen by outsiders as being part of the military community, and can be affected by the same views and prejudices that are directed towards soldiers themselves. Some army wives complain of discrimination when they apply for jobs, and even when they try to enrol their children in local schools in Britain. A recent chairman of the Army Families Federation (the body that lobbies on behalf of army families) observed that some schools think the children of 'squaddies' are 'trouble'.

But despite all the warnings and the obstacles, there have always been women who have thrilled to the idea of marrying a soldier, complete with glamorous uniform and tales of wartime glory. Equally, many women have fallen for a man despite, rather than because of, his military calling. The forces of military and parental disapproval, the spectres of danger, dislocation and poverty, frequently failed to overcome the powers of love and attraction. Indeed, one story, related by Peter Henly, a soldier who first enlisted in the army in 1858, illustrates the lengths that some girls would go to in order to follow their soldier sweethearts.

A young recruit in Henly's regiment was caught stealing turnips from a farmer's field while the regiment was on the march from Brompton to Portsmouth. The soldier was sentenced to 200 lashes for the offence but, before the punishment began, suddenly announced that she was in fact a young woman. An officer's lady was called upon to examine her and verified her claim: she was discharged. Before leaving, the young woman explained the reason for her elaborate charade. It transpired that she was from a wealthy family but had fallen in love with a soldier. He proposed marriage but, when her father discovered the relationship, he was furious. Hearing that a draft of soldiers from his regiment was to be sent abroad, the father persuaded the commanding officer to include his daughter's beau in their number. He accordingly left the city and his distraught lover could not discover where he had been sent. She resolved to find him and 'therefore left her father's house, dressed herself in men's attire, and went in pursuit of her love. Hearing of our encampment at Brumpton [sic] when on her travels, she thought she would go and see if probably she might find him, and was on her pursuit when she enlisted, and supposing our regiment was going abroad, she enlisted, to have a better chance of finding him, whom she so much adored.'

Married men were not supposed to be knowingly recruited, though many recruiting sergeants ignored this prohibition and urged them to enlist as a way of escaping their domestic ties. A ditty from George Farquhar's play *The Recruiting Officer*, popular in the time of Queen Anne, urged that:

> *We then shall lead more happy lives*
> *By getting rid of brats and wives,*
> *That scold on both night and day,*
> *When o'er the hills and far away.*

In the play, first performed in 1706, the wily Sergeant Kite beguiles potential recruits with the patter: 'If any 'prentices have severe masters, any children have undutiful parents, if any servants have too little wages, or any husband too much wife, let them repair to the noble Sergeant Kite, at the sign of the Raven in this good town of Shrewsbury, and they shall receive present relief and entertainment.' Other recruiting officers enticed young men with the idea that as soon as they donned their dashing uniforms they would possess an irresistible attraction for the fairer sex – an incentive still being exploited towards the end of the nineteenth century. 'My lad, you've only to 'list,' promised one silver-tongued recruiter for the 14th Hussars, 'and . . . you'll get your fun and plenty to drink free gratis; for the girls will fight for you, and you'll always find a Christian ready to stand treat. The Fourteenth,' he added, with a wink of his eye and a cock of his head, 'get the pick of the girls wherever they go.'

So who were the women who were prepared to follow their men across the globe to countries that many of them had barely heard of, or to wait at home for months or years for the return of a husband who might die from disease or in battle before they were reunited? How did they meet, fall in love and marry?

The army cannot but reflect the society from which it recruits. As General Sir Michael Walker says of today's military, 'It would be as wrong for it to try and be a beacon of social behaviour for others to follow, as it would be for it to fail to inculcate the standards and values that are important for the conduct of the brutal and terrifying, life and death, environment in which it must conduct its ultimate business.' Likewise, women who marry into the army come from right across society's spectrum, in the past strongly reflecting entrenched class divisions of society in the relationship between officer and rank and file.

Until the army became more professionalised in the latter half of the nineteenth century and the system of purchasing commissions was abolished in 1871, the majority of officers came from the wealthy or landed classes. A public school education and a suitable family back-ground were prerequisites. They were expected, when they married, to take wives from the same social class, women who were schooled in etiquette, who were respectable and unblemished by scandal, could be relied upon to hold a dinner party, run a household, dance a quadrille and, should their husbands reach senior rank, assume a role that lay some-where between vicar's wife and lady of the manor, dispensing pastoral care and occasional beneficence to the bachelor officers and soldiers' families. If an officer erred in his choice of mate and his regiment disapproved, he could be forced to choose between the two. As recently as the 1970s many regiments persisted in closely vetting their officers' fiancées to ascertain whether their character and background were 'suitable'. Some even claim that those whose fiancées failed the test could find themselves receiving hints that perhaps they might like to find another girl, or another regiment.

Ordinary soldiers, from 1685 onwards, had to ask formal permission from their senior officers before they could marry (and still do today). They were not eligible until they had amassed a certain length of service and a record of good conduct. The character of their bride-to-be was also carefully examined before approval was given. While being against soldiers' matrimony on principle, James Wolfe insisted that if his men must marry, they should at least choose wives who would pull their weight: 'Many Women in the Regts are very inconvenient,' he complained. 'Specially as some of them are not so industrious, nor so useful to their husbands, as a Soldiers wife ought to be.'

As well as being industrious, prospective soldiers' brides had to be morally acceptable. Soldiers who fell for women of dubious morals were likely to be refused permission, as the entry for 2 December 1727 in the Gibraltar Garrison Order Book records. 'Yesterday, a private gentleman [i.e. soldier] desired leave to marry a woman of the town that was the friend [i.e. mistress] of a pretty fellow in the town – not a soldier – but instead of receiving an answer in the affirmative, was sent to cool his courage in the black hole for the night and this morning for breakfast received one hundred lashes for presuming to marry a lady of no good reputation.' Next day the soldier, though 'his back was like raw head and bloody bones', was back again before his Commanding Officer, renewing his request 'to marry the lady for whom he had the honour to suffer'. The CO, 'in consideration of his sufferings and undaunted gallantry', relented and the nuptials were celebrated 'with great pomp and splendor [sic] that afternoon'. Although not, perhaps, by the discarded civilian lover.

Even if the fiancée concerned was morally unimpeachable, industrious and capable and her husband had earned the requisite rank and good conduct badges, the marriage would still not be allowed unless a vacancy existed on the 'married roll'. From the late seventeenth until the twentieth century, only a small number of soldiers were permitted to marry. In most regiments the limit was set at around 6 per cent of the strength, although sometimes it was only 4 per cent and in other cases 12 per cent or higher. It was estimated that an equal number of soldiers married without permission. Their wives were deemed to be 'off the strength' and were denied the recognition and privileges of officially sanctioned wives. They were not eligible to sleep in barracks, to undertake such regimental duties as cooking, cleaning and laundry (thus denying them one of the few sources of income open to soldiers' wives with their highly mobile lifestyles). They were forbidden either to travel abroad with the regiment when it was sent overseas, or to remain in barracks as official wives were sometimes permitted to. The 'off the strength' wife was left, quite literally, out in the cold.

Despite all the efforts to convince them otherwise, many soldiers considered that a wife was indispensable to their comfort and welfare, and were not even too fussy about who and how they wed. The history of the King's Own Regiment records that, shortly before the regiment departed Hythe for Canterbury in March 1805, a drummer of the regiment went to the market-place and for sixpence bought a labourer's wife of not more than twenty years of age and 'of a likely figure'. The uxorious John Shipp, who served both as a soldier and an officer in the nineteenth century and wrote a memoir of his military life, would have understood the man's motive for acquiring a wife (if not his unromantic manner of doing so). Shipp was a firm believer in the beneficial effects that women had on soldiers. 'What is a man's life, debarred the pleasure of female society?' he asked rhetorically. 'Men are little better than monsters without it. Wherever modest women are, there will always be a becoming decorum and decency; but men, when long estranged from their society, dwindle into gross habits; and the hilarity of an immodest song, and the cup of inebriety, form their pleasures, and the summit of their felicity.'

Those women who did satisfy the criteria still had to work hard to earn their place with the army. Regimental standing orders frequently refer to this bargain. Those of the 90th Perthshire Light Infantry in 1831 are fairly typical: 'No woman is to be allowed in Barracks who objects to making herself useful in cleaning the rooms, cooking etc. It cannot be too often repeated to the men that they are on no account to marry without leave and their marriage must at all times be discouraged as much as possible. It is impossible to point out the inconveniences that arise, and the evils which follow a Regiment encumbered with women. Officers, therefore, cannot do too much to deter their men from marrying; and there are few men, however hard they may think it at the moment, that after a short period will not be much obliged to them for having done so.'

Among the plethora of 'evils' was the problem of housing the women, transporting them when the regiment went overseas, and the question of what to do about the ones who were left behind. Other officers pointed to the near impossibility of supporting a wife and family on a soldier's lowly wage when it was difficult enough for the soldier to survive on it (in the nineteenth century the army was known as 'the Hungry Army'). The fact that the number of unofficial marriages kept steady pace with those officially permitted, and that every time a regiment embarked overseas a party of distraught wives and children were left behind, shows how little such admonitions were heeded. The dire warnings of poverty and uncertainty, discomfort and roughness held less potency for those who were either too captivated to care or, coming from tough, impoverished circumstances, had too little to lose. Living in a barrack room with fifty soldiers was less of a hardship for women who had spent their lives in smoky hovels, sharing beds with their siblings and labouring hard for a living.

Moreover, to expect every private soldier to remain single and celibate at the prime of life was far from realistic, especially as soldiers enlisted for life (in practice this meant twenty-five years). In Victorian times a combination of the idealisation of marriage and motherhood, the soaring rates of venereal disease and their catastrophic effect on manpower, and concerns about recruitment, led for calls to allow more soldiers to marry. Rather than increase the size of the married establishment, in 1847 limited enlistment was introduced allowing soldiers to serve only ten or twelve years, and in 1870 this was reduced to six years. The rationale was that although men still might not be able to marry while in the army, they would still be young enough when they left to start a family. This had the result of reducing the married establishment to only one in twenty-five of the rank and file. Marriage became a perk reserved largely for senior non-commissioned officers (two-thirds of sergeants and all staff sergeants being allowed to marry).

Officers also had to seek permission from their commanding officers before they could marry, and could not join the married strength until they had attained a certain age and seniority (which varied over the years). Men who fell in love 'before their time' had to resign themselves to a long engagement, while their fiancées waited at home. (And even if they were eligible to marry, they often found that their salary was insufficient to support a wife and family to the expected standard.) Permission to marry did not, however, depend on the size of the married establishment in their regiment. Nor were their wives subject to the quota that dictated how many could live within barracks, or how many could accompany the regiment abroad.

One very basic obstacle to matrimony, especially for soldiers, was the difficulty of meeting a suitable girl in the first place. Many returned to their home town or village on leave and used the opportunity to rekindle the flames of a childhood romance. Others, however, found that by the time they had amassed the necessary years and badges of good conduct to qualify for permission to marry, their former sweethearts might have been deterred by family opposition, or become anxious about being left on the shelf, and married someone else. Furthermore, many regiments spent long periods on overseas service and soldiers might not see their home country for a dozen years. If they became eligible to marry 'on the strength' they had to find a bride from among the local population, or within the regimental community. In Gibraltar, Minorca and other garrisons close to home, and in America and Canada too, soldiers found a ready supply of brides. Corporal William Todd, who fought in the Seven Years War in the mid-eighteenth century, noted that during a long spell of fighting in the German states, several of his comrades took German wives – just like their counterparts in the twentieth and twenty-first centuries who, spending large parts of their careers in Germany, have often intermarried with the local population. In the nineteenth century a large number of soldiers' brides came from Ireland, partly reflecting the large proportion of Irish recruits in the army, but also the fact that a substantial part of the British army was stationed in Ireland (in 1871 a quarter of the army's home-strength was there). In Ireland, as on the British mainland, these women were generally from the poorest neighbourhoods: those who had least to lose by marrying a soldier.

Local brides were not always considered suitable marriage material, at least by the authorities. When the 11th Regiment spent a long period on garrison duty in Minorca, from 1763 to 1771, many of the soldiers married Minorcan women who, complained the officers, were unsuitable material as soldiers' wives, being 'too lazy and good for nothing to earn their own livelihood'. Conversely, marriage might be opposed by the woman's family. In the Peninsular War, many British soldiers pursued romances with Spanish and Portuguese women, some of whose families – particularly those from the higher social classes – strongly objected. If the soldiers were Protestant then they were even more unsuitable, regarded as heretics by the Catholic Spaniards.

Such opposition did not deter one young Spanish girl, Jacintha Cherito. The daughter of a wealthy landowner, she fell in love with the handsome drum-major of the 88th Connaught Rangers, a man named Thorp, and determined to marry him despite the objections of her father. The night before the regiment left her town she took her jewellery and stole away to the British camp. Her enraged father, finding her missing, presented himself to the regiment's commanding officer and requested that he be allowed to search the departing column for his daughter, determined to prevent an elopement. Captain Grattan, an officer in the regiment, reported, 'The cars were examined, the baggage-mules were overhauled, the commissariat mules, carrying ammunition, biscuit, and rum, were looked at, but amongst all these no trace of the fugitive could be found. What, then, was to be done? There was but one other chance of finding the girl, and this was a survey of the officers' horses, as the officers rode at the head or in rear of the column.' To the father's puzzlement, his daughter was nowhere to be seen.

'The band played a quick march; Thorp, as Drum-Major, flourished his cane; the daughter of the Juiz de Fora, in her new and disguised character of cymbal-boy, with her face blacked, and regimental jacket, banged the Turkish cymbals, and Thorp, who as Drum-Major was destined to make a noise in the world, was for obvious reasons silent on this occasion. The regiment reached Monte Forte the same day, and the *padre* of that town performed the marriage ceremony in due form.' The couple were not destined to enjoy married life for long. Thorp was cut in two by a roundshot in the final battle of the Peninsular War, at Toulouse, and his young Spanish wife became a widow. 'The day after his death the English mail brought the [London] Gazette, in which poor Thorp's name was seen as promoted to an ensigncy in his old regiment [an officer's rank]; and though this announcement came too late for him to know it, it was a great consolation to his poor afflicted widow, and it was the means of reconciling her father to the choice she had made, and her return once more to her home was made a scene of great rejoicing; but nothing more of her was ever heard by the regiment.'

The alternative to intermarrying with the local population was to import potential British brides. In the earliest days of the British presence in India, the East India Company had followed the example of the Portuguese settlers in shipping out women from England to India to provide a ready supply of suitable wives for soldiers and Company employees. Classed as 'gentlewomen' and 'other women', they were given an allowance to maintain them for a year in India, during which time they were expected to find a husband. Those who failed either had to return home 'empty', or eke out some kind of existence in India. Those who stayed on and behaved immorally were warned that they faced being arrested and fed with bread and water. By the nineteenth century these cargoes of hopeful young damsels, known derisively as the 'Fishing Fleet', were still attracting scorn. A verse of 1813 ridiculed the girls who, after a year or so in India's harsh climate, had already lost the fresh bloom of youth and were trying desperately to repair their jaded looks.

> *Pale faded stuffs, by time grown faint*
> *will brighten up through* art
> *A* Britain *gives their faces paint,*
> *For sale at India's mart.*

More than a century later, these luckless lasses were still the object of satire. A poem published in the *Illustrated Weekly of India* in 1936 mocked:

> *Now sail the chagrined fishing fleet*
> *Yo ho, my girls, yo ho!*
> *Back to Putney and Byfleet*
> *Poor girls, you were too slow!*
> *Your Bond Street beauty sadly worn*
> *Through drinking cocktails night and morn*
> *With moonlight picnics until dawn*
> *What ho! My girls, what ho!*

By then the days of the East India Company paying the board and lodging of prospective brides had long since passed, and it was the girls and their families who had to bear the expense and shame of their failed fishing trip. Even in the seventeenth century some had entertained doubts about the expediency of encouraging boatloads of marriage-hungry young women to land on India's shores. Rather than having to bear the expense of supporting them, and the embarrassment of what to do with them if they failed in their matrimonial mission, the Madras government decided to 'induce by all means our Soldiers to marry with Native women because it will be impossible to get ordinary young women to pay their own passages'.

Many soldiers, officers and civilians needed little encouragement to take local women as mistresses or even wives (although not all went through official marriage ceremonies). The renowned soldier, diplomat and explorer Richard Burton, who served in India in the mid-nineteenth century, explained the charms of the native consort. 'She keeps house for him, never allowing him to save money, or if possible to waste it. She keeps the servants in order. She has an infallible recipe to prevent maternity, especially if her tenure of office depends on such compact. She looks after him in sickness, and is one of the best of nurses, and, as it is not good for man to live alone, she makes him a manner of a home.' But even by Burton's time, the heyday of the native consort was all but over. The advent of the steamship, combined with a new sense of racial superiority and evangelical fervour that disdained other cultures and religions, made the idea of actively encouraging intermarriage with the 'natives' anathema to the Victorian establishment.

Fears that the dearth of European women in India and Burma encouraged intermarriage, threatening the purity and power of the empire, were recorded by Sergeant MacMullen, stationed in India in the 1840s. The government, he thought, 'ought, therefore, attentively to consider this matter; and if they would prevent the threatened danger, should send annual cargoes of women, suitable to be the wives of soldiers, to India . . . our dominions in the East would thus be saved [from domination by half-castes].' In his memoirs, MacMullen, who served in the 13th (Prince Albert's) Light Infantry, made many sharp observations on the (often unhappy) lot of his comrades' wives and children.

In the absence of any government-sponsored scheme for wife-importing, men might trawl for a bride in the British orphanages or girls' schools in the larger Indian cities, or in cantonments. (Some schools acted as unofficial marriage markets, holding regular dances to which men freshly arrived on the troopships were invited.) Soldiers' daughters, particularly those in remote stations where there was no other European community beyond the regiment, could expect to be besieged by suitors as soon as they reached marriageable age. A man with several daughters was not to be pitied as he might be in England or Ireland, where getting them all married off could prove a troublesome business, but envied. 'He is a fortunate man,' thought Sergeant MacMullen, 'who has two or three tolerable looking daughters on the eve of womanhood; he requires no fortunes to get them off his hand; but, on the contrary, propitiatory presents shower upon him from a dozen individuals, all ready to pay handsomely in that way, or any other, for being permitted to marry into his family.'

The marriage and baptism records of the 1st and 2nd battalions of the 14th Regiment of Foot in the early nineteenth century, when both battalions spent long periods stationed abroad, give credence to MacMullen's observations. While many soldiers' sons enlisted in the regiment at a very early age, often as young as ten (they were taken on as drummer boys), a large number of the regiment's daughters became army wives in their turn. Often they married men who, as fairly senior NCOs, must have been twice their age or older, either from the 14th or from regiments that were posted at the same station, such as the 11th and 8th Light Dragoons with whom there was much intermarriage. Both phenomena probably resulted from their parents' difficulties in supporting several children on a soldier's meagre pay. For the girls, the price of embarking on married life so young, beginning childbearing when they had barely reached puberty and giving birth to half a dozen children before they reached their mid-twenties, was often poor health or even early death.

Mary Anne, the daughter of Private Samuel and Eleanor Brown, was only fourteen years and two months of age when she married the Apothecary of the 11th Dragoons at Fort William, Bengal, on 15 April 1822. Ann Potter was fourteen when she married Private Halliday at Meerut in 1818, and bore him six children before she was twenty-five. Ann McNally married Assistant Steward Morrow of 11th Dragoons in 1812 at the tender age of thirteen years; her brother had enlisted at ten. The fact that their father, a private in the 14th, had died probably led to these two siblings having to make their own way in the world as they had no other means of support. Younger still was Hannah Hartman, daughter of Private Frederick Hartman, only twelve years old at her wedding to a soldier of the 11th Dragoons. Some nineteenth-century wedding photographs feature bewhiskered old soldiers next to tiny, delicate girls who look as though they should be in the schoolroom, not bedecked in bridal finery. The practice was commented on by a lady who observed the regularity with which 'a grizzled bombardier of forty unites himself to a girl of twelve'. Meanwhile their civilian counterparts were, generally, waiting another decade before marrying: the average age of marriage in Britain was twenty-five (nearer twenty-one among the aristocracy) in Victorian times, and the average age gap between husband and wife was four and a half years.

Officers also frequently found their brides within the regimental family. Dances, polo matches and later 'the club', the hub of every Indian station's social life, all provided fertile ground for romance between daughters of senior officers and bachelor subalterns (junior officers). In the pre-railway era the long journeys across India that ensued when a regiment was posted to another station could provide romantic opportunities. In December 1845 the 28th (later the Gloucestershire Regiment) marched 623 miles from Dum Dum to Cawnpore. Most women and children remained at Allahabad but some more privileged officers' wives were allowed to go all the way, riding in their carriages at the rear of the column. Beside one carriage a Lieutenant Hudson's horse could often be seen as he was courting the youngest daughter of the colonel, Maria Burnside (although his style must have been somewhat cramped by the presence of her vigilant mama), and he was always at her side during the shooting and cricket matches that took place along the way. His persistence paid off: the marriage took place soon after they reached their new station.

Sometimes army wives were vehemently opposed to their daughters following in their footsteps. A lady who spent a year in India in the middle of the nineteenth century noted: 'More than one senior officer's wife has said to me that she would never advise any girl to marry a subaltern, nor would she ever consent to a daughter of her own doing so; for though she was now at rest, yet she had herself passed through the ordeal, and knew by sad experience what a wearying and painful one it was.' Today the tradition continues of regimental daughters becoming regimental wives in their turn, despite in many cases firmly resolving never to do so. Tor Walker was one modern army daughter who was determined not to become an army wife because of the peripatetic lifestyle it entailed: 'After moving around as a child you actually feel you want a bit of stability.' But when her father went to Cyprus for his final posting she went too and fell in love with his aide-de-camp: they were duly married. Although initially a reluctant army wife, she soon grew to enjoy the variety and friendships that came with army life, while the young aide-de-camp she married became Chief of Defence Staff.

Even if they lacked a military father, girls of a marriageable age with other relatives in the British or Indian army could make their way out to India to stay with them for prolonged periods. Although they seldom admitted that marriage was the purpose of their visit, for many of them their enthusiasm for seeing their brother or uncle was secondary to their fervent hope that India would prove fertile hunting ground for a husband. As the country abounded with unattached officers (and civilians) the ambitions of even the plainest girls were often realised. Emily Eden, with her sister Fanny, accompanied her brother George (later Lord Auckland) to India when he was appointed Governor-General in 1835. She wrote to another sister in England to warn her, only half-seriously, that should any of her own sons go out to India and spend several years at a remote station, they should not let their longing for companionship lead them to propose to the first girl they saw. She cited the example of a newly married couple she had encountered in Simla, 'the husband being an object of much commiseration. Not but what he is very happy, probably, but he married the very first young lady that came up to the hills this season; she was "uncommon ordinary" then, and nothing can look worse, somehow, than she does now.'

Pretty girls, meanwhile, had no difficulty in attracting suitors. Those whose financial situation precluded them from making good matches in England could be confident of success in the marriage market of India. In Meerut, one of the larger military stations, the Edens attended a ball at which Emily met two young women who had come out from England to join their sister, the wife of an officer in a Lancer regiment. The object of their sojourn in India was clear to Emily. The married sister, she wrote, 'is very poor herself, but has eight sisters at home, so I suppose thought it right to help her family, and luckily, I think, they will not hang long on her hands. They are such very pretty girls, and knowing-looking . . . They are the only young ladies at the station, so I suppose will have their choice of three regiments; but it is a bad business when all is done. They arrived just in time for this gay week, which will give the poor girls a false impression of the usual tenor of their lives.'

However, despite inauspicious beginnings, lasting unions were sometimes forged even in the horror and turmoil of war. One such wartime romance began during some of the bloodiest fighting of the Peninsular War, when British forces under Wellington stormed the critical fortress town of Badajoz in Spain in April 1812. Although the British were victorious, the cost in blood was terrible: they and their Spanish allies lost more than a quarter of their number. Many of those killed storming the breaches had suffered horrible deaths, being trampled on by their oncoming comrades or burnt beyond all recognition by exploding shells. Even the Iron Duke himself broke down in tears when he visited the breaches after the battle and saw, in the piles of horribly maimed men that lay all around, the awful toll that victory had taken. Almost more terrible than the fighting itself was the mayhem that ensued when the victorious troops entered the town and began plundering it. Many of the terrified Spanish inhabitants were raped, robbed and murdered. Even children were bayoneted. Desperate to escape such fates, refugees began pouring out of Badajoz and throwing themselves on the mercy of the nearest British officer they could see.

A pair of Spanish sisters, obviously of high birth, their ears bleeding from where their earrings had been torn off, approached two young officers of the 95th (Rifle Brigade), Lieutenants Harry Smith and John Kincaid, for help. Their home had been taken over by looters and they had nowhere to go to. The younger of the two girls, Juana Maria de los Dolores de Leon, was fourteen and strikingly pretty: both officers were immediately captivated. Kincaid, writing many years after, described the moment he saw her. 'A being more transcendingly [sic] lovely I had never before seen — one more amiable, I have never yet known . . . her face though not perhaps rigidly beautiful, was nevertheless so remarkably hand-some, and so irresistibly attractive, surmounting a figure cast in nature's fairest mould. That to look at her was to love her — and I did love her; but I never told my love . . . '

Smith was less inhibited and proposed almost immediately. In two days they were married and spent their honeymoon on the march, Juana sleeping in the open field next to her husband in all weathers. She waited at the rear of the army while Harry went into battle at Salamanca in July 1812, and shared the hardships of the retreat to the Portuguese border later that year, during which the army was without provisions for several days and men were forced to eat acorns and grass. So charmed were the officers by her beauty and uncomplaining resilience that they used to swarm around her horse, vying for the honour of helping her dismount. At the end of the war, when the victorious British were quartered at Toulouse, Juana was at the centre of the social scene, in great demand at balls as she was an accomplished dancer, and again after the victory the following year at Waterloo, she graced the balls in Paris, even dancing the fandango with the Duke of Wellington himself. In later years Harry Smith became a general and the governor of the Cape of Good Hope; the town of Ladysmith in KwaZulu Natal was named after his wife.

My great-grandmother, Lucy Twining, was also destined for a blessedly happy marriage – but only after an engagement of six years. In 1907 Lucy's future husband, Esmond Venning, an officer in the 31st Punjab Regiment of the Indian Army, finally amassed enough funds to support a wife. He reportedly sent Lucy a telegram saying simply: 'Come'. Undaunted by the brevity of his message, she purchased a wedding dress, packed her trunks, and sailed for Ceylon (now Sri Lanka) where Esmond met her and the long-awaited wedding took place. Throughout their marriage they were separated for long periods, during which they would write to each other often several times a day, passionate letters brimming with emotion and tenderness. Great bundles of their letters still exist, the addresses on them ranging from 'Chin Hills, Burma' to 'Basra, Mesopotamia', pouring forth endearments and telling each other of their respective doings. 'How grey and dull everything is when you are away, precious,' Lucy writes in one letter. 'Only the children become more instead of less delightful – other things lose their lustre.' In reply, Esmond reassures his 'darling little wifie' that 'I feel so lonely without you.' The strength of their feeling for each other is evident, and a perfect example of the truth of the statement made to me by one army wife, that the frequent separations of married life in the army 'either kill your marriage or they make it stronger'. For Lucy and Esmond, the latter was quite obviously the case.

The pain and disruption of separation – and the hope that it might even strengthen the bond between husband and wife – applied to the unions of both officers and rank and file. For all the superficial distinctions, the vast differences in their roles, living conditions and rules to which they were expected to conform, officers' and soldiers' wives shared many common experiences. Whatever their breeding, background or standing within the regiment, all these women had, and still have, to undergo the same uncertain lifestyle, frequently uprooting their families, packing their possessions, and acclimatising themselves to new communities and countries. And when their men are sent to war, from private's wife to colonel's consort they are all glued together in mutual discomfort at the long separation that they will have to endure, the same fears for the safety of their men, and the same dread that few like to articulate but of which all are aware: that their husbands might not come back.

In earlier centuries, though, it was the wife of the common soldier who had to face a particularly harrowing ordeal if the regiment was on the move. However much she might wish to follow the man she had chosen, she would have to face the prospect of being forcibly torn from his side.

2

To Stay or to Go

The distraction of the poor creatures at parting with their husbands
was quite heart-rending. Some clung to the men so resolutely that
the officers were obliged to give orders to have them separated
by force. The screaming and howling of their farewells rang in
our ears after we were in the boats, and even far out at sea.

Rifleman Benjamin Harris

One of the heaviest burdens that army wives have to bear is being
separated from their husbands for weeks, and months, at a time. The
pain of separation is, of course, intensified in times of conflict. Nowadays,
postings in conflict zones are unaccompanied and nobody would countenance the idea of soldiers' families following them on to a plane bound
for Iraq, Afghanistan or Bosnia. But 200 years ago or more, wives did
their utmost to be among the number allowed to travel abroad with
the regiment, as much in wartime as in peace. The sight of women and
children tagging along behind the army, in Flanders, South America, Portugal
or Spain, in peace and in war, was not just commonplace but entirely
expected. As British soldiers marched across wilderness and desert, forest and
plain, acquiring and defending territories, so the number of foreign garrisons
swiftly multiplied. Every new patch of red on the world map meant another
contingent of Redcoats would be dispatched to secure this possession, fend-
ing off competing claims from local inhabitants or rival powers. Behind the
Redcoats came the petticoats, crammed into troopships, perched atop baggage

carts, promenading on the decks of steamships, hushing fretful children in sweltering railway carriages, staggering under the weight of their worldly possessions or filling teak chests with china, linen, satins, laces and stays to be unpacked many months and many miles away.

Some of the first women to accompany the army overseas in modern times were those who followed their soldier husbands to one of England's first permanent overseas garrisons. By 1670 British explorers and merchants had established colonies in Virginia and Maryland, Bermuda, Antigua, Barbados and Jamaica, and the Hudson's Bay Company and the East India Company were trading in Canada and India respectively. In addition to these outposts, which were evolving semi-independently, there was the port of Tangier on the North African coast, given to Britain (together with Bombay) as part of the dowry of Charles II's queen, Catherine of Braganza. Across the water from Spain and surrounded by hostile Moors, it proved to be a troublesome wedding gift as it had to be defended at great expense. Troops were raised in England and sent to garrison it but their maintenance was too costly for Parliament's liking. Memories of Charles I – whose attempts to impose his own personal rule led, ultimately, to the emergence of two armies, for King and for Parliament, and the civil war – were still very raw. Parliament was reluctant to give his son any tools that he could fashion into a King's Army and thus bolster his own power. By 1683 it was clear to Charles II that, in the face of Parliament's obduracy, he could no longer afford to keep his Mediterranean outpost. The soldiers' pay was several months in arrears, and many officers and their families had already made their own way home rather than stay there unpaid. There seemed to be nothing for it but to evacuate the Tangier garrison.

In its short life, many of the men had been joined by their families and a community was flourishing, complete with a garrison school, church and the inevitable brothels. So when the evacuation began there were several hundred women and children who had to be transported back to English shores. In October and November 1683 the first party of married men and their families were embarked on a flotilla of ships including a large number of sick, who had to be accommodated aboard a hospital ship, the *Welcome*. In October 1683, 104 women and children were packed into the *Unity* under the charge of John Eccles, the garrison schoolmaster, together with 114 invalid soldiers. The following February, the remaining members of the garrison departed. Captain and Mrs Collier and their three children, subalterns' wives Mrs Lindsay, Mrs Ramsay and Mrs Duncan, and dozens of soldiers' families climbed aboard the *Happy Return* and the

Woolwich that lay waiting in the harbour. Keenly observing the preparations for the evacuation were the Moors, who prowled around the perimeter of the town with a menacing air. Fearing that they would use the confusion of the evacuation to launch an attack on the departing English, sailors from the ships of the evacuation fleet were hastily dressed in soldiers' uniforms to parade around the town in order to impress and deter the enemy. Before the last ships departed, the forts and walls around the town were blown up, sending masonry and debris high into the sky. If the English no longer wanted Tangier, they were going to make certain that no other power could use their fortifications for their own purposes.

As the passengers clambered aboard the departing ships, smoke from the demolished forts hung in the sky and their ears rang with the thunderous booms of the explosions. Some were no doubt regretful at leaving the homes they had made within the mud walls of the fort, but others must have been only too pleased to wave farewell to a town that Samuel Pepys, no stranger to the seamier side of life, depicted as full of 'nothing but vice of all sorts, swearing, drinking, cursing and whoring, the women as bad as the men'. Colonel Kirke, the garrison commander, had tried unsuccessfully to contain this immorality by meting out floggings for even the most trivial of offences such as having a dirty face, but these harsh measures had failed to stem the tide of depravity and disease.

Yet those who raised a cheer as the ships set sail may soon have wished they were back in port when, a short distance out, a violent storm blew up. The *Woolwich*'s topmast was snapped, forcing her and the *Happy Return*, also in difficulties, back into Tangier Bay for a refit. A few days later they ventured forth again, only to be driven back once more by a fierce gale. Five days later the ships braved the tempest again and were nearly driven on to the coast of Morocco. On deck the sailors battled to keep the rolling ships upright, while men, women and children, crammed together in the airless space below decks, moaned with fear and sickness. Six weeks after departing Tangier the battered, exhausted convoy limped into the Plymouth Sound.

The horrors of that voyage did little to deter those passengers and their descendants from following the drum to the furthest outposts of Britain's expanding empire in conditions every bit as difficult and dangerous. Despite all the stern warnings of commanding officers, men continued to wed and their wives generally did everything they could to follow them wherever they were sent. Only twenty years after the mass evacuation of women and children from Tangier, wives were again accompanying English and

Irish troops sent on an expedition to Portugal in 1703. In explaining why additional space was needed in the transport ships, the secretary to the Lord Lieutenant of Ireland wrote: 'That which adds to the number is the necessary allowance of four women to a company, which is the least that has been permitted and cannot be avoided.'

The quota of women allowed applied only to the wives of soldiers; officers' wives were at liberty to follow their husbands abroad, though they were generally expected to pay for their own food and keep. Soldiers' wives, however, were entitled to half rations, their children a quarter or a third depending on their age. They took up room in the ships, they had to be housed if abroad and protected if at war. They constituted a logistical and financial burden on their regiments and their numbers had therefore to be severely restricted. Those in charge of keeping the army supplied often resented the drain that women and children ('useless mouths' as they were termed because they had to be fed but did not fight) constituted on scarce resources. This attitude is apparent in a letter from Daniel Wier, the Commissary for the Army during the American War of Independence (then known as the American Revolutionary War), written to the Secretary to the Lords of the Treasury to complain of the expense of feeding the women and children with the army 'which are indeed very numerous beyond any Idea of imagination; and although the former are victualled at the rate of a moiety of each man's allowance, and the latter at a fourth only, yet the expence is very considerable. As it is my Duty as well as my inclination, to reduce this, as well as every other extraordinary expence, consistent with propriety and humanity, I hope we shall be able, with the advice and concurrence of the General to adopt some plan in order to curtail in some degree this enormous Expence.'

If such measures seem harsh or parsimonious, it is worth remembering that keeping the army supplied abroad was an extremely difficult business. Often food and clothing were in such short supply that there was not enough for the men themselves, let alone the 'useless mouths'.

The usual method of choosing who was to go and who was to be left behind was to hold a ballot. This was often done the night before embarkation, or even on the day itself. While the bands played stirring marching tunes, and munitions, horses, cattle and food stores were loaded on to the ship by dockhands, lots were drawn at the quayside on the head of a drum. The fear was that if it were done any sooner those men whose wives had drawn 'not to go' would disappear before the time came to embark. Colonel John Maunsell, overseeing the embarkation of troops from Cork in the

1770s, commented that it was important for women to accompany the troops as it discouraged them from deserting.

The tension must have been unbearable as the women crowded round the drumhead on which the hat or ballot box was placed and plunged their hands in to pull out the piece of paper on which their fate was written: to go or not to go. When 'not to go' (or 'to be left') was drawn, as it was in the majority of cases, it heralded the splintering of a family who would probably not be together again for many years, if at all, and the prospect of destitution for the women and children left behind. One officer, speaking of the time of the American Revolutionary War, commented, 'There is no part of the Expedition I so much dread as the parting of the Soldiers from their Wives and Children, nor is there any thing more discouraging for the Men that their Cries and Lamentations [for] the greatest part of them have it not in their power to subsist otherwise than from Hand to Mouth.'

Such a dire fate was indeed common for many wives and families left behind. While of course love for their men drove these women – many of them unsophisticated and illiterate – to brave hazardous journeys in leaking ships to alien lands, another compelling factor was the very real alternative: poverty at home.

There were some efforts to relieve their plight. In 1800 the Duke of York, as Commander in Chief of the Army, formalised the convention that six women per company of hundred men could accompany troops on foreign service 'to obviate the distress to which the families of Soldiers are liable to be exposed'. For companies of sixty soldiers, four women were allowed. When troops were sent out to India, China and New South Wales, the ratio was increased to twelve women per hundred soldiers. In peacetime, when for example the regiment was bound for garrison duty, more women were allowed to travel than in wartime (and could also take children with them). If vacancies occurred, that is if wives died while overseas, those at home who were next on the list could come out to fill the dead women's shoes. The Duke also decreed that those left behind should receive an allowance to enable them to return to their families: one guinea each for the wives and ten shillings for each child under ten. In 1818 this travel allowance passed into law when an Act of Parliament decreed that parishes should provide subsistence and travelling expenses to soldiers' wives passing through on their way back to their homes, on production of a pass certifying their identity. Even so, the prospect of hauling their family across the country, depending on the charity of notoriously ungenerous

parish authorities and of families who were perhaps in straitened circumstances themselves, held little appeal for most women, who preferred to
take their chances with the regiment and follow them overseas, whatever
the risks and dangers that lay ahead.

But first was that uncertain hurdle of the ballot. George Gleig, a
subaltern during the Peninsular War, remembered the effect of the ballot on
a devoted young couple when his regiment with the 85th (Buckinghamshire
Volunteers) Regiment embarked for Spain in July 1813. Duncan and Mary
Stewart were childhood sweethearts from the Highlands who had married
in the face of bitter family opposition. His father was a smuggler, hers an
exciseman who was reluctant to see his cherished daughter throw herself
away on a private soldier. When Mary journeyed south to join Duncan
at Hythe, the regiment was already under orders for embarkation to the
Peninsular War. Mary was by now heavily pregnant and approached the
ballot box in a state of high anxiety, stretching out a trembling hand for
the piece of paper that would determine her fate. Gleig reported what
happened next: 'When Mary unrolled the slip of paper, and read upon it
the fatal words, "To be left," she looked as if Heaven itself were incapable
of adding one additional pang to her misery. Holding it with both hands,
at the full stretch of her arms from her face, she gazed upon it for some
minutes without speaking a word, though the rapid succession of colour
and deadly paleness upon her cheeks, told how severe was the struggle
which was going on within; till at length, completely overpowered by her
own sensations, she crushed it between her palms and fell senseless into
the arms of a female who stood near.'

After a last night together, Duncan took his place in the ranks while
Mary was shut away in a barrack room by some well-meaning fellow
wives who wished to spare her the agony of waving him off. 'But, just
before the column began to move, she rushed forth; and the scream which
she uttered, as she flew towards Duncan, was heard throughout the whole
of the ranks. "Duncan, Duncan!" the poor thing cried, as she clung wildly
round his neck: "Oh, Duncan, Duncan Stewart, ye're no gawn to leave
me again, and me sae near being a mother! O, Serjeant M'Iintyre, dinna
tak' him awa'! if ye hae ony pity, dinna dinna tak' him! O, sir, ye'll let me
gang wi'him?" she added, turning to one of the officers who stood by;
"for the love of Heaven, if ye hae ony pity in ye, dinna separate us!"'

Her pleas fell on deaf ears — there could be no question of overruling
the ballot — and the men marched off with the band playing loudly to
drown out the cries of the women left behind. Mary persuaded her husband

to let her march with him as far as Dover. Three miles into the journey she was suddenly seized with labour pains. Duncan and the kindly Sergeant McIntyre hurriedly took her into a cottage on the roadside where, gasping in the agony of childbirth, she expired. She was only eighteen. Despite an attempted caesarean section the baby perished too. A compassionate officer told Duncan that he might remain behind to bury his wife and catch up with the regiment later, but the distraught widower, still reeling with the shock of his double bereavement, refused the offer. Having gained the officer's assurance that she would be decently buried, he embarked with the rest of the troops. According to Gleig, 'he scarcely spoke after; and he was one of the first who fell after the regiment landed in Spain'.

Joseph Donaldson of the 94th Scots Brigade tells a similarly tragic tale of a soldier called Sandy and his young wife. As the regiment prepared to depart for the Peninsula in 1809, the hour of the ballot drew nigh and the women came one by one into the room in order of seniority to draw their ticket and discover their fate. The soldiers stood around watching, the single ones out of idle curiosity, the married men anxious to know the result. A sergeant's wife, little liked in the regiment, drew not to go. Then a corporal's wife, an equally unpopular woman, drew 'to go'. Both results were received with apathy by the crowd. Next up was another old hand, a woman universally despised for her ill temper and renowned for hitting her husband and creating disturbances in the cookhouse. She drew 'to go', to the obvious displeasure of the onlookers, including her husband. After her came Sandy's wife, who was mother to a small child, and was 'remarkable for her affection for her husband, and beloved by the whole company for her modest and obliging disposition'. With shaking hand she withdrew her ticket and, unable to look at it herself, asked a man nearby to tell her the result. It was 'Not to go'. At once she fell into a paroxysm of grief. 'O Sandy, you'll no leave me and your poor babie, will you?' she cried to her husband. 'The scene,' according to Donaldson, 'drew tears from every eye in the room.' She became convinced that he would be killed in the Peninsula and grew hysterical with grief that he would never see her and their 'poor babie' again. Nothing that anyone could say would shake her conviction. She and Sandy spent the night sitting on their bed, with their child between them, alternately embracing it and each other and lamenting their cruel fortune.

In the morning, when the regiment set off for port, she trudged the weary six miles to the sea. Here she managed to accompany Sandy on to the ship and threw herself on to her knees before the commanding officer, begging him to let her stay on board. Although clearly moved by her plight, he refused, explaining he must abide by the rules that stipulated that six women only could go. In utter despair she said farewell to her distraught husband. Handing him the baby, she told him, ' "Give him a last kiss, Sandy." He pressed the infant to his bosom in silent agony, "Now, a's owre; farewell Sandy! We'll maybe meet in heaven" and she stepped into the boat [to take her back to shore] with a wild despairing look . . . as we got the last glimpse of her, she uttered a shriek, the knell of a broken heart, which rings in my ears at this moment. Sandy rushed down below, and threw himself into one of the births [sic], in a state of feeling which defies description.' Tragically, his wife's premonition proved all too accurate. Sandy was one of the first to fall when the regiment reached the Peninsula.

Hard as it was to strike lucky in the ballot, some women were not even allowed to participate in it. Apart from those who were 'not on the strength' because their marriages had not been sanctioned, others were debarred because they had children or were deemed to be of the wrong sort of character. Regulations made this very clear: 'In making the selection of women, care is always to be taken that those of the best character, and most likely to be useful to the troops, are first chosen; and no greater proportion of serjeants' wives is to be selected than the serjeants' wives bear to the wives of the corporals, drummers, and privates of the battalion'. Some commanding officers gave preference to the soldiers who had been married the longest, 'provided they and their wives are of good character, and that the latter by their known steady and industrious habits, are most likely to be useful to their respective Companies. Should there be any of equal claims, they will draw lots until the authorized number is complete.' Others, mindful of conditions at the other end of the journey, stipulated that only wives who were able-bodied and robust should be allowed to embark. In May 1778 Sir Henry Clinton, one of the British commanders in the American Revolutionary War, ordered: 'Commanding Officers of Corps will be allowed to keep a few women on shore & are desired to keep as few as possible & those to have no children & known to be good marchers,' while a general order of April 1807 specified that women being sent to the continent with the troops 'should be carefully selected, as being of good character and having the inclination and ability to render themselves useful; it is very desirable that those who have children should be left at home'. This last stipulation was, however, frequently ignored.

Both soldiers' and officers' wives were forbidden to embark if they were six months pregnant or more; the number of births that took place on board ship points to the fact that this rule was not universally observed. More generally, as awareness of hygiene and the need to curb the spread of disease grew, regulations came into force requiring that ladies must 'produce a certificate showing that she (and her children and servants, if any) is free from infectious disease, and in all respects medically fit to embark'.

Often commanders decided to reduce the number of wives accompanying expeditions, or better still leave them behind altogether. In May 1798 a British force was sent to destroy the French fleet at Ostend where it lay waiting, it was feared, to invade Britain. (In fact Napoleon, who was still six years away from becoming Emperor, had no intention of attacking England at this juncture.) Major General Eyre Coote, the commander of the expedition, was insistent that on such a lightning raid 'not one woman must on this occasion accompany the soldiers . . . The General is sure that every thinking good soldier will readily see the convenience to themselves and propriety of this order and cheerfully submit to a short separation.' To sweeten this pill, General Coote announced that he had given fifty guineas for distribution to the wives and children of the soldiers. As it transpired, it was as well that they had been left behind for the raid was a semi-disaster. The force managed to destroy some shipping but was prevented from re-embarking for Britain by the adverse tide and weather. Stranded on the beaches, the majority was forced to surrender to the enemy and marched away to spend several years as prisoners of war, a fate that their families would have shared had they been in tow.

A debacle of a different kind occurred in 1809, when an expedition was sent to Walcheren, in Flanders, once again triggered by fears of Napoleon invading England with the fleets he had assembled in Dutch ports. The matter of providing for the families left behind had been addressed. General Coote (this time second in command) decreed that all women and children must stay in England. Six women per company were allowed to remain in the vacated barracks together with their children. The rest had to return to their family homes but would receive monetary help to get there and to maintain them while they were there. In the event, a large proportion of the soldiers were struck down by 'Walcheren Fever' (probably a strain of malaria) that thrived in the swampy marshes on the island of Walcheren on which the port of Flushing was located. In a little over a month the expedition had to be abandoned because the illness had incapacitated the army. Of the 45,000-strong force, 4,500 men died of Walcheren fever and nearly 11,500 were hospitalised for weeks on their return to England. Once again the wives and children had had a lucky escape, although it is doubtful whether those left widowed or fatherless by the expedition saw it that way.

Despite the best efforts of the army commanders, the quota of wives was frequently exceeded as unauthorised numbers managed to smuggle themselves on board. Occasionally wives would bribe their way aboard ships or manage to exchange places with women who had succeeded in the ballot. Some even stowed away, to emerge only when they were well clear of the English coast and there was no chance of the ship turning back to deposit them. Mrs Courtenay Ilbert, who in July 1807 set sail for Quebec (where her husband, a captain in the Royal Artillery, was to do garrison duty), wrote in her journal of the voyage about a 'most affectionate couple', Corporal and Mrs Burns, who were badly injured when the sailors aboard the *Thames* dropped a marlin spike from the top of the foremast which struck their heads. Mrs Burns, wrote Mrs Ilbert, had drawn a blank in the ballot, 'which was a great distress to them both, among those who had the prizes was one woman who was not anxious to go to Canada. Mrs Burns directly offered her all the money she could raise, which was two guineas, which to her represented an enormous sum. The woman accepted it but afterwards hearing another say she would give more, she tried to recall the bargain, however the matter was represented to Captn Glegg, who of course decided for Mrs Burns, & the pair seemed so happy on the occasion that it did my heart good to see them . . . ' Happily they recovered from their injuries.

Private John Pearman, a new recruit to the 3rd Light Dragoons, sailed for India in June 1845 and noted that four young married women managed to smuggle themselves on board the *Thetis* and accompany their husbands to the sub-continent. Had they not managed to do so, they would have been apart for nearly a decade as the regiment did not return to England until 1853.

When the British fleet set sail in 1854 for the Crimean War, journalists were on hand to convey the emotion – and skulduggery – that accompanied the fleet's departure. Several of the newspapermen noticed the efforts of certain wives to circumvent the ruling of the ballot. *The Times* reported on one wife who managed to make her way on board ship, hair cropped close and dressed in a rifleman's uniform, before being discovered and promptly evicted. Luckily for her, the Countess of Erroll was on board the same ship and, hearing of her plight, persuaded the officer in charge to allow her to stay on board. Another soldier's wife, Mrs Longley, whose husband was a sergeant in the 17th Lancers, had failed to gain a place in the ballot. But she had once worked as a servant to Lord John Russell, who interceded on her behalf and got her a passage on board the Lancers' ship. Meanwhile Mrs Williams, whose husband was Sergeant Major of the 8th Hussars, had prevailed upon the paymaster's wife, the young and beautiful Fanny Duberly, to employ her as a lady's maid in order to secure her passage. Fanny, who remained at the front throughout the Crimean War and published a journal of her experiences that brought her fame (and notoriety), was later to bitterly regret her act of charity as Mrs Williams considered herself to be above the menial tasks of a maid.

One soldier, John Wager of the Rifle Brigade, was so distraught at leaving his wife and their young child that a few hours before the ship sailed he cut his throat, unable to live with the knowledge that he was abandoning them to destitution. His fears were well founded. A Portsmouth resident wrote to a newspaper that 'about two hundred wives and children of this gallant corps [the Rifle Brigade] are left destitute'.

Pressing for better support for the families left behind, *The Times* argued that 'The sorrow of separation, the agony of the last farewell, was felt as deeply by the wife of a common soldier as by that of the noblest officer. When the soldier heard that those he had left behind him were well cared for, he would feel more strongly than ever that he had a country worth fighting for.' Lord St Leonard took up the theme, telling the House of Lords in April 1854, 'Excepting the idea of dishonour before the enemy, nothing weighed so heavily on the mind of a soldier as the thought, that, while he was in a foreign land fighting the battles of his country, those nearest and dearest to him were receiving parish relief in a workhouse.' Later in the war an MP reported that he had received letters from soldiers' female relatives stating that unless they received some money to set themselves up in business they would have to resort to prostitution or the workhouse.

That some chose the former over the latter is unsurprising. Workhouses began their notorious reign when the government decided to centralise poor relief with the Poor Law Amendment Act of 1834, taking over its administration from the individual parish authorities. To discourage idleness and dependency, the poor would have to work for their welfare and a chain of workhouses was set up across the country (although in practice many continued to receive poor relief elsewhere). A workhouse, wrote the Reverend H.H. Milman, an enthusiastic supporter of these establishments, 'should be a place of hardship, of coarse fare, of degradation and humility; it should be administered with strictness – with severity; it should be as repulsive as is consistent with humanity'. Many workhouses adhered faithfully to this harsh doctrine and some of their administrators seem to have been devoid of humanity. Mothers were forcibly separated from their infants. Men, women and children were forced to work long hours in hard physical labour, surviving on scraps of food.

The scandalous conditions eventually provoked an outcry and an inquiry into their administration, which culminated in the abolition of the Poor Law Commission in 1847 and a move to reform the workhouses. But reform did not come quickly and conditions in these mini 'Bastilles' as they were known remained terrible, their grim presence in the villages and towns of England sending a chill through the wives who were forced to fend for themselves when their soldier husbands departed for foreign shores.

Even before the regiment departed overseas some women and children were left out in the cold. Women who were abandoned by their soldier husbands or sweethearts often found it impossible to track them down and pursue them for maintenance for their children, particularly if the men enlisted under false names. As regiments moved town frequently, 'going for a soldier' was an effective means for men who would not or could not support their families, to escape their responsibilities. Since Elizabethan times, relatives were obliged by law to maintain those who were unable to work. The Poor Law Amendment Act of 1834, as well as centralising poor relief, enshrined the obligation of a man to support his wife and his children, though illegitimate children had to be supported only if the woman was receiving poor relief (this requirement was dropped ten years later). It also changed the old system by which women could claim the money directly from the men: instead the absent husbands and fathers had to pay the money to the Poor Law authorities who then dispensed it on the women's behalf.

Concerned at the effect that these provisions might have on their manpower, the army authorities sought to circumvent the acts with one of their own. In 1837 a clause was added to the annual Mutiny Act that established military law during peacetime, stating that 'no Person whatever enlisted into His Majesty's Service as a Soldier shall be liable to be arrested or taken therefrom . . . for not supporting, or for leaving chargeable on any Parish, Township or Union, any Wife or any Child or Children'. Objectors pointed out that this clause turned soldiers into 'legalised seducers' in the words of one outraged newspaper correspondent, who were free to traverse the country leaving behind them 'a sure and certain track of blighted virtue' in the shape of illegitimate children, as well as destitute wives. Yet defenders of the exemption pointed out that a soldier's pay, after all the stoppages for uniform, weapons and other necessaries, was simply not adequate to maintain a family, and to imprison him for this inability would be unjust. It was not until the programme of army reforms introduced by Edward Cardwell, the Secretary for War, in the early 1870s that the army authorities took practical steps to discourage soldiers from abandoning their women and children. It became mandatory for a soldier to contribute to the maintenance of his wife and children, including any illegitimate children that he was proved to have fathered. However the measure was subject to so many qualifications and loopholes, that in practice it was seldom enforced and large numbers of women and children, deserted by soldiers who had gone 'over the hills and far away', continued to face destitution.

When the Crimean War brought the plight of soldiers' families to the public eye, several charitable bodies were set up to try to bring them relief, the foremost of these being the Central Association in Aid of the Wives and Families of Soldiers Ordered on Active Service. The Association set about disbursing aid to the many needy cases that came its way. Before the Crimean War was over it had given aid, in the form of weekly allowances as well as clothing, bedding, furniture and 'medical attendance', to 6,701 women, 9,321 children and 232 'dependent female relatives' of soldiers at the front, and rescued numerous wives from the cruel embraces of the workhouse.

Despite the efforts of the Association and of some parish councils to persuade the government to provide relief for these unfortunate women, ministers remained unmoved. Replying to a letter from the Birmingham Board of Guardians who, concerned at the number of soldiers' families applying for aid in the parish, requested that some assistance be provided to them from the national purse, Lord Panmure, the Secretary of State for War, rejected the suggestion. He insisted that 'any attempt to offer a maintenance to the wives of soldiers who are engaged in active operations in the field, would not only be an encouragement to marriage, but would deprive the woman of that incentive to industry by which she must maintain herself while her husband is on duty at home'. Soldiers at the seat of war, he believed, had sufficient funds to enable them to make 'much larger remittances to their wives than those who have been employed elsewhere have been hitherto enabled to make. Lord Panmure is not, therefore, disposed to propose any alteration in the existing law regarding the wives of soldiers.' He did, however, concede that he would submit to the Queen a proposal to pay soldiers at the front a field allowance 'by which means such soldier will have the power of more easily providing, to a certain extent, for the maintenance of his family'. The field allowance was duly implemented and the Association encouraged soldiers to send money home to their wives by withholding their relief from those whose husbands failed to. This tactic seems to have had the desired effect, judging from one soldier's letter home. 'Camp, Sebastopol, Nov 30th 1855. My Dear Wife, – It is in general orders, for all married men to send their field allowance home to their wives and families. I am glad it is so; for if it was gave to me, you would not have it, for if I had money in my pocket I would spend it.'

The Crimean War was the last time that women were allowed to accompany the army to war. For the last 150 years, although army wives have had to wave their husbands off to war and endure long months of anxiety while they pray for their safe return, they have not been subjected to the awful suspense of not knowing until the last day whether they might go with them or not. There are few wives today who would wish to expose themselves or their children to the dangers of a war zone. Now they have their own quarters, in which they can remain until their husbands return (or, if widowed, for six months after his death, in most cases). They can keep in touch with their men via telephone, letter and 'e-bluey' as the electronic versions of the old blue airmail letters are known, and their husbands' pay continues to appear in their bank accounts throughout their absence: the terrible spectre of poor relief or the workhouse no longer looms.

Yet despite the relative 'comforts' of modern army life, mothers can still be left for as much as fifteen months out of a two-year period to raise young children alone. When, to their relief, their husbands return, they have to adjust to their worlds being turned upside-down again. Modern wives talk only half-jokingly of having to 're-train' their husbands when they return. 'They can be totally different. They're used to lots of army banter and being quite aggressive. They can be quite uncivilised.'

Marion Weston, whose husband undertook several unaccompanied 'tours' in Northern Ireland while she and other wives remained at home in Germany, remembers the reunions at the end of such tours as being 'one of the most difficult times . . . If your husband had been in Northern Ireland or on a long exercise, you really had to step back because for six months you'd run everything, you'd made all the decisions, you'd brought up the children, and suddenly he came back and he expected to be kingpin again . . . suddenly you couldn't make the decisions, or you could, but it was much better that you didn't, and he had to be allowed back into the fold, into the place that he thought was his . . . It's quite a tricky time and especially if you've got a tiny child, as six months is quite a long time in a child's life, and he comes back and expects it to be exactly as it was. And you've made decisions and you've moved on.'

Midge Lackie, a soldier's wife who began her army life in 1960, remembers that when her husband returned from long periods living in the field he found it almost impossible to communicate with his family, and to move from the military to the domestic sphere. 'I used to say to my children, "Salute your father" because he didn't switch off . . . I soon realised I wasn't Number One, the army was. It was a horrendous mistress.'

Hard though it might be for wives and families, the problems encountered by the men themselves have been well documented. They have to readjust to normal life, returning from combat zones, or even from long exercises, when they have been in almost exclusively male company and completely removed from the ties of hearth and home. Servicemen who have witnessed horrifying sights or incidents describe the difficulties of then having to immerse themselves in domesticity. One soldier, the father of a young child, described seeing evidence of children being massacred in Kosovo – toddlers' clothing ripped by bayonets, tiny shoes lying abandoned among bones – and finding that on returning to England the only way of drowning out such horrors was to go drinking and socialising with his fellow soldiers who could empathise with his emotions.

It can be hard for families to understand that their husbands and fathers sometimes need time and space to come to terms with what they have witnessed and experienced. The army recognises such difficulties and provides support services to help families deal with them.

Little in the way of support services existed for army families in earlier years, whether materially or emotionally. The ordinary soldiers' wives left at home would have to cope as best they could with uncertainty, loneliness, and the inevitable poverty and hardship. But what of the 'lucky' women who managed to get on board the ships? For many of them, especially new wives, they were embarking on journeys that gave them a foretaste of the hardships and difficulties they would encounter in a life of following the drum.

3

Travels and Travails

Those who have not been at sea can never conceive the
hundredth part of the horrors of a long voyage to a female
in a sailing vessel . . . Our cabin was just the width of a gun over
which the cot was slung, but it could not swing, there being
not sufficient height . . . We were in constant darkness
and we have much putrid water on board.

> Mary Sherwood, wife of a captain in the
> 53rd Regiment, on sailing to India in 1805

For today's army wife, the journeys to and from postings are, thanks to
the advent of air travel (and the paucity of far-flung postings), fairly
painless and quick, albeit rather unromantic. But in years gone by 'troop-
ing', as the movement of troops and their families was known, involved
long marches across country or months at sea in rickety, overcrowded
ships. Sea voyages were dangerous, uncomfortable and long. Life aboard
troopships consisted, according to a private in the army of Queen Anne's
time, of 'Continual Destruction in ye foretop, ye Pox above board, ye
Pleague between decks, Hell in ye forecastle, and ye Devil at ye Helm'.
Others referred to them as floating slaughterhouses – and little wonder,
when at the end of many a voyage as much as one-third of those who
had embarked had died from scurvy, dysentery and other diseases.

In 1706 a force of 8,000 sailing from Lisbon to Valencia was reduced
by half by the time it arrived, while of 5,000 men who were shipped from

the West Indies to Newfoundland in 1702–3 nearly 4,000 died in transit. In 1710 a Commissary of Musters (the official responsible for provisioning the troops) complained that 300 men who disembarked in Portugal were in such an unhealthy state, after a distressing journey, that fewer than a hundred survived to join their regiments. Between 1776 and 1780 the death rate on the troopships transporting men to the garrisons of the West Indies was still 11 per cent.

Troops were usually transported in converted merchant ships that, though often packed with more passengers than they were designed to hold, were generally more comfortable than war ships; these allowed even less room for passengers, as much of the space was taken up with armaments. Sometimes the cargoes that the ships carried as a means of recouping some of the cost of transporting the men, took up so much room that the troops and their families were even more cramped. On occasion, the cargo even caught fire, endangering the lives of all those on board.

Soldiers and their wives were consigned to the airless space below decks while officers' families were assigned cabins, although these were often far from grand. Mrs Ilbert, her husband and young son William paid extra for 'state rooms' on their three-month voyage to Quebec aboard the *Thames* transport in 1807, while latecomers such as a very 'vulgar-minded' Captain B and his wife, also of the Royal Artillery, were forced to inhabit a leaky servant's quarter. Even state rooms were seldom as luxurious as their name implied. 'A state-room!' expostulated one Major Patterson, writing of the early-nineteenth-century troopships. 'What a lying definition for such a wretched, loathsome, murky, and abominable hole! where every misery that it is possible to think of, or that it is possible to compress within the smallest space, or that could be battened into an area of six square feet of dirty planks nailed up and tarred, is to be found.'

Mrs Ilbert soon found out that paying extra did not guarantee being leak-free when she was awakened one night by 'a wave dashing through the little scuttle hole which serves as a window to our state room – I was wet to the skin but after having changed my shift & nightcap I ventured to sleep again . . . but from this slumber I was most disagreeably roused; a sea broke over us, so violent as to break the window & deluge our bed & Cabin with water; at the moment this happen'd I believe Courtenay thought as well as myself we were going down.' Nor did it protect her from the ravages of sea sickness that she described vividly in her journal: 'I feel as if the bottom of my stomach with all its contents (which are little enough, God knows) were quietly ascending to my throat, when they arrive there, they send a speedy express to my head, and the moment the giddiness of my brain proved its knowledge of their vicinity, they then descend into their proper situation, until another swell calls them again into action, when they immediately obey the summons, & so on to all "Eternity".'

At least Mrs Ilbert was able to empty her stomach in some privacy. The junior officers' ladies, consigned to the outer berths at the sides and stern of the ship, were less fortunate. They were forced to perform their toilet and ablutions behind a ragged piece of sailcloth hung up across the corner of the cabin, which had a habit of falling down whenever the ship lurched, 'disclosing to the impious stare of sundry shipmates on the other side, a melodramatic entertainment, partly recitative, and partly vocal' as an evidently titillated Major Patterson (who disapproved of wives being allowed to accompany the army, and of soldiers' marriage in general) put it.

Even these ladies' miseries paled into insignificance beside the sufferings of the wretched inhabitants of the lower decks. Here the soldiers, women and children were crammed together in gloom and damp, the spaces between decks so small that only the shortest could stand upright. Their sanitary arrangements amounted to a few buckets that were regularly upturned by the movement of the ship, their contents sloshing across the deck. The lower decks were frequently awash with water and vomit and other effluents as men, women and children were thrown against each other by the violent rolling of the ship, while nearby horses lunged and screamed in terror and chickens, pigs and sheep squawked and squealed.

A German officer who fought with the British in the American Revolutionary War was shocked by the conduct of the soldiers on the transports out to America. He was particularly appalled to note 'what promiscuous exchanges were made with their wives', although there was a certain inevitability about such behaviour when it is considered that two or three couples often had to share a bed.

Even by the mid-nineteenth century conditions had improved little in this regard. Sergeant MacMullen travelled to India on a troopship at this time and was horrified by the indignities suffered by the soldiers' families, particularly the lack of adequate sleeping berths for women. Forced to sleep in hammocks that they found hard to climb into while preserving their modesty, many preferred to lie instead on the bare boards of the deck. Here they were regularly soaked by water coming through the hatchways, causing their cowhair mattresses to float around in sodden masses. 'There was not even a screen to separate their quarters from ours,' complained MacMullen, 'a gross violation of common decency; and the poor women, lowly as their condition was, felt bitterly the indelicacy of their situation, and often murmured that their feelings should be thus outraged.' The government of India, he pointed out, gave the wives of soldiers free passages and could easily afford to give them separate sleeping berths which, he insisted 'would prevent many an immoral and indecent occurrence on shipboard, alike disgraceful to the military service and to human nature. Convicts, if I mistake not, are kept separate; and why not the wives of soldiers, allowing none but their husbands or families to occupy the same apartment with them? . . . It is in vain that every soldier is provided with a bible and a prayer-book . . . if this Spartan indelicacy be forced upon women, the demoralisation of them and of the men must follow.'

In the damp, overcrowded conditions of the lower decks it was unsurprising that those descending below would be hit by 'sickening, foul repulsive breath'. In an effort to increase the circulation of air within the hold, the women were forbidden to put up blankets and sheets as screens during the day so they were forced to sleep, dress, cook, eat and even give birth under the gaze of their fellow passengers. Although they were allowed up on deck in calm weather, when the sea grew rough they were ordered down below. Captain Thomas Browne of the 23rd Royal Welch Fusiliers kept a journal of his voyage on board a troopship to North America in 1808. One day there was 'a dead calm . . . . the band began to play country dances, and the soldiers with such women as were embarked, danced till past midnight'. By the next day the scene of gaiety had been replaced by one of alarm when the ship collided with another transport in the convoy and their rigging became entangled. Thinking they had struck a rock, Browne and some other officers ran on deck 'where a great scene of confusion prevailed, [and] ordered down all the women who were screaming at their wits' end, & many of the men also, and thus succeeded in restoring order' while the ships were disentangled.

Added to the discomfort and lack of hygiene occasioned by such overcrowding was the problem of fresh food and water. Fresh water could seldom be spared to wash clothes, or bodies, so washing was mostly done with seawater during the voyage. Not surprisingly, the smell of unwashed bodies, slops and damp grew increasingly fetid as the voyage progressed. Lieutenant John Le Couteur travelled by transport ship with a detachment of wounded soldiers returning from the Peninsular War in March 1812. His job was to accompany them from Spithead to the military hospital in

Deal in Kent. He was horrified by the severity of their injuries: 'some of the Sergeants had no legs, another one arm. One man no legs, another no arms.' But what really revolted him was going below decks where 'the heat and stench were so great from a number of women and children being among the men, that it was quite unbearable'. Why he thought that the stench must be the fault of the women and children rather than the sick and probably gangrenous men they accompanied is not clear.

If the voyage took longer than anticipated, as it often did when the weather was stormy, food was rationed even more strictly. Flour, water and biscuit with small amounts of salt pork or beef constituted the main components of the diet for those below decks, while a few feet above them the officers and their ladies, who often brought their own supply of food, feasted comparatively sumptuously. Mrs Courtenay Ilbert was invited to dinner on board the *Blossom*, another ship in their convoy, six weeks into her voyage to Quebec and was pleasantly surprised by the epicurean delights on offer. 'You will wonder what sort of a dinner we could possibly have in the middle of the Atlantic,' she wrote, 'not a bad one I assure you. I will give you a bill of fare . . . some excellent soup, & at the bottom a roast leg of mutton, between the top & middle a couple of roast ducks, at one corner a Tongue opposite some sort of fry, the two other corners potatoes roasted & boild on one side of the soup a Ham stuck with cloves, on the other a dish of boiled rice, afterwards an excellent baked rice pudding and one of the richest and finest boiled plum puddings I ever saw. I forgot to mention, below the ducks was a stew of sheepshead & to correspond Pig's feet & ears which were excellent.'

Six weeks later, however, they were still at sea, sheltering among some barren islands off the Canadian coast while they waited for the weather to improve. Supplies began to dwindle: 'We have seen our comforts gradually drop off during the last three weeks, and now our necessaries are disappearing rapidly, we have no chance of getting a supply, the wind being directly against us; Of the ship's provisions there is neither flour, cheese nor rice, not quite a week's bread, very little oatmeal or Pease & only Rum enough for three days – We shall drink our last bottle of wine today (our Porter has been gone long ago). My fowls are not all eaten, & there are two left of those Capt Butterworth gave us, we have also a ham, a round of Beef and half a large Cheese; while any of these remain we cannot experience starvation.' She pitied the 'poor souls suffering with hunger' on the lower decks, where supplies of meat were running out. However, she comforted herself, there was no sense in trying to help them because 'all our stock divided among the soldiers would not give each of them a breakfast'.

The spectre of starvation was banished when the ship reached the small settlement of Percy on the Newfoundland coast a few days later and they were able to buy supplies, including some tea which Mrs Ilbert gave to the soldiers' wives. They were 'delighted with the present & I am convinced any other thing of double the value would not have pleased them so much'.

A lack of fresh food often resulted in scurvy, a particularly unpleasant disease. Limbs swelled up 'as big as drums', gums protruded beyond the lips, the tongue became too big for the mouth making it almost impossible to eat or drink. There was little anyone could do about it: once fresh food had run out it was a case of waiting until they reached the next port. In the mean time the corpses of those who succumbed to the illness were flung overboard for the sharks.

Other diseases found their way on board and flourished in the damp overcrowded conditions. Frequently smallpox and other infections would break out during the voyage and decimate the passengers. Indeed, soldiers disembarking at Mediterranean ports were sometimes taken on to small picquet ships and examined for signs of the pox and other diseases before they were allowed to land. There was often little time to spare between decanting one sea-weary, sickly load of soldiers from a ship and embarking the next lot of troops to take them home to England or straight on to another campaign. This meant that ships that had become infected with disease were sometimes not scrubbed clean and fumigated properly. As a result disease quickly spread to the incoming passengers who, in their turn, arrived enfeebled and infected at the other end, if they arrived at all.

The ordeal of being confined within those 'crazy floating prisons' frequently exacted a mental as well as a physical toll. Nerves were frayed by sea sickness, the fear of shipwreck and the pressure of being cooped up at close quarters for several months with other men and women, and could sometimes break. A couple on board the *Draxall*, another ship in the Ilberts' convoy, quarrelled soon after leaving port and the fuming wife decided to punish her husband by refusing to eat. After thirteen days she died of starvation. As Mrs Ilbert commented acerbically: 'She chose a bad method to vex her husband . . . she would have succeeded much better had she lived, she must have been blessed with a most persevering disposition.' A soldier named McCowen squabbled with his wife on board the *Three Sisters* while en route to Minorca in 1777 and was arraigned before a court martial in Gibraltar. According to the prosecution, the officer in charge of the detachment, Captain Squire, was informed 'that the Prisoner was cruelly treating his wife. That he had a drawn knife in his hand, and threatened to cut her in pieces.' Squire had duly gone below decks to investigate, commanded his sergeant to search for the knife and clapped a pair of handcuffs on McCowen. The soldier, drunk and indignant at his treatment, began to jeer at Captain Squire, mocking the young officer for never having seen combat and 'desired him to kiss his arse'. McCowen tried to plead in his defence that the captain threatened to make free with his wife while McCowen was being examined on board a picquet ship. His story was not believed and 'Crazy McCowen' was sentenced to 500 lashes with a cat-o'-nine-tails for insubordination.

It was not just disease that could threaten survival: ships inevitably faced whatever the hostile elements could throw at them. In 1711 a British force set off on an expedition to Canada to seize Quebec from French hands (a mission that failed: Quebec remained in French hands until General Wolfe's successful capture of the city in 1759). The fleet sailed up the St Lawrence River in thick fog. On 2 September a strong wind struck the fleet as it struggled towards the shore. Several ships including the *Colchester*, on which some companies of the Queen's Royal Regiment were travelling, struck the rocks and within two hours eight transports had been dashed to pieces. Desperate efforts were made to rescue the passengers as they clung to rocks and floating debris in the freezing water. Some of those on board the *Colchester* were saved but many were not: 11 officers, 10 sergeants, 18 corporals, 13 drummers, 166 privates and 20 women were drowned. Many of the survivors were 'so mangled and bruised as to be quite unfit for service'. The equipment, food and money were lost and had to be replaced rapidly. At first no money was refunded to cover the cost of victualling the women on the expedition as no particular orders had been issued on the subject. But when Queen Anne was told of the plight of these starving, ragged women she immediately directed 'that the same allowance be made as usual, that is rations for three of four women in each company'.

Home waters could be equally treacherous. On 25 January 1816 a small convoy of ships carrying soldiers of the 59th (2nd Nottinghamshire) and 82nd (Prince of Wales's Volunteers) Regiments, veterans of the Napoleonic Wars and such epic battles as Corunna, Vittoria and Waterloo, set off from Ramsgate for Cork. The waters were calm and the victorious soldiers, heading for garrison duty after years of war, must have been in a merry mood. One transport, the *Seahorse*, carried 246 men and 12 officers of the 59th Regiment together with 33 women and 38 children. The ships made their way along the south coast of England and by 29 January the *Seahorse* was twelve miles off the south coast of Ireland when, with terrifying force, it was hit by an easterly gale. The only member of the crew who knew the coast well was blown from the rigging and smashed on to the deck where he lay writhing in agony from his splintered bones. The ship was now floundering in a fierce gale as the sailors struggled to control her and to navigate the unfamiliar coastline. As they tried to round Brownstown Head the *Seahorse* was buffeted by towering waves and relentless wind. Her masts creaked and snapped, then her rudder was lost. She limped on as her crew struggled to make for land. It seemed that deliverance was finally at hand when they came within a mile of the shore at Tramore Bay. But then, with a deafening crash, the *Seahorse* struck a rock. The icy Celtic sea quickly swamped the crippled vessel and before long she went down, taking with her all but thirty of the 374 souls on board. Not one woman or child was saved. Two other ships in the convoy, the *Boadicea* and the *Lord Melville*, also met their ends on the rocky Irish coast a few hours later, although many of those aboard the latter ship were saved.

The previous year a three-masted sailing ship, the *Arniston*, was transporting sick and wounded soldiers from Ceylon to England together with some wives and children returning home. It was wrecked on a reef off the southernmost point of Africa with the loss of 372 lives. Only six crew members survived. All the passengers including fourteen soldiers' wives and their twenty-five children drowned, together with officers' wives Mrs Taylor and Mrs James, returning home with their children, the four sons of Colonel Geilles of the 73rd (Perthshire) Regiment, and Major General Lord Molesworth and his wife Lady Molesworth whose bodies were washed ashore locked in each other's arms. The bay in which the *Arniston* sank was later named after the doomed ship.

Until the massive loss of life aboard the passenger ship the *Titanic*, the most famous shipwreck and one that became a byword for gallantry and self-sacrifice was that of the troopship the *Birkenhead* in 1852. A 1,400-ton iron steamship, converted from a frigate to a troopship, she was considerably more spacious and drier than the cramped, damp wooden ships in which veterans of the Napoleonic era had suffered. On 5 January this imposing vessel, only four years old and pronounced by inspectors to be in efficient condition, lay at anchor in Cork Harbour while coal, food, water and troops were loaded on board. The soldiers were mostly fresh recruits wearing their new scarlet tunics with a mixture of pride and trepidation. Enlisted only a few weeks previously, they were now heading for Port Elizabeth in South Africa to reinforce the troops engaged in the 8th Kaffir War (the British campaign to 'pacify' the Xhosa people of southern Africa). After the troops had marched up the gangplank the women and children embarked, making their way to the portion of the lower deck that had been allotted to them. The officers' families were housed in cabins on the upper deck. After two days of frantic activity the ship was ready to sail and on 7 January she steamed out of Cork harbour, leaving behind crowds of wellwishers and tearful relatives on the quayside, waving hats and handkerchiefs until the ship became a speck and vanished into the distance.

Within hours of leaving harbour the ship was engulfed in a storm. Men and women, most of whom had never put to sea before, huddled in terror below decks as for ten days the ship was buffeted by a savage Atlantic gale, juddering atop towering waves before tilting sharply and plunging down with a terrifying crash into the following trough. Six of the women who had embarked (contrary to regulations) in advanced states of pregnancy were sent into labour by the shock of the storm. The more experienced wives, such as Mrs Darkin, wife of the Drum-Major of the 2nd (The Queen's Royal) Regiment of Foot, and Mrs Zwyker, wife of the Bandmaster, comforted the suffering women and aided the surgeons attending them. With the pain of childbirth compounded by the awful yawing of the ship that flung them around in their agony, three of the women died before their babies could be brought into the world. But for the other three, relief from their sufferings came in the shape of three tiny, bawling bundles. Eventually the storms subsided and in the calm days that followed the bodies of the women who had died were committed to the sea.

The *Birkenhead* finally reached Simon's Bay, near Cape Town, on 23 February 1852. Here some of those suffering minor illnesses disembarked, as well as thirty-six women and children not going on to the final destination, Port Elizabeth, further along the coast. A few fresh passengers joined the ship, which set off again on the evening of 25 February. All was calm and quiet aboard as the *Birkenhead* steamed peacefully through the night while the soldiers slept soundly in their gently swaying hammocks and the women and children in their bunks. There were now 643 people on board. Within hours 436 of those were dead.

Just before 2 a.m. the ship struck an uncharted reef off the aptly named Danger Point. With an ear-splitting crash she shuddered to a halt. Officers and men hastily pulled on what clothing they could find and rushed on deck. The captain's efforts to move the ship off the rock only succeeded in ripping her apart and hastening her demise. Water quickly rushed in, stopping the engines and drowning many men on the lower troopdeck. It then became a race to embark as many people as possible into the cutters that served as lifeboats before the ship went down. While the soldiers were assembled on deck, standing quietly in their ranks and listening to the orders of the ship's captain, sailors went below to rescue the women and children who were huddled together, clutching each other and their frightened children. Most were dressed only in nightgowns and were crying out pitifully for their husbands. They were ushered on to the upper deck and assembled to wait while the cutters were lowered. This in itself was problematic as the tackle was rotten and rusty and in some cases broke. Of eight lifeboats only three, two cutters and a gig, were successfully launched and it was soon obvious that only a few souls could be saved. The captain immediately directed his crew to save the women and children by embarking them into the second cutter.

As the women waited to embark, some soldiers were engaged in the painful task of driving the horses overboard, blindfolding the terrified animals as they struggled and screamed before being pushed into the sea, where their writhing bodies were quickly torn apart by waiting sharks. In the darkness soldiers and sailors worked frantically to get the seven women and thirteen children on board the cutter before it was too late. Some women had to be forcibly separated from the husbands to whom they clung sobbing, while the men themselves remained motionless, standing in their ranks. Most women were so exhausted or paralysed with fear that they had to be carried across the slippery deck which tilted madly first one way then the other. The senior army officer on board the *Birkenhead*, Lieutenant Colonel Alexander Seton, stood by the gangway with drawn sword lest any of the men try to rush on board the cutter, endangering the women and children. But none tried to do so and he soon sheathed his sword. One woman was hysterical, screaming for her two missing children, until a young officer rushed to the side of the cutter just before it was lowered and handed her the two terrified infants. He had found them weeping and clutching each other in the darkness of a cabin as he made a last check of the rooms not under water.

The cutter finally pulled away from the ship, its crew rowing hard to get it far enough from the stricken steamer that it would not be pulled under when she finally went down. One more cutter was launched before time ran out and the captain shouted to the men on the deck of the now sinking ship to jump overboard and make for the three boats. But their officers, realising the danger to the women and children if the lifeboats were rushed by too many men, implored them to 'stand fast' where they were. Incredibly, these young men, many of them raw recruits, who had been subjected to the discipline of the army for only a matter of weeks and never had their courage tested on a battlefield, obeyed his request to a man. They stood fast in their ranks, shaking hands with each other while water lapped around their feet as the ship sank slowly down, before she finally see-sawed and plunged beneath the waves.

The cutter holding the women and children had been damaged during its launch and was leaking, so those men on board frantically baled out water with their hats. Women wept and prayed while children screamed with hunger, cold and fear. They could see the *Birkenhead* disappearing beneath the waves and with her the husbands and fathers they loved. Some men managed to struggle to the surface and start swimming for the shore, but many of these were eaten by sharks or died of exhaustion and cold before they could reach it. Forty men survived by clinging to the portion of the mast that remained above water. The cutters made for the shore but became entangled in seaweed so were forced to head further up the coast. Eventually a passing schooner, the *Lioness*, spotted the cutters and picked up their weary, traumatised passengers before going back for the survivors of the wreck still clinging to the mast. They were brought ashore at Cape Town and the few men who had made it to the shore were eventually found and rescued.

The heroism shown on that night quickly passed into legend and was celebrated back in England where newspapers delightedly retold the story. A charitable fund was set up to aid the widows and orphans of the *Birkenhead*, although there was much indignation that the government failed to give any official recognition or compensation to the families of those who had died or to the survivors. One couple, Private Patrick Mullens and his wife, both survived the wreck, as did their two children, yet both somehow believed the other had perished. It was not until seven years later that they met by chance in the Eastern Cape and went on to have five more children.

Even beyond the reefs and in calm seas hidden menaces lurked. Until the mid-nineteenth century, the danger of being attacked by pirates or enemy privateers was constant. A detachment of the 4th, or The King's Own Regiment, sailing back from North America in September 1797 aboard the transport *The Three Sisters*, was just off Land's End when she was sighted by a French privateer. Since 1793 Britain had been at war with France and would remain so (with brief pauses) until Waterloo in 1815. During this time French and British ships considered each other fair game and would seek to capture each other and their cargoes both for motives of profit and propaganda. The unfortunate passengers were taken captive and held in prison for months if not years. On board *The Three Sisters* were twelve officers, thirty-two non-commissioned officers, and four rank and file. Also on board was Mrs McGuire, who had been born to the accompaniment of cannon fire and musket shot during the Battle of Bunker Hill in 1775, the first major engagement of the American Revolutionary War. She had grown up within the regiment and married its surgeon with whom she had already had one son and was shortly to bear another child.

True daughter of the regiment that she was, Mrs McGuire was keenly aware of the symbolic significance of the regimental colours and the importance of not allowing them to fall into enemy's hands. The colours, two large flags depicting a regiment's crest and bearing its battle honours, acted as a rallying point in battle, carried proudly aloft by young officers and defended to the death by the escorting soldiers. Loss of colours was regarded as the ultimate disgrace. The regiment's honour would forever be stained. So this redoubtable woman determined not to allow her own regiment's colours to be taken. As the French ship drew nearer she took out the heavy flat irons with which she pressed her husband's uniform and, wrapping the colours around them, dropped them through a porthole into the sea. Better that they should be lost to the murky depths than that the French should have the opportunity to insult them by flying them mockingly aloft. The privateer drew alongside and captured *The Three Sisters*, taking on board the men as well as Mrs McGuire and her young son. They were taken to Brest and flung into prison where Mrs McGuire was the only woman among six hundred men. In an attempt to preserve some privacy, coats were hung round her bed, but as they were so closely cramped that the beds touched each other it was no more than a gesture. In these conditions, notes the regimental history, her first daughter was born.

Yet all was not doom, discomfort and danger on board ship. By the time of Queen Victoria's reign, Britannia's dominance of the seas was assured and removed the threat from enemy shipping. The Empire was ascendant. The East Indiamen, as the small wooden ships that took men and their families out to India were known, took between four and six months to complete the voyage round the Cape of Good Hope to Bombay. But by the mid-nineteenth century the Peninsular and Oriental Line (the P&O) and the other major shipping companies were converting to steamships, which were larger, faster and less prone to leaking, despite the initial misgivings of the Admiralty which had been darkly suspicious of steam.

The first steamer sailed from Suez to Bombay in 1830. The opening up of the overland route through Egypt at the same time considerably reduced the length of the voyage to India and provided a more appealing and less dangerous prospect than the long and treacherous voyage around the Cape. Passengers disembarked at Alexandria, and took in the palaces of Cairo, the Sphinx and the pyramids before proceeding to Suez where they would embark once more by ship. By the mid-1830s steam was also being used on transatlantic crossings, reducing them from six weeks (or even twelve weeks in bad weather) to two weeks and, by the 1880s, just ten days. In 1869 the Suez Canal was opened, cutting the voyages to India by several weeks. Shorter journeys alleviated the problems of hunger and scurvy, and more spacious accommodation reduced the scourge of contagious diseases. An air of prosperity and optimism, engendered by peace in Europe which had prevailed since Waterloo in 1815, combined with these more comfortable physical conditions to make sea voyages, especially those to India, rather jolly affairs particularly for the officer class, whose conditions remained considerably more comfortable than those of the soldiery and their families.

In 1845 Harriet Earle was returning to India after spending her school years in miserable and austere exile in England. Filled with excitement at seeing her parents and India, her country of birth, after an absence of six years, she was enthralled by the social whirl of life on board a P&O steamer, although scandalised by the profligacy she saw: 'I have seen stewards pouring good whisky into blacking bottles to clean the boots with. Champagne flowed like water on Thursdays and Sundays at dinner. On these occasions I took especial care as to whom I danced with, for half the young fellows were much the worse for it.'

The steamer was filled with young officers going out to join their regiments in India as well as girls of an eligible age like Harriet, returning to India after receiving an English education. Romance flourished, encouraged no doubt by copious quantities of champagne, and the enchantment of moonlit walks on the deck (for those young ladies brave enough to evade their chaperones). During the afternoons girls, dressed demurely in white muslin, promenaded on deck, twirling their parasols while attentive young officers proffered their arms under the eyes of watchful mamas. Harriet fended off overtures from several young subalterns but her companion on the voyage, a 'sweetly pretty' girl named Miss Moresby, was thrilled to be proposed to by a young officer one evening. The next day she waited eagerly for her beloved at their appointed rendezvous, but he did not appear at all that day or the next. Finally on the third day she saw him on the stairs and was devastated when he passed by her as if she were a stranger. Harriet later discovered that he had remembered his proposal when he sobered up the next morning and confided to his friend that it had been a drunken error as he did not want to marry the girl. His brother officer advised him to ignore her, which he did, effectively ending the engagement.

Frances Wells, the rather staid and pious wife of an army doctor travelling to India for the first time in 1853, was less entranced by the experience. Writing to her father at home in Bristol, she described the after-dinner entertainments: 'We have plenty of music but I always dread playing before strangers . . . My husband will not let me sing tho' I have been often asked to do so. He says I am not to make myself cheap.'

Whether their sea voyage had been enjoyable or unpleasant, its conclusion was not always the end of the women's journey. In times of war they were frequently ordered to remain at the port where they disembarked. Even those who managed to get a place on the ships and travel with their men out to India, Spain or the New World could find themselves left behind when the army moved inland. In North America, faced with the problems of keeping the troops adequately supplied through the vast stretches of wilderness, British generals sometimes decided that fewer women must accompany the troops, so wives were left behind disconsolate on the ships by which they had arrived. Often they would disobey orders and rejoin the column, only to be sent back to the ships again if they were found out. General Clinton complained in July 1778 of 'many of the women who were sent on Board the Transports from Philadelphia being at Present with the army'. And in 1781 General Cornwallis, commanding the campaign in the southern states, sent half the women away from the column and back to camp. But their camps were many miles away and because men could not be spared to accompany them through hostile territory filled with enemy troops and Indians, many simply hid for a while and then stealthily rejoined the march. If discovered, they would not only be denied rations but risked being flogged before being sent away again.

Twenty-three years earlier General Braddock, commanding the British troops in their fight to evict the French from North America, had faced a similar problem and, conscious of the scarcity of rations and the dangers of the campaign, decreed that any woman who was found to have rejoined the column a second time would be executed. In 1772 a captain commanding a garrison in Halifax reported that they were very low on water and added that he was 'more sensible of it, as the 14th [Regiment] is now 400 men – 70 women & 90 children'.

During the Peninsular War senior officers often tried to persuade the women who had sailed out to remain in Lisbon while the troops went inland, but most ignored the advice and followed their men. In the Waterloo campaign of 1815 the Duke of Wellington took a tougher line with the soldiers' wives, insisting that a proportion of them remain in Ostend to avoid the regiments being too cluttered up with women. Despite the prohibition many soldiers' wives managed to evade their guards and make their way to Ghent, where they were promptly rounded up and sent back to Ostend, only to escape again. This time they were allowed their liberty and many of them followed their men as far as the battlefield of Waterloo itself.

By the time of the Boer War the practice of women accompanying regiments on campaign had ceased, although many wives, mothers and sisters who could afford to pay their passage travelled out to the Cape to be as close as possible to the action. However, they mostly remained in Cape Town.

For women who were going in peacetime to join husbands or fathers, disembarkation was generally followed by a journey by road, rail or river to their new home, often several hundred miles away. Harriet Earle had to travel 900 miles across India without a chaperone and only the bearers of her palanquin (a covered litter) for company, which was, she conceded, 'an awful risk, but in those days the peasants of India would no more have thought of harming an English woman than of flying'. When they came upon a large tiger lying across the path one night, her bearers were appalled to find that she was not carrying a gun. Luckily, the beast had just gorged itself and lumbered off without molesting them.

When a regiment moved from one station to another it travelled in a long column, marching by day and camping by night. The officers and soldiers marched in ranks, drums beating and band or pipes playing marching tunes. Behind the orderly files of men came the women: soldiers' wives, cooks and camp followers. Often they were as numerous as the soldiers and their presence was much deplored by officers who felt that it detracted from the smart military appearance of the column.

In wartime the procession was even more unruly. After the marching columns, the artillery wagons and the store carts came the baggage train. In the Peninsula, Wellington expressly forbade soldiers' wives to ride on the baggage wagons as the space was needed for vital equipment, but despite edict after edict to this effect the drivers could seldom resist taking pity on the hapless women and small children who found it hard to keep up on foot. Some fortunate wives managed to procure donkeys or mules for themselves, their children or their baggage. Some stowed infants into panniers that they fastened on to donkeys, others were forced to trudge along beside the wagons carrying their possessions and one or more children on their backs as they marched mile after weary mile in worn-out shoes, over-sized men's boots or even barefoot, wearing shabby red coats taken from fallen soldiers, now patched and tattered beyond recognition.

Other wives travelled in rather more style. A French officer, Colonel Lejeune, described the elegant little procession he saw as he watched the English troops pass by him during the Peninsular War. 'The captain rode first on a very fine horse, warding off the sun with a parasol: then came his wife, very prettily dressed, with a small straw hat, riding on a mule and carrying not only a parasol but a little black and tan dog on her knee, while she led by a cord a she-goat, to supply her with milk. Beside madame walked her Irish nurse, carrying in a green silk wrapper a baby, the hope of the family, a grenadier, the captain's servant, came behind and occasionally poked up the long-eared steed of his mistress with a staff. Last in the procession came a donkey loaded with much miscellaneous baggage, which included a tea-kettle and a cage of canaries; it was guarded by an English servant in livery, mounted on a sturdy cob and carrying a long posting-whip, with which he occasionally made the donkey mend its pace.' One can sympathise with the exasperation that some military commanders felt when they saw their orderly ranks interrupted by such bizarre if elegant additions to their corps. As well as detracting somewhat from the military appearance of the ranks, this incongruous little procession would have also diverted the efforts of the captain and his soldier-servant from other duties with which they could perhaps have been more usefully employed.

Troops on the march proved fertile ground for the satirical artist William Hogarth, in his famous painting *The March to Finchley*, depicting English forces heading north to take on Bonnie Prince Charlie's forces in the Jacobite rising of 1745–6. When he saw the painting George II, the 'soldier king' who had often led his troops into battle and whose son the Duke of Cumberland was in command of the army, was incensed by Hogarth's unflattering portrayal of his soldiers. Not only is the procession thoroughly disorderly, filled with obviously drunken soldiers in dishevelled uniforms but its martial appearance is also comprehensively compromised by the presence of several women in its ranks. Some of them are obviously prostitutes; one appears to be the pregnant wife or mistress of a grenadier, while another clings desperately to the arm of the drummer, her child by her side, clearly pleading with him not to abandon them.

The real-life women who did march to Scotland with the army had a tough time ahead of them. In April 1746, after camping in the bleak Highlands while the Duke trained and drilled his men, the army marched through the River Spey towards Culloden Moor. The water, still icy cold from the winter snows, came above the waists of the men who held their muskets aloft to prevent them from getting wet. After the men came the women, carrying their spare clothes on their heads to keep them dry. A few days later, the battle of Culloden took place. The women were left guarding the baggage while the Highlanders and the Government armies clashed in a bloody contest that left around a thousand Highlanders and 300 of Cumberland's men dead in less than hour. Cumberland instructed his men to show no mercy to the wounded Jacobites and for months afterwards bloody reprisals were carried out on the Highlanders.

In peacetime moves, soldiers' wives might well procure a space on one of the baggage wagons even if orders forbade it. Viscount Cranley, Colonel of the 2nd Queen's Royal Regiment, used to give lifts to soldiers' wives he saw marching along the road and take them to their barracks in his carriage. The officers' wives went mainly by carriage, although more adventurous sorts might choose to ride. In pre-railway India, regiments would commonly take several weeks to move from one end of the country to the other. Because of the searing heat the march usually began early in the morning before the sun was up and halted around midday.

Some women enjoyed the long marches, relishing the slight relaxing of the strict etiquette and myriad rules that made garrison life so stifling. In normal life an officer's lady had to watch her conduct carefully: the merest whiff of impropriety was enough to attract ire and opprobrium, not least from her fellow wives. Even offering a gentleman caller refreshment was out of the question as it was considered 'an act of glaring impropriety in a lady to invite any gentleman to stay and partake of tiffin who is not either a relative or an intimate friend of the family'. Nor were ladies allowed to socialise with their husbands' colleagues in the officers' mess as this building was strictly out of bounds to females, except when they were invited in on special occasions. But on the march ladies were often allowed to breach the walls of that male bastion and take their meals in the mess tent. Vivacious, sociable women relished the opportunity to escape briefly from the oppressive protocol and domesticity that suffused garrison life. Nor did the bill of fare in the mess tent disappoint. Being on the march was seen as no reason to lower standards and complaints were made if the wine served was not of the usual fine vintage. If ladies did not want to eat in the mess a cook would bring them meals in their tent and they were usually attended by an ayah (maid) and other domestic servants who would sweep and clean their tents, shooing away unwanted visitors such as rats and cockroaches, bring them tea before a march and water for washing. Marches also offered opportunities for sightseeing for those ladies who were interested in life beyond the confines of their cantonments.

A column on the march in India presented a particularly colourful spectacle. Behind the orderly column of soldiers trailed a disorderly, clamorous army of servants, followers and wives. Syces (grooms) rode the officers' spare ponies or drove their gharries (pony traps) while others perched on top of the camels and elephants used to transport heavy baggage. Behind them came the water carriers, grass cutters, cooks, sweepers and washerwomen, bullock carts with squeaking wheels and drivers cracking their whips and shouting curses. The rear guard followed behind, restoring some semblance of military orderliness to the tip of this extraordinary tail.

It was with such a column that Margaret Hannay traversed India, accompanying her husband Lieutenant Simon Fraser Hannay, Adjutant of the 50th Regiment Native Infantry (NI). The regiment left the station of Mysopoorie in January 1829 for their new posting at Mhow in the United Provinces, and Simon was in charge of the daily logistics of the two-month march. Like many officers' wives of that era, Margaret travelled in comparative comfort in a palanquin, carried by eight bearers, at the rear of the column. Although sorry to be leaving her home in Mysopoorie and particularly her garden where she had become attached to 'every tree and shrub . . . and all my beautiful flowers [which] will now in all probability go to ruin', she soon threw herself into the excitement of the march, her second in the space of nine months.

A typical day would begin at 3 or 4 a.m. when the tents were disman-tled and packed and, after a hasty brew of tea, the column would set off across the countryside, usually stopping at around 9 a.m. in time for breakfast. Then she would read her Bible for an hour before receiving visits from some of the officers: 'They are all so attentive and so anxious to please me . . . ' she wrote happily. After socialising, she often went for a ride or a walk to look at nearby villages and mosques and was delighted and intrigued by all she saw. When they passed near military garrisons or large European settlements the Hannays paid social calls to acquaintances and in turn received them in their tent. They visited Agra, where Margaret was overcome with awe on seeing the marbled splendour of the Taj Mahal, but disappointed by the Red Fort.

A fierce downpour drenched the column on one morning march, but inside her palanquin Margaret was dry and snug and, she smugly noted, much envied by the officers. In fact she enjoyed the march so much that she felt, as she wrote to her mother, that 'I must have been cut out for an Officer's wife.' So confident did she feel in the military sphere that she even took upon herself the role of Adjutant one day. Her husband had sneaked off to go fishing early one morning and the irascible Colonel who commanded the column decided to begin the day's march even earlier than usual at 3 a.m. 'The Colonel was cross as an old bear, and I was afraid in his ill humour he might say something about Hannay's being out so long. Therefore took it upon me to give the parole and countersign and then sent about the orders. Fortunately it was all right and no one knew that my husband was not at home.'

Frances Wells also felt enlivened by life on the march. For her, being an army wife in the station of Barrackpore was somewhat monotonous, so she was relieved when her husband's regiment, the 48th Bengal NI, was posted to Allahabad. She was by now a mother and was besotted with her new baby, Walter (known as Dickey). She looked forward eagerly to the march, busily knitting clothes to keep the baby warm in the cold nights under canvas. As she had anticipated, she found the mobile life 'very delightful, indeed after being so long restricted to the two drives at Barrackpore I feel like a liberated prisoner'. She was thrilled to see more of the country beyond the confines of the Little England that Barrackpore, like most European stations, contrived to be, and described with delight watching a caravan of 'hundreds of camels laden with merchandize carrying cotton, rice, grain and indigo'.

Her march routine was similar to Margaret Hannay's except that she travelled by carriage rather than palanquin: 'We drive our horse half the distance and then we change and put in the mare so that we get along famously and all into camp before it gets hot. The Mess khansamah [bearer] goes on half way and prepares tea and coffee for us which is always most acceptable . . . The Regt . . . march in and out [of camp] with the band playing and all their bayonets flashing in the sun: a dozen elephants follow carrying the Sepoy's tents and there is a little one a few weeks old, such a funny little creature and so full of mischief . . . I dress baby myself and feel very glad if I get my toilet over by 12 o'clock. The worst part of the business is that horrid bugle call when it is so cold and dark. I thought of you all a great deal on Christmas day and wished I had been with you, we were encamped in a ploughed field where we could make nothing stand steadily and it rained all day; however we managed to get a suitable dinner comprising roast turkey, boiled hump [beef], plum pudding and an iced cake which we brought from Calcutta . . . '

Although officers and their wives travelled in a great deal more comfort than the lowlier ranks, life on the march had its drawbacks for everyone. The heat could be exhausting and, as many men died from heatstroke during those long, dusty treks, it can be imagined that the women suffered greatly too. The dust generated by hundreds of horses, camels and marching men rose in great choking clouds that filled the eyes, ears and mouths of those in the column, especially at the back where the women usually marched. Weakened by exhaustion, soldiers frequently fell prey to illness, but as halts usually lasted only a night or two they had little opportunity to recover before they were on the road again. This too was the lot of any women who fell ill. Most ladies travelled in carriages or pony traps, or like Margaret Hannay by palanquin. In this respect they were better off than the men but in other ways they were at a disadvantage, notably in the clothing they wore. While the men sweated in their tight breeches, woollen tunics and high, stiff collars, the women had to endure the discomfort of numerous tight-fitting under and outer garments.

Another hazard came in the form of thieves who were attracted to the easy targets provided by the vast tented camps. These midnight marauders reputedly shaved and oiled their bodies so that if caught they could slip like eels from the grasp of their assailant and slip away into the night. So nimble and skilful were they that they were said to be able to strip the clothes off their sleeping victims without waking them. According to Harriet Earle, the thieves usually worked in pairs. 'One of the fellows would tickle the sleeper on the ear with a feather, who would then move and turn over to the other side, upon which they would draw out the clothes a little from under her. Then, giving her time to go off into a sound sleep again, they would repeat the trick until they had taken everything from her, leaving her without a scrap of clothes either about or on her person.'

Implausible as this sounds, Harriet claimed that her mother had been on a march when such a crime was committed against a Mrs Beckett, the only other officer's wife accompanying the regiment. Awaking one night shivering with cold, she was astounded to find that thieves had not only taken her bedclothes but had removed her nightdress too without disturbing her. On calling for her ayah, the woman was mortified to find that she too was naked and had been divested of every scrap of clothing she possessed. When they lit a lamp Mrs Beckett saw that all her possessions and those of her children had gone. They had nothing to wear and had to borrow clothes from Mrs Earle (Harriet's mother) until the end of the march. As Harriet relates, there was a comical side to the story: 'When Mrs Beckett appeared at the mess breakfast next morning, there was a shout of laughter. She was a great favourite, and joined in it, though at her own expense, for it was really too funny a sight for gravity and good manners. My mother's dress was too short by nearly a foot, for Mrs Beckett was an immensely tall woman and my mother the reverse.' Mrs Beckett was clearly a 'good sport' and possessed two important attributes of an army wife: a robust sense of humour and a hearty resilience.

The kind of larcenous indignity inflicted on Mrs Beckett became less likely with the arrival of the railway in India in 1853. The first railway line was opened between Bombay and Thane twenty-one miles away, and by the turn of the century India was criss-crossed by 24,000 miles of gleaming railtrack. No longer did regiments have to spend months trekking across India to take up a new posting. Now at least some of the journey could be completed by rail (although even by the twentieth century railways did not penetrate the further reaches of India and Burma and the last leg of the journey would still have to be undertaken by road). No longer would those long columns snake their way along the Grand Trunk Road that ran the length of India, accompanied by the jangling of camels' bells, the trumpeting of elephants and the crack of the bullock drivers' whips in the misty dawns.

These journeys, romantic, eventful, exhausting and terrifying though they might have been, were no more than the beginning of another adventure for the wives who made them. If they survived the rigours of the voyage or the march they would find themselves with a fresh challenge to face: that of making a home in the garrison or outpost that they had struggled for weeks or months to reach.

4

A Home from Home

Ten men, ten women, and eight children are to be found occupying
one hut . . . preservations of decency are impossible. The double
beds nearly touch each other, without even the scantiest
attempt at screen or curtain.

**Charles Dickens describing the married
quarters at Aldershot in 1856**

Most army wives would agree that the existence of married quarters
is not just a boon but an essential cornerstone in the peripatetic
life of military families, even though the accommodation itself may fall
short of expectation. A survey was carried out in 1986 in response to
mutinous rumblings in the ranks of army wives: most had a poor opinion
of quarters and of their state of repair, decor and furnishing. 'Often, colour
schemes make no sort of co-ordinated sense,' concluded the report, adding
a plea for quarters to be decorated in more neutral shades. As a child I
can remember a look of horror often coming over my mother's face as
we entered a new quarter to be assaulted by a kaleidoscope of clashing
colours: lime-green sofas vying with purple curtains and mottled orange
carpets. Usually, after some negotiation, the Quartermaster's office would
replace some of the more offensive objects with quieter colours.

   The report also found that the rules governing their entitlement to
quarters and furnishings aroused feelings of irritation and incredulity; for
example, officers' quarters had fitted carpets while those of other ranks
did not. Many of those petty distinctions were subsequently abolished,

though officers' families are still housed according to rank while soldiers' quarters are allocated by size of family. Quarters, now referred to as Service Families Accommodation, continue to vary greatly in terms of quality, a fact tacitly acknowledged by the Chief of the General Staff, when, in a statement in December 2003 regarding the army's future, he promised to improve the state of army accommodation. Increasing numbers of army families (nearly a quarter according to a recent survey of army spouses) are choosing to live in their own houses.

Army wives in earlier centuries would no doubt have been happy if all they had to complain about was tacky interior decoration. Their plight was more basic: they had to find their own accommodation. The army authorities' only contribution was to try to restrict their presence; they certainly did not want to encourage it by providing housing for them. In fact, in the seventeenth and early eighteenth centuries, there was no such thing as quarters at all, even for the soldier himself. Regiments moved regularly from town to town in their role as keepers of public order (in the days before a police force), and their men were frequently billeted on private households as well as in inns and livery stables. But this created enormous resentment in towns where some householders were incensed to have their homes invaded, their wives and daughters insulted and their drink consumed by a rabble of rowdy soldiers. In an effort to appease angry burghers, the practice of billeting soldiers on private houses was stopped in England, Scotland and Wales. The Mutiny Act of 1703 stipulated that soldiers should be billeted in 'inns, livery stables, ale houses, victualling houses, and all houses selling brandy, strong-waters, cyder or metheglin to be drunk on the premises, and in no other, and in no private houses whatsoever'. An additional grievance as far as the civilian authorities were concerned was the 'great number of women and children the soldiers always carry with them'. The matter was referred to a board of General Officers, who recommended that commanding officers 'take care that all women not legally married be chased away'.

Abroad too the problem of housing troops and their families sometimes caused friction with the civilian population. In Montreal in 1764, one of the town magistrates, a merchant named Thomas Walker, strongly objected to the presence of British troops and took every opportunity to harass them. He ensured that soldiers and officers were given the least comfortable quarters possible and turned men and families out of billets. Once, in midwinter, he refused to allow women of the 28th (later the North Gloucestershire) Regiment to stay in the billets that they had been allocated, leaving them to trudge through the snow with their children to find alternative housing. So enraged were the soldiers when they learnt of this treatment that they broke into Walker's house one evening. A scuffle ensued, culminating in Walker's ear being cut off. When an inquiry was launched the soldiers closed ranks, refusing to reveal the culprits, so nobody could be brought to trial for the crime. The incident of 'Walker's Ear' as it became known led to the 28th's nickname of 'the Slashers'.

In overseas garrisons the problem of billeting was sometimes overcome by constructing barracks, but these were frequently of poor quality. During Queen Anne's reign in the early 1700s a report noted that the army was haemorrhaging manpower in cold climates where men were dying from exposure due to inadequate shelter. In New York in 1711 one-third of the garrison perished from sheer cold in a single winter, while in Newfoundland and Nova Scotia, where the temperature was frequently well below freezing, the barracks were so shabby that they fell apart over the soldiers' heads. These were the conditions shared by their families.

In some ways life was easier for soldiers' wives when the army was on the march. Then wives on the strength were permitted to pitch their tents to the rear of the camp although in practice many shared tents (when tents were available) or huts with their husbands. Those 'off the strength' did not, as far as the army was concerned, exist. If they were found in camp or barracks they were turned out and punished severely if they had the temerity to return. Viscount Molesworth in his 'Short Course of Standing Rules for the Government and Conduct of the Army, 1745' warned that women must not be allowed to sleep more than one to each tent, perhaps on moral grounds but more likely it was another way of limiting their numbers.

By the end of Queen Anne's reign in 1714 there were still no barracks in England. For the most part soldiers continued to be billeted on pubs and inns. When their regiments took part in 'manoeuvres', as training exercises used to be called, which usually took place in the summer months, they were housed in tents on the field. Officers' ladies could generally afford to stay in inns if they wished to follow the regiment around the country, but this was not always an option for their poorer sisters.

Whenever the idea was mooted of building barracks to house the soldiers, it was strongly resisted by the political establishment, both on the grounds of cost and the instinctive abhorrence of anything that smacked too much of a permanent standing army. The spectre of Charles I and his King's Army still loomed large. Even in 1786, when Prime Minister William Pitt (the Younger) urged the construction of defensive military works including barracks, he was rebuffed. Some barracks were built in Scotland and Ireland: huts about seventeen or eighteen feet in length with five double beds accommodated ten soldiers who ate, lived and slept there. No other arrangements were made for the married men, except that those who had married with permission were given passes enabling them to visit their families as long as they were back in barracks before dark. The families themselves continued to live on the margins of army life, although soldiers were later given a lodging allowance that enabled them to house their families in nearby inns or boarding houses.

In 1792, with the threat of French invasion appearing imminent, attitudes changed and a formal programme of barrack building at last began in England. In these barracks married soldiers were allowed to install their families in a corner of the room on a couple of beds (regardless of the size of their family or the age of the children). A makeshift screen or curtain provided the barest modicum of privacy. The barrack room, festooned with soldiers' washing that drooped from lines strung across it, would reek of the strong smell of clay pipes smoked by the soldiers and many of their wives. It was not the most comfortable way of starting married life.

And the lack of privacy inherent in barracks undermined the army's insistence on the propriety of its women. While young boys thrived on the rough and tumble of barrack life, wearing cut-off uniforms, petted by the soldiers and able to slip into their vacant beds while they were out on drill, girls were often more vulnerable. It became a source of concern to moral campaigners that girls of thirteen and young brides sometimes only a few months older were forced to sleep inches away from unmarried men, dressing and undressing, making love and giving birth behind a flimsy curtain.

The question of whether married women ought to be accepted and decently accommodated continued to be debated throughout the early nineteenth century. By the 1850s, Charles Dickens was throwing his considerable weight and reputation behind the issue. In 1851 he published an account in his journal *Household Words* from a lady correspondent (an officer's wife) describing the scene that a new soldier's wife might encounter. 'Picture her making her entry into married life over the threshold of a barrack-room, containing twenty or thirty men. She hesitates, she trembles; some are laughing, some are singing, some swearing, and some dressing for parade. She hurries through the throng; and, 'ere a month is past, necessity has reconciled her to her new position. A thin curtain is all that screens her from the gaze of her husband's comrades . . . '

She went on to describe a typical married corner of a barrack room that she had inspected: 'At the end of this room, near the windows, was the narrow space allotted to the sergeant – a married man. Two iron bedsteads lashed together, formed the family couch. Four iron rods, fastened at the corners, supported a cord on which hung some curtains looped up. The screen which separated this nook from the men's quarters was also drawn back. The place was scrupulously clean . . . ' The sergeant's wife, a 'slender, delicate-looking creature with a pretty, cleanly dressed infant in her arms', had tried hard to add some homely touches to her sparse habitation: a jar of flowers, various articles from foreign climes and a patchwork quilt. She was, it transpired, only nineteen and her baby of nine months had been born in that barrack-room at midnight with all the men around her.

The lady correspondent was convinced that if the government would only improve the living conditions of soldiers' wives, their morals (commonly deemed to be low) and those of the soldiers would improve too. 'It would be but commonly prudent,' she pointed out, 'if Britannia would permit the fortunate one in twenty [soldiers who were permitted to marry] to have decent accommodation for his wife . . . It is not of much use,' she scolded, 'to educate the soldiers' children, while their mothers are committed to pollution . . . Britannia has, of late, made some wise regulations for the moral and intellectual improvement of the soldiery; she has established regimental schools . . . [But] Be decent . . . not the bitterest enemy of army expenditure, would grudge you the cost of a few separate cells – cheaper than the cells you offer to the use of those who have offended your laws – whereinto there your soldiers could bring, as into a little home, a modest wife. Here . . . might the woman remain pure, and exercise her humanizing influence over her husband and his comrades . . . '.

By this time, there were calls for more soldiers to be allowed to marry, with Charles Dickens adding his voice to those who insisted that preventing soldiers from marrying was both unnatural and immoral. The movement still had to counter the intransigence of certain military authorities who persisted in the view that introducing married quarters would only have the deleterious effect of making marriage more appealing to soldiers. In 1852 one officer, Captain Hugh Scott of the 92nd (Gordon) Highlanders, was censured by the Duke of Wellington (then Commander in Chief of the Army) for breaching the Articles of War when he called for the construction of married quarters for soldiers. But the old Duke, with his entrenched resistance to change, died that year, removing one major barrier to reform.

Then in 1854 the Crimean War brought the plight of soldiers into the public's horrified gaze and turned the tide decisively in favour of reform. In response to the growing clamour, the government appointed several commissions to look into the living conditions of soldiers; their findings concurred with those of Charles Dickens's lady correspondent. Barrack rooms were indeed less spacious than jails. Convicts enjoyed 1,000 cubic feet of air while soldiers were given only 300 or 400. Rates of death among soldiers during peacetime reflected such insalubrious, cramped conditions. Infectious diseases spread quickly among the men and the married families living alongside them. A report to the House of Commons in 1858 revealed that mortality rates in the Foot Guards were 20.4 per thousand whereas the average for the civilian population of military age was only about nine per thousand. This concurred with the findings of the Barrack Accommodation Committee which had published a report in 1855 stating that barracks were overcrowded, with several families living together alongside the bachelor soldiers. Moreover, in the whole of the United Kingdom there was only one barrack bath.

The report recommended that separate accommodation be provided for married families within barracks rather than outside as this would enable the regiment to keep a tighter control on the married soldiery, as well as saving the considerable sums spent on lodging allowances for married men.

In the meantime some regiments, such as the 11th Hussars, had already begun to address the problem by setting up separate married quarters on their own initiative. The officers of the Brigade of Guards were particularly progressive. In 1852 they raised £9,000 between themselves to build a lodging house in London for fifty-four of their married privates and families at a rent of 2s 6d a week for each man. The War Office later bought the lodgings from the Brigade, although with typical parsimony they would only pay £8,000 for them. Following the Barrack Accommodation Committee's report, a programme of building works began and within two years twenty military stations in Britain had separate married quarters. In the other 231 stations the families continued for the time being to live in the barrack rooms.

The married accommodation was often little improvement on the old mixed barrack rooms. Seven families were crowded into fourteen beds; though each woman was responsible for the men's washing she had nowhere to dry and iron it; and all the children had to shelter behind the parental screen. Some observers noted that there was now more immorality among married people than ever before as they made use of the relative seclusion of married quarters to indulge in illicit behaviour. By 1857 nearly all regiments had reverted to the old arrangement. In 1860 married quarters were built at Chelsea Barracks in London while Queen Victoria personally demanded that some be constructed at Victoria barracks in Windsor, anxious perhaps that the scenes of degradation that she had heard took place in mixed barrack rooms should not occur on her doorstep.

In 1856 Charles Dickens, who continued to take a keen interest in the living conditions of soldiers' families, visited the newly built Aldershot Camp and was appalled by the overcrowded, squalid married huts where privacy was utterly lacking. Children screamed and cried while men cursed and quarrelled and the women attempted to carry out their domestic chores amid the squalor and brawling. 'The result of this degradation,' he thundered, 'is that the modest, innocent girl soon succumbs to the shame and obscenities around her and step by step she becomes the drunken, dissolute, fear-inspiring and slatternly brawler of our barrack yards. What good are chapels and schools before this systematic training in depravity?' By 1864 a report by the *United Services Gazette* found the situation unchanged.

Ironically, not all the inhabitants of the new married quarters would themselves have seen much to complain about – at least at first. Often the accommodation was a vast improvement on what they had left behind. Many recruits, particularly those from England's city slums, the impoverished crofts of Scotland, and famine-struck Ireland, joined the army to escape desperate poverty. A soldier jailed for cowardice in the Egyptian campaign in 1882 was asked why, if he had no appetite for fighting, had he joined the army. His response was simple: 'Starvation.' To them and to the wives who came from similarly humble backgrounds, who had grown up in the hovels of London, Highland crofters' huts or the smoky dwellings of Galway where they shared beds with their siblings, the lack of privacy and the shabbiness of their surroundings mattered little. It was a home and was in many cases no worse and sometimes rather better than what they were used to.

But, slowly, married quarters did begin to improve. The new accommodation shared certain characteristics with the married quarters of today in that their size and standards varied greatly according to the rank of their inhabitants. Soldiers' families were housed in two-storey buildings divided into flats and sparsely furnished. The privy was of course outside

and the fireplace was often shared with at least one other flat. Officers'
quarters were somewhat larger and more generously furnished with
regulation tables and chairs, coal scuttles, fire irons and cupboards, while the
commanding officers' houses often verged on the palatial and sometimes
adjoined the Officers' Mess. Abroad, senior officers sometimes did literally
live in palaces converted into quarters. Later on allowances were made for
the size of families and those with a lot of children were entitled to larger
quarters. But even so the regulations and the disparities between what
different ranks could expect remained marked, even in the late twentieth
century. In the 1960s officers' married quarters were not supplied with
ironing boards as traditionally officers' wives had someone else to do such
menial tasks.

While all the progress (as some, if not all, saw it) towards decently
accommodating families 'on the strength' was going on, the lot of the
unauthorised wives remained sadly unchanged. As they were not on the
'married roll' they were not entitled to any sort of housing and remained
relegated to lodgings or squalid shacks outside the camp perimeter where
ragged children with sunken cheeks played and scavenged for food. Wives
of private soldiers were particularly badly off as a private's pay was scarcely
enough to keep the man himself fed and watered, let alone provide for a
wife and children. The best they could do was to save scraps from their
meals to take to their families. Despite the bland assumption of people
like Lord Panmure that wives could keep themselves and their family with
their own 'industry', this was often impossible for women encumbered
with small children and perhaps pregnant too. Some of them were forced
to turn to the trade for which the army always supplied plentiful customers:
prostitution. Even those who managed to survive without resorting to
such measures could be treated with disdain by wives on the strength and
by the local inhabitants.

By the early twentieth century married quarters continued to be
restricted to those 'on the strength' and those who did not qualify had to
pay for their own lodgings or resign themselves to living separately until
they took their place on the married roll. When Dorothy Cook met her
future husband Tommy in 1924 they quickly became engaged but as
Tommy had not served long enough to qualify for married quarters they
waited for three years before marrying. Their first married quarter was in
Whittington Barracks, Lichfield. 'In reality,' remembered Dorothy, 'it
was a dreadful place but to us it was paradise. We were given an "A" type
quarter comprising two rooms. One with a large kitchen range, which

served as Dining room, sitting room and Kitchen. In it were a Kitchen table, and chairs, and brown linoleum. The Bedroom was linoed in the same depressing way . . . There was no bathroom, so we bathed in the scullery, or kitchen according to the weather, in a galvanised bath. We had a separate WC and our own front door. This was "Our Blue Heaven" where we could do just as we liked, and we loved it.'

Often the standard of army accommodation failed to keep pace with that in the civilian realm. The married quarters built by the Victorians to replace the squalid huts in Aldershot were barely updated over the next century so that by the 1960s some soldiers' families were still living in quarters with no running water and an outside lavatory. Quarters abroad were sometimes no better. Melissa Cordingly (whose husband Patrick was to command 7th Armoured Brigade in the 1991 Gulf War) remembers visiting a soldier's wife in Germany in the early 1970s who had been housed in a shabby Portakabin and was so depressed by her surroundings that she had taken to the bottle.

Most wives, like the young sergeant's wife with her jar of flowers and patchwork quilt, tried hard to add a personal, homely touch to their quarters. The curmudgeonly Major Patterson, who had been so horrified by the indecent situation of women on board ship, grumbled at the home improvements made by barrack-room wives who 'nail up, and pull down, so many shelves and brackets, pegs and pins, that, were they to continue long at this work, the barrack-department would soon arrive at hopeless bankruptcy'.

Those living abroad often tried to anglicise their dwellings in an effort to recreate a little corner of England in the foreign field to which they had been exiled. Leonora Starr, an officer's wife living in India in the 1930s, observed that officers and their wives were divided into two groups. There were those whose bungalows 'were filled with brass elephants, amateurish sketches of Kashmir, carved tables with brass tops, screens carved in minute detail . . . and curtains of Indian silk. The other variety clung rather pathetically to every tradition of Home, disguised their cheap furniture (hired from the Government or a dealer in the bazaar) with flowered cretonnes and made their bungalows look as English as they could.' Another officer's wife remarked that 'once you stepped inside the home [in British India], you were back in Cheltenham or Bath or wherever'.

Iris Portal was somewhat disappointed by her first married quarter when she arrived in Poona, India, in 1927 as the bride of Major Gervas 'Squire' Portal of the 2nd Royal Lancers (Gardner's Horse). Iris's father,

Montagu Butler, was a senior mandarin in the Indian Civil Service and at the time of her marriage was serving as the Governor of the Central Provinces. The Butler family, including Iris's older brother Rab, lived in some splendour in Government House at Nagpur and it was a rude awakening for Iris when she arrived in Poona and was shown to her new home. 'Cavalry Lines, Poona' she wrote, 'lay on the edge of the cantonment through an exceptionally noisome bazaar called Ghorpuri. An open drain from this bazaar ran along the back of the row of bungalows in which the officers lived. A dusty road lay in front . . . This, my first home, was small and dark and had no electric light or water. The rooms were ceilinged by a cloth, behind which animals of various sorts galumphed and scratched. . . . If you looked up you could see the little feet of rats or bandicoots or maybe a mongoose padding over your head.' Yet when the time came to move to a new station the following year, she became sentimental about the little house where, although it was far removed from the luxury to which she had been accustomed, she had been extremely happy.

For some wives, the hardest thing to get used to when they moved into their new house was managing the small army of servants that they were obliged to employ commensurate with their station – most particularly in India.

For Rosemary Montgomery, who came to Cawnpore as a new bride in 1931, managing her staff was almost a full-time occupation. When she first arrived, she was tutored by another officer's wife in the art of house-keeping in India. The main principle of this instruction was that she must not trust the servants with anything even of the smallest value or they would steal it. As Rosemary wrote home to her mother: 'You have to give out every single thing each morning including dusters, etc, boil all your milk and water and inspect every corner to see that it is clean. She has been most kind and given me hours of advice and help and I think I'll be able to manage more or less though I foresee that it will be hard work at first. It takes her two hours a morning and she's had six years' practice.'

Rosemary soon settled into her daily routine, which she described in another letter home. After her husband left for the office after breakfast she began her day 'by visiting the kitchen and seeing a boiling "detchie" (an aluminium pan with no handle) of water. I consider coal and look to see whether there is permanganate of potash ready to soak the vegetables and whether the earthenware saucers on which the larders stand have been filled with water and disinfectant – I am also expected to inspect any fowls that we may be going to eat, a heartrending spectacle and waste of energy

as I've no idea what a chicken unplucked should look like. Then I go to
the Kelvinator to see what's left over, how much butter, milk, etc and
whether there's soda water and then armed with keys and account books
march to my storeroom and fling wide the cupboards where I give out
what is needed for the day, so much sugar for the pudding and so much
for cakes, tinned food when we need it and sticks of macaroni in cereals
and vinegar. I'm really getting quite expert on how much a cornflour
shape takes. Then I write out and explain, with drawings to translate to
our rather inadequate cook, tomorrow's menu and take down yesterday's
expenses and give out milk and butter coupons and kitchen cloths – the
kitmagar, who corresponds to butler, then appears and I give out lump
sugar, ham, biscuits, etc, fill up the decanters and cigarettes and matchboxes
and give out dusters and clothes for each man – Finally I go to the linen
cupboard and give out napkins, towels and bedclothes as we lose them.
As you can imagine all this takes some time, but I still find it very
amusing and far too difficult to be boring.'

The problem of 'losing' household items was frequently referred to by
wives in India who complained that light-fingered servants would steal
anything that was not locked away or nailed down, and this sometimes
coloured their view of all Indians, causing them to caricature them as a
race of thieves and liars.

Frances Wells, arriving in India nearly a century earlier, was initially
enthusiastic about setting up home for the first time and was delighted
with her servants, writing to her father, 'I must say on the whole I like
the native servants. There is no impudence, no finery with them and I
think ours will soon get into order as they see that we are very punctual
in our meals and that I am very particular about having all things in proper
order.' Only weeks later she had changed her views, complaining that all
Indian servants were 'idle and disloyal'.

Margaret Hannay, the energetic adjutant's wife living in India in the
1820s and 1830s, was particularly scathing about women who relied too
much on their servants. 'You would be quite astonished, dearest Mama,'
she wrote, 'could you see or know how selfish ladies are in India. They
would not give up one comfort which they have been used to for anyone.
I hope I am not selfish for I do despise it in others. Laziness too is what
grows on one almost imperceptibly. I try to guard against it as much as I
can. I always dress myself, brush and dress my own hair, and take care of
my own clothes. I am not praising myself, dear Mama, but only wish you
to know that it is quite possible for a lady to exert herself in this Country.'

I keep no ayah [lady's maid], which diminishes the expenses of our establishment not a little. Hannay often insists on my having one, but I will not indulge in such laziness unless obliged by ill health.'

Dorothy Cook, who had begun married life in such humble but happy style, was not naturally at ease in the role of mistress of a large household. She was alarmed to find that as her husband's rank increased so must the number of servants they employed. By 1935 they were in Meerut, India, where her husband was Lieutenant Quarter-Master of the Military Hospital. Much against her inclination they were forced to exchange the bungalow they loved for an officer's quarter for which they paid twice as much rent, plus higher bills for lighting and coal. Furthermore, she had to employ twice the number of servants.

When Annie Lee went out to India in 1909 as a corporal's wife she was not troubled by the question of how many servants to employ. She had far more pressing problems. After an uncomfortable journey by dhoolie (a rather humbler kind of litter than a palanquin) into which the monsoon rains had poured she arrived in Dalhousie to find that there were no quarters available. She was given a tent with two charpoys (string beds) and an oil stove outside it on which she had to cook supper while beating off the insects. She was not the complaining sort: the daughter of a Boer War veteran, her philosophy was simple: 'You got used to it. You get used to anything in time if you have to.'

The canvas solution was frequently applied to the problem of insufficient married quarters. Ruth Barton had been married only a few weeks when in 1931 her husband's regiment, the 6th Rajputana Rifles, was sent to Burma to deal with a rebellion. After a few weeks Ruth and some other wives followed and she travelled up country to join her husband, Pete, at the battalion's headquarters on the Irrawady river. Ruth, who was the only wife to have come this far, was allowed to share a small tent with Pete near the mess from where they were supplied with meals. Blissfully happy at being able to live once more with her husband, she revelled in the beauty of her surroundings, which amply compensated for the shortcomings of their primitive home.

'The tent was pitched on the river bank beneath a little grove of wild plum trees which gave welcome shade in the heat of the day . . . As Pete was always up for early parade, I wakened early and looked straight out through the tent opening on to the shadowy river below. All the colours were veiled and dim, but soon the sun had risen behind the tent and the river glowed with the vivid reflections of the wooded banks, carrying them like a delicate bridge in long, straight columns from shore to shore. At each faint breath of wind the columns shivered and blurred, blending the colours together. In the first few minutes after Sunrise the red-brown hills beyond the river glowed softly pink, and then their outlines took on the sharp clarity of an eastern day. In the deep stillness of early morning a long procession of boats came down the river, paddy boats with high, carved prows, gaily painted, and colourful sails set to catch the variable wind. In the welcome coolness of late afternoon we sat outside the tent and officers came to call, glad of a chat with a woman, not having seen one for nearly a year. As the sun was setting the river caught fire and molten gold ran up the little creeks on the shore below us. After the sun had set, and the afterglow faded, a grape-soft, mauvish flush spread round the rim of the sky, deepening and spreading upwards before it ebbed gently away, leaving one to wonder if it had ever been . . . '

For young couples in love, the most mundane surroundings could take on a romantic aspect. On campaign soldiers and their wives frequently slept under the open skies with nothing more than their cloak to cover them and tents were considered a luxury. It was not until the campaign of 1813–14 that proper tents were supplied to the army in the Peninsula. Until then most soldiers and their families had to sleep under open skies with only a blanket rigged up as an improvised tent. In inclement weather they made rough huts or shelters but on brief halts they seldom had the chance to do that and many perished from exposure. Even when tents were issued, the baggage wagons bearing them might be several hours or even days behind the main body of the column, so there was nothing for it but to lie down on the ground when a halt was called and sleep as best they could.

When tents were available they were often horribly overcrowded and insalubrious, particularly for young wives who had not had time to adjust to living cheek-by-jowl with their husbands' comrades. Mary Anton had not long been married when she accompanied her husband James of the 42nd Highlanders (the Black Watch) to the Peninsula in 1813. The first night she spent under canvas was far from comfortable, as James recalled. 'Eleven soldiers lay in it that night with us, all stretched with their feet to the centre and their heads to the curtain of the tent. Every man's knapsack below his head, and his clothes and accoutrements on his body, the one half of the blankets under, and the other spread over the whole, so that we all lay in one bed. Often did my poor wife look up to the thin canvas that screened her face from the night-dew, and wish for the approaching morn.' Not only was Mary troubled by the indelicacy of her situation; she was also alarmed by the thought of catching a skin complaint from her sleeping companions, many of whom were afflicted by dermatitis, caused by seldom washing or changing their clothes.

The next day James set about constructing a small hut where he and Mary could enjoy some privacy away from the snoring and itching of the other soldiers. Although it was barely big enough to lie down in it was their own little home. Mary hung her apron up in lieu of a door and when it was 'closed' none of the men attempted to enter. The first night a strong wind blew the roof off their hut and they were forced to spend the rest of the night sheltering under a rock, with Mary trembling in her husband's arms. But when daybreak came they rebuilt their hut and here they remained, blissfully content for several days. When James was posted on picquet (outlying guard) duty some two miles away, Mary took him bread and mulled wine. Their happy domesticity was rudely interrupted when the order came to strike camp. 'On leaving the camp that night, many of the married people set fire to their huts,' recalled James, 'but I left mine with too much regret to become its incendiary; and my poor Mary shed tears as she looked back upon it, as a bower of happiness which she was leaving behind.'

Officers' wives were seldom expected to submit to the indignities of a shared tent, although those who, like Juana Smith, accompanied their husbands into the field often had to sleep in the open. Although they were spared from sleeping beside their husbands' louse-ridden, skin-itching comrades, there were plenty of other hazards inherent in tent living. Lady Harriet Acland spent many months sharing a tent with her husband during the American Revolutionary War. The third daughter of the first Earl of Ilchester, Lady Harriet had married the Grenadierand MP John Dyke Acland in 1771. At the beginning of 1776, aged twenty-five, she sailed with her husband to North America, where the war was already going badly for the British, commanded by General John Burgoyne. Arriving in Canada, she quickly forsook the gracious living to which she had hitherto been accustomed for the trials of life on the march, adapting cheerfully to living in tents and huts in the wilds of North America. Indeed her endurance, fortitude and kind nature made her the idol of the troops, who were amazed to find a lady of such noble birth sharing their hardships and privations.

One night in 1777 the Aclands had gone to sleep in their tent, together with the Newfoundland dog they had acquired, when the tent suddenly caught fire. Major Acland's orderly sergeant managed to drag his master out of the flames while Lady Harriet herself succeeded in crawling out under the wall of the tent, only to see her husband plunging into the flames to search for her. Again the faithful sergeant dragged him out, but not before he had suffered severe burns on his face and body. The fire, it transpired, was started by the dog, which had overturned a table on which a candle was burning. Lady Harriet was typically stoical about the episode despite the destruction of all their possessions, although her wealth and comparatively privileged position must have made it easier to bear such losses.

By the time of the Crimean War in 1854, the difficulties of providing accommodation on campaign for the army's women had not been resolved. Officers' ladies could not be expected to share tents with men other than their husbands, while soldiers' wives, though they might be prepared to bed down alongside their husbands' comrades, sometimes found that there was not enough room for them. When the army sailed East to fight the Russians it was not at first apparent that the Crimea would be its final destination. Indeed it had stopped at Malta, Constantinople, Scutari (in Turkey) and then Varna on the Bulgarian coast before the order came to sail for the Crimea.

On arrival at Scutari, many of the soldiers' wives spent a miserable night wrapped in blankets or cloaks and seeking what cover they could in ditches or under bushes. Some tried their luck in the Turkish hovels around the harbour but were soon discouraged by the many resident rats. Reprieve came in the shape of an announcement by the Commissary General that from now on two tents would be provided for the women of each regiment. Many women were still driven to take shelter in the vast Turkish barracks that was shortly to become the army's general hospital, but was still filled with vermin of every description at this stage. Here they stayed in the cellars, where rats ran helter-skelter across filthy, badly ventilated rooms that regularly flooded and filled with waste from the sick rooms above. On one occasion a pipe was found to have been blocked by the body of a newborn baby. Despite the squalor, many of the soldiers' wives remained here rather than travelling on to Varna and the Crimea.

When Florence Nightingale arrived in Scutari in November 1854 with her small band of nurses the women were still there, though many had now filled unmarked graves around the barracks. The following month Lady Alicia Blackwood, whose husband was chaplain to the forces in the Crimea, volunteered her services to Florence Nightingale and was given responsibility for the 260 women and children who had made the reeking cellars their home.

In her journal she described the situation as 'a Pandemonium full of cursing and swearing and drunkenness. The arrangements of a barrack room for married soldiers in those days were such, that other than this result could hardly be expected. They were certainly as much sinned against as sinning!' The mixing of men and women in a barrack room (common as this was in England) appalled her almost more than the legions of rats. The fact that women had to give birth in such circumstances was particularly horrifying, as was the alarmingly high death rate. On her first day she found one woman 'in the agonies of death; she was lying on a heap of filthy black rags on the floor in a dark room containing about sixty women, from twenty-five to thirty men, and some infants. There were no beds or bedsteads whatever, a piece of Indian matting and a heap of rags was all any one had, and these were strewn all over the floor, as may be imagined, when so many occupied the space. The poor dying woman was gasping for breath. I spoke to her, but she was past all human aid, and as I stood and looked upon her the spirit took its flight. I inquired what medical advice she had had? how long had she been ill? "A week," was the reply; "but no doctor had seen her, she could get none." ' There were not even enough doctors to perform amputations on the soldiers, let alone tend the women and children.

While the soldiers' wives were slumming it in Scutari, some officers' wives took up residence a little further up the coast in Therapia where the Hotel d'Angleterre proved to be so comfortable that many elected to stay there for the duration of the war. Others, however, were not interested in taking the soft option. One such was Lady Erroll, whose husband was a captain in the Rifle Brigade. The Errolls pitched their green marquee in the middle of the brigade's camp, where it aroused great interest in the soldiers and passing Turks, as did Lady Erroll herself. The *Naval and Military Gazette* had reported that Lady Erroll 'was an object of great curiosity and wonder to the Turks as she rode from the beach'. Lord Erroll, it seems, was less appreciative of her charms for he slept in the only bed that could fit in their small marquee. His wife was left to make herself comfortable on the ground.

Fanny Duberly was another hardy soul. She had travelled with her husband to Scutari on the *Shooting Star* (having made the generous but unwise offer of employing the wife of Sergeant Major Williams as a maid to enable her to accompany the regiment), and had elected to stay on board. Fanny had married Henry Duberly in 1850 and, despite their sharply contrasting personalities, the marriage proved to be an enduring and affectionate one. Fanny was extremely pretty, with corn-coloured hair and a shapely figure, enhanced by stays and a wardrobe of well-tailored clothes. Vivacious, high-spirited and brimming with charm and wit, she captivated the officers of her husbands' regiment who admired her looks and spirit as well as her skill as a horsewoman. Fanny was not averse to encouraging her devotees and happily held court in the garrison towns where the regiment was stationed. Henry, ten years her senior, was decent, easy-going, unambitious and, possibly, a rather uninspiring man. But he was a good husband to Fanny, standing by her when her actions occasioned criticism. She in turn provided unwavering support to him, staying by his side through the bleakest of conditions, although her habit of becoming rather too intimate with some admirers occasioned some adverse comment.

When the orders came for the army to sail on from Scutari to the Bulgarian port of Varna, Fanny managed to wangle her way there too, thanks to Lord Raglan, the kind-hearted, rather elderly commander-in-chief of the army. He overruled Lord Lucan, the commander of the cavalry, who had tried to prevent Fanny from sailing. When she arrived, she and Henry spent a comfortable night in a tent to which Fanny's growing band of admirers brought such provisions as ham, brandy and beer.

A couple of days later the cavalry, to which Henry, as paymaster of the 8th (King's Royal Irish) Hussars, belonged, went on to Devna, a full day's march away. Arriving just before nightfall there was no time to pitch tents. Captain Tomkinson, a young admirer of Fanny's, spread his cloak and a sheepskin beneath a bush for her. This elegant and hitherto pampered daughter of a Wiltshire banker, who had spent her early life in gracious, if not grand, surroundings, lay down on this makeshift bed, put her hat over her eyes, and slept.

Driven by a sense of adventure, unencumbered by children (Fanny and Henry were to remain childless) and keen to provide comfort to her husband, Fanny was prepared to defy any commander's orders in order to fulfil her wifely duty as she saw it. Throughout the two years she spent in the Crimea, Fanny lived variously in a tent, on board ship and latterly in a hut. When the cavalry were encamped at Devna, after her first comfortless night under the bush, Fanny was able to share a tent with Henry, which she soon embellished by adding an arbour built of boughs and foliage. Here she received callers and sat reading, writing or occasionally doing needlework. Their tent, she noted happily, was a marquee, more comfortable than the bell-tents that most of the men had, and was double-lined to keep out the heat (and to prevent men wandering through camp at night from being able to see her undressing through the flimsy canvas). But canvas was no defence against a hurricane that struck the camp in July 'filling our tents, eyes, dinners, hair, beds, and boxes with intolerable dust'. The cavalry moved camp several times and each time Fanny's brigade of admirers would painstakingly erect the pretty arbour that made her tent conspicuous among the orderly rows of military bell tents.

While encamped inland from Varna, Fanny went to call on the wife of an officer in the 11th (Prince Albert's Own) Hussars, a Mrs Cresswell, who was reputed to be a hearty, stout-hearted lady, a brilliant rider and a keen shot. Curious to meet this Amazon for herself Fanny, who was always at pains to keep up appearances even in the roughest conditions, was appalled to be confronted by a woman, as she wrote to her sister Selina 'with such uncombed, scurfy hair, such black nails, such a dirty cotton gown open at the neck, without a sign of a collar or linen sleeve. Oh, you never had a kitchen maid so dreadful. She calls the officers "boys" – and addresses them as "Bill and Jack" – talks of nothing but her horse – found fault with my saddle, which happens to be a particularly good one. Told me I was "a fool" to have a marquee, a bell-tent was quite good enough for anyone – that my husband would vote me "a bore" if I didn't cook his dinner – that I was foolish to wear collars and sleeves as they were unnecessary – and that if I wished my husband to like me – "I should always the night before a march strike my tent, and sleep either wrapped in a cloak or "anywhere" – I should like to see Henry sleeping out! In fact, she took my breath away so completely that I doubt if I shall not be broken-winded all my life. I do not exaggerate when I say that her neck and bare arms were earth colour with dirt . . . Mrs Cresswell allows no woman near her tent – so who empties her slops – or how she manages about etc, etc I can't divine. I suppose the soldier servant does it!'

Unlike Mrs Cresswell, Fanny employed a soldier's wife, Mrs Blaydes, as a maid (replacing the altogether unsatisfactory Mrs Williams). Mrs Blaydes, however, was to die of fever before they left Bulgaria. Fanny was upset by her death but soon employed another soldier's wife in her place.

After several moves of camp, the army received orders to embark once more and sail on to the Crimean Peninsula. This time Raglan refused Fanny permission to go, but once more she managed to circumvent an order. Here she was encouraged by Lord Cardigan, the man who was to command the Charge of the Light Brigade and who was loathed by many officers as a bully and a martinet, but who clearly had a soft spot for Fanny, whom he had already visited in her charming bower and chatted to on evening riding excursions from the camp. Disguised as a soldier's wife, Fanny sneaked on board ship, arriving at the Crimea two weeks later.

It was the start of many long months spent living on board. Fanny found that it was impossible for her to live in lines with Henry as she had hoped, since Henry shared his tent with three other men. As she could not obtain a separate tent she decided to remain on board ship, and make the six-mile journey to the camp each day, along a route that became steadily more muddy and impassable as the weather deteriorated. She loathed being confined to her cramped (and bitterly cold) cabin in the crowded harbour of Balaclava, where ships sometimes caught fire or exploded when their stores of powder ignited. A vicious storm on 14 November 1854 sunk many ships at Balaclava, causing much loss of life. Fanny herself made it to the safety of the shore by scrambling from ship to ship through the howling wind and rain. It was not until March 1855 that she was able to move on to dry land.

The ships were ordered into the outer harbour of Balaclava, making it impossible for Fanny to continue her daily visits to shore. She had already begged Lord Raglan to allow her to live in the camp but he had refused her permission. Notwithstanding this prohibition, one of Fanny's most devoted admirers, a naval officer, Captain Stephen Lushington, volunteered the services of his sailors to build a hut for her in the Light Brigade lines. The hut was only twelve feet square but had a large plate-glass window and was furnished with a stove and a little table, with a cookhouse and stable at the back. It was not nearly large enough to entertain the many visitors who came to pay court to Fanny, so a marquee was erected alongside to act as a receiving room, and she employed a Maltese cook to cater for her dinner parties. Here Fanny was happy. Once more she was in the thick of things and far more comfortable than she had been in the harbour. She set about decorating their humble hut as best she could, papering the walls with pages from the *Illustrated London News* which she coloured in by hand, and set Henry's soldier servant the task of making a garden. The soldiers' wives at the front, who had shivered through winter in flimsy tents or in the trenches, must have looked enviously at the comfortable huts of Mrs Duberly and her ilk.

As the icy winter rains abated and spring arrived in the Crimea a steady stream of officers' ladies began making their way across the Black Sea to join their husbands. Lady Agnes Paget, whose husband, Lord George, commanded the 4th Light Dragoons, came out in April 1855, and lived on board ship in Balaclava harbour. Charlotte, the petite, pretty wife of Brigadier General Van Straubenzee (a British officer) arrived later in 1855 and, like Fanny, shared a hut with her husband which she decorated with pages from *Punch* as well as the *Illustrated London News*. Major Forrest, the second in command of the 4th (Royal Irish) Dragoon Guards, brought his wife out in June 1855 and installed her in the hut that he shared with his commanding officer, Colonel Edward Hodge (known as 'Little Hodge' because of his diminutive stature). The arrangement was most unsatisfactory for all concerned. Hodge, like many officers, was strongly opposed to the presence of ladies at the front, believing that they distracted their husbands' attention from their military duties (although he approved of soldiers' wives because they were industrious and useful). Lord George Paget, he noted in his journal 'looks more after her [his wife] than after his brigade'. Forrest, he observed sourly, was 'not a very active officer' at the best of times and his wife's presence would only encourage him to further neglect his duties and 'let his regiment go to the dogs'.

But it was Mrs Forrest's personal habits that really aroused Hodge's ire. The hut was divided down the middle, Hodge having one half and Forrest the other, but the partition was thin and Hodge was driven to distraction by having to listen to their domestic routine every day. 'Forrest had his wife to sleep with him, in his half of our hut,' he scribbled furiously on 10 June. 'In my mind a very disgusting *exposé* to put any lady to. However it only confirms my opinion of the two . . . .' A few days later, in a letter home, he stormed: 'That horrid Mrs Forrest is still here. She has no maid, nothing but a great he-dragoon to do all she wants. I have not spoken to her for the last ten days. I always avoid her. I think her coming to live here so disgusting. I believe that she expected that we should ask her to breakfast and dine with us, but that I will not stand, so they get the things after we have done with them, and they send an old jam pot down to us to have their rum put into it, for this, I know, is the only liquor there is in his tent. Considering that there are no rations drawn for her, all this is to me a wonderful proceeding, and not quite what a lady ought to do.' Still more disgraceful was the fact that, like Mrs Cresswell, she had no female servant to perform some of the more intimate tasks, which devolved instead to Forrest's soldier servant. Hodge was appalled to see that 'she has no female attendant about her. The dragoon still empties the leather [i.e. slop] bucket'. On 14 October he noted with horror, '*The batman* was seen yesterday picking the fleas out of Mrs F's drawers, after which he hung them out to air. The latter part I saw. Her infernal cackle nearly drove me out of my hut today. Her laugh is quite like that of an idiot.'

Even in peacetime married couples were regularly called upon to share accommodation. Long after the days of several families sharing a cramped barrack room had gone, a shortage of married quarters frequently led couples to move in with each other in a quarter designed for one family. Midge Lackie was a naive young bride of nineteen when she arrived in Aden in 1960 to begin married life with her husband Alex, a soldier in the Royal Signals. She had never been more than a few miles out of her Highland village before, never travelled on a train let alone a plane. When she stepped off the plane she was stunned first by the heat, and then bewildered to be herded, along with the other wives, into a 'sort of cattle pen . . . and they shouted the men's numbers, '23510313, Wife Of, Corporal Lackie.' Her next shock was that the couple with whom they had to share a flat (her husband Alex was not yet eligible for a separate married quarter) were naturists. 'They walked around the flat in the nude. They were from London, so I thought all Londoners did that.' A fortnight after she arrived Alex went off on desert patrol leaving Midge to acclimatise as best she could to her new quarters.

While sharing with other couples could be problematic, women who were left on their own for long stretches while their husbands were away at war or on exercise found that moving in with another wife tempered their loneliness and isolation. During the Second World War many of the wives who found themselves abandoned in India pooled their resources and moved in together. These 'grass widows' found enormous solace in each other's company, particularly in times of war. When Peggy Pusinelli's husband, a gunner officer, went to North Africa in 1941 with his regiment, most other wives left Mhow, the station where they were posted, to go and stay with friends or family in other parts of India. Peggy and one other wife, Betty Gibbon, stayed in Mhow and within a few weeks Betty had moved into Peggy's small bungalow. Neither had children and as there were still other regiments left in Mhow their social life remained vibrant. They lived together for two years, during which time they 'never had a cross word and I think that for two women to live for two years in harmony was pretty good'.

However humble or palatial the accommodation, and however happy or unhappy they had been there, leaving their homes for the next posting was, and remains, a time of high emotion for army wives. They were abandoning the tried and tested for pastures unknown and a house that might or might not be an improvement on their current home. Before they left they also had to face the trial of 'pay, pack and follow' – in the famously terse message from Richard Burton to his wife Isabel when he was suddenly called from Damascus to London: that is, the process of settling up with servants and local tradesmen and packing the contents of their household into dozens of stout boxes.

Even the most robust wives shrank from the prospect. Fanny Pratt was an old India hand, the wife of Thomas, a Lieutenant Colonel on the staff of Lord Tweedale, the Governor of Madras. Yet even she was greatly dismayed when in May 1846 Thomas was ordered to proceed to the Nilgiri Hills some 400 miles away, Lord Tweedale having decided to move his administration to escape the worst of the summer heat. Writing to one of her sons, who was being educated in Britain, Fanny complained of the upheaval this move entailed. 'Our comfortable house must be emptied and closed up – its contents be either sold or placed in the care of different friends, all our servants to be given warm clothing with woollen garments, and in between all the packing up, the host of tailors! Paying bills! Making out lists of things to be taken or left and purchasing all the requisites for our journey. I feel quite confused and have but little leisure for letter-writing. All day the thermometer has stood at 91 and I need scarcely say, the least exertion is far from according one cooler.'

In recent years the business of moving house was no less exhausting. Penny Little, married to an officer of the 2nd Gurkha Rifles, found the regular house moves the most trying aspect of her thirty years as an army wife. 'Every two to three years the call to arms would arrive (or even if it didn't there was always the possibility). The MFO [Military Forwarding Organisation] boxes would appear ready to be assembled . . . this would just be the start of the nightmare. Boxes eventually erected, the packing could begin. I well remember on one occasion being seven months heavily pregnant and therefore somewhat top heavy. While delving [into an MFO box], I toppled in headfirst and lay there like a crab on its back until my husband eventually arrived back from a boozy mess meeting and somehow managed to retrieve me from the depths.'

Once the packing had been completed there came the 'ritual humiliation', as Penny remembers it, of the 'March Out'. This was when the Quartermaster or his subordinates took possession of the married quarter from its departing occupants and undertook a minute inspection of its walls, floors and furnishings to ensure that it was fit for its next occupant. The 'humiliation' of this inspection derived from the fact that if the cleanliness of the quarter did not meet the standards demanded, or if there was so much as a fork missing from the detailed inventory of the furnishings, the hapless wife would not only be treated to a look of withering scorn for her domestic failings but would have to pay for the 'damage'. So exacting were the standards expected that most wives spent the weeks preceding the move in a frenzy of spring-cleaning in an effort not to be caught out when the gimlet eye of the barrack officer scrutinised every skirting board and bedspring for dust.

For Marion Weston, a veteran of eighteen moves during her twenty-two years with the army, it was 'a sort of thing of pride that you jolly well didn't get any fines for holes in the wall or dirty carpets or stained mattresses. You really tried extremely hard and spent *hours* cleaning your cooker so that everything shone, and every saucepan you'd shine with Brillo. You learnt from other people, they told you what to do. Toothpaste was very useful in holes in the wall . . . You washed every wall, you filled every hole and then on the morning you had everything laid out, the beds had all the blankets laid out, all folded, so they could just count them, all the cutlery laid out, all the crockery laid out in the kitchen. It was quite a performance. If you were lucky you moved into a friend's house the night before so you could get it all ready. And sometimes the march out was at 9 o'clock in the morning and then you'd get in the car and drive back to England or wherever' – where a new quarter would be awaiting and the whole cycle would start again.

In all these moves, the army wife would have to make the family home anew, creating an environment where she and her household could settle down into domesticity, a sanctuary from the instability of their mobile life. For a mother, it was particularly important to have somewhere, however basic or temporary, in which she could raise her children in as much security and comfort as possible. However, this natural aspiration was very often thwarted – in the most extreme of circumstances – by the exigencies of war.

5

Mothers and Children

Having children certainly increased the hardships that the poor women
were fated to endure. Excess of suffering, which tore asunder
every other tie, only rendered maternal love stronger,
and it was amazing what hardships were voluntarily
endured for the sake of their offspring.

> Joseph Donaldson, a soldier with the 94th
> (Scots Brigade) during the Peninsular War

In the days before effective healthcare, bringing children into the world
was always a hazardous business for both baby and mother, even in times
of peace and even in the wealthiest households. Infant mortality was high,
particularly in cities and among the poor. In London in 1764, 49 per cent
of all recorded children were dead by the age of two, and 60 per cent by
the age of five. During the second and third decades of the nineteenth
century around 30 per cent of English infants failed to reach the age of
five. In Victorian times 15 per cent of babies were still failing to reach
their first birthdays – and twice as many as this in the poorest city slums.
Childbirth itself was the single most common cause of death in women
aged twenty-five to thirty-four.

But bringing a child into the military world was a still more perilous
venture. Infant mortality was higher among army families than in any other
segment of English society during the latter part of the eighteenth century.
As the historian Sylvia Frey has noted, 'The cramped conditions of barracks,
the frequent exposure to extremes of weather while on campaign, and

poor diet and the extreme poverty of many soldiers' families all contributed to the higher death rate.'

Apart from the unhealthy physical conditions, women and children could find that living in a male-dominated society placed them in a highly vulnerable position. Usually, even in the direst of circumstances, men were moved to compassion by the sight of women and children whose plight was even more desperate than their own and did their best to help and protect them. At other times, however, mothers and their children received no such quarter and in a few cases the army community let them down brutally when those on whom they must have thought they could rely abused this trust.

Wives who went off to war with the troops were supposed to be childless (although of course this prohibition was often ignored). But those accompanying soldiers to garrisons in peaceful parts of the Empire were generally allowed to bring their children too. Army wives and children were to be found in the garrisons of Canada, the West Indies, Aden, Ceylon, Burma, Malaya and New South Wales. They thronged the cantonments of India, the children trotting beside their ayahs (nursemaids) and often chattering in Hindi or Tamil with a great deal more fluency than they spoke English.

Soldiers' children were generally educated in regimental schools. These had existed from the days of the Tangier garrison but were officially recognised in 1811 and began to flourish in garrisons at home and abroad, often staffed by the more educated soldiers and their wives. Regimental schools were designed to serve the soldiers' families and were not considered suitable for officers' offspring, certainly not beyond the age of eight or nine. Boys who were destined for the usual 'gentleman's careers' of the Church, civil service or army needed to attend schools in England that would qualify them for these professions; they would usually attend boarding school and spend their holidays with relatives or friends. Girls, it was thought, could develop into young ladies fit for English society only if they received an English upbringing, although their education was generally deemed to be of less importance. Naturally, this entailed a long estrangement of parents and children, painful for both, but most parents considered this a sacrifice worth making for the sake of their children's futures.

Nowadays the boarding school allowance (which pays a proportion of the fees) provided by the army is greatly valued, as are the subsidised flights for army children returning to spend their holidays with parents living abroad. But in the 1950s and 1960s when my mother was an army child the army would pay for only one passage a year, so she and her brothers spent two out of three school holidays living with an aunt, returning to see their parents in Malaya just once a year for the long summer holiday. They were lucky: their aunt was kind and generous and had two children of similar ages. But others were less fortunate and spent miserable holidays with relatives who resented their presence and the expenditure it entailed, even though most received an allowance from the absent parents. Sometimes no such accommodating relative could be found and the children had to spend their holidays at school, a miserable fate for those who disliked their boarding school and for whom 'Home' was not England, a land they had often never seen before, but was a cottage in the foothills of the Himalayas or a bungalow in Burma: wherever, in fact, their parents happened to be.

Before the Second World War and the advent of air travel there could be no question of children returning for the holidays (indeed it was not until 1961 that the troops themselves were transported by air). By the time the steamship arrived in harbour the holidays would be all but over so it was simply not an option. During the eighteenth and early nineteenth centuries, officers' children whose fathers were posted abroad seldom saw their parents from the time they were sent back to Britain (usually between the ages of six to ten) until the day came for them to return, by now on the cusp of adulthood. Few officers' wives could afford to make the journey back to Britain to visit their offspring more than once (if at all) and in any case most felt that their place was at their husband's side. So their children could spend the greater part of their childhood without ever seeing the distant parents whose faces became ever more blurred in their memory as the years passed by.

Not all army wives subscribed to this doctrine. Some, like my great-grandmother Lucy Venning in Burma, preferred to educate their children at home rather than send them across several continents for an English education. The Duke of Wellington's wife, Kitty, also felt strongly that 'the dreadful evils which the loss of a Mother inflicts upon Children' precluded her from exposing herself to danger by following her husband to war, even when she felt drawn to accompany him, if only to keep him from the arms of other women who were happy to take advantage of her absence. 'Let no degree of Suffering O my God tempt me to forsake my Children!' she vowed. But the Wellington marriage was far from happy. The initial attraction between them did not weather their long engagement:

Wellington was heard to mutter when he met his bride-to-be after a decade's absence, 'She has grown ugly, by Jove!' Other army wives preferred to devote themselves to their marriage and to settle for a long-distance relationship with their children.

Some women even chose to part with their children in early infancy rather than expose them to the dangers of a long voyage. In 1805 Mary Sherwood decided reluctantly to leave her first-born child, a daughter just under a year old, with her mother and sister when her husband's regiment was sent to India, so fearful was she of the effects of the voyage and of India's climate and diseases on her adored daughter. The child had just taken her first faltering steps and could say 'Mamma', and Mary's anguish at parting from her for several years was almost unbearable: 'Oh my baby! My little baby!' she wrote in her journal in bitter despair. For Mary the parting was akin to a state of bereavement, for it would be so many years before they met again that 'we are as dead to each other. My mother, my sister, you who have taken my infant under your care, you will feel for her and be tender with her . . . My beloved baby – oh my God! Bless my baby!' When she next saw her daughter she was nearly grown up.

Some children coped with the absence from their parents with extraordinary resilience, while others found the dislocation harder to bear. To them, England was a foreign country: they found it difficult to adjust not only to life without their parents, but to a land where the food, climate and people were all strange. Mollie Kaye, who became an army wife – and, as M.M. Kaye, famous as the author of the epic India-based love story *The Far Pavilions* – was born in India in 1908. She spent a supremely happy childhood growing up in Simla under the snowy peaks of the Himalayas and then in Delhi where she revelled in the dry, dusty expanses of the plains around the capital. India to her was home and when at the age of ten she was 'banished', as she saw it, to boarding school in England, along with her younger sister Bets, she was plunged into misery. Like many foreign-born English children she was appalled by her first sight of England. As she travelled by train from the docks at Tilbury to London she gazed 'horrified, from the rain-spotted window, it seemed to me as though there were no open spaces here at all. Nothing but mile after mile of squalid, soot-stained walls, warehouses and dingy streets lined with small, grimy terraced houses in which, unbelievably, my native people, Angrezis [English] – 'Sahib-log' – actually lived . . . .' Bullied mercilessly at boarding school by the other girls, Mollie and Bets resorted to speaking to each other in Hindustani, which the other pupils could not understand. Mollie's life from then on became a countdown to the day when she could return to her real home, India, and end her hated exile.

I experienced similar feelings of dislocation and bewilderment when I returned to an England I had left at the age of six and of which I had only dim memories. I had had an idyllic two years, living first in Hong Kong and then Brunei attending the army schools there. My days were spent playing barefoot amid banana and coconut trees, listening to the incessant clicking of chopsticks and clattering of mahjong pieces in the markets of Hong Kong, jumping from waterfalls in the Brunei jungle into deep, limpid pools, and laughing at the monkeys that squatted along the road next to our house. In the monsoon I would swim along the road and go to school in a rubber dinghy. Arriving in England in the bitter December of 1981, I was at first entranced to see snow and then stunned by the sensation of cold that I had almost forgotten. My first term at boarding school was one long culture shock. In place of juicy pineapple and papaya for breakfast I was confronted with a small, wizened apple pockmarked with wormholes. The bitter wind whipped around my bare knees as I trudged to chapel every morning so that soon my berry-brown skin was so chapped that it took on a hard, grey appearance not unlike an elephant's skin. The bed linen and duvet that my mother had sent ahead by sea mail months earlier had inexplicably failed to arrive, so I shivered in borrowed sheets and a blanket in a draughty dormitory. 'Dear Mummy and Daddy,' I wrote home that first Sunday. 'I hope you are well. I am fine but I am VERY COLD. Please, please can you send blankets?' Although I was one of the fortunate ones who did 'settle in' and was happy at boarding school, to this day my abiding memory of those early weeks is of biting, bone-chilling cold.

Letters were a lifeline for boarding school exiles and for their anxious parents separated by many miles of ocean. For children the excitement of espying that pale blue airmail packet containing longed-for news from their far-off home was intense and letters would be read, re-read and tucked into sleeves or pockets, to be read yet again till they were so creased and smudged as to be almost indecipherable. Parents too lived for the arrival of an envelope bearing the familiar childish scrawl, hoping that it would provide reassurance that all was well and that they had indeed made the right decision in sending their children away. This correspondence was their only means of retaining some hand in their children's upbringing while they were apart, and many parents used it to try to influence their children's behaviour from a distance.

Fanny Pratt was one such assiduous letter writer. She and her husband Thomas had spent some years in India, where their first son had died, before returning to Britain for a brief interlude. When they sailed for India again in December 1843, for Thomas (by now a Lieutenant Colonel) to take up his post on the staff of Lord Tweedale, Governor of Madras, they left behind them three surviving sons, Tom, Frank and Torrens, and a daughter, Annie, to be educated in Britain. Acutely conscious that she was missing her children's formative years, Fanny's correspondence with them was her one great solace. A devout Christian, her piety comes across strongly in her letters. She used her correspondence to impart advice, admonishments and encouragement to her sons as they made the transition from boys to men without her. Her missives were filled with exhortations to the Almighty to spare their health and keep them on the path of righteousness and she constantly beseeched them to read the Bible and behave piously. Fanny never missed a mail to England during the years she spent in India and later Australia, and she expected her children to be equally conscientious correspondents. She would wait impatiently for the next steamship to arrive with its precious cargo of mail from England and was bitterly let down whenever it failed to bear letters from her absent offspring. 'We are much disappointed at not hearing from one of you by the last mail,' she admonished her sons in March 1844, a few weeks after arriving in Madras.

She was clearly torn between doing her duty, as she saw it, by giving her children a good education and upbringing in England, and her natural instinct to want her children at her side. 'Were it possible and consistent with your welfare, my darling boys,' she writes, 'to have you and our precious Annie with us, I should be quite happy, in spite of the heat and the many disadvantages of our life. But duty is very positive in this instance and we must therefore hope and pray that our necessary absence will not diminish our darling children's affection towards us.' A few months later she was ecstatically happy: 'I have just received letters, one from dear Tommy and the other from Torrens. I love to get them and bless the writing of my darling absent boys.' Their letters, she explained in another missive, were 'a source of the greatest comfort to Papa and I'.

Desperate to know every facet of her children's lives, she asks Tom in one letter, 'Have you made any particular friendships amongst your companions and who are they?' On another occasion she begs the boys to send her a list of their relative heights so that 'we shall fancy we see you all grown'. Her preoccupation with their well-being occasionally takes on rather morbid overtones. 'My darling children,' she writes, 'I yearn to see you around us once more. May God watch over and bless you and grant that we may all be spared to meet in health and with affection. It would break my heart to think you can forget us.'

Fanny and her husband went on to have three more boys, Sisson, Chalmers and William, during their absence from England. She drew enormous solace from the presence of her little sons and her letters are full of fond pride in their antics as she sought to acquaint her elder children with the little siblings they had never met. But despite her hopes and prayers, Fanny's relationship with her children was not all that she wished. Tom, the eldest, often found it difficult to respond to his mother's devout outpourings in the way she clearly expected. Annie too failed to share her mother's excessive piety, while Frank, her second son, rebelled by living rather too well and getting into debt. But although Fanny can at times seem overbearing and more interested in imposing her own beliefs on her children than in listening to their preferences, her maternal devotion cannot be faulted. She did at least manage to install her children in happy homes, with relations who seem to have been kind and hospitable to their charges. When those relatives were no longer able to continue their guardianship of her elder children, Fanny lost little time in returning home to England to provide a home for them herself, reluctant as she was to abandon her husband in India for two years. When she returned once more to India in 1853, ten years after she had first parted from her elder children, she left behind her two youngest children with relatives in Dublin. She missed her small sons so painfully that she confessed she could hardly look at other people's children as to do so reminded her of her own absent sons. Yet for all the years of separation and despite being subjected to their mother's pious outpourings in every letter, her children were in many ways much more fortunate than other little exiles.

To Harriet Earle, the gaiety of her steamship voyage to India and the experience of travelling by palanquin would have been all the more exciting after the life she had left behind in England. Sent back from India aged eleven, Harriet and her younger sister Emily were deposited for six unhappy years with an aunt in Birmingham who had no children of her own. This woman was clearly more interested in the allowance she received for the girls' upkeep than she was in their welfare. The schoolroom where they spent their days was unheated and these two refugees from the tropical warmth of India suffered terribly from chilblains. Harriet and Emily were kept in a state of near starvation, being forced to run around the yard and swoop down like birds for the crusts of bread laid out for them. Harriet was frequently beaten and sent out every day to play in the nearby cemetery where she regularly had to witness the sad spectacle of a baby's burial. The resolutely positive Harriet managed to derive some benefit from these grim experiences: 'I can honestly say that other people's troubles become my own, which I attribute greatly to this early training amongst the graves.'

Distraught as most mothers were at lengthy separations from their infants, they were firmly convinced that the parting was in the best interests of the children, not only in terms of education but health. Frances Wells, expecting her first baby in 1854, was appalled by the health and habits of British children in India, writing to her physician father in Bristol, 'The more I see of Indian children [she means India-born British children] the more I hope to be able to send mine home before it is very old as they contract such bad habits in this country, all look so pale and sickly, and get to speak with such a dreadful twang, indeed many speak no English which I think is a great pity, as they cannot be instructed in any pretty little hymns or Bible stories which I think it will be such a pleasure to teach.' Fanny Pratt, sweltering in the heat of Madras, was both proud and relieved that Sisson, born four months after her return to India in 1844, was 'a strong, healthy little fellow'. But even this robust little creature, petted and cosseted by his fond mama and numerous servants, suffered from the oppressive heat and humidity of Madras. In place of the rosy apple cheeks that most toddlers boasted his complexion was, his mother noted sadly, 'pure white'.

Devoted mothers like Frances Wells and Fanny Pratt happily delegated the more menial aspects of childcare to their ayahs but were nonetheless closely involved in their babies' upbringing, reading to them, playing with them and taking them out for drives in their carriages. Even so, that the children spent many hours a day in their ayahs' company is evident from the fact that they spoke the servants' native tongues more fluently than English. Lucy Venning's daughter Mollie mainly spoke Burmese, even to her mother.

Some less conscientious mothers were only too pleased to delegate the care of their children almost entirely to ayahs or (as became more common in later years) to imported English nannies. Many officers' ladies chose to hand their babies over to wet-nurses rather than breastfeed them themselves. Even by the nineteenth century, when wet-nursing had become rare in England (it persisted only among the very wealthy upper classes after the mid-eighteenth century), the custom remained popular among English ladies in India. Mary Sherwood was advised that white women in India, even if they had a plentiful milk supply, should employ an Indian wet-nurse if their child was at all delicate. When she enquired what became of the wet-nurse's own children, who were thus deprived of some if not all of their mother's milk, she was told that they almost always died: 'But this can't be helped, the mothers never fret after them. Whenever they nurse a white baby they cease to care for their own, they say, "White child is good; black child his slave."'

While most ayahs and wet-nurses were devoted to their young charges, there were inevitably some who were neglectful or abusive and others who harmed them by passing on diseases. The most prevalent fear among English mothers was that their ayah would feed opium to their children to keep them quiet, a phenomenon that, according to a report published in Calcutta in 1828 by a British doctor, Mr Corbyn, was disturbingly common. He believed, moreover, that most Indian wet-nurses were cruel, depraved women whose appetite for smoking drugs and drinking alcohol was extremely harmful to the babies in their care. 'I trust that ladies in India will see the necessity of nursing their own children,' he concluded.

Evidence that his advice was frequently ignored comes from such contemporaries as the soldier and diarist John Shipp, who observed that the practice of employing native wet-nurses remained common. As a result, he reported, large numbers of babies caught syphilis from their native wet-nurses, while scores of others were killed when opium was used to pacify them. He claimed to know of two who had died this way. 'One of them was in the regiment I was in, and in its little stomach, after death, was found more than the eighth part of an ounce. The nurse merely urged, in her own vindication, that the child was so cross she could not pacify it.' Another couple left their baby home alone while they went out to a dance, dispatching a servant during the course of the evening to check on the child. When they returned it was sleeping soundly but the next morning when they tried to waken it they found that it was dead. The post-mortem again revealed a quantity of opium in its stomach. Frances Wells feared to let her woman servants near Georgie, her third child, when he became ill and 'scarcely ever let him out of my sight as I am so afraid of opium', while Mary Sherwood was distraught at finding her one-year-old son, Henry, being dosed with the drug by his ayah. Under medical supervision he recovered.

Even the most dedicated mother who breastfed her own child and kept a watchful eye over the ayah at all times was no match for the many diseases that prevailed in tropical climates. Young children were particularly susceptible to such illnesses, especially in the summer months when the intense heat sapped the strength of even the most energetic individuals. Every garrison cemetery from the West Indies to the Far East contained gravestones carved with angels and marking lives that were all too fleeting, cut short by cholera, dysentery, sleeping sickness and sometimes just the excessive heat. Besotted by her children and attentive to them as she was, Frances Wells and her doctor husband Walter could do nothing to prevent their adored eldest son Dickey from contracting dysentery, aged seven months. Writing home to her father, she described how 'for four days we had but little hope of saving him: one night his bowels were moved fifteen times and for fourteen hours we could not induce him to take a drop of food: Walter says he never saw so obstinate a case in his life or one which so completely baffles all remedies. The poor little fellow is so reduced, instead of beautiful fat rosy cheeks they are now so pale and wan and his little form is wasted almost to a skeleton. He has been too weak to smile or cry and would do nothing but lie in a sort of stupor in my lap . . . I have been so miserable dear Papa since my precious boy has been ill and if I were to lose him I do think my heart would break . . . '

After several days of hovering on the brink of death the little boy rallied and recovered. Frances was overwhelmed with relief and joy and effusive in her thanks to the Almighty for sparing him. But just a few months later she was prostrate with grief when she had to bury her second baby, born prematurely. After what must have been a difficult labour in the remorseless heat of August in India, the baby, tiny and weak, survived for only five days. Writing to her father, Frances gave vent to her grief and desolation. 'What sorrow it is to lose a child however young it is: that little infant seemed all the dearer to me from being so weak and sickly and every day I fancied that it's [sic] cry sounded stronger until it became so very quiet and then I heard that it was dead. Walter filled its little coffin full of roses and he says it is buried in a very pretty spot in the cemetery, but there is something dreadful in being obliged to bury the dead so quickly, only a few hours between death and burial.'

Harriet Tytler (as Harriet Earle had become after marrying a widower, Captain Robert Tytler, of the 38th Native Infantry) suffered from severe shock when her second child, a 'fine, bonny' baby, died after contracting lockjaw, and even religion brought her no solace. 'My husband brought me my Bible, knowing I loved it, but my heart was too rebellious. I threw it from one end of the room to the other, saying, "Take it away. God has taken my darling baby from me, the baby I loved so dearly. Why did He not take someone else's baby?" But I found comfort a week later in my Bible and then I was truly ashamed of myself.'

Fanny Pratt too suffered terribly when her son Chalmers, born three years after Sisson during the Pratts' second stint in India, succumbed to the effects of diarrhoea and heat. At first, little Chalmers was 'just as fat and happy as an infant can be, and is such a pet with Papa, he crows with delight when he sees him'. Up until the age of two and half he remained a healthy, contented child, but a combination of the oppressive summer heat, together with the exertions of a two-week journey by palanquin into the hills of Ootacamund, took a terrible toll on his constitution and by May 1849 Fanny had become seriously worried. 'My darling Tom,' she wrote to her eldest son, 'we have had much anxiety about our dear little Chalmers, he had become worse and weaker every day and when we reached this place was so utterly prostrated and so emaciated that we had many reasons to fear for his life. But already the rest, and the pure air has been helped by our merciful God in soothing his feeble frame.' Two weeks later the cooler climate of the hills seemed to have had the desired effect and pulled him back from 'the very brink of his grave'. He was now making steady progress towards recovery and Fanny nursed him tenderly. 'I feed him like a little bird. Every hour, he has a wine glass or less of some nourishment, and his poor wasted limbs chafed by the fire, then rolled in shawls and carried into the garden, where he seems to inhale strength, and can now smile at the flowers, and at my efforts to amuse him. My heart is relieved of a heavy load, we have been so painfully anxious about him for three long months.'

Tragically, all her tender nursing and optimism were in vain. On 7 August 1849 she wrote to Tom from Bangalore: 'Our darling Chalmers breathed his last on the morning of 30th inst [July]. His happy spirit was released without a struggle or sigh from his poor emaciated little frame, and as we knelt near him we could bless God and wish our darling joy of his glorious exchange . . . If love and tenderness could have prolonged his life he would be still with us. We are quite resigned to our Heavenly Father's will. He gave us our lovely child, and He has taken him and made him an heir of everlasting Glory, but still we mourn for his loss. I often feel as if my heart could burst, we loved him all too well. He was the fairest of our flock and the frame of a splendid boy, his forehead very beautiful and showers of golden curling locks. So gentle in temper, that he took every medicine without hesitation, "enough Mama dear" was his only remonstrance.'

Mary Sherwood, who had rescued her small son Henry from a near-fatal overdose of opium, found that her reprieve was all too short when, just two months later, he became gravely ill at Dinapore in India. She had doted on Henry, whose arrival eased her pain at the separation from her daughter, but he was a weak child and although she fed him herself, when she finally weaned him at fourteen months when her third child, a daughter, was born, he quickly declined. Although it was plain that he was dying, the two surgeons who attended him would not let her be with him in his last moments and kept sending her away, perhaps fearing that the shock would dry up her milk. But at last she could bear it no longer. 'I hastened to his side. He was changed during the few minutes in which I had been absent from him. Someone said to him, "Henry, kiss your mamma." We supposed he had passed all knowledge of present things, but he turned his lovely eyes to me and smiled. Oh! What a smile! I kissed his lips; they were already quite cold and clammy. I was again drawn from him, but soon after, returning, I sat down and took him on my lap, stretched as he was on his mattress. He was breathing hard; his breath became slower and slower. He suddenly raised his eyes, as if to heaven and they became fixed. He fetched his breath at longer and longer intervals, and soon it ceased for ever. Oh! My baby! Oh! My Henry! I saw the remains of my precious baby for a few minutes that same night; he was laid out on the sofa of the parlour. They would not suffer me to stay with him. They tore me from him.' Only her faith, and her new baby, a pretty, sweet girl she called Lucy, sustained her. But a few months later Lucy too succumbed to a short but violent illness, and Mrs Sherwood was holding another life-less little body in her arms. 'Oh my God! I thank Thee for the composure and comfort which Thou bestowed upon us in that hour of greatest need,' she exclaimed, more in hope than in truth for both she and her husband were almost poleaxed by this new bereavement. Of their seven children, one died at birth and three in infancy.

While India was considered too hot and unhealthy, particularly in the summer months when the mortality rate among children rose, the climate of the West Indies was dreaded even more keenly because of the prevalence of infectious diseases. So high were the death rates among soldiers and their families (up to 40 per cent in the early eighteenth century) that men would desert in droves as soon as they heard the rumours that their regi-ment might be sent there, and many parents chose to leave their children behind with relatives or in orphanages rather than risk their health. To prevent desertion, men were sometimes embarked on board troopships supposedly heading for America or India, only to be informed several days out to sea that their actual destination was the dreaded West Indies. The soldiers' wives, usually so keen to embark with them, showed a marked reluctance when it came to the pestilential islands of the Caribbean.

The Gordon Highlanders arrived in Jamaica on 4 June 1819 after three months at sea. The population of Kingston turned out to watch the kilted soldiers march through the town to their quarters at Up-Park Camp, their bonneted wives bringing up the rear with their children who trotted beside them. Many of them were veterans of years of hard fighting against the French, but even these hardy survivors proved no match for the contagion and climate of Jamaica. Their arrival in the hot, unhealthy season was, as the regimental history notes, ill timed: 'The intrepidity which enabled them to defy the legions of France was of no avail against a more subtle foe.' Yellow fever struck the regiment and filled the sick rooms to such a degree that the guardship HMS *Serapis*, on which the regiment had its headquarters, had to become a convalescent hospital. The disease, transmitted by mosquitoes, turned men and women into shivering wrecks, racked by violent vomiting, chills and a high fever. Sometimes the sufferers vomited blood, sometimes they went into shock. Some recovered but many did not, succumbing to liver failure and jaundice that earned yellow fever its name.

The women and children suffered particularly badly. Five officers' wives, five officers' children, seventy-two soldiers' wives and fifty-nine soldiers' children had embarked with the regiment when it left in April 1819. Only six months after their arrival in Jamaica, around half of them were dead: two officers' wives, two officers' children, thirty-two soldiers' wives and twenty-nine soldiers' children had succumbed to yellow fever. Ten officers, thirteen sergeants, eight drummers and 254 rank and file were also buried from the same cause. A feeling of utter despondency and despair gripped the remaining members of the garrison, summed up by one soldier who, sitting down by the side of the road, buried his face in his hands and cried, 'My wife is dead, my bairns are dead, and I wish I was dead.'

As well as heat and disease, poisonous creatures posed a grave threat to infants and babies. Frances Wells was horrified when her first baby, Dickey, began screaming as she undressed him and 'when I lifted up his clothes to see if he was wet there was an immense centipede longer than my hand on him, I was so terrified as the bite of these horrid things is often fatal but we could not discover any sign of a bite on him, you may fancy how thankful I felt.' Another infant was less fortunate. Harriet Tytler recounts the sad tale of a couple who had left their baby in the charge of the ayah while they went out for their evening drive. Returning a short while later, they were confronted by the hysterical ayah and found the baby, whom they had left in perfect health less than an hour earlier, now lying dead. The ayah told them how she had bathed the child and put on its nightdress as usual 'when the poor thing gave a fearful cry. The ayah never thought of anything being wrong with the nightdress and tried to pacify the child by hugging it closer and closer, but each time she did so, the child gave a fresh scream, until it went into violent convulsions and died.' The parents were sceptical about her story, but when they undressed the baby to be laid out in its coffin, they found a scorpion and realised what had occurred. 'Evidently the ayah disturbed it each time she clasped the child to comfort it, resulting in a fresh sting, till the agony was more than the little life could bear.'

Florentia Sale was another mother for whom the cost of defending the empire was measured in the little gravestones left in her trail as she followed her husband around India, Mauritius and Afghanistan. Florentia's utter disdain for self-pity and her refusal to be bowed or diminished by disaster sustained her through some terrible ordeals. Born in Madras in 1787, the daughter and granddaughter of men who had served the East India Company, she was twenty-one when she married Captain Robert Sale, or 'Fighting Bob' as he became known. Soon after they married he was posted to Mauritius and later years saw the Sales in Ireland, England and from 1823 back in India, from where Sale went to fight in the Burma campaign of 1824–6. During this time Florentia bore twelve children, four of whom died in infancy. A fifth, their eldest son, died aged ten. The *Dictionary of National Biography* describes Lady Sale as 'par excellence a soldier's wife. She was the companion and friend of her husband through-out a life of vicissitude, sympathising with him in all that concerned his profession, quick in perception, self-reliant and practical.' She needed all those qualities to endure the domestic tragedies that befell her as well as other ordeals.

Frailer women found that climate, disease, childbirth and the exhaustion of an uncertain, peripatetic existence all took a toll on their health. Many died young, leaving motherless children whose fathers were at a loss as to how to bring them up alone when they themselves were seldom at home. Babies who lost their mothers at a very young age frequently did not survive. Sergeant MacMullen, who chronicled the sufferings of soldiers' wives on board ship in the 1840s, tells of one wife who gave birth during the extreme heat of the summer months in Sukkur, Baluchistan, where the temperature reached 107°F (42°C) in barracks and 128°F (54°C) in tents. Three weeks afterwards she died, leaving behind three children including the baby who, deprived of its source of nourishment, expired soon afterwards.

Often widowers left with young children managed to muddle through with the help of other regimental wives. Major Sainsbury of the Duke of Cornwall's Light Infantry lost his young wife in Burma in 1892, leaving him with two young sons. Sainsbury found it hard to carry out his duties as well as look after two small boys, but was rescued by a friendly neighbour, a Mrs Saunders, wife of the battalion's pioneer sergeant who, 'having no children of her own, took a great interest in my sons, and with my two native servants helped me considerably, and I managed to carry on . . . ' Rather than continue to rely on the charity of his neighbour, Sainsbury got a posting at the depot back in England where he would receive help from his family.

John Shipp's adored wife Ann was only twenty-two when she died giving birth to their second child in Dinapore. Shipp, who was about to be dismissed from the army after being implicated in a crime of which he claimed to be innocent, was utterly bereft at the loss of the woman he called 'my best friend and guide'. Moreover he had a four-year-old son and the tiny newborn boy whose birth had caused her death. Without a mother's milk the baby must surely have perished too. Luckily Shipp had kind and compassionate neighbours, a Captain Marshall and his wife. Mrs Marshall, wrote Shipp, became a foster-mother to the baby and 'divided her maternal attentions equally between him and her own infant, who was only a few days older than my orphan boy'. After a few weeks the baby was given into the care of Shipp's brother-in-law who also lived in India. Shipp himself was sent back to England, dismissed from the army. He had hoped to take his elder boy with him but was unable to afford his passage so he too remained in India, to Shipp's everlasting grief.

Not all foster mothers were as devoted as Mrs Marshall. Mary Sherwood rescued the motherless infant of a soldier in her husband's regiment whose foster mother was systematically starving it. She also took in several other motherless and orphaned children to save them from neglect, and found that caring for them helped to salve her grief for her own dead children.

Such solicitude typified the ethos of the close-knit military community:

the regiment as extended family. Sometimes, however, this guiding principle broke down, and the most vulnerable members of the 'family', its women and young children, were exposed to the brutal, unsavoury elements that lurk within almost every society, military or civilian. An act passed in 1701 enabled men convicted of capital offences to be enlisted into the forces. Criminals were often given the choice of serving a term in the army or in jail. Swelling the ranks with such men did little to raise the moral character of the army or the public perception of soldiers. Nor can it have cheered the army's wives to know that the men whom they and their children lived alongside might be convicted thieves or rapists.

Such concern would naturally focus on children. Any attack on them would be particularly shattering – carried out by men they would probably have trusted because, like their fathers, they were soldiers, wore a similar uniform and belonged to the same garrison. In the case of Frances Berney, the nine-year-old daughter of Corporal Berney of the 1st Foot, her attacker would have lived close by and would likely have been known to her.

He was Michael Golougher, a soldier in the 2nd or Queen's Royal Regiment, who was brought before a court martial in Gibraltar on 8 August 1775 and accused of 'attempting to carnally know or abuse Frances Berney . . . & for giving her the venereal disorder' on Whitsun Monday. Frances had come across Golougher one afternoon while she was carrying her baby brother in her arms. He forced her into the bedroom of an absent officer and, ignoring the girl's frightened protests, locked the doors and windows before snatching her brother from her arms and laying him on the bed. He then threw Frances on the same bed and, as she told the court, lifting up her clothes he 'used her in a very bad way'. A few days later, the court heard, she developed a pain in her 'private parts' and only then confessed to her mother what had occurred. Upon being taken to the doctor it was discovered that she had been molested and infected with venereal disease.

Golougher was found guilty of molestation and was sentenced to 1,000 lashes with the cat-o'-nine-tails, but was not drummed out of the regiment. Frances Berney would have been forced to come face to face with her tormentor until either he or her father left Gibraltar.

Another nine-year-old girl, Mary Nicholls, was bitterly betrayed by a man alongside whom her stepfather, Sergeant Downs of the 28th Foot, had served in battle only weeks earlier. In the autumn of 1777, the 28th had played an important role in the American Revolutionary War, contributing to British successes at Brandywine, Philadelphia and Germantown. But instead of following up such victories by pursuing and destroying the American army, Howe and his army had settled down into winter quarters in Philadelphia for rest and (particularly) recreation.

It was during this period that Sergeant Downs and his wife decided to go out one evening and asked Private Thomas Lilly, billeted in the same house as them, to babysit their nine-year-old stepdaughter until they returned. (Both Mary's natural parents were dead and she had long since been unofficially adopted by the sergeant and his wife.) Lilly agreed but he was tired, and when another soldier, Corporal John Fisher, came calling at the house, Lilly asked him if he would mind sitting with the girl while he went off for a sleep. Fisher agreed and, as soon as Lilly was safely in bed, he pounced on Mary and raped her, growling at her not to scream and, afterwards, to tell no one of what had occurred. The terrified girl must have stayed silent throughout her ordeal as Lilly was not awakened. When her parents came back she told them nothing of what had occurred. Indeed the crime was not discovered until a week later when Mary's stepmother saw the 'evidence' that something had been done to the child. Reluctantly, Mary confessed the 'secret' and the regimental surgeon confirmed that she had been raped and was infected with VD.

In the court martial's record Fisher comes over as devious and unrepentant, attempting by turns to justify and deny his actions. Her failure to scream when the attack was taking place was, he asserted 'acknowledgement that she was perfectly willing'. He even accused her of lying about her age. The court, evidently disgusted with his evasions and explanations, found him guilty and sentenced him to be 'hanged by the neck'. Mary at least would not have to face her tormentor again.

If bearing and raising children was difficult enough in peacetime, motherhood in times of war demanded seemingly endless reserves of tenacity, devotion and self-sacrifice. Those qualities were never needed more than in one of the most harrowing episodes in the British army's history: the retreat to Corunna in the winter of 1808–9, during the Peninsular War, in which Britain, with varying degrees of local support, sought to evict Napoleon's French armies from Portugal and Spain. Britain had been at war with France, intermittently, since 1793, as the new republic sought first to consolidate then expand her borders. With the British victory at Trafalgar in 1805, any French hopes of dominating the seas were crushed, but in 1807 Napoleon, who had become France's emperor in 1804, turned his attention to the Iberian Peninsula, invading first Portugal (Britain's only remaining ally apart from Sweden) and Spain.

In October 1808 British troops commanded by General Sir John Moore had advanced from Portugal into Spain, planning to join up with Spanish forces and engage the French army under Marshal Soult. However, it soon became clear that the British supply lines were dangerously inadequate, while the troops were falling ill with dysentery and typhoid. Their Spanish allies failed to deliver the promised support – and winter was starting to bite.

Moore, reinforced by fresh troops, had planned to attack Soult's force of 17,000, encamped nearby. But when Napoleon, who was advancing on Lisbon, realised Moore's intention, he turned north, intent on finding the British army and destroying it. On hearing that Napoleon was bearing down upon him with a force of 80,000, Moore saw at once that his situation was impossible. His only hope now was to prevent the army from being cornered and obliterated by a superior French force, and this he determined to do. By rapid forced marches, overriding the protests of his subordinates who wanted to stand and fight, Moore made for Corunna where the British fleet would be able to evacuate his men – and the women and children with them.

Moore had done his best to persuade the women to stay in Lisbon or, better still, to go back to England, before the army went into Spain. In a General Order published on 10 October 1808 he warned presciently that, as carts would not be available to transport the women and children on the roads into Spain, they would be subjected to 'the greatest hardship and distress' in the coming winter. Veterans of the fighting against the French in the Low Countries could testify to this. In January 1795, in the early stages of the wars against France, the British army was in retreat from the enemy, crossing the icy, barren wastes of Gelderland in the Netherlands; those who took part remembered the terrible sufferings of the sick and wounded, and the women and the children. It was the harshest winter anyone could remember – the dams were frozen and birds fell from the trees, dead from cold. One morning the soldiers awakened to see, scattered over the whitened plain, the frozen bodies of hundreds of men and horses who had died in the night. 'There a group of British and Germans round an empty rum cask; here forty English Guardsmen huddled together about a plundered wagon, there a packhorse with a woman alongside it, and a baby swaddled in rags, peering out of the pack, with its mother's milk turned to ice upon its lips – one and all stark, frozen, dead.' Six thousand men, and countless women and children, perished within four days.

Now, in Spain, it was again a bitingly cold winter, and Moore was deeply conscious that the women and children would be most vulnerable. He told his commanding officers to 'use their endeavours to prevent as many [women] as possible, particularly those having young children, or such as are not stout, or equal to fatigue, from following the army'. As a further inducement to remain behind the women were to be offered rations, a free passage to England and an allowance to enable them to reach their homes. But Moore refrained from issuing an outright prohibition and most women ignored his blandishments and set out with the army, taking their children with them – as Moore found, to his alarm, when the army reached Sahugun (in northern Spain). They were ordered to stay behind in the town while the troops went on to attack Soult's force. When the men returned to the town, sullen and exhausted, having marched through the night only to be turned back when Moore heard of Napoleon's advance, the women and children rushed out from the buildings, overjoyed at the unexpected reunion with husbands and fathers.

On 24 December, amid lashing rain, the retreat began in earnest. The soldiers, bitterly resentful at being made to turn and flee, were simmering with insubordination and some commanders resorted to brutal methods to keep them under control. At almost every town and village soldiers would unearth casks of wine, vainly concealed by the inhabitants, and drink themselves into a stupor, ignoring the furious prohibitions and pleas of their officers. Houses and convents were looted and vandalised, villages set on fire and the Spanish inhabitants, supposedly the allies of the British, abused. In an effort to curb such behaviour, floggings were meted out by disciplinarian commanders like Brigadier General Robert 'Black Bob' Craufurd. As the weather and the roads worsened, stragglers who could not keep up with the column were left behind to the mercies of the enemy. So closely did Soult's army snap at the heels of the British force that the rear guard, commanded by Craufurd, was often forced to turn and fight to keep the enemy at bay. Halts were brief, allowing the exhausted men little time to rest and sleep. Food was scarce and even clean water was seldom to be had. The women and the children marched, as usual, with the baggage train at the end of the column and many, unable to keep up with the rapid pace, simply collapsed by the wayside and did not rise again. Mothers staggered along carrying babies and dragging young children, crying with fatigue and hunger, beside them.

Sergeant Anthony Hamilton of the 43rd (Monmouthshire) Regiment of Foot (Light Infantry) was horrified by the sufferings of the women on this retreat. 'Some of these unhappy creatures were taken in labor [sic] on the road, and amid the storms of sleet and snow, gave birth to infants, which, with their mothers, perished as soon as they had seen the light. The wife of Sergeant Thomas, my pay Sergeant, of Capt Dalziel's company, was among the unfortunate sufferers. Others, in the unconquerable energy of maternal love, would toil on with one or two children on their back; till on looking round, they perceived that the hapless objects of their attachment were frozen to death.'

Benjamin Harris, a Rifleman of the 95th (The Rifle Brigade), recalled one particularly devastating scene that even years afterwards caused him 'a sore heart' to remember. After a rare but brief halt next to a turnip field, where the ravenous men had broken ranks to tear turnips from the frozen earth, the rear guard was ordered to move on again. As they began to march once more, Harris heard the screams of a child and turned to see a woman of the 95th who was 'endeavouring to drag along a little boy of about seven or eight years of age. The poor child was completely exhausted, his legs failing under him. Up to this moment, the mother had occasionally been assisted by some of the men, who had taken it in turns to help the little fellow on, but now all appeal was in vain. No man had more strength than that necessary for the support of his own carcass. Although the mother could no longer raise the child in her arms – as her reeling pace too plainly showed – still she continued to drag the child along with her. It was a pitiable sight, and it was wonderful to behold the efforts the poor woman made to keep the boy amongst us, even though she was like a moving corpse herself. At last, the little fellow had no strength even to cry. With mouth wide open, he stumbled onwards until they both sank down to rise no more. When the shades of evening came down, they were far behind, amongst the dead and dying.'

As the column wove its way along roads that had become muddy quagmires, through rugged mountain passes in bitter cold and snow, Rifleman Harris noticed another woman belonging to his regiment struggling forward in the ranks with her husband.

'She presented a ghastly picture of fatigue, being very large in the family way. Towards evening she stepped from amongst the crowd and lay herself down amidst the snow, just off the main road. The enemy were not far behind and the night was coming down. Her husband remained with her, and I heard one or two hasty observations from our men that the two had taken possession of their last resting-place, for to remain behind the column of march in such weather was to perish. We soon forgot about them, but a little time afterwards, to my surprise (I then being in the rear of our party), I saw the woman and her husband hurrying after us. In her arms she carried the babe she had just given birth to. Between them they managed to carry that infant to the end of the retreat. The woman's name was McGuire, and luckily for her and her babe, she was a sturdy and hardy Irishwoman, for that night the cold and sleet were sufficient to try the constitution of most females. When darkness came on I lost sight of her, but with the dawn I noted with some surprise that she was still amongst us. It is said that God tempers the wind to the shorn lamb – that boy I saw many years afterwards when he was a strong and healthy lad.'

Even in the most harrowing, tumultuous of circumstances, the sight of a small child in need would arouse the protective instincts of the most hardened soldiers, to the point of flouting the rules. On the retreat to Corunna, Mrs McClelland, wife of a sergeant in the 28th (North Gloucestershire) Regiment, was trudging along the snow-covered roads with two desperately ill children in her arms. Weak with exhaustion, she placed one of the children, a little girl, on to a passing commissariat wagon, only for her to be removed immediately by the captain in charge as it had been strictly forbidden for women and children to travel on the baggage carts. Mrs McClelland was shattered: 'I think the light left my eyes when I saw this pale dying child, laid down upon the cold iced snow. All were passing on, I could not carry both. I was too ill. I could not leave my child, though the French were following close and perhaps might find but me living when they passed! Colonel Browne used to be sadly fond of this child and often had her to play with him when at mess, and during the voyage would take her on deck, amuse her and be so kind to the little thing for she was still a pretty child when dressed – he was passing at the time and seeing who it was he stopped; and turning to General Paget, who was with him (and who was formerly the Colonel of our Regiment), he said, "There's a little child belonging to a brave soldier, a man you much respect, her mother is ill and the little creature does not weigh more than fourteen pounds, may she not be placed in one of the wagons?" He replied, "By all means have the child taken up." His order was obeyed directly. We arrived at Toro, but there my little girl died and during the night I had with me one dead child, another dying, and was obliged to remain in a dark room all night without fire or candle!'

Other babies were snatched from death. The regimental history of the Gloucestershire Regiment (formerly the 28th/61st Foot), tells of an officer of the 28th who was so exhausted he could take no more and decided to kill himself. Leaving the ranks, he wandered into a little spinney to shoot himself, but before he committed the deed he noticed the body of a soldier's wife lying in the spinney, and beside her, still alive, a tiny baby. He covered the body of the woman and picked up the baby, went back to the column, and took the baby right through to Corunna, finally seeing it safely on to a ship for home.

August Schaumann, a somewhat libidinous commissariat officer who enjoyed flirting with soldiers' wives in happier circumstances, observed a similarly harrowing sight during the same retreat. The army's progress had been slowed by terrible weather and having to cross swollen mountain streams. The presence of many wounded and sick men, as well as 'wretched women and still more wretched children', further delayed its advance, much to Moore's consternation. On 6 January, they were again climbing up a mountain pass. Snow covered the ground and fell upon men and animals who both staggered and collapsed with fatigue, exposure and hunger. Amid this universal misery Schaumann noticed an upturned bullock cart by the side of the road, its Portuguese driver lying dead beside his fallen bullocks. 'A soldier's wife had sought shelter beneath his cart, but she, too, was lying lifeless; and the tragic part of it was that her child, who was still alive, was whimpering and trying to find nourishment at her frozen breasts! One or two officers had the child taken from her, and wrapping it in a blanket, carried it away.'

Both British and French soldiers could show compassion, even to each other. While capable of extreme barbarity, hacking and firing at their enemy mercilessly in the heat of battle, they could fraternise happily together when the flag of truce was raised in order for both sides to collect their dead and wounded or to exchange prisoners. On one occasion, on 27 February 1814, a couple of British soldiers were passing through the town of Orthes a few hours after the battle at which Wellington had defeated Marshal Soult, at the cost of 2,000 men to Soult's 4,000. The French had retreated, leaving behind some of their wounded. It was one of these abandoned men who cried out to the passing redcoats as he lay severely injured in a ditch a little way from the town. The corporal, who told the story to Joseph Donaldson, gave the man a drink of wine from his canteen. As he stooped to do so he noticed something moving beneath the Frenchman's cloak. Drawing it aside he found a boy of about four years old, dressed in English style, nestling beside the French officer. It transpired that when the British column, advancing up the road, had come under heavy fire the child had become separated from his mother in the confusion. The French officer, lying wounded in the ditch, saw the danger that the child was in and enticed him over to the side of the road and out of the line of fire. He kept him amused to distract him from the battle until the exhausted child fell asleep, whereupon he wrapped him in his cloak.

So attached had he become to his protector that the little boy, whose name was James, at first clung to him and refused to be parted from him. But when they arrived at the British camp inquiries were made and the child reunited with his mother. She told the corporal that she had come into Orthes with the rear of the army and, while she was suckling her younger child, James had wandered off. As soon as she realised that he was missing she had begun searching frantically for him all through the battle-scarred town. Eventually after her searches had yielded nothing she was forced to leave the town and march on with the army to the camp beyond.

In the confusion of a march or a battle, it was easy for children to become separated and lost. One of Benjamin Harris's comrades, a rifleman named Richard Pullen, came out to Portugal at the end of 1808 with his wife and their two teenage children, Charles and Susan. Pullen arrived with the troops that had come to reinforce Moore's army but merely ended up joining it in its retreat. His wife and children soon began to lag behind and within a few days he had lost them altogether. When the survivors of the march reached Corunna, they were evacuated back to England's shores in safety.

By the time the army finally reached Portsmouth, Pullen still had not found his family. A little while after landing he was overjoyed to see his wife clambering on to the beach, her feet like his still lacerated from the long march without shoes, her face bearing the ravages of the trauma she had suffered. They hobbled towards each other and embraced passionately, weeping tears of joy at being reunited. But these soon turned to tears of sorrow as the horrible realisation dawned that neither had their children with them. He had believed that they were with her while she had assumed that they were with him. Pullen's comrades told them to give up all hope of seeing the children again as they would undoubtedly be dead or left behind in Spain and there was nothing that a soldier with no money or connections could do to get them back.

But the Pullens would not be deterred and at once began making inquiries, asking every returning soldier whether they had seen the children and even scraping together enough money to place advertisements in local papers. To their intense joy, one of these advertisements yielded a response from a battery of artillery at Plymouth. They had found a girl on the side of a mountain in Spain, screaming with fear and all alone, and had picked her up and taken her with them. Susan Pullen was duly reunited with her parents. Of their son Charles, however, nothing was heard. Pullen himself died a short while afterwards on the Walcheren campaign and Mrs Pullen and her daughter were sent to their parish in Warwickshire to eke out an existence on poor relief. After she had gone the regiment received a letter from her son Charles who, it transpired, had been captured on the retreat and was now a prisoner in France. But nobody forwarded the letter on to Mrs Pullen so it seems that he was left to his fate while his widowed mother remained in ignorance of his whereabouts.

Sometimes it was the mothers who went missing. Charles Stevens of the 20th (East Devonshire) Regiment tells of how one of the regimental women, a delicate creature who was well-liked in the regiment because of her respectable demeanour and irreproachable conduct, simply vanished in the dark one night on the retreat to Corunna, leaving her young daughter all alone. Presumably she had become exhausted and collapsed by the roadside, or perhaps she feared that her daughter would endanger her own life by staying behind to help her and so slipped quietly away to die. Her daughter made it safely back to England.

When mothers died, in wartime as in peace, widowed fathers strove to protect their children, prepared to put their own survival on the line. Joseph Donaldson recalled one man whose wife died on a march in the Peninsula, leaving him with an infant of only a few months old. Instead of consigning it to the care of one of the other women, the man preferred to take care of it himself and carried it on top of his knapsack for many days, staggering under his load even when he fell ill, until he was sent to the hospital at the rear. What eventually became of him and the child Donaldson was unable to learn. Another soldier, back in the days of Marlborough's Wars (when, once again, the English were fighting the French in Europe), even went so far as to carry his little boy into battle with him at Malplaquet, a particularly murderous contest in 1709. Donald McBane, a swordsman in Orkney's Regiment, carried the infant in his knapsack and the terrified boy remained so quiet that McBane thought he must have been killed by one of the musket balls that he felt pass through his own clothing. It was not until the end of the battle that he could take off his knapsack and found to his relief that his son was still alive, though injured in one elbow. Having had the wound dressed by a surgeon, McBane returned the boy to his anxious foster mother back in the camp.

Until women were banished from the front, the incongruity of babies being born in the midst of the turmoil and mayhem of war continued to be a feature of camp life. Few women can have given birth in circumstances as extraordinary as Kate Hutton, who brought a son into the world in the midst of battle during the Seven Years War (1756–63). Her husband, Samuel, described how the infant was 'saluted by cannon on his entrance into the world, and the ball of one was near taking off his head. The day after he was born, we were ordered to march. I wrapped my wife and child in my cloak, and placed them on a baggage wagon, and the only favour I could obtain was that of marching by the side of the baggage wagon, instead of marching in the ranks.'

The Crimean War was the last time this strange proximity of life and death occurred, in which in one corner of a tent a mortally wounded man might be gasping his last painful breaths, while in another a newborn baby was being ushered into the world. While some women gave birth in the squalid, fetid air of the Scutari barracks, others did so in the even more basic surroundings of a tent at the front.

The often rather brusque Major General William Codrington wrote to his wife on 15 January 1855, with noticeable emotion, that, 'In the midst of the snow storm that night, covered by a little patrol tent which is above a deep and square hole in the ground, was produced – a baby! . . . I heard of it this morning and went to take some few things and see the "place of confinement" . . . a heap of blankets and other odds and ends horizontal showed the situation of the lady of the mansion. I took her some tea as an introduction to my seeing if she was in want of anything; and of course I desired to see the baby itself; when Mrs B pushed the blanket from over her own head and there was the little affair in all warmth, face making, redness, and happy ignorance! A curious scene indeed and much to be commended to the notice of ladies who have broad beds, monthly nurses, warm fires, change of linen, warm water and Dr Locock . . . I have taken her some portable sup, a good blanket, some gloves . . . I think the Major General will have to be Godfather to this child of snow! The fact is, I believe she ought not to have been remaining in camp at all.' Less than three months later Codrington wrote to tell his mother that both the corporal and his wife had died and their baby girl had been taken in by another woman of the regiment.

While many mothers and their children did suffer terribly during war, life on campaign was not always filled with misery and oppression. The atmosphere in camp could often be jolly and relaxed if battle was not imminent and the weather fine. When a halt was called or when duties had finished for the day, the men might play a game of cards or cribbage while wives bustled around the camp fires cooking dinner for their husbands in the large camp kettles they carried with them. A fifer or fiddler might strike up a tune and some of the men and women dance a jig beneath the trees. The children too would often join in, or sit by the campfires being petted by their fathers. Little boys would strut around the camp in their sawn off uniforms while the girls helped their mothers or played with dolls. These happy scenes of domesticity, temporary though they were, served to cheer battle-weary soldiers and gave them a sense of normality that was welcome to many who had long ago left the family home for the vicissitudes of a soldier's life.

Children who accompanied their mothers to the American Revolutionary War certainly endured their fair share of hardship and hunger. But, as in most wars, most of the time the army was not actually engaged in battle but was marching, camping or preparing for it. During these activities some sort of normality would reign during which the children of the camp (and at this time they and their mothers accounted for between 10 and 20 per cent of the camp populations) would indulge in the same pursuits that would have entertained them back home in England. Excavators at battlefield sites have uncovered a variety of children's toys. Marbles, doll dishes and doll parts, earthenware sheep and 'whizzers' – metal discs that whirled on strings, made by soldiers by pounding musket balls flat – were found in evacuations at one defence line. It is not difficult to imagine a gruff soldier deriving pleasure from taking a few minutes to fashion a whizzer for one of the little scamps who tore around camp with his playmates.

Harriet Tytler found a novel way of amusing one of her children, in the grimmest of circumstances – during the Indian Mutiny in 1857. By now she had got over the heartache of her dead baby to produce a daughter, Edith, aged nearly two when the Mutiny broke out, and was pregnant with her fourth baby. (Her eldest son, Frank, had been born in 1849.) The family was living in Delhi when some of the city's population joined the rebel sepoys in turning on the Europeans in their midst and massacring them. A fortunate few escaped, Harriet and her family among them. After a few weeks sheltering with friends at other stations she decided to return to Delhi with her husband Robert, who was part of the field force sent to retake it.

A few miles short of the city the force halted on a ridge and prepared to lay siege to the city. Meanwhile, in the blistering heat of a Delhi summer, Harriet (who, because of her advanced state of pregnancy, had been allowed to remain with the army when all the other women and children had been sent away) gave birth to her baby, lying in an upturned bullock cart with a makeshift thatched roof. The baby developed dysentery and was not expected to live more than a week, but remarkably he survived the whole siege and was christened, no doubt to his intense embarrassment in later life, 'Stanley Delhi-Force Tytler' (Harriet had at least resisted pressure to call him 'Battlefield Tytler').

A few days after the birth an enormous shell exploded close to the cart, and a large fragment fell almost on top of Harriet and the baby, but miraculously neither was hurt. Then the monsoon broke and water poured through the thatched roof, drenching Harriet and baby to the skin. She was sure that after such an experience, and with no dry clothes to change into, they must both die but they did not, and Captain Tytler found them better accommodation in a small stone tower. This was the family's home for the next three and a half months, where they sheltered from the shot and shell that rained down around them as the enemy repeatedly attacked the British to try to force them from the ridge.

One of Harriet's most pressing problems was this lack of clothes. When their only garments were being washed she and the children had to wrap themselves in sheets and much of her time was spent darning furiously. Another difficulty was keeping her children occupied – no marbles, whizzers or other toys for them. Her son Frank was less trouble as he ran around happily in the sun playing with soldiers who were delighted to indulge in some lightheartedness. But little Edith had recently recovered from an abscess on the liver and was still weak. She found the oppressive heat intolerable and frequently fainted. To keep her out of the sun Harriet had to find some way to amuse her, and was at her wits' end as to how to distract her. 'At last a bright idea entered into my head. It was rather a unique one, which was to scratch holes in my feet and tell her she must be my doctor and stop their bleeding. This process went on daily and for hours. No sooner did my wounds heal, when she used to make them bleed again for the simple pleasure of stopping the blood with my handkerchief. But it had the desired effect of amusing her for hours.'

The 'unconquerable energy of maternal love' that Sergeant Anthony Hamilton had witnessed on the retreat to Corunna was what drove devoted mothers on again and again, through siege, starvation, sickness and battle, in stifling heat or bitter cold, when they must have often felt like giving in, lying down and dying. They persevered even when their own bodies were racked by fatigue and hunger, impelled by the urge to protect the precious children in their care.

Like most mothers, they felt that their first duty was to their children, but their determination to protect them could bring them into conflict with the army authorities. Military priorities sometimes had to take precedence over compassion: it was not cruelty that caused commanders to prohibit children from riding on the baggage wagons, but the fact that every corner of space was needed for supplies. In peacetime too army wives often found that their domestic life was constrained by regulations and codes of behaviour that were part and parcel of military life, for them as well as the soldiers.

6

On Parade

The Wives of non-Commissioned Officers must set an example of neatness and cleanliness, both in their own persons and those of their children, and in their rooms or lodgings. They will all, as well as the wives of the private soldiers, curtsey whenever they meet the Commanding officer or the Captains of their husbands' Companies, and teach their girls to do the same, and their boys to salute.

From the 1859 Standing Orders of the 13th (Somerset) Light Infantry

In the early days of the modern army, from the moment she married her soldier sweetheart the army wife entered into a bargain with the military. Her place on the strength earned her certain privileges, such as the right to a home of sorts (in barracks or quarters) and the chance to compete in the ballot when the regiment went abroad. In return she had to perform whatever duties were required of her and conform to a code of behaviour that infiltrated almost every aspect of her life, from her dress to her morals. The army governed her behaviour from the time she arose to the sound of the bugle call to the time she extinguished her light at night on the same signal (a convention that was still in force in the 1930s in many garrisons). For the army authorities, keeping control of the wives and families – whose presence they did not always welcome – was important for the successful functioning of the regimental community. If wives were not to constitute too much of a drain on resources, they must be made to pull their weight.

Senior soldiers' wives might take on more elevated occupations such as acting as maid to an officer, or even nursing or midwifery. Wives of lowlier standing had to undertake tasks such as sewing, washing and cleaning, not just for their husbands but also for the other soldiers who shared the barrack room. The barracks themselves had to be kept spotlessly clean and were inspected daily by officers: wives who failed to have the blankets folded correctly on their beds when the duty officer made his inspection would be censured. Laundry was scrutinised to ensure that it came up to the expected standard – needing many hours' work ankle-deep in mud in damp wash-houses to do so. Women were warned that the privilege of washing (and the extra money it earned them) would be taken from them if their work did not come up to scratch, a serious punishment as soldiers' families relied on this extra income to survive. As one averred, 'Without her earnings at the wash-tub they could not live, and some soldiers frankly avow that they chose their wives as a carter would choose his horse, with an eye to strength and endurance.'

As well as providing the army with useful services, it was thought that such labours were beneficial for soldiers' wives who would otherwise be liable to descend into idleness and immorality. They were frequently seen by the military authorities as 'useless sloths . . . miserable drabs who are to be seen sauntering and smoking [clay pipes] in the yard', as the *United Services Gazette* described them in 1857. If they were made to work hard and be obedient, went the prevailing wisdom, their characters would be improved.

Even when the traditional tasks of a soldier's wife such as laundry, sewing and cooking were devolved on to support services set up by the army for that purpose, both soldiers' and officers' wives were expected to perform a range of other duties from the practical to the pastoral. In recent times the expectation that wives would 'do their duty' and attend sports days, organise dances and carry out social work within the regimental community was much less overt than formerly, but it was there nonetheless.

In the eighteenth and nineteenth centuries army women, as well as performing the duties prescribed, had to ensure that their behaviour and general demeanour conformed to a code of conduct befitting their station, showing due deference to wives whose husbands ranked senior to their own. (Even today some complain of fellow wives who 'wear their husbands' ranks on their sleeves'.) Senior wives must not be seen to be too frivolous, while wives of junior ranks should not give themselves graces. Above all, they must conform. Extraordinary as these attitudes might appear, it is worth remembering that in few other professions are the families so closely caught up in the dangers, anxieties and frequent moves that characterise a soldier's life. Thrown in on each other's company and resources, a special social code has grown up over the years among the families, in which certain mechanisms have evolved as a means of coping in difficult times. Sticking closely together, abiding by the rules, written or unwritten, of their society, all helped with maintaining unity and taking decisions, and some of these customs have endured.

In some respects, although life on campaign was hard and dangerous, it lacked the monotonous drudgery of barrack life. In the field there were no floors to scrub, and only the most fastidious martinet of an officer would complain if his shirts were not ironed to perfection. Moreover, opportunities often arose for the soldier's wife to supplement her income and perhaps assert her independence to a small degree. Many women made healthy profits by setting themselves up as sutlers (selling food and liquor) or as maids to officers or ladies. But regimental work took priority over all other activities. And on occasion their duties could go well beyond domestic drudgery and take them into the military sphere.

In the Seven Years War   when Britain and France jockeyed for domin ation in the nascent colonies of India and North America as well as the traditional fighting grounds of Europe – women showed that they could go beyond their traditional domestic labours and take on military tasks. In June 1758, a British expedition was mounted to capture Louisburg on Cape Breton Island (off French Canada) from the French. When the soldiers landed, they had to wade through the rough surf and drag all their supplies and heavy artillery guns up the rocky beach and across the uneven ground to the walls of Louisburg. Second-in-command of the force was General James Wolfe, well known for discouraging his men from matrimony. Now, he was determined that if wives did have to come along, they should be put to good use. So he dragooned the women who had landed with the force into helping their men pull the cumbersome guns across the difficult terrain. As daylight dawned the guns were in place and the bombardment of Louisburg began. The French garrison held out bravely but was forced to surrender after fifty days. Wolfe later acknowledged the women's good work in helping to get the guns into position.

By the end of 1759 Wolfe had gone, dying a hero's death in the battle of the Heights of Abraham that secured his place in history and delivered Quebec into British hands at last. But still hostilities between France and Britain dragged on, in North America, Europe and beyond. Now the British found themselves besieged at Quebec by a French force of superior strength. General James Murray, who had been Wolfe's second-in-command at Quebec and was now the city's governor, did his best to defend the city, working his soldiers hard and issuing edict after edict reminding the women that they too must earn their rations (from which one deduces that there were some shirkers among them) by nursing, cooking and washing. On one occasion he had to insist that they remain in the barracks. One officer present at the siege explained why it was forbidden to venture into the woods outside the city walls. One soldier who had done so was found, 'killed and scalped, one of his arms cut off and his bowels taken out and cut into shreds and a log skewer thrust through his upper lip, nostrils and the crown of his head. His heart had been carried away.' Meanwhile, typhoid, dysentery, scurvy and frostbite reduced the garrison's strength and it became even more critical that every man – and woman – should pull their weight. As the noose drew tighter around the besieged garrison Murray gave orders for ten women from each regiment 'immediately to join the artillery they will be employed in sowing [sic] up sand-bags, and making wads from old junk for the guns'. Just when the situation seemed hopeless, Quebec was relieved by a British force coming up the now unfrozen River Saint Lawrence in May 1760. The French were routed; Britain's naval superiority had once again saved the day. But had it not been for the resilience of the small, besieged force of men in Quebec city who hung on through bitter cold and shortages, and perhaps in a small way to the women who worked in the hospitals and on the ramparts, Quebec would have fallen before the spring thaw brought deliverance.

Whatever commanders thought of women on campaign, many men had good cause to be grateful that their wives had succeeded in accompanying them to the front. Not only did they enjoy their companionship (if the marriage was a happy one), but the more loyal and resourceful women could do much to ameliorate the hardships of life on campaign for their husbands. The army wife may have been subject to military rules and regulations, but she needed no official injunction to care for a wounded or sick husband.

Until the advent of modern medicine, medical care was rudimentary at best, with military surgeons having more in common with carpenters than their counterparts today. But keeping wounds clean, slaking the thirst of sick and injured men, giving them food or blankets or even a comforting touch could often make the difference between life and death. In America, the Peninsula and the Crimea wives would venture on to the battlefield as soon as the fighting had ceased to find their men. Even with no medical skill they might be able to save their lives if they found them lying injured and could protect them from the body-strippers, who descended like vultures to remove uniforms and valuables from the dead and dying.

Sometimes the hospitals themselves were scarcely better than graveyards. Lieutenant Thomas Anbury, who kept a vivid journal of his experiences in the American Revolutionary War, described the horrific scenes that ensued at the close of battle when the wounded were carried in from the field. 'Some of them begged they might lay and die, others again were insensible, some upon the least movement were put in the most horrid tortures and all had near a mile to be conveyed to the hospitals; others at their last gasp, who for want of our timely assistance must have inevitably expired. These poor creatures, perishing with cold and weltering in their blood, displayed such a scene, it must be a heart of adamant that could not be affected by it.' Many wives braved the filth and infection of hospitals to tend their wounded husbands (often they were reluctant to nurse the other men and would only do so under duress). Sergeant Thomas Sullivan of the 49th Regiment noted that after the battle of Bunker Hill (also known as Breed's Hill) in June 1775, in which British casualties were heavy, the hospitals had 'a sufficient number of Nurses, who were mostly the Wives of the Wounded'.

One of the most celebrated women who followed their husbands to war was Lady Harriet Acland, whose escape from a burning tent did not deter her from life on campaign. During the American Revolutionary War she nursed her husband with a devotion that earned her the admiration of an entire army. In July 1777, British forces commanded by General Burgoyne captured Fort Ticonderoga, a strategic fort on the southern shore of the great Lake Champlain in Vermont. Flushed with this triumph, the army went on to defeat a rebel force at nearby Hubbardton. But during that battle Major Acland was severely wounded and when Lady Harriet, who had with some difficulty been persuaded to remain behind on the northern shore of the lake, heard the news she immediately rushed to her husband's side. Only at great expense could she induce a boatman to take her across the stormy waters of the vast lake to the southern shore, where she found her husband lying in a miserable log cabin. Here she nursed him until he was sufficiently recovered to undertake the journey to rejoin the army.

Her commitment was widely applauded. Thomas Anbury was moved to observe, 'Such instances of connubial attachment, in the levity of the present day, are rarely to be met with; but that such characters do exist, and that the pleasure and gaieties of the beau monde have not altogether vanquished the social virtues, is to be instanced in that pattern of her sex, Lady Harriet Acland.' Anbury's allusion to the 'levity of the present day' is a reminder that while Lady Harriet was sharing the trials of the army in America, back in England other members of the aristocracy were distinguishing themselves in very different ways. The fashionable circle around Georgiana, Duchess of Devonshire (only a few years younger than Lady Harriet), whose members included the pleasure-loving Prince of Wales, was giving rise to gossip and scandal as they gambled, partied and conducted extra-marital affairs with abandon.

Having nursed her husband back to health, Lady Harriet was determined not to let him out of her sight. As she was by now heavily pregnant, she commissioned two artillery gunners to make a carriage for her out of an old ammunition cart. As Anbury relates, 'in this impromptu carriage she resolved to follow throughout the campaign the fortunes of her husband, who could by no entreaties prevail upon her to remain in the rear, or in a place of safety'. The army continued its march south. As it drew near the settlement of Freeman's Farm on 19 September, Major Acland finally prevailed upon his wife to detach herself from his side and go with the artillery and baggage that was taking a route that would be less exposed to enemy fire, should it come. And come it did.

A rebel force that had been awaiting the arrival of the British now attacked. As a burst of musket fire rent the air, Lady Harriet and three female companions hurriedly took shelter in a small hut close to the action. For the next four hours they waited anxiously, listening to the thunder of cannon and all the chaos of battle. Soon after the fighting began some surgeons arrived and took possession of the hut for care of the wounded. Now the ladies had to watch as a succession of men with injuries of the most horrific kind were carried in. Here a man with half his face blown away, there a poor soldier gasping for breath as his punctured lungs filled with blood. They drew closer together and prayed for their husbands' safe deliverance.

Deeply as she felt for the misfortunes of her fellow women, Lady Harriet must have been overwhelmed with relief when, at the battle's

The aftermath of battle: women undertaking the melancholy task of searching the battlefield for their husbands, hoping to find them alive.

A soldier's wife, dancing in camp: life on campaign was not all tragedy and horror. Drink, music and dancing helped to banish some of the horrors of war.

The Light Dragoons' barrack room, 1788: women and children lived and slept alongside single soldiers until the advent of married quarters in the mid nineteenth century.

The camp at Aldershot: a soldier carrying out his domestic duties. Charles Dickens visited the camp in 1856 and was appalled by the living conditions of soldiers' families in the married huts.

The 'pretty dragoon': Christian Welsh, or 'Mother Ross', disguised herself as a soldier to search for her husband, and spent more than a decade fighting in the army under Marlborough.

Fanny and Henry Duberly: this photograph was much in demand among soldiers in the Crimea who admired Fanny for staying at the front throughout the war, but not everyone appreciated her presence there.

Harriet and Robert Tytler: Harriet was the only Englishwoman present at the Siege of Delhi in 1857. As well as caring for her two small children, Harriet had to give birth under an upturned bullock cart.

The cookhouse of the 8th Hussars, the Crimea: the woman in the background was one of many wives who accompanied the army, cooking and washing for the soldiers, often in miserable conditions.

Molly Ellis, an army officer's daughter, had been in India only six months when she was kidnapped by tribesmen on the North West Frontier and held hostage for ten days in 1923.

A Sergeant Major's wedding: soldiers' daughters in India often married men in their father's regiment, sometimes at a very young age. 'A grizzled bombardier of forty unites himself to a girl of twelve,' commented a lady visitor in the early nineteenth century.

Lucy Venning, the author's great-grandmother, as an army bride in Ceylon (Sri Lanka) in 1907.

Beryl and Walter Walker, the author's grandparents, at a polo match in India, 1938. Not all wives enjoyed the army social life: one described such occasions as 'stultifyingly dull'.

The Raj at play: fancy dress party, Shillong, India, 1937.

close, she saw her own major walking towards her, alive and well. But by now she had been an army wife long enough to know that her reprieve might be only temporary. As long as the war continued the Damocles sword of death would hang over their heads. As the admiring General Burgoyne later wrote, 'Lady Harriet, with her usual serenity, stood prepared for new trials; and it was her lot that their severity increased with their numbers.'

On 7 October 1777, the two armies clashed again on the same battle-ground as before. This was the battle of Bemis Heights, sometimes known as the Second Battle of Saratoga. As there was no hut or shed near the battleground that had not been razed to the ground in the previous action, Lady Harriet and her companions had to take shelter in the hospital tent among the dead and dying. Here they again listened to the noise of battle with mounting anxiety. Bemis Heights was a bloody contest involving desperate hand-to-hand combat. Then at last came the terrible news: the troops were defeated, and her husband, desperately wounded, had been taken prisoner. According to Anbury, Major Acland had paid some British soldiers fifty guineas to carry him from the field and the men had been in the act of doing so when they were intercepted by American troops and captured.

Filled with despair, tortured with anxiety for her beloved John, Lady Harriet spent a restless night. By the morning, encouraged by her companions and fortified by a little brandy and dirty water that a kindly soldier's wife had pressed on her, she had made up her mind what she must do. General Burgoyne takes up the tale: 'When the army was upon the point of moving, I received a message from Lady Harriet, submitting to my decision a proposal (and expressing an earnest solicitude to execute it, if not interfering with my designs) of passing to the camp of the enemy, and requesting General Gates's [the American General commanding the opposing army] permission to attend her husband.' Burgoyne was amazed at her proposal. After all, he noted, this was a woman 'of the most tender and delicate frame; of the gentlest manners, habituated to all the soft elegancies, and refined enjoyments, that attend high birth and fortune; and far advanced in the state in which the tender cares, always due to the sex, become indispensably necessary [he is referring to her pregnancy]. Her mind alone was formed for such trials.' What was more she had spent the last twelve hours racked by anxiety for her husband, unable to sleep, unable to eat (there was no food to be had) and drenched in rain. But seeing her determination Burgoyne promised to do all he could to help. Though he had no food at all to offer her he did manage to find her a small rowing boat in which to cross the Hudson River to where the rebel force were encamped on the other side. He then wrote a short letter on a scrap of paper to General Gates commending her to his protection.

Taking with her the major's valet, her own maid, and Mr Brudenell, the chaplain to the artillery, Lady Harriet rowed down the river to meet the enemy. Night had fallen by the time the little party reached the enemy's outposts. Mr Brudenell hoisted the white flag of truce and called out to the sentry, telling him the nature of their mission. But the sentry, suspecting a trap, threatened to fire into the boat if anyone stirred before daylight. So Lady Harriet, heavily pregnant and keenly aware that even the smallest delay might prove fatal to her husband, was forced to wait in the boat for eight hours, tantalisingly close to John but unable to go to him, shivering with cold as her unborn child stirred within her. When daylight dawned they were finally allowed ashore and Lady Harriet was received by General Gates 'with all the humanity and respect that her rank, her merits, and her fortunes deserved'. Like his rival commander, and almost everyone with whom she came into contact, General Horatio Gates was bowled over by the charming, gracious demeanour of the woman who stood before him. After briefly scanning Burgoyne's scribbled note he declared that he was happy for her to remain in the rebel camp for as long as it took to nurse her crippled husband back to health.

Had she been a humble soldier's wife, perhaps she might not have been received quite so graciously. But General Gates, who was a former British officer and every bit as susceptible to being impressed by high birth as Burgoyne, was clearly delighted to be able to assist such an 'amiable piece of quality' as he described Lady Harriet. Moreover, her endearing manner and high birth aside, Gates was keenly aware of the propaganda value of being seen to treat his fair petitioner magnanimously. His audience with her came a short while after the murder, on 27 July 1777, of Jane McCrea. She was the auburn-haired fiancée of a loyalist officer with Burgoyne's column, who had sent for her believing that she would be safer with the army as the fighting drew near her home. Accordingly he sent two Indians to fetch her and escort her safely to the English camp. As she neared the English camp a quarrel broke out between her two escorts as to who would claim the lion's share of the reward for delivering her to safety. One of the warriors, determined that his fellow should not cheat him of what he was due, seized the petrified Jane McCrea and attacked her with his tomahawk. When she was dead they hacked off her scalp, believing that her long auburn tresses would fetch a goodprice. According to some versions of this story, and there are many, her broken-hearted fiancé purchased the scalp and would gaze tenderly on the long locks of his murdered beloved for many years afterwards.

Burgoyne had decided to engage the services of warriors from the Seneca tribe ('a necessary evil' he called it) because of their skill at fighting in dense forests. Yet, like the French a generation before, he was unable to exert sufficient control over these capricious allies, and their actions, particularly their habit of torturing and scalping captives, soon brought his army into disrepute. The killing of Jane McCrea provided the rebels with the perfect propaganda stick with which to beat Burgoyne. Within days of her murder she had become a cause célèbre and a recruiting tool for the rebels, who used it as evidence of British inhumanity. Volunteers flocked to the rebel camps to avenge the death of an innocent American girl, never mind that both her brother and fiancé fought for the British.

So when Gates received Burgoyne's letter, commending Lady Harriet to his protection, he must have seen another chance to rile his opposite number and make reference to the crimes committed by his troops. On 12 October he sent a note to Burgoyne, somewhat sanctimoniously declaring that his request that Gates treat Lady Harriet kindly had been unnecessary since 'The respect due to her Ladyship's rank, the tenderness due to her person and sex, were alone sufficient recommendations to entitle her to my protection; considering my preceding conduct with respect to those of your army whom the fortune of war has placed in my hands, I am surprised your Excellency should think that I could consider the greatest attention to Lady Ackland in the light of an obligation.' His underlying message was clearly: 'I do not need any lessons in humanity from you.' By treating Lady Harriet with such accommodation and civility he would be able to claim the moral high ground. (American writers later denied that she had been kept waiting in the boat for eight hours.)

The British army, keen to claim her heroism for their own cause, leapt at the chance to celebrate her fortitude and praise her 'connubial attachment' at a time when their situation seemed grave. Roger Lamb, a sergeant in the Royal Welch Fusiliers, explained why Lady Harriet became an icon for the beleaguered British. 'There is scarcely an instance,' he wrote, 'either in ancient or modern history, that more finely depicts the resolution, affection, and fortitude of woman toward the husband of her heart and vows than this. If war sometimes in bad men, calls forth all the viler passions of our nature, in woman it is otherwise; it rouzes into action an heroism, otherwise unknown, an intrepidity almost incompatible with the sex, and awakens all the dormant susceptibilities of their mind.'

The postscript to Lady Harriet's story is sadly ironic. With the major nursed back to health, the Aclands rejoined the British column and proceeded south with Burgoyne. But after surviving all these ordeals Major Acland then threw away the life that his wife had strived so hard to preserve when he quarrelled with a fellow officer over a comparatively trivial matter. The squabble escalated into a duel in which Acland stumbled as he made a sword thrust and fell forward, striking his head on a stone. In this rather banal and unnecessary manner he died. It was Burgoyne's niece, a Miss Warbuton, who reported the sorry ending to this romantic tale and implored her readers to imagine 'the wretchedness of Lady Harriet on this unhappy event. Attached to him as she was, having suffered so much for his sake, and having, as she hoped, brought him home to safety and a life of future happiness, to have all this cheering prospect dashed at once in so miserable a manner, was, one would have thought, more than human nature could support or sustain. But she had a mind superior to every trial, and even this, her severest infliction, she bore up under with resignation and fortitude'. Miss Warburton happened to see Lady Harriet several years later, and observed that while she was still a handsome woman she had 'a look of tender melancholy mingled with resignation that made her the most interesting object I had ever beheld'. There is, however, one final and rather romantic postscript to Lady Harriet's extraordinary story: she ultimately became the wife of Mr Brudenell, the chaplain who had so bravely accompanied her on her mission to the enemy camp.

The wifely devotion of Lady Harriet was by no means restricted to the officer class. Dan Skiddy, who went to the Peninsular War with the 34th (Cumberland) Regiment, had an equally staunch spouse, a squat little Irishwoman named Biddy who was 'as broad as a big turtle' and was known to the men of the 34th as 'Mother' Skiddy, or 'Mrs Commissary General' because of her superior foraging skill. She was far from popular with commanders because of her habit of going ahead of the column on a donkey named 'the Queen of Spain' and holding the whole army up, in order to be ready with a cup of hot tea for Dan, who suffered badly from rheumatic pain in his joints. Wellington eventually gave orders that women who did not stay in the rear would have their donkeys shot. But the irrepressible Biddy refused to be deterred from doing what she saw as her duty. To the amusement of the whole division, she and two other wives were on their donkeys again the very next day, leading the way ahead of the army. Unluckily for them the Provost Marshal, the man who enforced military law, was lying in wait and ambushed the little party, killing and wounding two or three of the donkeys. Yet the very next day Biddy was foremost on the line of march again. 'We must risk something to be in before the men,' she explained, 'to have the fire an' a dhrop of tay ready for the poor crathers after their load an' their labour.'

As well as looking after her husband's comforts she washed and sewed for other men in the company. One of these was the young Lieutenant George Bell, later a major general. After the battle of Toulouse in 1814, the final action of the Peninsular War, some of the troops began to return to England (others were sent to America). Bell, who had grown to admire Mother Skiddy, sought her out to bid her farewell and pay her for a year's worth of washing and darning. But she was reluctant to accept any money, saying, 'O, sir, sure you always belonged to me own company, an' you're welcome to the bit av washing.'

With her broad beam and torrent of curses, Biddy Skiddy might not have had the traditional appearance of an angel of mercy. Yet her devotion to her Dan not only leavened the miseries of war for him but, on one occasion, saved his life. Although her husband had sworn her to silence on the subject, she revealed to George Bell how the painful back she was complaining about had been caused. 'Yer honour minds how we were all kilt and destroyed on the long march last winter, and the French at our heels, an' all our men droppin' and dyin' on the roadside, waitin' to be killed over agin by them vagabones comin' ater us. Well, I don't know if you seed him, sir, but down drops poor Dan, to be murdered like all the rest. Says he, "Biddy dear, I can't go on furder one yard to save me life." "O, Dan jewel," sis I, "I'll help you on a bit; tak' a hould av me, an' throw away your knapsack." "I'll niver part wid my knapsack," says he, "nor my firelock, while I'm a soger." '

It was a serious offence for a soldier to lose either his knapsack or his weapon and Dan Skiddy, veteran that he was, could not bring himself to commit such a crime, even as the sound of French firing drew closer. Biddy made one last effort to persuade him to move, but it was no use, 'The poor crather hadn't power to stir a lim'.' So, helping him up a bank, she coaxed him to get on her back, warning him that unless he got on ' "the French will have ye in half an hour an' me too, the pagans" '. Dan climbed on Biddy's broad back, still holding tightly to his knapsack and his firelock, despite her pleas that he throw the weapon away, telling her,

'I'll shoot the first vagabone lays hould av your tail'. Off she set with her husband on her back, knapsack, firelock and all 'as strong as Sampson' as she put it, 'for the fear I was in. An' fegs, I carried him half a league after the regiment into the bivwack. Me back was bruck entirely from that time to this, an' it'll never get strait till I go to the Holy Well in Ireland, and have Father McShane's blessin', an' his hand laid over me! An' that's all the thruth, her honour, I've told ye.' She attributed her feat to the fact that fear gave her strength she would not have otherwise possessed. No doubt she was right: adrenalin is known to overcome fatigue by producing a surge of energy, and this probably helped Biddy make that superhuman effort. But love too clearly played its part, impelling her to risk her own life to save his.

Even in camp women risked their lives merely carrying out the most mundane of domestic duties, as evidenced by a tale told by Private William Wheeler of the 51st (King's Own Yorkshire Light Infantry). One day in October 1812, during the Peninsular War, the British were encamped near Valladolid in Spain. Mrs Maibee, a sergeant's wife, was preparing breakfast for her husband when the enemy began firing their heavy artillery on to the British camp. She was in the act of taking some chocolate off the fire when a shot carried away her arm and right breast, killing her.

Washing too could be a high-risk occupation. Margaret Kirwin, a private's wife, and a sober, stoical West Country woman, accompanied the 19th Foot (The Green Howards) to the Crimea in 1854. En route, Margaret had had to spend twelve hours a day standing in a stream doing the washing of the 101 men in her allotted company. As a result she became dangerously ill: her distraught husband John had been forced to leave her lying apparently near death on the shores of Turkey when the regiment sailed for the Crimea. However, thanks to the ministrations of an army doctor, Margaret recovered and journeyed on to the Crimea to join her husband a few months later. Within a few hours of arriving in Balaclava (where she and her husband set up home in a tent pitched in the unwholesome surroundings of a graveyard), she had to resume her duties as a laundress. A general who heard that there was a woman nearby sent his servant to ask if she could do his laundry. Margaret was soon washing his clothing on one of the tombstones and hanging it out to dry on a clothesline she rigged up in the graveyard. It was while ironing some officers' shirts that she had a brush with death. 'I was on my knees ironing, my little goat lying beside me, four shells exploded on my tent and I was covered with earth. In the clearing at the back of my tent there were

28 sheep and 14 bullocks torn to pieces, and a dozen shirts belonging to Mr Beans were quite spoiled. He had got them as a present from his mother in Malta . . . General Darling and Mr Beans galloped up hard from Balaklava and when they came up they asked if I was killed but I said, "Mr Beans; I am not thank God sir, but look at your fine shirts riddled with holes". The General said "Mrs Kirwin, you must have something very lucky about you." '

Not only was Margaret kept busy earning her keep, she also had to look after her husband, cooking his meals, doing his laundry too and nursing him when he was sick. Out of 1,050 men of the 19th who set sail from England in 1854, only 185 returned to England. The others perished in battle and from disease, inadequate shelter and clothing and lack of food. That John Kirwin was one of the lucky 185 was due, he said later, to his wife, without whom he would not have survived. For her part she felt that, despite the horrors she had seen (the *Times* correspondent William Howard Russell lent her his telescope to watch the fighting for Sebastopol on one occasion but Margaret could not stand the sight of men bayoneting each other and handed it back), and despite the many close calls she had had – including the occasion when a sergeant let off his pistol by mistake and shot her bonnet off, stunning her – she had been lucky because she was with her man. 'You see, sir,' she told her interviewer in 1896, 'providence has proved kind to myself and my husband to leave us so long together, both of us being in our seventies. If I was young tomorrow, I would take the same travels; but I would be a little wiser.'

Every theatre of war saw soldiers' wives proving their quality. Especially admired in the Crimea were Mrs Elizabeth Evans and Mrs Becky Box, both married to private soldiers in the 4th (King's Own) Regiment. Mrs Evans followed the men on to the battlefield of the Alma until she was ordered to the rear. In the tense moments before the battle commenced, a major told her, 'Look well at that, Mrs Evans, for the queen of England would give her eyes to see it.' She obeyed and gazed upon the awesome spectacle of the British army drawn up for battle. Within minutes the scene of splendour had become one of confusion. Smoke billowed from the battlefield, cannons thundered, horses screamed and men shouted. Mrs Evans watched along with the other women as the infantry launched attack after attack on the Russians, all praying for their husbands' survival.

Elizabeth Evans had begun her life a soldier's wife living in a curtained-off corner of a barrack room, so the lack of modesty, the earthy smells and language to which she was exposed held few horrors for her. Moreover, by day she had the tent largely to herself and it was here that she set about the task of mending the regimental colours that had been badly torn in the battle, a task that took her several days to accomplish. When the regiment took part in the Battle of Inkerman on 4 November 1854 Mrs Evans stayed behind in camp to guard the precious colours that she had worked on so painstakingly. Like Mrs McGuire in the American Revolutionary War, who had wrapped the colours round her heavy flat irons and dropped them into the sea to keep them from the French, she well knew their symbolic value to the regiment and was determined to defend them with her life. When she was not darning or washing she joined her husband on picquet duty, a position that took her within speaking distance of the Russian trenches. As this was highly irregular she would creep out at dusk, past the officers who gave up trying to stop her and just looked the other way as she groped her way forward. So respected had she become that when she succumbed to a violent fever in 1855 and her husband was away escorting a prisoner ship to Varna, she was tenderly cared for by the men for whom she had done so much. She survived to be reunited with her husband in England at the end of the war. She went on to endure the siege of Lucknow in the Indian Mutiny and when her husband retired, she ran a laundry in Richmond, Surrey. After her husband's death she was granted special permission to wear his Crimean medals, and when she herself died she was buried with full military honours.

Becky Box was equally intrepid. As well as being a regimental wife she was, in the latter stages of the war, employed as a nurse by Florence Nightingale. She was known to be as strong as an ox and could pick up a six-foot man and carry him on her shoulders to safety. She secured her place in the affections of the soldiers by regularly joining the men in the trenches where she tended the wounded. On more than one occasion she braved shell and shot to pick her way across open ground to the friendly French lines, where she would procure brandy for the sick men in her camp. The men repaid her kindness by sharing their rations with her when food was short.

Before Florence Nightingale and her small band of trained nurses landed at Scutari, it was left to army surgeons, invalid or pensioner soldiers acting as untrained medical orderlies, and the brave wives of soldiers to administer what care they could to the men. Mrs Longley, who had managed to embark with the 17th Lancers only thanks to the intercession of her former employer Lord John Russell, more than justified her presence in the Crimea. She devotedly nursed the sick and wounded, going out on to the battlefield of the Alma to tend the wounds of those who lay bleeding there.

Very often sickness ravaged an army and its followers as much as battle wounds – and, in the days before effective medical treatment, just as fatally – and women's nursing skills were similarly called upon. Elizabeth Webber Harris was the wife of the colonel of the 104th Bengal Fusiliers (later The Royal Munster Fusiliers), when the regiment was stationed at Peshawar in North West India in August 1869. She had gone up to the hill station of Murree to escape the stifling heat when she received word that cholera had broken out within the regiment. Rather than thanking Providence that she was safely removed from danger, Mrs Webber Harris at once set out for Peshawar and, on arrival, set about administering what care she could to the sufferers. At first it seemed that the danger was receding as the death rate began to diminish, although in one week the regiment lost thirteen small children and some women. Suddenly, around 10 September, it became more virulent again and Colonel Webber Harris was ordered to take the regiment out of the town and encamp in the countryside so as not to spread the dread infection to too many of the population. At 3 a.m. the next day they marched, taking care to avoid main roads. Just as she arrived at camp Mrs Webber Harris saw a soldier fall to the ground. 'I called my servants; we picked him up and sent for the Doctor. Unhappily we had only one with us, so he was sometime coming. The poor man was in a collapse from cholera, and quite unconscious. While waiting, I got some mustard, tore my handkerchief in half and put on 2 mustard plasters, and the Doctor arriving, he was sent off to hospital, and am thankful to say he eventually recovered.' That night twenty-seven men died and were buried on the spot.

Throughout the three months she spent in quarantine with the soldiers, Mrs Webber Harris worked ceaselessly to nurse the sick and raise morale. By the time the regiment returned to Peshawar in December it had lost a third of its men. Both Colonel Webber Harris and his wife had survived. The colonel's lady had shown enormous courage by staying with the regiment at great personal risk when she could have remained safely in Murree. This, after all, was not wartime and she had no need to follow the troops. How much they appreciated her act of solidarity soon became evident. As she modestly put it:

Everybody made much of me, because, I think, I had not seen another woman's face for three months! and then I heard that the officers of the regiment had sent home for a gold Victoria Cross for me. When it arrived, it proved to be an exact replica of a V.C. in gold, with this inscription on the back –

> *'Presented to Mrs. Webber Harris by the officers of the*
> *104th Bengal Fusiliers, for her indomitable pluck,*
> *during the cholera epidemic of 1869.'*

It is a most beautiful ornament, and will always be my most cherished possession.

As a book on British gallantry awards points out, it is the closest a woman has ever come to winning the Victoria Cross.

Even after the Army Nursing Service was created in 1881 to formalise nursing care, recruiting and training women to work in military hospitals for a regular wage, many army wives continued to provide their services on an informal basis. In the Boer War several senior officers' wives, as well as some society ladies who had no connection with the army, professed their wish to go and help in the hospitals at the front. But, as one journalist sourly noted, their lack of training or experience meant that they were often liabilities. 'I have heard many Society Women thinking that they would like to do a little work, say "O! I love nursing" and then go pottering about the wards in flounces and furbelows, hindering the nurses and irritating the patients. All this is wrong, and should not have been allowed. If ever there is another big war, a good deal of attention, I should think, will be paid to the keeping back of Society women.'

But while the society butterflies were getting in the way, other wives worked hard in the dirty, disease-ridden hospitals at places such as Bloemfontein and Vryburg, like Mrs Buckley, a colonel's wife who lived with her husband in a tin shack in Vryburg for over a year. A committed Christian, she had already spent many years in England caring for the sick and outcast members of society. In South Africa she worked from dawn until dusk, driving carts of supplies and nursing weary, fly-tormented men, and then going home to her hut where she cooked and cared for numbers of convalescents who stayed with her after leaving hospital to recharge their strength. Eventually her health gave way and she had to return to England. Mrs Buckley gained no reward or acknowledgement for her services, although her husband was awarded the DSO.

★   ★   ★

A world away from the filth and blood of battle and disease, one of the most important roles of officers' wives was to look and act the part, to support their husbands and to be a social asset to them. Iris Portal once arrived at a social function in India in the 1930s to be told by one of her husband's fellow officers that she was not wearing enough make-up and 'looked awful. I found this rather amusing and dashed back to slap on the rouge and mascara and returning in time to do my stuff.' A contemporary described the life of officers' wives as 'excessively boring, trivial, claustrophobic, confined and totally male-oriented. The army wife was not expected to do anything or be anything except a decorative chattel or appendage of her husband. Nothing else was required of her whatsoever. She was not expected to be clever. It didn't even matter if she wasn't beautiful, so long as she looked reasonable and dressed reasonably and didn't let her husband down by making outrageous remarks at the dinner table. She certainly had wonderful opportunities for riding and participating in all sorts of horse sports, but apart from that and looking after her children and running a fairly decent dinner party, there her role ended.'

They were both speaking of pre-war India, but the descriptions evoke hollow laughs from many post-war wives who resented the expectations placed on them, that they should turn out to every official function and be available for such duties as arranging the flowers in the mess, running the jumble sale and hosting coffee mornings. They felt that they were treated as appendages of their husbands rather than individuals. The habit of referring to women as 'wife of . . . .' rather than Mrs X, and demanding their husband's name, rank and army number whenever they contacted the military authorities (even on such personal matters as seeing an army doctor) continued to enrage army wives well into the 1980s and only ceased when a consultation exercise revealed the great resentment it caused.

The tradition of officers' wives taking on a pastoral role and visiting the wives of soldiers under their husbands' command was one duty that could cause emotions to run high on occasions. Some officers' wives felt awkward taking on the role of the 'Lady Bountiful' to women who were several years their senior, while others enjoyed the contact it brought them with the wider regimental community. Similarly, some soldiers' wives were appreciative of such visits while others fiercely resented the intrusion and the condescension they implied.

Some wives were flummoxed when, as their husband progressed up the ranks, they found themselves propelled into a semi-public role for which they felt unprepared and unsuited. When Elizabeth Howlett's husband

Geoffrey became the commanding officer of the 2nd Battalion of the Parachute Regiment she found herself having to chair meetings and give talks, which filled her with horror. 'I went and had public speaking lessons because I couldn't do it, I just couldn't. I froze.' Even more demanding was the task of keeping up morale among the families left behind in Aldershot when the regiment went to Northern Ireland. Over a period of two years in the early 1970s 2 PARA went on four unaccompanied tours to Northern Ireland of four months each. It was a time of spiralling violence in the province and on the mainland. The Bloody Sunday killings in January 1972 were followed by the IRA's bombing of the Officers' Mess in Aldershot in which six civilians and an army padre were murdered. Elizabeth and her three children had armed guards posted around their house as her position as CO's wife made her an obvious target.

In such a tense atmosphere, friction sprung up between the Irish-born wives, who had met and married soldiers from the regiment on a previous tour of duty, and the other wives who, increasingly anxious for their husband's safety as the regiment began to suffer casualties, became hostile towards the Irish women whose countrymen were carrying out the attacks. As Elizabeth remembers, 'None of the English wives liked the Northern Ireland girls. They were really quite nasty to them, because they got so fed up with their men always . . . [dying]. We lost people. And it was difficult, it was a very difficult time.' One morning at three o'clock she was awakened by the telephone. On answering it she heard a woman sobbing incoherently down the line. It was a soldier's wife, an Irish girl, who had become tormented with anxiety about her husband, as well as feeling isolated in a community miles from her home. 'She was going to put her head in the gas oven, so I said "Wait, wait till I come and we'll do it together." '

Waking her three sleeping children and taking them round to a neighbour, Elizabeth frantically raced to find the woman's house in time to prevent her committing suicide. When she arrived Elizabeth realised that she was serious about her threat. To buy time she asked for a cup of tea. They sat down and it all came pouring out: 'How no one accepted her here and she didn't have any friends and she couldn't live without her husband being near and she was worried about him. Well we all were, because it was a dangerous time . . . She poured it all out and that's what she wanted, she was lonely, she wanted to talk to somebody. And then it was getting on and I said, "Now come on, let's get on with it. If we're going to do it let's get on with it, because if we're not going to do it I must get back to my children." And so she said, "Oh well, perhaps now you've talked to me I feel better" . . . So I felt I'd done something then. It was jolly difficult to think what to do. And you know I wasn't trained, it was just common sense. I hated the wives' clubs – I hated doing that [but] it was assumed if you were the CO's wife that you did it. You got on with it. It was very good for one I suppose, very character-forming.'

Furthermore, she saw it as her duty to help Geoffrey by ensuring that the wives were happy: 'Because if they were all complaining to their husbands, Geoffrey had his hands full anyway out there, he didn't want a lot of disgruntled soldiers, so I had to do the best I could.'

With so many written and unwritten codes, it was not always easy for wives to find the right balance. In recent years, wives still felt that if they complained too much about the frequent postings, the condition of their quarter, or the long separations, or if they failed to 'fit in', they might be dubbed a 'problem wife', possibly damaging their husbands' careers. Yet by the standards of earlier centuries, such sanctions were mild indeed. Women who were attached to the army were subject to much more severe punishments for disobeying the rules, although equally their crimes were often of a far graver nature than merely transgressing social boundaries.

7

Crime and Punishment

The wives of non-commissioned officers and soldiers must consider
themselves just as amenable to military discipline as their husbands,
repeated infringements of which will render a woman liable
to be deprived of her privileges, and her name struck off
the roll of the married establishment.

From the Standing Orders of the
Durham Light Infantry, 1891

The conflict between the martial and marital obligations of soldiers
has always been a source of potential unrest. Regimental standing
orders frequently reminded the men that they were 'responsible for the
conduct of their wives, and for the cleanliness of their quarters. When
more than one family is located in the same room, it will be the duty
of the senior non-commissioned officer or oldest soldiers to report any
irregularity or neglect of orders.' If a family's behaviour was found wanting and the soldier was deemed to be 'too weak' to control his wife and
children, he 'must suffer for his weakness'.

When women accompanied their men in time of war, maintaining
order was of crucial importance, with discipline being strictly enforced on
both sexes. But even in peacetime commanding officers sought to impress
upon the men that their military duties must come first. Their wives were
similarly expected to defer to the demands of the army. While women
who distinguished themselves by industry and devotion were appreciated,

those who threatened the cohesion of the regimental community by insubordinate or immoral behaviour, those who interfered with its operations in the field by delaying its progress, those who stained its reputation by engaging in looting or robbery, those who provoked disturbances by selling or partaking too freely of alcohol, and those who undermined discipline by inciting desertion or mutiny among the men, could all expect to be dealt with severely.

One perennial scourge for the army authorities was sexual licence. In the seventeenth and eighteenth centuries soldiers' wives often suffered from being tarred with the same brush as the camp followers and prostitutes who attached themselves to armies in the field. 'Loose' women were detested by commanders, not merely on moral grounds but for practical reasons too. Their habit of spreading venereal diseases severely affected the capability of a force by rendering large numbers of soldiers unfit for service. Samuel Pepys noted on a visit to Tangier that a girl named Joyce, a 'mighty pretty creature', was reputed to have transmitted venereal disease to some 400 soldiers. In Victorian times the problem reached alarming proportions. In 1859 for every thousand men there were 422 admissions to hospital for venereal disease. While recognising that soldiers, the majority of them unable to marry, had to have some outlet for their sexual urges and that prostitution was the obvious solution to this problem, the damaging effects of VD had to be checked and means of regulating prostitution were therefore sought.

Some senior officers, like many members of the middle and upper classes, were apt to look on all working-class women as prostitutes, actual or potential. Indeed, when in the 1860s the government sought to tackle the problem with the iniquitous Contagious Diseases Acts, it was soon apparent that almost any working-class woman, prostitute or not, was liable to be rounded up and subjected to an intrusive and unpleasant physical examination for disease.

Long before the introduction of these widely loathed Acts and the advent of the equally inhumane 'lock hospitals', in which women were detained until they were deemed to be disease-free, military commanders had been taking their own measures to combat the problem of sexually transmitted disease. In 1746, while commanding the army in Scotland against the Jacobites, the Duke of Cumberland, as part of his efforts to mould the men under his command into the smart, disciplined troops he required, awarded 200 lashes with a cat-o'-nine-tails to a number of 'disorderly women' and had them drummed out of camp. As 'disorder' was often used as a euphemism for venereal disease, it is quite likely that their crime was to have spread infection, although they may have committed other offences too. His subordinate and protégé, James Wolfe, may have been influenced by Cumberland's actions when, as a young major in Scotland in 1749, he took a hard line towards the wives and camp followers who cluttered up his orderly garrison, announcing that 'If any Woman in the Regt has a Venerial Disorder, & does not immediately make it known to the surgeon, they shall upon the first discovery, be drum'd out of the Regiment, & be imprison'd in the Tolbooth, if ever she Returns to the Corps.' Wolfe, a fastidious, intense young man, probably felt a degree of moral revulsion towards these loose women, but it was their effect on the physical health of the regiment that was of most practical importance and inspired him to take such harsh, though not unusual, measures.

Even the most worldly commanders were troubled by the problem. General Braddock, who commanded the British army during the early years of the French and Indian Wars that led to the semi-global Seven Years War, was sorely vexed by the problem of venereal disease among the troops during his expedition to take Fort Dusquesne from the French in 1755. Three times in one month he ordered the soldiers' wives to be examined to make sure they were 'clean'. Those found to be harbouring infection or who refused to be examined were barred from the march. His successor John Forbes, who had briefly trained as a doctor, was equally convinced of the importance of curbing the venereal scourge. During his own expedition to Duquesne in 1758 he insisted that 'Any women suspected to be infected with the Venial Distemper are to be sent to the Hospittal. To be examind & those who are found disorderd are either to be kept in the hospital till Curd or Turnd out of Camp.'

The other great bane of commanders trying to keep their troops in order was the demon drink. In November 1759, twice within ten days pairs of women were whipped through the streets of Quebec for selling liquor to the troops. That same year on the other side of the Atlantic, in another theatre of the Seven Years War, the Commander of the Royal Scots Greys (then known as the Royal North British Dragoons) was grappling with the same problem. A regimental order was issued in Gronenberg that 'as there are great complaints of Drunkeness among the men It is believed to be owing in some measure to so many of the women being allowed to sell Liquor, It is again Repeated that the Commanding Officer of troops be answerable that no women be allowed to sell Liquor but the one appointed to be the Sutler . . . if any women Persists in selling Liquor after these orders they will be Ducked and Drummed out of the Regiment.'

In peacetime, too, when garrison commanders struggled with the problems caused by widespread drunkenness, the finger of blame was frequently pointed, and justly, at the soldiers' wives. Stuck in the sweltering heat of the Indies or Burma with little to distract them by way of entertainment, many soldiers and their wives devoted much of their energies and nearly all their pay to procuring enough drink to render themselves insensible to their miserable situation. Sergeant MacMullen, who served in India in the mid-nineteenth century was, for all his sympathy for soldiers' wives and their sufferings, a deeply moral man and was revolted by the intemperate behaviour of some army wives at Colabah Barracks, near Bombay. Their husbands were being invalided home, having been wounded in recent fighting. But when it came to embarkation it was not the invalids who had difficulty getting on board the ship but their wives. Some of these women were so paralytic with drink that they had to be hoisted on board by a teakle, a kind of crane.

During the ten months spent by MacMullen's regiment, the 13th (Somerset Light Infantry), at the hot and inhospitable station of Sukkur more than fifty soldiers died, and at least half of those deaths were due to alcohol. The army authorities tried to regulate drinking by limiting the amount that soldiers could be served in the regimental canteen, the only place where they were allowed to purchase alcohol. But inevitably they found other sources of supply, principally the married women of the regiment who sold lethal home-brewed spirits at inflated prices. Although the punishment for being caught supplying alcohol to the soldiers was banishment from camp and a fine of five rupees, the huge profits that could be accrued from such a trade persuaded many women to run the risk. Sergeant MacMullen knew of one wife who had managed to amass savings of £200 (about £11,000 in today's money) from selling liquor at Sukkur, while Sergeant Pearman of the 3rd Light Dragoons, who served in India at the same time, cites the example of Paddy Burns, or 'the old tin kettle' as she was known. When the regiment was stationed in Ambala, India, this enterprising woman had a tin baby made with a wax face. She would take it to the regimental canteen in the evenings and mimic the cry of a child, whereupon she would give it a dose of rum to soothe it until the 'child' was filled with a gallon of the liquor. Later in the night when the canteen was closed and the soldiers were desperate for drink Paddy would sell the grog at four times the price she had paid for it. Eventually the scheme was uncovered and she and her husband were hauled up before the colonel. The man got his discharge and they returned to London and bought a pub with the proceeds of their racket.

In wartime the appeal of alcohol, both as a means of profiteering and of relief from the vicissitudes of life on campaign, was stronger still. Men and women living constantly in the presence of death, and suffering from fatigue, hunger and exposure, sought refuge in the rum bottle. In one incident during the Peninsular War, a young lieutenant, William Grattan of the 88th (the Connaught Rangers), was more tolerant than a senior officer might have been towards a soldier's wife who had indulged too freely. Grattan had been seriously wounded at the storming of the fortress town of Badajoz in April 1812. On the first morning of this fierce two-day battle, the women had taken leave of their men and remained in the camp. Here they sat and waited, some confidently predicting victory and rubbing their hands in anticipation of the spoils that their men would bring back from the vanquished city. Others, listening to the furious thundering of the cannon and seeing the desperate state of some of the wounded who were being carried back to camp, felt sick with apprehension as they prayed that their husbands would be spared. Some tried to quieten their nerves with a little rum, or in the case of Nelly Carsons, whose husband Dan was Grattan's batman, a great deal of it.

When Grattan returned to camp after being severely wounded, he was helped into his tent by two soldiers who intended to put him to bed. But when they entered the tent they found that his bed (a straw truss) was already occupied. Nelly, 'by the way of banishing care,' as Grattan tactfully surmised, 'had taken to drinking divers potations of rum to such an excess that she lay down in my bed, thinking, perhaps, that I was not likely again to be its occupant; or, more probably, not giving it a thought at all.' One of the soldiers attempted to wake her, in vain. 'A battery of a dozen guns might have been fired close to her ear without danger of disturbing her repose! "Why then sir," said he, "the bed's big enough for yees both, and she'll keep you nate and warm, for, be the powers, you're kilt with the cold and the loss ov blood." I was in no mood to stand on ceremony, or, indeed, to stand at all. I allowed myself to be placed beside my partner, without any further persuasion . . . Weakness from loss of blood soon caused me to fall asleep.' But before long he was rudely awakened by Nelly who, 'discharging a huge grunt, and putting her hand upon my leg, exclaimed "Arrah! Dan jewel. What makes you so stiff this morning?" It required but few words from me to undeceive her.' Unabashed, Nelly got up to make tea while Grattan laughed so heartily that his wound began to bleed again and, had the surgeon not made a timely appearance, he might have died.

At other times the consequences of what would now be described as 'binge-drinking' were more tragic than comic. As discipline deteriorated on the retreat to Corunna in the winter of 1808–9, more and more soldiers, women and children strayed away from the column, ignoring the commands and entreaties of their officers. Desperate to get their hands on food to dull the aching hunger in their bellies and drink to quench their thirst and relieve their misery, they plunged into cellars and dug away the earth to find the hastily concealed supplies left by fleeing inhabitants. Whenever they found a hidden stash of alcohol they drank themselves insensible.

One of the worst instances was on New Year's Day 1809 when the rear guard reached the miserable little town of Bembibre. Here the soldiers found hundreds of casks of wine that had been concealed in vaults beneath the streets and fell upon them. When the order came to move on more than a thousand men had to be left behind, collapsed in heaps on the streets too drunk to move. Beside them, prostrate on the ground, lay women and children with wine oozing from their lips and nostrils, making them appear as though they had been shot. Neither slaps nor the prodding of bayonets could rouse them. Within hours of the British rear guard leaving Bembibre a regiment of French dragoons clattered into town in pursuit. Furiously they rode through the streets, slashing with their swords at the defenceless bodies that lay all around, killing or wounding everyone in their path. One soldier's wife who had been left by her husband in the town's convent 'stupid with intoxication' was discovered by the French and thrown from a high window on to the hard stone ground. Only a few managed to crawl out of the town to catch up with the British force. An officer who came across one such unfortunate survivor described him as 'the most shocking spectacle I ever beheld. It was impossible to distinguish a single feature. The flesh of his cheeks and lips was hanging in collops, his nose was split, and his ears, I think, were cut off. In addition to his wounds, it is probable that his limbs were frost-bitten.' Sir John Moore ordered these mutilated survivors to be paraded past the regiments as a deterrent to straggling.

The problem of alcohol was still troubling commanders forty years on, in the Crimea. Major William Forrest of the 4th (Royal Irish) Dragoon Guards wrote to his mother in March 1855 that he had been 'obliged to apply for a passage to England for Mrs Field; she was constantly smuggling spirits into the camp, and was incorrigible. I fancy she thought that there was no method of punishing her. I applied to have her sent away, and my application was successful . . . I suspect that she will give us the slip yet, for I see her stalking over the hills with a carpet-bag in her hand in the opposite direction to Balaklava [harbour]; however I shall take care that she does not return to our camp.'

Another difficulty was restraining drunken or battle-crazed troops from plundering and ransacking the houses of local inhabitants. Long before the doctrine of 'hearts and minds' was established, British generals sought to restrain their men from doing anything that would poison their relationship with the local populace. The Duke of Marlborough was one of the first generals to grasp the importance of having an organised supply system that would prevent his troops from stripping the countryside bare as they passed through. He insisted that his army be kept supplied with sufficient funds to enable his commissaries to purchase the necessary pro-visions. While the essentials of bread, fuel, and fodder for the animals were supplied by the commissaries, other items such as vegetables and meat were generally supplied by sutlers who bought local produce and sold it on to the soldiers. Soldiers' wives also bought food from outside the official supply chain to supplement rations – women could move much more freely around the countryside in a way that men in uniform could not.

However, a woman could overstep the mark. General Pulteney told of a woman who was convicted of petty larceny and received swift justice during the War of the Austrian Succession (1740–8). 'Her tail was imme-diately turned up before the door of the house, where the robbery was committed, and the Drummer of the Regiment tickled her with 100 very good lashes, since which time the ladies have behaved like angels. The sex is not the worse for correction.' During the American Revolutionary War the rebels were keen to paint the British army in as bad a light as possible and their propaganda made much of the 'war crimes' committed by the Redcoats who, they claimed, systematically plundered the countryside, looting and burning houses. Travelling in the rear of the column and with greater opportunity than the soldiers to stray away from it, the women came under regular suspicion. One contemporary described them as a 'swarm of beings – no better than harpies' who 'distress and maltreat the inhabitants infinitely more than the whole army. At the same time they engross, waste and destroy at the expense of the good soldier, who keeps his ranks.' General Henry Clinton, Commander-in-Chief of the British

Army in America from 1778 to 1782, announced that any women found among the houses or buildings on the line of march would be punished.

These were no idle threats, as the records of courts martial from this period demonstrate. A general court martial held at Freehold, New Jersey, on 27 June 1778 heard charges against Mary Colethrate and Elizabeth Clarke, followers of the army, who were accused of plundering a house belonging to a local farmer. Having allegedly beaten the farmer's wife to discover where she kept the valuables and stripped her children bare of all their clothes, the women then proceeded to denude the house of all its valuables, even cutting open feather beds to discover hidden treasures. Mary Colethrate was acquitted, but Elizabeth Clarke was found guilty and sentenced to receive one hundred lashes on her bare back with a cat-o'-nine-tails 'and then to be drummed out of the Army, in the most public manner possible'. The commander-in-chief, Lord Cornwallis, railed against the petticoat contingent, calling them 'the source of the most infamous plunder' and ordered regular inspections to uncover stolen property. All items for which the soldiers and women could not provide proof of purchase were confiscated and burned on the spot. When this failed to deter them, Cornwallis ordered all women to attend executions and floggings, but ten days later relented and rescinded the order.

In the Peninsular War the same discipline problems arose and soldiers' wives were once again among the miscreants. Wellington was adamant that all produce, from fodder to meat and vegetables, must be paid for, conscious that the Portuguese and Spanish whom they came to liberate would swiftly turn against them if the British came to be viewed as an army of locusts. But often the Spanish peasants and traders would supply food only at grossly inflated prices. Moreover large expanses of the Spanish countryside were barren desert, making the job of the commissariat still harder. Soldiers' wives were sometimes driven to defy Wellington's prohibitions and dig up potatoes, turnips or any other vegetable they came across, scrabbling in the hard earth with bare hands for something that would nourish them and their children. Even when they paid for food, the women came in for Wellington's ire, as they had a habit of ranging far ahead of the column, buying up all the bread supplies for several miles around and leaving nothing for the commissariat to purchase for the troops. Several orders were published reminding them to desist from this practice, but they had limited effect.

Sometimes it was not hunger that drove the women to plunder, but avarice – in which case they would try to evade the scrutiny of the prize agent, who took charge of the spoils. He distributed the proceeds on a sliding scale according to rank, a system that many lower ranks considered grossly unfair. Although plundering was sometimes allowed, soldiers, high on victory, incensed by the slaughter of their comrades, were wont to indulge in orgies of destruction after a hard-won fight. Their wives, equally keen to get their hands on some item of silver that could net them a fortune or a casket or two of wine that would transport them to oblivion, sometimes joined them on the rampage.

The sack of Badajoz was one of the more frightful displays of bloodlust and plunder. While the future Juana Smith and her sister were saved by British officers, their compatriots were treated mercilessly by the maddened soldiers. Troops sent into the town to bring order merely joined in the plundering and threatened to kill any officers who tried to stop them. An officer in the King's German Legion observed around 200 women pouring into the town when it was barely taken to have their share of the plunder and was 'sickened when I saw them coolly step over the dying, indifferent to their cries for a drop of water, and deliberately search the pockets of the dead for money, or even divest them of their bloody coats'.

Wellington too was shocked by the audacity of one pair of looters, a soldier and a woman (presumably his wife), whom he found so laden with plunder and so addled with drink that they could scarcely speak or move. He addressed the woman, asking her what business she had there. 'She said nothing, but the Soldier looked him in the face, & said "Now that what I calls right you see that we poor fellows fight and gets nothing, & that these here devils, comes & carries of all as belongs to us". Ld Wellington added, that the effect of these two creatures, thus curiously brought under his eye was so irresistably ludicrous, that it was quite impossible for him to say a word & he rode off.' In an effort to halt the carnage Wellington decreed that anyone caught plundering would be flogged and even erected a gallows (though it is thought no one was actually hanged).

Kindly Sir Rowland (later Lord) Hill, known to his men as 'Daddy' Hill because of the paternal concern he displayed towards their welfare, was on one occasion so angered by the utter disregard for orders shown by some soldiers' wives that even his renowned tolerance snapped. In July 1809, during Wellington's tactical withdrawal into Portugal following the battle of Talavera, his Spanish allies failed to keep his army supplied with the promised rations. The famished British army came to the Spanish town of Zarza Major and were soon met by a delegation of townspeople who presented themselves to the officers and angrily complained that some of the army's women had already been through the town, helping themselves to vegetables and other foodstuffs without paying. It was established that the women were wives belonging to the 29th (Worcestershire) Regiment, who had gone ahead of the column contrary to orders. Angered at the breach of discipline and embarrassed by the diplomatic faux pas, Hill ordered that the delinquents should be turned over to the provost who, as Colonel Leslie of the 29th recorded in his journal, 'exercised schoolboy discipline' on a few as an example to the rest.

Yet women continued to steal and loot, and to be punished for it, throughout the Peninsular War. John Spencer Cooper tells of an Irishwoman who was caught stealing and sentenced by the provost marshal to be flogged. After this she left her husband, a sergeant named Bishop, and took up with a colonel from another regiment, perhaps thinking that he would have more power to protect her or that, living with a man of more means, she would have no need to steal. She had already been married before Bishop, to a drummer who had been ordered on foreign service, leaving her behind in Ireland where she met and married Bishop, presumably bigamously. She must have possessed great powers of attraction for a colonel to have risked opprobrium (or even dismissal) by taking up with a woman who was not only married to a soldier but was a convicted felon to boot. Wellington's Provost Marshal became so infuriated with the women who believed that they could plunder with impunity that he once flogged more than a dozen at a time, giving them 'sax and thirty lashes a piece on the bare doup. And it was lang afore it was forgotten on 'em', according to a Highland soldier who witnessed the punishment. One of the women who was flogged was Meg Donaldson 'the best woman in our regiment, – for whatever she might tak', she did na' keep it a' hersel".

Years later, stung by criticism that his army had flogged women, Wellington defended himself in a letter to his confidante Lady Salisbury, insisting, 'There was no order for punishing women! But there was certainly none for exempting Women from punishment! It is well known that in all armies the Women are at least as bad, if not worse, than the men as Plunderers! And the exemption of the Ladies from punishment would have encouraged Plunder.' Furthermore, such treatment of the fairer sex was not limited to Wellington's army. It was not until 1817, two years after Waterloo, that the flogging of women was outlawed in England.

Occasionally an opportunity for plunder arose that proved irresistible. On the road to Corunna the retreating army, lacking oxen to draw carts up the mountain passes, steadily divested itself of all unnecessary baggage including the military chests, containing £25,000 (around a million pounds in today's money), to be used for paying the soldiers and purchasing supplies. The men at the rear of the column watched wistfully as these chests, containing more money than they could have earned in several lifetimes, were hurled into the ravine below. Their wives were quick to spot their chance and several scrambled over the mountainside to chase after the chests. Mrs Malony, the wife of the regimental tailor of the 52nd (Oxfordshire Light Infantry) and a popular woman who 'often beguiled a weary march to the men with her tales' scrambled down the mountainside and stashed so many coins about her person that it seemed that her fortune was made. Although she managed to stagger all the way along the retreat with her burden, when she got to Corunna and began to embark on one of the ships of the evacuation fleet, her foot slipped as she stepped from the rowing boat to the ship and 'Down she went, like a shot, and owing to the weight of dollars secured about her person, she never rose again.' She was not the only woman to suffer this fate.

On another occasion, after the battle of Vittoria (1813), the French army's baggage train fell into the hands of the victorious British. The troops themselves, having driven the enemy off the battlefield, were now in full pursuit so the greater part of the booty was appropriated by the non-combatants: paymasters, commissaries, purveyors and soldiers' wives who fell on the contents of the baggage with glee and abandon. As soon as Wellington heard about this unlicensed free-for-all he hurriedly sent up guards to prevent the remainder from being stolen. Evidently by the time the guards arrived on the scene most of the booty had already been disposed of and it was soon obvious who the beneficiaries were. According to Captain Browne, 'Soldiers' wives were seen for weeks after the action in muslins, three or four gowns one over the other, trimmed with fine lace, several pairs of earrings dangling from their ears, reticules, watches & fans as part of their costume. The contrast of these decorations with their brazen tanned faces and brawny arms was ludicrous enough.'

In the matter of discipline and justice, military society diverged most widely from civil society in the fact that, within the army, women could be tried and sentenced for crimes that simply did not exist in civilian life. Crimes that undermined the discipline and obedience of the army were treated with the utmost severity. Soldiers found guilty of desertion or mutiny were liable to receive capital punishment, usually by hanging to emphasise the ignominy of their crime, and any woman who played a role in such activities could face similarly harsh justice. In Tangier in 1664 a woman was found guilty of incitement to mutiny. She was sentenced by a court martial 'to be gagged and receive on her bare back 50 lashes, 10 at five different spots and to be sent out of the garrison by the first ship, being whipped also from the prison to the water side'. Another woman convicted of 'inciting desertion while in the field' in Ireland in 1691 was sentenced to death.

Sometimes a man could be torn between duty to the army and duty to his wife. Joseph Donaldson tells of a soldier in the Peninsula during the autumn of 1812, when Wellington was leading his army back into Portugal to secure communication lines. In driving rains, the supply wagons frequently failed to keep pace, leaving the troops to go hungry for days at a time. After nights of sleeping out in the wet and days of marching on an empty stomach this soldier's wife collapsed at the roadside, incapable of taking another step. A compassionate officer permitted her husband to fall out from the ranks and wait with her till the wagons came up and she could be loaded on to one. But when they came past they were already full, and numbers of people in the same predicament were already lying on the roadside. The man now had to decide whether to leave his wife to the mercy of the French soldiers, or to remain with her and be taken prisoner and know that if he ever saw his regiment again he would face the ignominy and punishment dealt out to deserters. The mere presence of the hapless woman was enough to make her party to a potential crime.

There was no time to lose: the French cavalry were close upon them. As Donaldson relates, 'In despairing accents she begged him not to leave her, and at one time he had taken the resolution to remain; but the fear of being considered as a deserter urged him to proceed, and with feelings easier imagined than described, he left her to her fate, and never saw her again; but many a time afterwards did he deprecate his conduct on that occasion, and the recollections of it imbittered his life.' Military honour had won over marital loyalty. His fears of being punished for desertion were well founded. Corporal William Todd who served on the continent in the Seven Years War relates the shocking tale of William Cross, a soldier who left the ranks to go to the aid of a woman who was being raped by another British soldier. Having driven off her attacker, he was arrested by the captain of the Provost Guard and immediately hanged without trial for deserting the line.

While a soldier's wife if so inclined could turn to prostitution, drink and plunder, there was an even more heinous practice: body-stripping. It was widely condemned but seems to have gone on virtually unchecked and seldom punished. While devoted women rushed on to a battlefield to protect their husbands from body-stripping, some of their unscrupulous fellow wives would be picking their way, vulture-like, through the ranks of the fallen, along with other soldiers and local people. Sometimes this ghoulish practice was from necessity: both soldiers and their wives driven to removing the uniforms from the bodies of dead, or nearly dead, men when their own clothing became ragged and they lacked the means to replace it. Often, however, the motive was simply mercenary: buckles, buttons, boots and other accoutrements could all be sold for profit. Not only was the presence of body-strippers on the battlefield demoralising and dangerous: it was also unhealthy. Contagious diseases were harboured in the fabric of dead men's clothing and often passed on to the new owner.

Some body-strippers were ruthless in the execution of their task, tearing off the clothes of badly wounded soldiers with little care and often hastening their demise as they did so. The practice was alluded to in a comedy written in 1701 entitled *The Funeral or Grief a la Mode*, in which an army wife named Kate, widowed no fewer than nine times, swore that, 'I never stripped a man 'til first I tried if he could stand on his legs, and, if not, I think 'twas fair plunder, except one adjutant, and he was a puppy, that made my eighth husband run the gauntlet for not turning his toes out.' An oil painting of the aftermath of the Battle of Malplaquet in the War of Spanish Succession in 1709 shows a brawny, rough-looking woman, presumably a soldier's wife, in the foreground of the picture, busily engaged in this odious practice, a ghoulish expression on her face. Behind her the battle rages and wounded men are brought in, to be pounced on by the body-strippers as soon as they are left alone.

George Gleig was shocked by their brazenness in the Peninsula. 'A man falls by your side and the very next moment, if you chance to look round, he is as naked as he was when he came into the world . . . ' Captain Browne witnessed the practice after the battle of Salamanca (1812). At the battle's end, when the bodies of 5,000 British and allied dead lay still warm on the field, the women swarmed onto the battleground and could be seen 'stripping & plundering friend & foe alike. It is not doubted that they gave the finishing blow, to many an Officer who was struggling with a mortal wound; and Major Offley of the 23rd Regiment, who lay on the ground, unable to move, but not dead, is said to have fallen a victim to this unheard of barbarity.' George Bell claimed that the soldiers encouraged their wives in the practice and even 'estimated them in proportion to their proficiency in these vices'.

As well as being the perpetrators, women were frequently suspected (often with just cause) of provoking soldiers to commit crime, as in a case heard by a court martial at New York City Hall in February 1781. The army was at war with the American rebels but in between the fighting the usual business of life continued, with soldiers and their wives indulging in the age-old pastimes of drinking, thieving, loving and fighting, sometimes with terrible consequences. The court heard that in November 1780 Peggy McGuire, the wife of a private in the 57th Foot, had been drinking and dancing with a group of soldiers including a private named James McCullough, in the barrack room one evening. After a while Peggy and McCullough slipped away to a nearby field, for what purpose the court was left to guess, and a short while later the men heard a cry of 'murder' and rushed to the scene. As the soldiers ran towards the field they came across Private McGuire running towards them. He ran straight into one of the men, a corporal, knocking him down. A few seconds later Mrs McGuire rushed towards them and in front of several of the soldiers swore to her husband that if he did not avenge her honour by killing McCullough she would kill him (McGuire) and furthermore would never sleep with him again – a rather superfluous threat it would seem. Aroused to a fury by her taunts and threats McGuire rushed at one soldier, striking him on the mouth with his bayonet, then smashed the butt of his firelock into Private McCullough's head. McCullough died some days later of a fractured skull, and no possessions of Mrs McGuire were found on his body. Surprisingly the court, despite all the witnesses that had seen the crime, acquitted McGuire because they could not be sure that it was he who had delivered the fatal blow to the victim. Whether Peggy McGuire, who clearly incited the crime, was subjected to any sanction is not recorded by the court. From the witness statements it seems clear that whatever McCullough was doing to Peggy McGuire in that field was not robbery, and was almost certainly consensual. On being surprised by her husband, she immediately accused McCullough of robbery in order to deflect suspicion. Yet Private McGuire preferred, publicly at least, to believe her version of events, and the court chose not to question her story.

Yet for every slattern whose behaviour provoked violent quarrels, there was a loyal wife who was ready to risk censure to defend her husband when he was in trouble. A veteran wife named Martha May was incarcerated in Carlisle jail in June 1758 for abusing Colonel Henry Bouquet, who had reduced her husband to the ranks for some minor offence, a humiliating punishment for an old soldier. Remorsefully she explained to the Colonel in a petition sent from her cell that 'seeing him taken out of the Ranks to be confined Put me in Such a Passion that I was almost besides myself but being informed, after that I abusd Yr Honour, to a high degree . . . I have been a Wife 22 Years and have Traveld with my husband every Place or country the Company Marcht too'.

Wives had to know their place, and even defending their husbands against what they saw as injustice was seen as no excuse for behaving in an insubordinate manner. In 1776 an Irish troop, nicknamed 'the White Boys' because of their white jackets, was stationed in Perth. These soldiers' pay was pitifully low, only three pence halfpenny a day after stoppages – hardly enough to buy food to supplement their rations, let alone to support their families. As a consequence many were driven to stealing and, when apprehended, were punished harshly, usually by flogging. One soldier in the regiment was arrested for the crime of stealing nine potatoes from a nearby potato field in order to feed his wife and four children (whether he was married on or off the strength is not known). The Commanding Officer directed that he be tried by court martial. He was duly convicted and sentenced to receive 500 lashes. He was brought out to the North Inch, an area of common land where the local women gathered to do their laundry. Many of the townspeople had gathered to watch the floggings, for there were several other offenders up for punishment. As the Commanding Officer made his way down to the Inch to oversee the flogging, the man's wife darted forward and accosted him on the road. With a baby at her breast and her three other children by her side, she begged him to treat her husband mercifully, for he had only been doing his best for his hungry babes. But the officer turned aside with contempt and, when in desperation she seized him by the arm, imploring him to relent, he pushed her away violently.

Word of this encounter soon reached the assembled spectators and a wave of disgust and anger swept through the crowd. As each soldier went up to receive his punishment the murmurings grew, especially as the men cried out in agony. By the time the potato-stealer was brought out the crowd was bristling with hostility towards the Commander. The soldier took off his shirt and submitted to being tied up, ready for the lash. He received the first twenty-five strokes without a murmur, but then a left-handed drummer took over and the different angle at which the strokes were inflicted had the effect of tearing up the skin and flesh with every stroke, causing him to cry out in agony. His wife, who had waited nearby, could not endure to see her husband suffer. Setting down her baby, she rushed through the crowd and grabbed the drummer's arm to prevent him from continuing. At once several soldiers rushed up, seized the woman and dragged her off, screaming. Seeing this, the washerwomen stepped in and, egged on by the crowd, they descended on the prisoners, including the soldier being flogged, and untied them all. The soldiers guarding them offered no resistance and the officers were forced to flee as the angry crowd turned on them. The adjutant, slower than the others to escape, was seized by the women who held him down on his belly while the spectators took it in turns to administer a vigorous thrashing on his bare backside. After that the floggings no longer took place in public but within the confines of the guardhouse.

Those women who, rather than being bystanders to a crime, were found officially guilty of misdemeanours had their sentences set down in the regimental records. Those of the Gibraltar garrison in the early eighteenth century are typical: a catalogue of punishments for such crimes as drunkenness, stealing, or, in the case of one poor woman named Mrs Childly, 'Beating better manners into several men, & a too frequent bestowing of her favours'. She was thrown into the 'black hole' (dungeon) for a night and in the morning led to the market place where she was confined to the whirligig in the market place for an hour. This device was like a round cage, fixed upon a spindle, which was indeed whirled round and round until the unfortunate woman was sick – and exposed to the ridicule of all. A fortnight later a Mrs Malone got two hours in the same contraption, 'for proper reasons', a spectacle that 'gave great pleasure to the spectators'. An officer's wife of the Foot Guards suffered a similarly public and unpleasant punishment. 'She was set upon a stone & an iron bar about five feet high supports her back, upon which bar is a chain or collar that moves up & down & is fixed to her neck. This made her sit in great prim, each hand being fastened to a ring on the sides of the stone. The Time of suffering is three hours, or more in proportion to the offence, & an inscription which signifies the nature of the crime is pinned to the stomach.'

Other records reveal that the sisterly harmony that was supposed to exist among the wives was often severely strained. Petty squabbles frequently erupted within the steamy atmospheres of the cookhouse or washhouse, and pride was nettled by the strict observation of hierarchy and privilege. An entry in the Wives' Punishment Book of the 82nd Regiment (Prince of Wales's Volunteers) on 9 November 1877, when the regiment was stationed at Limerick, records the misdemeanours of some of the more quarrelsome women and the punishments they received: Mrs Osborne was recorded as 'Using abusive language in the washhouse towards Private Wilks Wife, and striking Private Wilks.' Her punishment was to be struck off the strength of the regiment for a month. A few years later Mrs Wilks was hauled up for 'creating a disturbance and using bad language in the married quarters about 6.20pm' and 'severely cautioned to be struck off the strength'.

Other crimes detailed in the punishment books provide clues as to which aspects of women's behaviour most concerned the authorities, such as sexual impropriety. In Aldershot the 82nd's punishment book recorded the misdemeanour of Mrs Beuch who was severely cautioned for being absent from her quarters and 'found walking about the lines in company with soldiers at 10.20pm' on 24 September 1880. Married women must not only be virtuous but be seen to be virtuous – consorting with other men late at night fell well short of the mark. Quite apart from any question of marital infidelity in itself, the army was concerned that illicit sex between army wives and other soldiers could have highly divisive and even violent consequences.

8

Scandal and Strife

The military ladies . . . are always noisy, affected, showily dressed, with
a great many ornaments, *mauvais* ton chatter incessantly from the
moment they enter the house, twist their curls, shake their bustles,
and are altogether what you may call 'Low Toss'. While they are
alone with me after dinner they talk about suckling their babies,
the disadvantage of scandal, 'the officers' and 'the Regiment',
and when the gentlemen come into the drawing-room, they
invariably flirt with them most furiously.

Julia Maitland, *Letters from Madras, during the years 1836–1839*

For as long as armies have fought, and women have followed armies,
illicit affairs have been conducted within their ranks. In biblical times,
King David sent Uriah the Hittite into battle in the front line, knowing
that he would be killed and David could then take up with his beautiful
widow, Bathsheba. From that day to this, armies have traditionally taken
a dim view of adultery within the military community. Soldiers sleeping
with other soldiers' wives, officers sleeping with soldiers' wives, officers
cuckolding other officers and, more recently, female servicewomen
sleeping with their married male comrades: all such activities are seen as
detrimental to morale, breaking the bond of trust that should exist between
brothers-in-arms – and sometimes leading to bloodshed.

The proximity of death, and the close-knit nature of army communities in which men and women are cloistered together for long periods

with limited contact with the outside world, help create an environment in which extramarital sex can flourish. Add to this the fact that army life has always involved long periods of separation from spouses, it is unsurprising that the issue of marital breakdown continues to be a major concern for army families. Today it is seldom out of the newspapers, whose readers are regularly treated to titillating stories concerning 'randy majors', lustful warrant officers and betrayed spouses. Yet even before the advent of the tabloids and mass newspaper readership, tales of certain affairs would leak out beyond the confines of the regiment. And when injured parties resorted to violence, the matter would come before the court martial.

Sometimes, though, the niceties of a court martial were dispensed with altogether. Corporal William Todd, who served in the army from the 1740s to the 1760s, relates the case of a drummer in his regiment who killed his wife 'by Cutting her throat with a rasor' while the regiment was stationed at the village of Brompton near Chatham docks in 1756. 'He directly made of [sic] to the River in Order to drown'd [sic] himself, but was persued & taken & had [handed] to the Quarter Guard & Confin'd in irons. The next day he was sent to Gaol to Rochester where he was hanged & Gibbetted. This rash Action he Confessed too us all that he was Jealous of Serj Hemmington of their Company being too free with his Wife; they had been out together this Night etc.'

Usually, justice was not so summary and due process was observed. Courts martial were kept particularly busy attending affairs of the heart during the American Revolutionary War – leading to speculation that if the British had devoted as much energy to the pursuit of their enemy as to the pursuit of pleasure, then they might have fought a more successful campaign. Indeed, this was the accusation levelled against the British commander, General Sir William Howe – 'good-natured Billy', who seemed to prefer the comforts of Philadelphia and the arms of his mistress Elizabeth Loring, the pretty wife of a loyalist (American) officer, to the more onerous business of pursuing Washington's army after the battle of Germantown in 1777. As one ditty, circulated by loyalists frustrated at the way Howe continually allowed the enemy to slip from his hands, put it:

> *Awake, arouse Sir Billy,*
> *there's forage on the plain,*
> *ah leave your little filly,*
> *And open the campaign.*

Another rhyme mocked:

> *Sir William, he snug as a flea*
> *Lay all his time a-snoring;*
> *Nor dreamt of harm as he lay warm,*
> *In bed with Mrs Loring.*

Although Mrs Loring's cuckolded husband was prepared to tolerate her adultery for reasons of his own, other men in the same position were driven by jealousy to commit crimes of passion that brought them before a court martial. Those who found themselves betrayed within the bosom of their own regiment had to endure the added indignity that the affair was likely to be common knowledge. An urge to avenge the humiliation of such public betrayal drove some men to murder.

Such crimes were not dealt with consistently. Sometimes a court martial would view a wife's infidelity as extreme provocation, and accordingly exercise clemency. Such was the case with William Norrington, a private soldier in the 40th Foot, who came before a court martial in Staten Island in July 1776 accused of murdering John Corrigan, a soldier in the same regiment, by stabbing him in the back with a bayonet. Another soldier who had been with the victim on the night of his murder told how one evening they had gone in search of tobacco and come across Norrington's wife Sally lying asleep in a hovel in a drunken stupor. Corrigan confided to his companion that 'he had a mind to go and lye with her' and, so saying, entered the hovel. Within three minutes (no doubt tipped off by someone), Norrington had come upon the scene. On espying his wife with Corrigan lying on top of her he cried out, 'Sally, Sally, is this the way you serve me?' Rushing into the hovel, he drew his bayonet and a few moments later Corrigan came staggering out, screaming with pain. He was taken into a nearby house bleeding heavily from a stab wound in the back. A few minutes later Sally Norrington was also brought in with a wound on her right side, though her injury was less serious. Corrigan died shortly afterwards. Norrington, overcome with horror at what he had done, then tried to stab himself in remorse but, he told the trial, he failed to do so as his cartridge box was in the way. A second witness had actually seen Norrington plunge the bayonet into Corrigan's back and Norrington himself admitted doing so. But he maintained that, when he came across Corrigan lying on top of his wife with his breeches down and her petticoats up, he had decided to wound him to teach him a lesson. He insisted that had never meant to kill the man.

The court clearly believed him, for they decided not only to acquit him of murder but to let him go free, on the grounds that such provocation had caused his passion 'to have usurped the place of reason'.

But another apparently similar case, in which quartermaster Alexander Frazer of the 48th (later Northamptonshire) Regiment murdered Corporal James Dunn of the same regiment, was treated in a very different manner. The court martial took place in Havana in April 1763. The British had taken Havana from the Spanish who had belatedly come into the Seven Years War on the French side. The capture of Havana had cost a thousand British lives but within a few weeks 5,000 more men had died from disease. Garrison duty in Havana could have held little appeal for the men of the 48th, yet life there clearly had its compensations for Corporal Dunn, in the shape of the Quartermaster's comely wife. The affair between Dunn and Mrs Frazer soon became common knowledge within the regiment. Several men claimed to have seen them naked on a bed together, and the gossip soon reached Frazer. One evening, stung by the knowledge that most of the regiment knew that he was being cuckolded by a man junior in rank to him, Frazer went in search of his wife and, finding her with Corporal Dunn, drew his sword and struck Dunn a heavy blow. Dunn did not die immediately but lingered for two days in great agony. Rather than excuse him on the grounds of the provocation he undoubtedly suffered, the court found Frazer guilty of murder and sentenced him to death.

Were the officers conducting the court martial influenced by the fact that the regiment was not at war but merely undertaking garrison duty? Certainly the loss of a Quartermaster in peacetime was less damaging than in war, when maintaining supplies was a more difficult matter. Could the very different treatment received by William Norrington in such a strikingly similar case, only thirteen years later, have been related to the fact that his regiment was engaged in hostilities? With Britain a six-month voyage away and reinforcements hard to come by, could the need to hold on to every soldier have influenced the court martial's decision to let him go free? Or was it the fact that Frazer was a senior figure in the regiment and was therefore treated more severely than a junior man would have been? It is impossible to know.

If considerations of expediency did come into play in Norrington's case, they evidently did not weigh heavily in a case brought before a court martial in New York in November 1781. Another wronged husband, Private John Lindon of the 22nd Foot (later the Cheshire Regiment), was charged with murdering his wife after she left him and refused to return. The court heard that he had come to the field hospital where his wife was working to beg her to come back to him. This she refused to do. Glaring furiously at his wife Lindon shouted at her: 'If you do not live with me, you shall not live with any one else.' He then lifted the musket to his shoulder and shot her in the chest. It took several hours for her to die. Lindon's defence was that she had not only refused to live with him, or anyone else, but had robbed him of all his 'necessaries' and exasperated him. He was found guilty and sentenced to be hanged. Clearly, rejection was not considered so extreme a provocation as infidelity.

Edward Costello, a soldier in the Rifle Brigade during the Peninsular War, was witness to a case of wife-killing that went virtually unpunished. After the storming of Badajoz in 1812, Wellington moved to engage the French army under Marshal Marmont (one of five French armies, totalling 230,000 men, that were dispersed through the Peninsula at that time). He marched his troops north to Salamanca and then west, keeping pace with Marmont's army, often within sight of each other, watching and waiting for the perfect moment to pounce. It was around this time that Costello sat down for his evening meal at a camp outside Salamanca, with a sergeant named Battersby. The sergeant had with him a pretty woman called Nelly who seemed to be his wife. She sat down with the men under the branches of a clump of cork trees and, as Costello recalled, 'assisted much to keep up the spirit of our conversation'. The atmosphere was jolly and relaxed, the men enjoying the company of a lively, attractive woman, when suddenly they were interrupted by the approach of a tall, fine-looking man, a grenadier of the 61st (South Gloucestershire) Regiment, who was calling out for Sergeant Battersby. Costello relates the events that unfolded next.

> Casting sundry determined glances about him, more in anguish than ferocity, he drew near the woman, and seated himself on a knapsack near her. The latter, from the moment he had first made his appearance, I had perceived, seemed wondrously confused, and changed colour several times.
>
> 'Nelly,' said he, fixing a firm and deliberate look on her, his voice at first scarcely articulate with emotion, 'Nelly, why do you treat me so, how can you stoop,' and here he cast an almost contemptuous

glance of recognition on Battersby. 'How can you stoop to such a disgraceful, so dishonorable a protection?'

'I am with those,' said she, 'who know better how to treat me than you.'

'That,' rejoined the grenadier, 'may be your opinion, but why leave the child, it is but three years old, and what can I do with it?'

To this she made no answer.

'Do not think,' he again continued, 'that I wish you to return to me, that is impossible. But I cannot help my feelings!'

This was only replied to by reproaches . . .

The grenadier, at last, made a move to take his departure, and his wife, for such she evidently was, had agreed to accompany him a little of the way, and they walked together. I did not know how to account for it, but there was a certain uneasiness attended me, which had kept me, as it were, on their trail all the evening; and Battersby and myself followed in their rear. They had proceeded a few hundred yards, and were some distance in advance, when she turned to wish him good night. The poor fellow paused again, as if in deep thought, fixing on her the same cool, deliberate look that he had exhibited all the evening.

'So you are determined, Nelly,' said he at length, 'to continue this way of living?'

'Yes,' said she.

'Well then,' he exclaimed, holding her firmly by the left hand, which she had extended for him to shake, while he drew his bayonet with his right, 'take that', and he drove it right through her body. The blow was given with such force, that it actually tripped him over her, and both fell, the bayonet still sticking in her side. The poor woman gave a convulsive scream, and in a moment expired. The grenadier bounded instantly on his feet again, and stamping one foot on the body of his victim, jerked forth the bayonet reeking with her blood. Wheeling himself round on his heel, the fatal weapon tightly clutched in his right hand, his eyes instantaneously caught the direction Battersby had taken, and he flew after him with the speed and countenance of a fiend, to wreak a second vengeance. The sergeant fortunately arrived at the camp in time enough to call out the rear guard, who, of course, were instantly on the alarm to meet him.

According to Costello, the grenadier was brought to court martial and given three months' solitary confinement but served only one. He was later killed in action in the Pyrenees. Battersby was not punished but kept his rank. He survived until 1815 when he was shot in the head at the battle of Quatre Bras. 'As for Nelly, we buried her that very night near the post where she fell, having dug her grave with the same kind of weapon as that by which she had been deprived of life.' The Rifle Brigade's Quartermaster, William Surtees, who also witnessed the incident, believed that the jealous husband was not even brought to court martial, 'as her ill conduct probably had been considered as in some measure palliating what he did, and that he might be supposed to have been irritated to a degree of madness when he perpetrated the fatal act'.

Although it was frowned upon for soldiers to covet each other's wives, not least because of the violent consequences that often ensued, still more deplored were officers who indulged themselves with the wives of the other ranks. Not only did such activity entirely subvert the familial relationship that was supposed to exist between officers and the men they commanded. It was also considered unbecoming to an officer's station to consort with members of the lower classes, from which soldiers and their wives traditionally came. Such liaisons put the wronged husbands in invidious positions, for if they attempted to remonstrate with the officer they could be court-martialled for being disrespectful. Private James Cairns of the 18th (The Royal Irish) Regiment, stationed in Boston in 1774, found his position intolerable when his wife left him for Captain Evans of the same regiment. When he went to the captain to demand his wife back, Evans turned on him and thrashed him soundly. Cairns managed to wrest the whip from him to stop the beating, but for this action he was brought to court martial and sentenced to 800 lashes for his 'impudence', of which he received 500. What was more, he was persecuted from then on and 'punish'd upon every trifling Occasion'. Unable to bear it any longer, he deserted and, failing to find work in Philadelphia, when the Revolutionary War broke out he enlisted in the rebel army and was eventually captured and tried for desertion by the British. Although he pleaded that it was only Captain Evans's behaviour that had induced him to desert, the court showed no sympathy for his circumstances and sentenced him to be hanged.

A similar case was that of John Siborn who in 1757 complained in a petition to the (third) Duke of Marlborough that he had been reduced in rank from bombardier to matross (the rank below bombardier in an artillery battery, now abolished). The reason, he alleged, was that his wife had refused to sleep with Captain Thomas Ord, who clearly believed that he had droits de seigneur over the prettiest soldiers' wives in his company.

Another woman who exchanged a soldier husband for an officer lover was a Mrs Miller, wife of a sergeant in the 12th Foot (later the Suffolk Regiment), although she was clearly sorely provoked by her husband's behaviour. One morning in May 1761, when the regiment was in cantonments in Benninghausen, Germany, during the Seven Years War, she came running into Corporal Todd's quarter where he was chatting with Lieutenant Stappleton, 'with her Cap of & her hair all about her Ears, crying out that he would kill her. And directly Sergeant Miller came running after her with a Stick in his hand & was going to strick her. I catch hold of the Stick & broke it & the Lieutt drew his sword & swore he would Run him through if he presumed to Beat his Wife in his presence.' The Lieutenant allowed Mrs Miller to stay in his quarters as she was afraid of returning to her own. When Miller objected he was at once thrown into the guardhouse and brought before the court martial for slandering the lieutenant. The court martial pardoned him but his wife did not return to him and, as Todd relates, 'Serjeant Miller was Obliged to content himself without her.'

Not all officers got away with availing themselves of their juniors' wives. Richard Holmes in *Redcoat* cites the case of Lieutenant Kelly, who absconded with the wife of a private soldier. Kelly was tried before a court martial and cashiered, although his sentence was reduced to a reprimand by the Prince Regent (himself no slouch when it came to dalliances with married women). Kelly, who had risen from the ranks to become an officer, was allowed to sell his commission. As for the colonel who ran off with Sergeant Bishop's wife in the Peninsula after she was flogged for stealing, history sadly does not relate whether he was allowed to keep his command.

Mrs Bishop was by no means the first soldier's wife to have become disenchanted with her lowly station and sought to exchange her husband for a man of higher rank. August Schaumann, the lascivious commissary of the Peninsular War, rhapsodised about a woman named Anne Luke who, he thought, 'would have made a magnificent model for the statue of Venus'. Anne had come to the Peninsula as the wife of a soldier in the 3rd (King's Own) Dragoons but, endowed with extraordinary beauty and talent, she soon felt that she was not in 'her proper place' as the wife of a mere soldier, and quickly became the mistress of the regiment's commissary. Her husband was paid to keep quiet, and the affair continued until the commissary exchanged into the Spanish army, whereupon Anne took up with a more senior commissary, whom she 'married', presumably in an informal ceremony since Schaumann makes no mention of her divorcing her former husband. Not all women were able to carry off such a rise through the ranks but Anne Luke, with her cheeks 'like peaches, her mouth and teeth quite perfect, and her skin beautifully white', was 'quickly able to acquire the most refined manners. Nobody would have suspected her of being the wife of an ordinary dragoon.'

It could work the other way round too. Occasionally a man might be able to trade on his charm to gain the favour of an officer's wife who might then assist him through the ranks. One man was said to have won his captaincy thanks to the patronage of a senior officer's wife who had been impressed by his dancing skills. As Major Patterson, that staunch opponent of military marriage, remarked sourly, 'He got more by his heels, than ever he could by his head. Waltzing and quadrilling were better to him than years of fighting. Flirtations availed him more than the hardest service, and one bright glance of a lady's eye, was of greater value to him than even the claims of Waterloo . . . '

An officer's wife possessed of charm and looks could sometimes advance her husband's career via a spot of judicious flirting with his superiors. But it required a deft touch to avoid accusations of impropriety, and those who blatantly courted the regard of their husband's brother officers could quickly find themselves the subject of gossip and scandal, damaging their own reputations and their husband's careers. Fanny Duberly did not always manage to tread the fine line successfully. Her friendship with Lord Cardigan, the overbearing, arrogant commander of the Light Brigade, was a high-risk association. She could scarcely eschew his company, when he was her husband's brigade commander, and when it was his patronage and interest in her that enabled her to thwart Lords Lucan and Raglan and sail from Varna to the Crimea.

Would Lord Cardigan have stuck his neck out to enable Fanny to get to the Crimea had he not been captivated by her beauty and wit during their walks and rides around Varna? It seems doubtful. Yet she risked opprobrium by consorting with him, so noxious was the cloud of scandal that surrounded the disreputable earl. As well as being loathed by his officers (though not his soldiers) as a high-handed martinet, he had scandalised society at home by being cited as the third party in a divorce case and consorting rather too openly with other ladies (married and single). His own marriage, which had begun in equally scandalous circumstances, had long since broken down.

Yet, hated as he was by fellow officers, and excoriated by the press, at fifty-seven he was still an imposing and dashing figure. Tall, with long legs encased in their tight crimson overalls, his short jacket tailored to fit his wasp-waisted body immaculately, his proud, handsome face, golden hair and luxuriant moustache (which he was given to twirling furiously when angry) all combined to give him the appearance of the noble warrior he aspired to be. His biographer Donald Thomas notes, however, that he suffered from piles, constipation and swelling of the bladder. In England women had bombarded him with billets-doux, begging him for an 'interview'. To his subordinates he was withering, tyrannical, spiteful. But to ladies he could be charming, chivalrous, even kindly. When Fanny burst into tears on being told of Lord Raglan's order prohibiting her from sailing on to the Crimea he was probably genuinely moved, for he could seldom resist a lady in distress.

Fanny, for her part, was perhaps not quite so immune to his charms as she pretended. Though she frequently referred to him in unflattering terms and claimed to abhor him, yet she could not or would not avoid his company, telling her sister Selina, 'We take wonderful rides with Lord Cardigan, but not often, as I detest him.' When, thanks to his intercession, she sailed on to the Crimea, she certainly did not avoid his company aboard the *Himalaya*, taking walks with him around the deck. It was not long before this was commented on. 'How scandalous people are,' complained Fanny in a tone of injured innocence, 'even with only three ladies [Mrs Cresswell and Lady Erroll being the others] the gossip is intolerable.' Once at the Crimea, Lord Cardigan's attentions did not cease. He lent her his charger, Ronald (on which he later led the Charge of the Light Brigade), and generally behaved, as Fanny acknowledged, 'very well' towards her.

When Cardigan left the Crimea in December 1855, his health and his heart both broken down, as he confided to Fanny, by the loss of the Light Brigade, Fanny did not lack other escorts. As unofficial queen of the Crimea she had a little court, among whom were certain favourites. The easygoing Henry did not seem to object that his wife chose to go riding and walking with her parties of admirers, but others were less tolerant. Colonel Hodge was certainly no fan. In May 1855 he wrote to his mother, 'The grass in the plain is beautiful. Mr & Mrs Duberly and [Colonel] Paulet Somerset out grazing. The publicity of all this is very disgusting.' His second-in-command, Major William Forrest, found her 'an odd woman; the French 29th Regt have dedicated a Polka to her, as "the Amazone". I do not believe she is guilty of that which many say she is, but of course she has many "Followers" as the Servant Girls say, and her vanity causes her to encourage them: they tell a story of Col Shewell, 8th Hussars [Henry's commanding officer], who is really a very good Man, but He was one day riding with others in company with Mrs Duberly, when some Special Admirer of Hers joined the Party & upon which, they separated from the others. Shewell trotted away, saying "I cannot think what made me ride with that nasty dirty Creature" . . . '

A photograph taken by the Crimean War photographer Roger Fenton of Fanny on her horse with Henry beside her was in great demand. 'Every man I met seems to have one,' she informed her sister Selina, delighted to have become a kind of early forces' pin-up. Though Fanny certainly encouraged and revelled in attention, whether from ordinary soldiers or her officer beaux, there is no evidence to suggest that she actually did anything other than flirt with them (although the 1968 film *The Charge of the Light Brigade* portrayed her and Cardigan as lovers). Even so, merely riding *à deux* with another man was crime enough in the eyes of some and by preening herself rather too obviously in an age when modesty and decorum were highly prized female attributes Fanny laid herself open to such slurs.

Lord Cardigan was not the only officer who enjoyed the company of pretty young wives. One late Victorian Indian army officer, forced to leave his young wife alone at home while he went on duty in a fort guarding the North West Frontier, fretted terribly that his general, who delighted in flirting (and more) with the wives of his junior officers, would take the opportunity to pay a visit to his young bride. Crouched in his hill fort, he determined on sending a message to his wife, warning her to be on guard. It was the turn of the century and the only way of sending a signal from one remote hillside to another in the middle distance was by heliograph – using mirrors to flash sunlight. So the young officer set up the heliograph and sent a signal to his wife (who clearly knew her signals) that read, with wonderfully Edwardian restraint, 'Beware General X, he is a most immodest man.' According to legend, the general, who was indeed on his way to pay a call on the young wife, saw the signal flashing across the valley and, suspecting enemy activity, ordered his aide to translate. Blushingly, the aide obliged and the general, crimson with embarrassment, immediately announced a change of route that would not, after all, involve a detour via that certain officer's quarter. Even today many an attractive army wife will admit to have been on the receiving end of the rather too close attentions of an amorous senior officer, and there is one man who will be forever known to the wives of his former station by the sobriquet 'General Groper'.

But if matters progress beyond mere flirtation and unsolicited attention, senior officers who dally with junior officers' wives can face serious consequences, even dismissal. If such sanctions seem extreme in the context of the civilian world, it is worth considering the scenario of a soldier or officer having to follow into the battle the man whom he knows to be his wife's lover. Not only would it be difficult for him to feel respect and loyalty for such a man – he might also be sorely tempted to shoot him in the back.

Few junior officers were foolish enough to allow their affections to alight on the wife of a senior officer, fearing the consequences for their career. Major Patterson tells the tale of one young lieutenant, 'a youth of rather fashionable exterior, and on the most pleasing terms with himself', who saw a shapely young lady passing by and hurried to catch up with her, confident of making another conquest and impressing his companions with his powers of seduction. When he drew beside her he gazed under her bonnet and exclaimed winsomely, ' "What a charming angel! – what brilliant eyes!" ' The object of his admiration at once turned to him and, lifting up her veil, revealed herself to be none other than the general's wife. The young man at once withdrew, stammering his apologies, horrified at his faux pas, for the general was known to be an extremely jealous husband. Patterson, who met him soon afterwards, said that he had never seen a man so petrified. 'His countenance was the very picture of despair . . . "And this to the General's sposa," as he cried; "my commission is not worth a sous. – I shall be broke as round as a hoop; in short, the sooner I go and hang myself the better." ' Fortunately for him the lady was too discreet to tell her general of the encounter.

Discretion and even humour averted many a potential scandal. The members of one cavalry regiment like to tell the tale of a woman who cut a swathe through their ranks during the 1970s and 1980s, marrying and divorcing several officers in the regiment by turn. Eventually, on her fourth or fifth marriage, she took a husband from another regiment, whereupon the officers of her former husbands' regiment sent her a telegram saying 'What's wrong with us?'

Sometimes the adverse consequences of infidelity could go beyond the husband's reaction. Erring wives could face eviction from the regiment and the army if they conducted their affairs so flagrantly that they upset the stability of the community. In the eighteenth or nineteenth centuries 'lewd women' were subjected to the whirligig or a whipping and drummed out of camp. But even in the twentieth century the military authorities have not scrupled to intervene in cases of marital discord. Midge Lackie, whose early days as an army wife in Aden had prepared her for almost any surprise, was nonetheless shocked when an acquaintance, a corporal's wife, was evicted from her quarter in Minden in the 1970s. She was sent back to her parents' home in Austria because it transpired she had been holding car key parties while her husband was away. Another wife of Midge's acquaintance was thrown out when word reached the Quartermaster's ear that she had hit her husband with a frying pan. Little matter that he had beaten her regularly when he came back drunk from the mess: she was deemed to be a disruptive wife and as such had no place in the regimental community. Another favoured method of dealing with couples having problems was to post them elsewhere, removing them from temptation.

Even today many wives resent the paternalism that often characterises the army's attitude towards its soldiers' private lives, however benevolently intended. Indeed, some contend that soldiers do not have private lives at all, so entwined are the public and the private in the military world. Samantha Roberts became an army wife in 2001. When she first met her husband Steve, four years before they wed, he was still married to his first wife, although the marriage was in trouble. She was shocked when Steve told her that his superiors had called him in and told him to give his marriage a chance rather than pursue a relationship with Samantha. 'I thought, "What the hell has it got to do with them?"' When he ignored their advice and proceeded with his divorce, the army continued to involve itself, to Samantha's indignation. 'It's just really wrong, really wrong. We could have handled it and it would have been better if we'd handled it ourselves in our own way. That was the first sort of time I came into contact with it and I just thought, "Oh my God, what am I getting into here?" I was really angry and said, "I'm going to ring them" and Steve said, "Er, no. You don't do that." So, you know, it was really hard.'

Yet while Samantha resented Steve's employers intruding into their personal life, there are other wives who feel that the army does not do enough to discourage its soldiers from breaking up their marriages. Indeed, one charge levelled at the army today is that it makes it relatively easy for a soldier to walk out on his marriage and abandon his family. He is able to go straight into barracks, while his family must leave their quarter when the marriage is dissolved. In contrast, a man who leaves his family in the civilian world usually has to find alternative accommodation while his wife and children remain in the family home.

The intervention that so incensed Samantha Roberts stemmed from the obligation on a commanding officer to discuss with a soldier his reasons for wishing to change his, or her, 'married category'. The rationale for this policy was that, before it was introduced, some women had no idea that their marriage was over until they were asked to vacate their quarter as their husbands no longer had married status. The Army Families Federation (AFF) and Soldiers', Sailors', Airmen and Families Association (SSAFA) both lobbied to change this to ensure that abandoned families at least had due warning that they were about to lose their home. As Lizzie Iron, former chairman of the AFF, explains, the army is often caught between wanting to look after the welfare of its soldiers and their families and being accused of being too interfering: 'Is it paternalistic, or is it responsible, to intervene in soldiers' private lives?' she asks. 'The army has to find a difficult balance between allowing people to live their lives and ensuring that they are operationally fit. If a soldier is upset about a domestic crisis then he is less effective as a soldier.'

Another emotive subject for army wives is separation, widely held to be a major factor in marital breakdown and infidelity. Most army wives cope admirably in their husband's absence, running the household, giving birth and raising children with minimal fuss. Others struggle to cope. For some, loneliness is the hardest burden to bear. Midge Lackie saw many marriages come unstuck under the pressure of spending too many months apart. 'So many women had affairs because you're lonely. You're so lonely. These ladies didn't have any company so if some chap came along and paid them a compliment . . . I can understand how marriages split up. It either brings the family unit closer or it can go the other way. Loneliness was the biggest killer of all in army life.'

Valerie Fagg, whose husband served in the Parachute Regiment in the 1970s, was similarly sympathetic, even when her own husband was the target of advances from lonely women whose husbands were in Northern Ireland. 'Brian used to help the Families Officer, he used to get called out in the middle of the night. He'd get there and these girls [the wives] would be there in flimsy nightdresses saying, "I need help." I think some of them did make passes. I took to going with him if he was called out to a house late at night. If I arrived with him they couldn't try it on. We'd say, "Go and get yourself dressed" and often it turned out that they hadn't got a real problem, it was just their excuse to get somebody down to see them.

They were just ordinary housewives and I think a lot of the problem was that they were bored and lonely on their own.'

With troops being committed to such theatres of war as Iraq, Afghanistan and Sierra Leone where families cannot follow them, and increasing numbers serving two such tours within a two-year period, the issue of separation and its effect on marriages is likely to remain thorny. There have always, however, been some who have seen separation as less of a burden than an opportunity. In British India the summer months saw a mass exodus of wives from the heat of the plains to the relative cool of hill stations. Here they installed themselves and their servants in hotels or houses leased for the summer. Rates of disease and death always soared in the hot summer months on the plains and a few months' respite from the burning heat was thought essential for all who were not tied by duty to their stations. Emily Eden, who came to Simla in 1838, rhapsodised about the pleasure of breathing clean, fresh air again after the stifling heat of the plains: 'Now I come back to air again I remember all about it. It is a cool sort of stuff, refreshing, sweet, and apparently pleasant to the lungs . . . I see this is to be the best part of India.'

In 1863 the Viceroy of India, Sir John Lawrence, decided that he and his government would spend their summers in Simla and the relocation of the whole government machinery from Calcutta to Simla, a distance of 1,170 miles, became an annual event. In 1912 the seat of government moved to Delhi and the summer transfer to Simla ceased. Nonetheless, army and civilian families continued to make their pilgrimage to the cool of the hills at the beginning of summer. Here they would remain until the scorching heat abated in the autumn, while their men toiled on, paying the occasional visit to their families if they could spare the time. Throughout the summer the hill stations became whirls of social activity.

People who lived in pre-war India are divided between those who maintain that there was very little impropriety and that it was almost impossible for army officers or their wives to indulge in illicit affairs, and those who insist that the cantonments of British India were aflame with sexual intrigue. Whatever the rumour and counter rumour, it was doubtful that any scandal could match one that sent shock waves around the mid-nineteenth-century Raj – a case not only of adultery but adultery with one of the natives.

It involved the young Amelia Eliza Byrne, known as Bonny because of her good looks. Bonny was born in India in 1837, the daughter of an army officer, Captain de Fountain, and his second wife, Adolphine. The captain had died when Bonny was six and she and her widowed mother lived off his small pension in Fatehgarh, near Farrukhabad. The ruler of Farrukhabad, Nawab Taffazul Hussain Khan, was well known for his predilection for white women (although Bonny's father had been of mixed blood she would certainly have considered herself to be white), and Bonny was only fourteen when he began paying court to her at the family house, with her mother's encouragement. Adolphine and Bonny so outraged other members of the European community by their mixing with 'a native', prince though he might be, that they quickly intervened and Bonny was packed off to Kidderpoor Girls School in Calcutta. This finishing school-cum-marriage market organised regular balls to coincide with the arrival of shiploads of new officers in India (most passed through Calcutta). It was at one such ball that Bonny met and shortly afterwards married a young officer called Reginald Byrne. She was delighted when, soon after the wedding, Reginald was posted to Fatehgarh where her mother and, more importantly, her admirer the Nawab, were living. Adolphine promptly moved in with the newlyweds and began issuing invitations to the Nawab to visit. He needed little encouragement and soon began turning up at the house whenever Reginald was absent. News of his wife's close friendship with the Nawab was not slow to reach Reginald and one day in 1857 he came home unexpectedly, to find his wife and the Nawab 'in close and earnest conversation'. Furiously, Reginald forcibly evicted a smarting Nawab from the house, and no doubt felt he had settled the matter, though the Nawab's vows of vengeance rang in his ears.

A few weeks later the Mutiny broke out. Reginald was among those killed very soon after. But Bonny and her mother were taken in by the Nawab and installed in the women's quarters where, on account of Bonny's looks and the Nawab's favouritism, they aroused considerable jealousy. Other European men, women and children from the Fatehgarh garrison were also rounded up by the Nawab's troops, after a failed escape attempt, and ended up at the Nawab's palace, but in far less salubrious surroundings. They were imprisoned in stables and sheds, with starvation rations. The wounded were all in great distress.

Across the stable yard, in the comparative comfort of the women's quarters, Bonny and Adolphine's position was coming under threat. By now it had become clear that Bonny was pregnant and the envy of the senior wife became sharper still, as she feared that if the Englishwoman gave birth to a boy her own son might be disinherited from the succession. Determined to eliminate this unwanted rival, she began to lobby hard for the European prisoners to be killed, intending that Bonny and her unborn baby should be among their number. Reluctant at first, the Nawab eventually gave in to pressure and on 23 July the prisoners were led out onto the parade ground. The men were put to death by the sword, then the twenty-two women and young children were made to sit on the ground and face a gun loaded with grapeshot. Several discharges were needed to kill the prisoners (one girl eventually had to be beheaded as the guns persistently misfired at her). The callousness of their execution aroused intense fury when the British public and authorities came to hear of it. But neither Bonny nor Adolphine was among the dead.

In the aftermath of the Mutiny, suspicions grew that Bonny and her mother had not merely survived the massacre but had been its direct cause. Enraged at their perfidy and immorality, many other members of the European community urged that such collaborators deserved the ultimate punishment. The newly appointed local magistrate telegraphed to the Governor-General, George Canning, for 'permission to hang Mrs de Fountain and her daughter'. But Canning, nicknamed 'Clemency Canning' by some of his infuriated countrymen, refused to allow the executions, insisting that 'there has been enough bloodshed of this kind'. Bonny survived to give birth to her son and to marry again, to a British civil servant, but she died less than two years after the Mutiny, in February 1859, survived by her mother. Her story aroused such anger – scandal piled upon scandal – that it was seldom mentioned in polite society.

Some sixteen years after the Mutiny the idea of an Englishwoman taking an Indian as a lover was still utterly unconscionable. When the wife of a prominent British lawyer was discovered by her husband to be having an affair with a sweeper, not just an Indian but a low-caste Indian at that, he beat her so violently that she could not move for a week. He then had the sweeper tried for rape, and persuaded his wife to testify that he had attacked her. The sweeper was duly convicted and sentenced to transportation to the Andaman Islands.

Such outrageous women might flout every convention and cross the racial divide, but very few unmarried girls dared to risk social ruin by indulging in much more than a kiss – and that only with potential husband material. Forbidden from marrying until they reached the age of thirty, young officers were consigned to a rather monastic existence. As one officer was later to put it: 'Sex was a subject which, possibly because it was so difficult to get, did not occupy one's mind and was certainly not the universal topic it has become today. Marriage on a subaltern's pay was out of the question; the pill had not been invented; one-parent families were not acceptable; brothels only for the very foolish, and all that was left was lots of exercise.'

The only other alternative was to find an accommodating married woman, and the hill stations during the summer months provided the ideal hunting ground. For most women taking their children up to Simla or other hill stations for a relaxing summer, an affair was the last thing on their minds. But for some the chance to escape the sometimes stultifying, restrictive life they led in garrisons created such a feeling of liberation that the normal constraints and tenets of their existence were swept away in the rarified mountain air. For two-thirds of the year they lived a life so regimented and so public that, as Julia Maitland, living in Madras in the 1830s, observed, the smallest hint of scandal was hungrily seized upon and endlessly discussed. Or, as another wife, living in India a century later, described it, 'Every facet of your life was known – with the result that there was virtually no immorality whatsoever because of the extraordinary communal life we lived.' But in the hills all the rules changed. Even in Emily Eden's day hill stations had a burgeoning reputation for impropriety. 'I always think those wives who are driven by health to be so many months away from their husbands, are rather in a dangerous situation in this country, where women are seldom left to take care of themselves,' she commented knowingly.

Nan Warry, an Indian Army officer's wife in the 1930s, was shocked when she spent her first summer in Gulmarg, a popular hill station in Kashmir, to find herself plunged into a bubbling cauldron of illicit romance. With her young son in tow, she took a hut with her younger sister Avis, a renowned beauty and also an army wife, and observed with amusement how the hut quickly became the centre of attraction for all the young bachelors of Gulmarg who vied for Avis's favours. Their days were occupied with golf, tennis, picnicking and riding parties, while the nights were spent dancing at the club. Dancing was a particularly perilous pastime as 'to be constantly alone with one [man] might end in the inevitable dilemma'. Some found it hard to resist the constantly recurring temptations of ' "Ride with me today" – "dance with me tomorrow" – "Sleep with me the day after" '.

While Nan found the barrage of attention difficult to cope with, there were plenty of women who revelled in the racy atmosphere of the hills in summer. Their catalogues of conquests among the single subalterns earned them such descriptive sobriquets as 'The Charpoy Cobra' (charpoy being British–Indian slang for 'bed'), in the case of a 'languorous dark-eyed brunette, lissom-limbed, fingernails as scarlet as her lips'. 'The Passionate Haystack' was a 'pretty doll-like girl with untidy tawny hair piled high above a pair of china blue eyes'; and 'The Swedish Match Queen' was a platinum blonde permanently surrounded by a throng of admirers.

The writer M.M. (Mollie) Kaye also spent a summer in Gulmarg and encountered these temptresses, as well as one serially erring lady known as 'the Subaltern's Guide to Knowledge' and another as 'Bed-and-Breakfast'. A bachelor friend of hers later recalled somewhat wistfully that while sex with respectable single girls was unthinkable, 'Grass widows were considered fair game. Married women . . . who were left husbandless for weeks on end, had a field day. They used to mow us down in droves!' One such siren had spent a delightful summer entertaining her lover on her houseboat in Srinigar while her husband remained on the plains. When he came up to the hills for his month's leave she put the affair on hold. On hearing that her husband had decided to spend the first part of his holiday fishing on a stream twenty miles away, she hastily recalled her lover and their cosy entente was resumed. Unfortunately for her, word of her brazen behaviour soon spread and reached the husband who packed up his fishing rod and hastened up to Srinagar two days before he was expected. Slipping silently on to the houseboat, he surprised his wife and her Don Juan dining cosily à deux. Without uttering a word he marched through the dining room and disappeared into the bedroom, emerging a few moments later with his service revolver in his hand. The alarmed lover did not stop to offer excuses but dived fully dressed through the open window and into the lake, swimming away as fast as he could, ducking to avoid a revolver shot, which narrowly missed him. The occupants of the nearby houseboats, hearing the commotion, sprang to their windows or on to the roofs of their boats to watch. They observed the furious husband racing up to the top of his own boat from where, 'Only slightly impeded by his hysterical wife, who was clutching his arm and shrieking "No! No! No!" at the top of her voice, he proceeded to scare the daylights out of his onlookers, as well as the lover and the lady, by driving the former to swim under water and, every time the poor chump's breath gave out and his head showed, carefully placing a shot just near enough to force him to dive again.'

Such stories of faithless wives must have sown the seeds of unease in the minds of many a husband languishing in his sweaty exile on the plain, imagining his wife amid the gaiety of Gulmarg or Simla, surrounded by ill-intentioned admirers and finding their flattery hard to resist. One summer the story circulated of a handsome young man on his way down from the hills after leave. After heavy monsoon rain the road had been washed away, forcing him to spend the night in one of the many rest houses that lay along the two to three hundred-mile journey down to the plains. At the rest house he met a colonel, also stranded, on his way up to the hills. They ate dinner together, neither asking for nor giving any introduction. After several whiskies they became relaxed in each other's company and began to share confidences.

'Had a good leave, young man? the colonel enquired.
    'Ye-es. Just not quite perfect.'
    'Why was that?' asked his companion.
    'There was one woman I'd have given anything to possess. But, alas, she wouldn't succumb to my charm.'
    'Bad luck. Who was the siren? I'll let you know what I think of her should we meet again.'
    "Mrs—, I'm sure she would have been wonderful to sleep with.'
    'She is.'
    'How do you know?' the would-be lover asked in surprise, piqued to think that the older man might have succeeded where he had failed.
    'She is my wife,' was the reply.

The serious side to such stories, whether apocryphal or true, was that the lifestyle of British military society involved regular separation even in peacetime. In the uncertainty and anxiety of war the strains of long separations could create cracks in even the most solid of marriages. The policy of cohabiting with another abandoned wife during a husband's long absence was one time-honoured solution to the problem.

In the Second World War many wives opted to share a house in order to alleviate the loneliness of living alone and to take comfort from the presence of another woman sharing the same anxieties for her husband. Some women may have even recognised that if they did not share their life with a friend, they might be tempted instead to slake their thirst for companionship and comfort in the arms of another man. Denizens of wartime British India are understandably reluctant to talk about the seamier side to life among those left behind while their husbands and fathers were fighting in Burma, North Africa or Italy. As they describe it, most women were too busy bringing up their children, doing voluntary work for the Red Cross, or carrying out their other regimental duties among the wives and families, to have time to launch themselves into an affair, even if they had had the inclination. But if pressed, some will concede that, while the majority of army wives were stalwart and faithful, there were inevitably some for whom loneliness, anxiety, or even pure opportunity resulted in infidelity. The fact that while they were thus engaged their husbands were involved in savage, bloody fighting rendered their betrayal all the more profound.

Occasionally women were driven to risk their lives by having back-street abortions in a dark corner of an Indian bazaar, submitting to the questionable skill of an old woman with a hook and a needle to terminate a pregnancy that could have occurred only while their husband was at the front. One woman died because she was too worried about revealing her affair to admit that she was pregnant. When complications ensued, either from a botched abortion or because the pregnancy was ectopic, she refused to see a doctor. Her husband came back from the front for her funeral. Was he told the real cause of her death, or did a tactful doctor attribute it to some other reason to absolve him of the pain of discovering that she had not only died but had betrayed him?

Those women who shared their tribulations but did not give into temptation are markedly reluctant to condemn them. Nan Warry was typical in seeing such women as victims of war. Defending them, she points out that many of them were living a terrible purgatory: 'They did not know whether their husbands were alive or dead. Whether they were entitled to a widow's pension or could still draw on their husband's income. Some, to make a living, ran a boarding house or took paying-guests. Some who had young children to care for, or for various reasons could not earn a living, had no one to turn to but a kind friend – or a kind lover. Who shall judge them?'

Nan Warry's understanding of women in desperate circumstances finds an echo in earlier years. While separation, loneliness and opportunity (not forgetting the persuasive charms of a lover) all contributed to an atmos-phere conducive to infidelity, sometimes another, more prosaic, factor came into play. Necessity. Unable because of their highly mobile lifestyle to find work as domestic servants, the main occupation open to uneducated women before the Industrial Revolution, some soldiers' wives were impelled by penury and desperation to contemplate the only other viable form of employment open to a female of their background: prostitution. According to Francis Place, a tailor and radical campaigner who argued for improved conditions for the working classes in the late eighteenth century, 'poverty and chastity are incompatible', a theory known as 'Place's Law'. Although most women, soldiers' wives included, did manage to prove this maxim wrong, for others selling themselves provided the only answer. On campaign, when food became even scarcer, greater numbers of women resorted to this measure.

Those who witnessed this practice tended to attach little blame to the wives. August Schaumann paints a grim picture of the conditions after the battle of Talavera in July 1809. Tormented by leeches that clung to every part of the body, including the insides of their mouths, the men were glad to move on when the army struck camp in August. But after a few days of marching across mountains they were suffering from exhaustion, severe sunburn and hunger. Schaumann, as commissary, did his best to procure flour for the starving soldiers and their families. He observed that the soldiers' wives, 'who as a rule went about decently clad, and were most faithful to their husbands, now rode round hungrily in rags on starved donkeys, and gave themselves to any one who wanted them in exchange for half a loaf of bread'. Perhaps these women were influenced by the fact that some of their number had, the previous month, been subjected to Sir Rowland Hill's 'schoolboy discipline' for stealing food in Zarza Major, and chose prostitution rather than risk being flogged.

The Peninsular veteran Joseph Donaldson also absolved the women of blame, accusing instead the unscrupulous men who took advantage of their precarious situation. 'They were assailed by every temptation which could be thrown in their way, and every scheme laid by those who had rank and money, to rob them of that virtue which was all they had left to congratulate themselves upon. Was it to be wondered at, then, if many of them were led astray, particularly when it is considered that their starving condition was often taken advantage of by those who had it in their power to supply them, but who were villains enough to make their chastity the price?'

By the second half of the twentieth century no soldier in the British army could complain of starvation, although many still bemoaned the quality of their rations. There were, however, times when soldiers' pay packets lagged so far behind those of their civilian counterparts that, struggling to provide their young families with the basic necessities of life, many were driven into debt or to exhaustion from moonlighting as taxi drivers or labourers to make up the deficiency. In the 1970s and again in the 1980s army wives marched in protest at their husbands' low wages, some carrying the slogan 'better off on the dole'. Other wives found their own methods of boosting the family finances.

In the garrison town of Aldershot where, in the nineteenth century, moral reformers had been appalled to find soldiers' wives making a 'bare subsistence' by taking home up to ten soldiers each night, the problem of prostitution reared its head once again in the straitened times of the 1970s. Wives of the Parachute Regiment, whose husbands were frequently absent on dangerous and difficult duty in Northern Ireland, were astonished to find some of their number filling their lonely days by turning to the oldest profession. Elizabeth Howlett, whose sympathy and kindness had saved a soldier's wife from suicide, was once again confronted with a situation for which she was entirely unprepared when she was informed that two wives in 'her' regiment, 2 PARA, were running a brothel. 'It had really got going well, and I had to go and do something about it. I was a bit frightened because it was for the other soldiers that weren't in Ireland, the other regiments in Aldershot . . . Luckily Geoffrey always left a families' sergeant behind, which was a godsend. So I grabbed him and we both went in, and it was closed down. You couldn't have that.'

Marion Weston came across a similar situation when she took on the responsibilities of CO's wife in Detmold, Germany. 'I saw bits of society that I wouldn't have ever expected to see. You'd get [told by another wife] "There are a lot of chaps appearing at Mrs Snoggins's house." And . . . you'd have to go and investigate. She was entertaining gentlemen [other soldiers]. Her husband was away. She was being paid for it.' The woman concerned usually had to leave her home as she had forfeited her right to a married quarter. Not only was her trade disturbing the families who lived in her block of flats but, if word of her activities spread to the men patrolling the streets of Northern Ireland, the thought that the wives they had left behind might be betraying them, especially in so mercenary a fashion, could damage their morale.

Sometimes apparently trivial matters could escalate into a scandal that led to tragedy. In the nineteenth century the importance attached to honour and the acute sensitivity of gentlemen to any perceived slur on themselves or their families meant that such issues could have grave consequences. The celebrated diarist and Guards officer Captain Gronow recalled acting as a second in a duel that originated when one officer, a 'Mr N', proclaimed loudly that the wife of a brother officer was 'What she ought not to be.' A duel was fought, between the insulter and the defender of the lady's honour, and though neither man was killed Mr N had to leave the regiment.

A similar insult, levelled against the wife of a Captain Renshaw, an officer in the 6th Inniskilling Dragoons, led indirectly to the deaths of a soldier and his wife in circumstances that caused a national scandal. Captain Renshaw had arrived in India with his pretty young bride at the end of the 1850s and joined his regiment at the hill station of Mhow. At first the young couple were welcomed warmly into the regiment and were popular with the officers and their wives alike. But slowly rumours began to filter back from Britain. Mrs Renshaw, it transpired, had been married when the couple first met and Renshaw had been the third party cited by her first husband in their divorce case. Furthermore, the judge in the case had not only found her guilty of adultery, but of duplicity and profligacy that, he thundered, he hoped was rarely to be found among women. It was a shocking indictment of her character at a time when females, particularly those of the middle and upper classes and most especially the wives of cavalry officers, were supposed to be spotless and pure. (Moreover an officer was supposed to resign his commission if cited in a divorce case.)

The Renshaws quickly found themselves shunned by some of the officers and respectable matrons of the regiment who shrank from the society of such a tarnished woman. One couple in particular, Captain Smales and his wife, who considered themselves to be of rather superior social standing, took the step of warning the regiment's new commanding officer of Mrs Renshaw's dubious moral antecedents, which 'rendered her an undesirable association in the domestic circles of the regiment'. He and another officer even went so far as to demand the Renshaws' expulsion from regimental society, while Mrs Smales ostentatiously absented herself from regimental functions rather than mix socially with a woman who had been publicly branded immoral. But the commanding officer, Colonel Crawley, decided to take a more broadminded approach and, reprimanding his subordinate for believing gossip and slander, insisted that the Renshaws must be accepted and their 'scandal' should never be mentioned. The regiment quickly divided into pro-Renshaw and anti-Renshaw factions, the latter, led by Smales, seeking every opportunity to obstruct and question the authority of Colonel Crawley. The eventual outcome of the feud was a breakdown in regimental discipline and subsequently a court martial that involved several non-commissioned officers as witnesses.

During the court martial of Captain Smales, a Sergeant Major Lilley, in common with some other witnesses, had been confined to his quarters under close arrest, a sentry posted at the door of his one-room bungalow. His wife, Clarissa, a consumptive in the final debilitating stages of the illness, racked with diarrhoea and so weak that she fainted frequently, was subjected to the same scrutiny for, knowing how serious was her illness and anxious to support her husband, she decided to remain at home with him rather than go into the garrison hospital. Only when she retired behind a thin curtain could she gain any privacy from the sentry's gaze. She did not like to come out on to the verandah for air while the sentry was present, so was forced to remain in the stifling room. In addition to her current misfortune she had also suffered the tragedy of watching her two young children sicken and die only a few months before. Now, helpless with illness herself, she had to watch her husband, trapped like a caged animal in the tiny house, become increasingly restless and unwell, as he used alcohol to deaden his misery. After a month of house arrest Sergeant Major Lilley became apoplectic and died.

Two weeks later Clarissa followed him to his grave. She was only twenty-two years old, a kind, gentle woman, whose body was laid to rest alongside that of her husband and children in the Mhow garrison cemetery, victims not only of the oppressive physical climate but the equally harsh social climate of British India. The scandal that had led to the court martial was far removed from the Lilleys, yet the reverberations of an officer's wife's reputation coming under fire had almost certainly hastened her death, may have been responsible for that of her husband, and unquestionably caused their last days to be overshadowed with misery, discomfort and humiliation. When the scandal broke, Colonel Crawley was court martialled for causing Lilley to be imprisoned far longer than the eight days that army regulations allowed, a transgression that, the prosecution said, made him unfit to command a regiment. After a highly public trial in England he was found not guilty. The Renshaws, whose marriage had caused these fatal repercussions, eventually exchanged into another regiment. As for the Lilleys, their fate was soon forgotten by the public, but its impact on the regiment was more lasting. A large square tomb, now surrounded by long grass in the centre of a forgotten field in India, erected by the soldiers and non-commissioned officers of the 6th Inniskillings 'as a mark of their respect' to John and Clarissa Lilley, provides an enduring reminder of the scandal and of the terrible consequences that an unsuitable marriage could have.

The fascination that the military world held for civilians was evident again a century later when a court martial was convened in West Germany in 1955 for the trial of Mick Emmett-Dunne. This handsome sergeant of the Royal Electrical and Mechanical Engineers (REME) stood accused of killing his lover's husband, a sergeant in the same corps. The woman at the centre of the case was German-born Mia (Maria) Watters, who had married the victim, Reg Watters, in 1948 when he was stationed in the industrial town of Duisburg in north-east Germany. With her film-star looks and vivacious manner, it was easy to see what had attracted Reg. But after they were married, her short, fair-haired, husband became, she later claimed, morose and inattentive. Too fond of alcohol, he frequently left her sitting alone on social occasions while he drank himself into a stupor at the bar. Miserable and craving attention, she was vulnerable when, a little less than five years into their marriage, Reg introduced her to his friend and fellow sergeant, Mick Emmett-Dunne.

At six foot two, Emmett-Dunne towered over 'Titch' Watters, a diminutive five foot one. In addition he had been taken prisoner in the war but made a daring escape. He was a glamorous, exciting figure who knew how to turn on the charm. He delighted in flattering and flirting with the many bored, restless married women who sat listlessly in the sergeants' mess or in their quarters, waiting for some excitement to brighten their lives in the drab environment of post-war Germany. British soldiers and their families were initially forbidden from buying food from German shops as, explained an army families' booklet in 1948, 'Shops in Germany are practically empty and what little remains in them must be left for the German civilian population.' So soldiers and their families had to buy all their essentials through the army or the NAAFI (Navy, Army & Air Force Institute), using British currency. This opened up lucrative opportunities for black marketeering. Soldiers could buy goods from the NAAFI that could not be obtained in the German shops, and sell them at a profit to civilians. Mick Emmett-Dunne was involved in this racket and soon enlisted the help of several wives, including Mia Watters. It was easier for the wives, particularly Germany-born women like Mia, to make their way out of barracks with contraband alcohol and sell it in Duisburg without attracting attention.

But Emmett-Dunne's assignations with Mia were, it seemed, not purely to transact business. Within a few months of their initial meeting they had, she later confessed, begun a clandestine relationship, dancing in public and meeting in private. Mia was delighted to be feted and admired by an attractive and sought-after man. She later claimed that she was hoping to provoke her husband into paying her more attention, and at first her plan seemed successful. Watters reacted with furious jealousy, begging his wife not to see or talk to Emmett-Dunne any more. But by now she was too smitten to heed him. On every social occasion Mia and Mick could be seen dancing in each other's arms, while the humiliated Watters took refuge in drink, keenly aware of the whispers and pitying looks being cast in his direction.

In the early hours of 1 December 1953 Reg Watters was found hanging by a rope in a barrack block, an upturned bucket nearby. An army doctor pronounced it to be a case of suicide, and a brief investigation by the Royal Military Police concurred. Sergeant Watters' alcohol habit was well known and his wife's attachment to Sergeant Emmett-Dunne was the gossip of the camp (her neighbours reported hearing footsteps on the stairs when her husband was away). Such public humiliation, it was thought, might well have driven Watters to take his own life. He was duly buried and his apparently distraught widow left Germany to live with her sister-in-law in Leeds.

Meanwhile in Duisburg the affair continued to generate controversy. A rumour began to circulate that Watters had not hanged himself but had been strangled by Emmett-Dunne, who wanted Mia for himself. The authorities, however, seemed content to accept the verdict of suicide. And there matters might have rested, had it not been for the fact that some months later a military policeman, who had been involved in the Watters investigation but had since left the army to join the civilian force, happened to hear of a marriage that had taken place in England between a certain Mia Watters and Sergeant Mick Emmett-Dunne on 3 June 1954, just six months after Reg Watters' death. His suspicions aroused, the policeman alerted his superiors and Watters' body was exhumed. A further examination concluded that his injuries were not consistent with suicide and, in March 1955, Emmett-Dunne was arrested and brought back to Germany to stand trial.

A court martial was convened as the case involved members of the British army who, together with their families, came under military law, according to the Status of Forces Agreement (SOFA) between Britain and Germany. The attractive Mia Emmett-Dunne quickly became the focus of newspaper attention. Journalists from British newspapers thronged the court room, eager to relay salacious details of the case back to a hungry public in Britain. Beside them sat army wives, eagerly craning for a view of the man in the dock, and the woman at the centre of the case. Was she a femme fatale who had caused her lover to murder her husband, or an innocent bystander? Emmett-Dunne claimed that he had killed Watters in self-defence. The two men were in Emmett-Dunne's car when, he said, they began arguing over his bootlegging scheme and Watters pulled a gun on him. In trying to knock the gun out of Watters' hand he had accidentally hit him in the throat, killing him. Panic-stricken, he decided to make the death look like suicide, and enlisting the help of his half-brother, also a soldier, he had rigged up the body to make it appear that Watters had hanged himself.

Emmett-Dunne claimed that his subsequent marriage to Mia Watters was unrelated to her husband's death. He had bumped into her by chance when he returned to England on a posting and, he said, had offered to marry her because he felt sorry for her and wanted to provide her with a home. The court heard that shortly before Watters' death Emmett-Dunne had told a friend that someone in the camp 'would commit suicide if his wife did not behave'. He denied saying the words. He denied, too, telling an acquaintance that he was 'in love with a married woman'. He attempted to pass off his assignations with Mrs Watters as business transactions concerning his bootlegging scheme. Mia Emmett-Dunne too denied that after her first husband's death she had told friends 'Mick has done it'. She told the court that letters sent to her by Emmett-Dunne were purely related to the alcohol business. Although she was doubtful that her husband had committed suicide, she did not, she claimed, suspect that Emmett-Dunne had had any hand in his death.

The court found Emmett-Dunne's increasingly desperate explanations unconvincing. He was found guilty of Watters' murder and sentenced to death. A reporter from the *News of the World* noted 'the sobs from the throng of Army wives in light Summer frocks' that echoed round the court room when the death sentence was pronounced. Mia sold her story to the *Sunday People*. Under the headline 'My Love of Two Sergeants' she confessed to being 'heartbroken at the havoc I have caused' and at the discovery of Emmett-Dunne's guilt. 'The hands that have caressed me,' she sobbed, 'the hands that I have grown to love. These hands killed Reg.' The case held one more surprise in store. Although the death sentence had been pronounced, and although Emmett-Dunne was under British jurisdiction, it emerged that just eighteen months before Sergeant Watters' death the British and German governments had signed a convention prohibiting the enforcement of the death penalty on German territory by the Occupation Armed Services Authority. Emmett-Dunne managed to escape the noose, instead serving ten years in prison in Britain before being released and disappearing into obscurity.

Yet for all these intrigues and betrayals, the majority of army marriages managed and still do manage to weather the trials of separation and the temptations inherent in the highly communal, somewhat intense nature of military society. When soldiers' private affairs have affected their ability to discharge their duties, or had repercussions within the wider regimental community, the army has often (but not always) felt obliged to intervene. But in other cases the army hierarchy has been content to let matters take care of themselves. It is hard to imagine Wellington being taken to task for enjoying the favours of the courtesan Harriette Wilson, or the actress Marguerite Josephine Weimer – who had also been Napoleon's lover and added insult to the injury of his defeat by claiming that 'Monsieur le duc était de beaucoup le plus fort'. Perhaps commanders have recognised that the nature of army existence is not always conducive to marital stability. Indeed, even the lighter side of military life, the social activities and entertainments enjoyed by soldiers and their families, have frequently provided the opportunity and environment for romance, infidelity, gossip and jealousy revealed by many of these scandals.

Yet equally commanders have also understood the importance of allowing soldiers, and their families, the opportunities for relaxation or revelry as a way of relieving the pressures of their unique lifestyle. Enabling the men, and their women, opportunities to mix informally and enjoy themselves has often been seen as essential for good morale, promoting a sense of community and providing a break from the monotony of garrison life or the uncertainties of war. A vibrant social life has, therefore, always been at the heart of the army's existence, with women playing a vital role both by participating in it, and by helping to hold together their communities by supporting each other in difficult times.

9

Social Functions

Every day added something to their knowledge of the officers' names
and connections. Their lodgings were not long a secret, and at length
they began to know the officers themselves . . . They could talk of
nothing but officers; and Mr Bingley's large fortune, the mention
of which gave animation to their mother, was worthless in
their eyes when opposed to the regimentals of an ensign.

The Bennet sisters greet the arrival of a regiment
in town, in Jane Austen's *Pride and Prejudice*

When the 11th Hussars, commanded by Lord Cardigan, left Brighton
in March 1841, many citizens of the fashionable seaside resort turned
out to bid farewell with regret. During its eight-month sojourn the regiment
had, it was widely acknowledged, brought a dash and vitality to the
town's social life that would be sadly lacking when it departed. 'We have
seldom known a ball go off better in Brighton,' remarked the *Brighton
Gazette* on one occasion, 'a circumstance which it is only fair to add was
mainly due to the spirit with which the officers entered into the evening's
amusement.' The regiment's departure was lamented too by the town's
tailors, dressmakers, innkeepers and hoteliers, for the officers had been
billeted for most of the season at the town's finest hotel, the Royal York.
The cream of Brighton society, who had been favoured with invitations
to Lord and Lady Cardigan's private dinner parties, was also sad to see the
regiment leave.

The days are long gone when the arrival of a new regiment in town produces a flurry of excitement. No longer do young women pick out their prettiest bonnets and summon their dressmakers in anticipation of a social fiesta of picnics, dinners and balls to be attended by the smart young men in their scarlet coats and tight breeches. Yet to the outsider, regimental life can still appear to be one long round of socialising, a delightful prospect to those with deep pockets and extrovert natures. The army's capacity for pageantry and organisation has ensured that the social calendar is filled with mess nights, balls, dances, picnics, parades, family days and Christmas parties both at home and abroad. Even in times of war, this appetite for balancing the serious business of campaigning with more trivial pursuits has scarcely diminished. Indeed, possibly the most famous society ball of all time took place on the eve of Britain's most celebrated victory, the Battle of Waterloo.

The news of Napoleon's escape from his island prison in Elba, to which he had been consigned after the defeat of France in 1814, was the signal not only for Wellington to begin reassembling his army. It also saw the embarkation for Brussels of swathes of England's high society who swelled the ranks of the city's British expatriate community (it was widely expected that Napoleon would invade the Low Countries and strike a blow against the armies of the allies). When Napoleon landed in the south of France on 1 March 1815, Lady Caroline Capel and her family had already been in residence in Brussels for a year (to escape her husband's debtors), while the MP and diarist Thomas Creevey was also firmly established there. They were soon joined by other exiles who rushed to Brussels to partake in the excitement. The Duke of Richmond, who had been with Wellington in the Peninsula, had angled for an appointment to Wellington's staff for the Waterloo campaign. In this he was disappointed, but he nonetheless moved out to Brussels with his family where his wife, the Duchess, was soon organising a dizzying catalogue of social events, her energy for entertaining rivalled only by that of Wellington himself.

Indeed, after arriving in Brussels at the beginning of April, Wellington was soon seen to devote almost as much energy to socialising as he did to preparing the allied army for war. Kitty, his long-suffering duchess, remained at home in England as usual. In early June, when an attack by the French seemed imminent, Wellington was busily escorting the pretty Lady Jane Lennox, daughter of the Duke of Richmond, to a cricket match. He also took time out from planning his campaign to squire such alluring damsels as Lady Frances Wedderburn-Webster around Brussels, and hold dinners and balls aplenty to which all the most attractive society ladies were invited, regardless of their reputation. Caroline Capel wrote in disgust that the Duke had made a point of inviting 'all the Ladies of Loose Character' to his soirées. When one of his aides pointed out that a certain lady of doubtful reputation was not 'received', far from striking her from the guest list, Wellington at once declared, 'I will go and ask her myself' and, putting on his hat, went out to do so.

While the soldiers' wives had to make prodigious efforts to get to Brussels, circumventing the guards placed over them at Ostend and Ghent, officers' wives faced no such obstacles. Flotillas of packet boats and other craft made their way across the Channel bearing cargoes of fashionably dressed ladies, all eagerly making for Brussels. On arrival they set up home in hotels or lodgings, arrayed themselves in all their finery to ride out in the park, visited the theatre and angled for invitations to the most fashionable balls. They were not disappointed by the social scene that met them. At a grand cavalry review at the end of May it was, as Wellington's biographer Lady Longford records, 'hard to decide which was more memorable – the splash of scarlet uniforms at the time or of pink champagne afterwards'. Some old campaigners were beginning to be worried about the effects of all this revelry. 'Another such a day as yesterday, and we shall be ruined as soldiers – ruined with burgundy and champagne, and with all that, as the Duchess of Gordon says, carries a man off his legs,' wrote a concerned Colonel Sir Augustus Simon Frazer to his family. The socialites, however, were delighted. On 2 June one of the Capel daughters wrote excitedly to her grandmother: 'Tomorrow Lord Wellington gives a great Ball. Sir Charles Stewart Monday and the Duke again on Wednesday.' Her mother, expecting her thirteenth child imminently, added, 'Balls are going on here as if we had had none for a year.'

While Wellington certainly enjoyed a good party and relished the sight of his dashing young officers enlivening society and squiring its most attractive members, his motives for indulging in this hectic round of socialising went far beyond sheer hedonism. Brussels was at that time teeming with Bonapartist spies and sympathisers and those who did not believe that Napoleon could be held back from the city. By attending and encouraging social functions, Wellington was sending out a clear message of confidence. He even encouraged his heavily pregnant niece Emily, married to one of his young aides, Lord Fitzroy Somerset (who became Lord Raglan of Crimean fame), to remain in Brussels for her confinement. He was cautious enough to advise the Duchess of Richmond against holding a picnic too close to the French frontier, asking her to mention nothing to anyone for fear of causing alarm. But when she sounded him out about holding a ball on 15 June, Wellington replied confidently, 'Duchess, you may give your ball with the greatest safety, without fear of interruption.'

His prediction proved to be not wholly accurate. The ball did go ahead, but it was interrupted in spectacular style. When the officers, ambassadors and aristocrats trooped into the sumptuously decorated ballroom in the Richmonds' rented house in the rue de la Blanchisserie, Wellington had already learned that afternoon that the French army had not advanced in the direction he had thought most likely, but further to the east. He accordingly issued instructions for his army to be ready to march at a moment's notice. (Prussian, Belgian and Dutch forces were already positioned at strategic points close to the French frontier.) Wellington then told the Prussian liaison officer, General Müffling, that he would go to the ball as planned. 'The numerous friends of Napoleon who are here,' he explained, 'will be on tiptoe; the well intentioned must be pacified; let us therefore go all the same to the Duchess of Richmond's ball, and start for Quatre Bras at 5 a.m.' (Quatre Bras was a strategically important crossroads just south of Waterloo.) Besides, he reasoned, if he needed to distribute orders to his staff officers in a hurry, it would be convenient to have them all in one place, at the ball. Some officers whose regiments were already many miles from Brussels left the ballroom early on in the evening to make their way to where their men were bedding down on the ground for the night, or snatch a few hours' sleep in their billets. Others, following the example of their chief, stayed to revel in the array of beauty and entertainment on offer, as described in Byron's poem 'The Eve of Waterloo':

> . . . *And Belgium's capital had gathered then*
> *Her beauty and her chivalry, and bright*
> *The lamps shone o'er fair women and brave men . . .*

Just before supper, as Wellington stood ready to go in with his young companion Lady Charlotte Greville, another dispatch was handed to him. The news it contained was disturbing. The Prussians, on whom Wellington had been relying to hold off the French forces, had been repulsed at Fleurus, less than eight miles from Quatre Bras. Determined not to reveal any anxiety lest it cause panic, the Duke went in to supper, but a few minutes later another message was delivered, this time by the Prince of Orange, commander of the Dutch army. The Prince whispered in

Wellington's ear that the enemy had in fact advanced as far as two miles from Quatre Bras. Showing considerable sang-froid, Wellington remained at the supper table making conversation with the pretty young women who surrounded him, but after a decent interval he excused himself and retired to a private room to consult a map.

Within minutes messengers and aides were scurrying in all directions with orders for the regiments to march towards Quatre Bras, or to wake up those who were slumbering peacefully in their Brussels billets. Word spread quickly around the supper table and soon men were climbing into carriages, hurrying back to their lodgings to pack a few provisions before marching off. Wives and sweethearts clutched nervously at the arms of their departing beaux, many of whom did not have time to return to their lodgings to change into uniform and found themselves marching off to war in their stockings and dancing slippers and having had no sleep at all. Wellington himself slept for only two hours. The fourth verse of Byron's poem captures the mood:

> *Ah! then and there was hurrying to and fro,*
> *And gathering tears, and tremblings of distress,*
> *And cheeks all pale, which, but an hour ago,*
> *Blushed at the praise of their own loveliness.*
> *And there were sudden partings, such as press*
> *The life from out young hearts, and choking sighs*
> *Which ne'er might be repeated; who would guess*
> *If ever more should meet those mutual eyes,*
> *Since upon night so sweet such awful morn could rise!*

In the early morning mist, as bugles and bagpipes marshalled the men into their marching order, an English resident of Brussels, Charlotte Waldie – who was not herself an army wife but numbered many officers among her friends – saw the heart-rending scenes of farewell that ensued: 'Numbers were taking leave of their wives and children, perhaps for the last time, and many a veteran's rough cheek was wet with the tears of sorrow. One poor fellow, immediately under our windows, turned back again and again, to bid his wife farewell, and take his baby once more in his arms; and I saw him hastily brush away a tear with the sleeve of his coat, as he gave her back the child for the last time, wrung her hand, and ran off to join his company, which was drawn up on the other side of the Place Royale. Many of the soldiers' wives rushed out with their husbands to the field, and I saw one young English lady mounted on horseback, slowly riding out of town along with an officer, who, no doubt, was her husband.'

Within a few hours many of the young men who had danced the quadrille so gracefully at the ball lay on the fields of Quatre Bras and Waterloo, blood seeping through their smart scarlet tunics on to the ground. The pretty dancing partners on whom they had bestowed parting kisses had become widows, though it took some time for them to discover their fate.

In the years since the great victory some have wondered at the fact that men who were to command troops in battle, or in Wellington's case whole armies, should have spent the hours before the action not planning, not resting, but dancing and drinking. Yet, for centuries, war and revelry have gone hand in hand. There is something about the imminence of a conflict in which men would be maimed and killed and women and children left to mourn that only encourages (among some at least) an appetite for fun and frivolity while such things are possible. Danger and discomfort breed the need for relaxation and indulgence, and commanders keen to keep their men from the evils of drink and debauchery have often encouraged harmless pastimes as a way of keeping them, and their families, occupied and content.

One commander astute in this respect was the Duke of Cumberland. In Scotland, in 1746, he sought to deter his troops from indulging in unlicensed pillage and mayhem by organising a series of games for the men, including bareback horse races. The soldiers' wives too (just as liable to go on the rampage if left unoccupied) were invited to take part. James Wolfe wrote that the Duke had given 'a fine holland smock to the soldiers' wives to be run for on these galloways [Highland horses], also bare-backed, and riding with their limbs on each side of the horse, like men. Eight started and there were three of the finest heats ever seen. The prize was won, with great difficulty, by one of the Old Buffs' ladies.'

With or without official sanction, soldiers and their wives managed to find entertainment during lulls in the fighting wherever they were, in camps and towns from North America in the Revolutionary War to Portugal and Spain in the Peninsular War. Merely dancing a jig beneath the trees or sharing a pigskin of wine and a joke or two around the campfire of an evening helped to relax and reinvigorate jaded soldiers and their weary families, and remind them of the simple pleasures of home life. True, sometimes a little too much rum was drunk and the pressures of living, sleeping and eating among the same small set of men and women for years on end erupted into arguments and fights, though few ended so violently as the case of Sergeant Battersby and his Nelly. But in the main, such occasions served to introduce normality back into the lives of those who had not seen home for many long months and who had forged such close bonds with their companions that, for them, the regiment was truly a family.

A little further off from these campfires the officers might (supplies permitting) be enjoying a four-course dinner prepared by their soldier servants, perhaps dining on a hare that they had caught while out coursing earlier in the day. Senior officers regularly held dinners for members of their staff and other officers. Few officers' wives were present at these as only a small number followed their husbands on campaign. One of those who did was Mrs Currie, wife of Captain Edward Currie, an aide-de-camp of Sir Rowland Hill; she followed him on every expedition in the Peninsula. She was the only wife among the officers of Hill's staff to do so and her tenacity was rewarded by frequent invitations to dine at the general's table. Her presence, it was said, elevated the tone of the company who 'neither forgot the deference due to beauty nor the polished manners of the drawing room'. She was lucky that it was Hill's table she graced. Wellington declared that out of all his generals Hill gave the second best dinners (General Cole gave the best). His own were, he admitted 'no great things. And Beresford's and Picton's [two other divisional commanders] are very bad indeed.' Hill was also a great fan of the theatre and whenever his division was at rest he encouraged his officers to put on plays. Although several slim young ensigns gamely attired themselves in petticoats to play the heroines, the presence of Mrs Currie among the company was always greatly appreciated. She had many admirers in the Peninsula. Major Patterson lauded her kindness, while George Bell called her 'a fair and beautiful Englishwoman . . . always joyous and happy, a charming representative of those bright stars of Albion, whose presence was always cheering amongst so many red-coats'.

In the Crimea, for most of the women who accompanied the army, like Margaret Kirwin, Elizabeth Evans and Becky Box, there was generally too much work to do to even think about pleasure. As an officer's wife, Fanny Duberly could fill her days rather more pleasantly, entertaining visitors in her cabin on board ship and even giving dinner parties. Captain Nolan, who was later to play a controversial role in the ill-fated charge of the Light Brigade, enjoyed her hospitality ten days before he was killed.

In return she was frequently invited to lunch in the camp and, when spring came and she moved into her hut at the front, her social calendar became busier than ever. At the beginning of March the first race meeting was held, which Fanny attended, though it was interrupted by an alarm that the Russians were advancing (it proved to be false). Afterwards there was a wild dog-hunt, though Fanny did not join in a sport 'so cruel, so unsportsmanlike, as hunting a *dog*'.

Fanny was, of course, the only officer's lady present at the hunt meeting. Indeed, since the Countess of Erroll had gone home, together with the odious Mrs Cresswell, she reigned supreme as the only lady at the Crimea, to her obvious delight – although she was sorry to see Lady Erroll depart, having become firm friends with her. Fanny was full of sympathy too for Mrs Cresswell when she heard the news that she had been widowed in the battle of the Alma but that nobody had the courage to inform her: 'God help and support Mrs Cresswell under a blow that would crush me to the grave,' she wrote. In one letter to her sister, she boasted, 'The longer I live, the greater swell I become. When I look back at the time when I lived at Wycombe [as a girl], glad to get the companionship of Miss Saunder-Nash and Miss Whytt, etc, and find myself now much in the position of a Queen – feted by admirals, asked to meet ambassadors and generals – how strange are the changes of life!'

Cold as the winter was, miserable as the slippery ride from Balaclava to the British camp before Sebastopol became, uncomfortable though she found her cabin in a ship that was loaded with dynamite which on several occasions threatened to explode, Fanny rarely considered going back to England. Instead, ignoring her family's entreaties to return, she wrote to her sister Selina in January 1855 asking for provisions to see her through the coming spring. For Fanny, practicality was a consideration, but keeping up appearances and maintaining her position at the centre of the Crimea's social scene was equally important. Though she might have given up petticoats in favour of wearing men's trousers under her skirt (a more sensible option for wading through the mud of Balaclava), she still wanted to look feminine and attractive. So she continued to wear her whalebone stays and instructed Selina to send 'pretty' neck ribbons, a 'nice' looking gown, and conditioner for her hair, as well as more prosaic items such as 'durable' shirts, strong muslin sleeves and material for a tent lining. She also summoned a French tailor to measure her up for a new riding habit, which he made in the style of the uniform of a French cavalry regiment, the renowned Chasseurs d'Afrique. Fanny was so pleased with its effect that she ordered a plumed riding hat to go with it and delightedly sent Selina a sketch of herself, hourglass figure set off to perfection, in her new attire. 'It is (as you can imagine) – *Stunning*,' she concluded happily. False modesty was never one of Fanny's failings. Indeed, she boasted that her company was so craved that she was 'the never omitted guest where a dinner wanted to be amusing and brilliant'. She was delighted to hear the British soldiers refer to her as Mrs Jubilee and preened herself when she visited the French lines to be greeted with a roar of approval.

Her position was assailed only briefly during the winter when, on Boxing Day 1854, the *Caradoc* put into Balaclava harbour, bearing an Irish baronet, Sir Roger Palmer, and his heiress daughter Ellen, who had come to visit her brother Roger, of the 11th Hussars. The Palmers were met on the dockside by one of Lord Raglan's aides-de-camp, and the next day an invitation arrived from Raglan himself to visit the camp. He even sent horses for their party and lent Ellen his own charger. Indeed, no trouble seemed to be too great for Lord Raglan to go to where the Palmers were concerned. This, as one historian has noted, was at a time when his army was collapsing from sickness and exposure, with men and horses dying in their hundreds from inadequate food and shelter. His courtesy to Ellen Palmer and her party contrasted markedly with his treatment of the distinctly middle-class (and moreover rebellious) Fanny Duberly, to whom he not only refused permission to live in camp, but failed to issue invitations to any of his dinners.

The Palmers left for home after a few weeks. It was not until the end of the winter that any other ladies ventured to the bitterly cold, rain-soaked Crimea. Then, with the warm weather, came shiploads of ladies and gentlemen from the very highest echelons of society. Although Fanny did not admit to it in either her journals or letters, her reign as unofficial Queen of the Crimea had effectively come to an end. Many of the newcomers had come on cruises that encompassed Malta and Constantinople. Amid the gaiety and excitement, the dinners and fancy dress parties on board, it was almost easy to forget that they were going to a seat of war, where men had died and were still dying in their scores from cholera, enteric fever, shot and shell. Some ladies, such as Lady Agnes Paget, were married to officers at the front and could therefore escape the label of 'war tourists'. Together with the Pagets travelled Mrs Amelia Morris, wife of another participant in the Charge of the Light Brigade, and her sister Lady Ann Carew who had a son serving in Scutari, together with Lady Ann's daughter Bessie. These ladies had spent a pleasant winter in Constantinople before deciding to venture on to the Crimea when the weather grew warm. They were joined by the British ambassador to Constantinople, Lord Stratford de Redcliffe, and his wife and two daughters. Such persons of 'quality' were treated warmly and attentively by Lord Raglan and his staff.

Lord Raglan was particularly taken with the lovely Lady Agnes Paget. Agnes, aged twenty-three, was blonde, beautiful and demure, of impeccable breeding (the daughter of a baronet). Lord George, her husband and first cousin, commanded the Light Dragoons and had taken part in the Charge of the Light Brigade. Raglan had known the couple in England (indeed, when Paget asked him why he had not deployed the Light Cavalry at the Alma, Raglan replied sentimentally, 'Well, George, you see, I thought of Agnes during the battle'). When Agnes took up residence in the Crimea, Lord Raglan insisted that she dine with him regularly, ride with him to inspect the batteries or lines, and even stand by his side as he directed the bombardment of Sebastopol in June 1855. Agnes was at Raglan's bedside when, shortly after the bombardment of Sebastopol, he died. A few weeks after the Pagets' arrival, as summer arrived in the Black Sea, fresh reinforcements of society ladies, wives and others, descended on the Crimea's shores.

Having weathered the grim winter months, struggled through the mud, slush and mire of Balaclava in the winter in her trousers and heavy boots, and received nothing but rebuffs from Lord Raglan, it was only natural that Fanny Duberly should cast a rather jaundiced eye on the elegantly dressed newcomers. The ladies who now arrived in the Crimea in time to take part in the programme of race meetings, picnics and plays that now began, had not, like Fanny, endured bitter nights in a storm-tossed ship, or watched their friends ride off to the battles of Alma, Balaclava and Inkerman and not return. Nor had they had to pick lice from their hair and clothes, or shivered with fever, fearing that they might never see England again.

Lady Agnes Paget irked Fanny particularly. After encountering the Pagets one day she observed cuttingly, 'George is such a bore, and she (Lady Agnes) is not in love with him.' It must have grated for Fanny, used to having a monopoly on male admiration, to hear another woman being dubbed 'the belle of the Crimea' by Roger Fenton, courted and fêted not only by Lord Raglan but also by the ordinary soldiers. When these men were lying wounded in hospital, a visit from the exquisite Agnes, who stood by their beds like a beautiful blonde angel, seemed to have almost miraculous effects upon their morale. When Agnes left the Crimea, long before Fanny did, the latter took some pleasure in reporting to her sister that Lady George Paget had made herself extremely unpopular by insisting upon taking over three cabins in the ship, forcing several wounded men to share one small cabin.

As well as hospital-visiting, watching the action from the British batteries (just close enough to the Russian guns to give them the thrill of danger), attending race meetings and hunts, ladies could divert themselves with picnics and riding excursions (escorted by officers). The most popular picnic spot was the valley of the already legendary Charge of the Light Brigade. The custom of visiting battlefields, months, days, even hours after the fighting had ended, had been established many years before. After Waterloo many of those who had watched the troops march from Brussels lost little time in heading for the battlefield to see the scene of the terrible contest. Young Georgy Capel, whose uncle, Lord Uxbridge, was wounded in the battle and lost his leg, visited the field a month afterwards. She found it still covered with bloody tunics, caps filled with congealed blood, and letters from friends and families of the dead soldiers, some of whose corpses still lay undiscovered in cornfields. Most valuable items had already gone, seized in the hours after battle by plunderers and body-strippers. Alongside the looters, whose motive was profit, traipsed sightseers, impelled by curiosity. So numerous were these tourists, picking their way through the mangled bodies, that it was suggested that they should at least bring with them bread, wine and other refreshments to distribute among the wounded who still lay on the battlefield, day after day, awaiting transport to the hospitals.

By the time the Crimean ladies spread their picnic rugs in the valley of the Light Brigade's fateful charge, the blood of the fallen cavalrymen had long since trickled into the soil. Yet there were still a few skeletons lying unburied for curious eyes to see. Fanny Duberly, who visited the site seven months afterwards, observed the hooves of half-buried horses protruding from the soil and the headless skeleton of a Light Dragoon. She was now too well used to seeing bodies, both of horses and men, floating in Balaclava's stinking harbour to flinch at such sights. She even sent some souvenirs, a half-torn jacket, some buttons and a bullet, taken from the corpses, to her sister in England.

If the frivolity of picnicking parties amid the bleached bones of fallen men seemed incongruous, more disturbing in the eyes of some military men was the custom of ladies venturing into the batteries before Sebastopol to witness the bombardment at close quarters. Not only were they in danger from a stray shot, they might also witness the harrowing sight of men dying and being wounded before their eyes. To reduce such business to a theatrical spectacle seemed wrong to those who had seen men die in the trenches before Sebastopol. Lieutenant General Sir William Codrington wrote of seeing two ladies, Mrs Forrest and Mrs Handcock, up at one of the look-outs above Sebastopol in August 1855. 'It is all very well to come once or so, and look at the scene – but I do not like ladies coming there to see firing as if to a show, when they must feel that every shot may be mangling some poor fellow!' Yet Lord Raglan himself had several times sent his own carriage to convey Lady Agnes Paget up to a good viewpoint above Sebastopol to watch its bombardment in June of that year, when she won still more admirers by remaining cool and fearless though within range of the Russian guns.

The appetite of ladies for witnessing war at first hand was not confined to the British. Before the Battle of the Alma in September 1854, the fine Russian ladies of Sebastopol had driven out from the town to a ridge over-looking the battlefield at the invitation of the Russian commander, who promised them the fine spectacle of watching the British and their French allies being beaten by his army. Long lines of carriages bearing the elite of Sebastopol society drove out from the city and lined up on the ridge in eager anticipation. They retreated hastily when it became clear that, far from swiftly crushing the invaders, their army was being beaten.

Nearly half a century after the last of the war tourists had gone home from the Crimea, more shiploads of elegant ladies set out across the oceans, heading for a distant shore where, this time in South Africa, Britannia's sons were fighting to maintain the Empire.

Soon after the start of the war, reports began to filter back to Britain of inadequate medical staff and facilities. Moved by the plight of the suffering soldiers, and concerned for their own husbands, sons and friends at the front, numbers of ladies began arriving in the Cape, professing their intention of nursing in the field hospitals. Well intentioned but inexperienced, they mostly found themselves turned away (in fact the army medical staff were so doubtful that women could be useful in this capacity that even the services of many experienced nurses were rejected). Other women simply wanted to be near the action, and had to be restrained from venturing off into the hinterland to join their men at the front.

Violet Cecil, who had arrived in South Africa with her officer husband

Edward well before the war broke out, described these would-be heroines as looking 'as if they have dropped from the clouds, and no
opportunity for heroism likely to be afforded them, are bitterly disappointed. They had visions of battlefields, but even trained nurses are not
allowed to the front. Also this place is not organized enough to make a
splash in . . . '

Cape Town, however, offered ample compensations for such disap-
pointments. The vibrancy of its social scene can be gauged from the advice
that Lady Mabell Airlie gave to her sister, Alice Cranborne. Lady Mabell,
whose husband was serving in the 12th Lancers, was already in Cape Town
when she wrote to her sister, who was contemplating coming out to join
her husband, also serving in South Africa. She must, advised Mabell, ensure
that her wardrobe was up to scratch and pack 'about the same as [for]
Cannes, by then, and some furs. They want to be tidy, but not too smart
as it looks rather vulgar. It is better to have cheap things, as they get ruined
here, and not too long skirts. You want a sort of table d'hote gown for
dinner, old summer gowns would do. And I think it would be wise to
take one dinner gown with a high and low body [bodice].'

So much of high society descended on Cape Town that it began to
resemble the pages of *Burke's Peerage*. Some observers were appalled by
the number of women cluttering up the Cape. They crowded the best
hotels such as the Mount Nelson, making querulous demands of the staff,
organising endless dinner parties, tea parties, picnics and dances, to which
they invited bored staff officers, luring them away from their military
duties. It took the intervention of the stern General Kitchener for such
ladies to be deterred from their social activities. Arriving in South Africa
in December 1900 as Lord Roberts's Chief of Staff, he was appalled by
the hedonism he observed. 'You hear amazing stories,' reported the artist
and journalist Mortimer Menpes approvingly, 'of how Lord Kitchener will
suddenly enter a club, or the Mount Nelson Hotel, in mufti [civilian
clothes], and with a few words of command will sweep the place of young
staff officers who are more or less idling away their time, giving a choice
of starting for the front or for England within twenty-four hours . . . '

Violet Cecil exempted herself from such criticism both by virtue of
her connections, and by balancing her busy social life with work for the
war effort. Violet was a petite, pretty and vivacious woman whose marriage
to Lord Edward Cecil, son of the then Prime Minister Lord Salisbury, was
already becoming strained. They left their four-year-old son George in the
care of an aunt and arrived in the Cape in July 1899, taking up residence

in Government House as the guests of Sir Alfred Milner, with whom Violet soon developed a close friendship that later gave rise to much gossip. Although it is unclear whether they had a physical affair at this time (they married years later, after Edward had died), Violet and Alfred were certainly on very intimate terms, spending the afternoons riding together or enjoying walks and tête-à-têtes in the pretty gardens of Government House. Violet soon assumed the role of hostess for the bachelor Milner (to the ire of many other ladies). Soon after the start of the war Cecil Rhodes lent Violet Groote Schuur, his own comfortable house, where she lived together with her friend Cecily Bentinck. Edward, meanwhile, had journeyed to Mafeking with Colonel Baden-Powell, on whose staff he served. He remained there for eight months as the town was besieged by the Boers from October 1899 to May 1900.

In between fretting about her husband and enjoying the company of the Governor, Violet set up her own Field Force Fund (together with Cecily) for distributing comforts and supplies to the troops. She and Cecily opened their doors to convalescing officers, whom they nursed, cared for and flirted with until they recovered sufficiently either to return to the front or to be invalided back to England.

Groote Schuur quickly became the epicentre of Cape Town's fashionable society. Violet and Cecily's more smitten convalescents wrote them effusive letters after they returned to the front. Occasionally their behaviour raised eyebrows: Mabell Airlie muttered darkly that Violet wanted 'watching from the "intrigante" point of view . . . She is far too clever to have flirtations with small fry, but I believe there have been stories about her and Lady Charles [Cecily Bentinck] . . . ' Yet Violet proved an invaluable support when in June 1900, Mabell's husband was shot dead at the battle of Diamond Hill. That same month Violet set out for Mafeking and her reunion with Edward. Mafeking had been relieved on 16 May and Edward, though happy to be released from his 'prison' of eight months, was feeling downcast at being passed over for promotion. Violet had had a far more successful war. Not only had she deservedly won admiration for her war work, she had also carved out a place as the pre-eminent hostess in expatriate British society.

If social life assumed a frenetic dimension in war time, in peacetime it frequently took on a rather more staid aspect. In their urge to recreate English society in Canada, India or Burma, perhaps to compensate for the sense of dislocation and strangeness of their new surroundings, army communities often adhered more rigidly to the rules and mores that governed social intercourse than at home. In communities where everyone knew each others' rank, income and to what kind of house they were entitled, this could make social life formal and constrained.

On arrival at a station, a newcomer could expect to be visited by a procession of ladies from her own regiment and any others at the same station, all keen to size up the newcomer and make her acquaintance. Although this was an effective way of meeting people, more retiring sorts found it an ordeal. 'I wish there was no such thing as calling in Kashmir,' exclaimed one irritated wife in 1889, 'but we Britishers are so stiff & ceremonious!' Frances Wells, who seldom lost an opportunity to assert her lack of interest in the social scene, declared that she had been 'quite overwhelmed with morning visitors since our arrival [in Allahabad] and quite dread returning them all, it is such a bore making new acquaintances: there is only one regiment here besides ours [the 11th] and a great many civilians; I do not admire any of the 11th . . . ' Furthermore, Allahabad, she was informed, was 'a very stupid place, but at any rate it cannot be worse than Barrackpore and I am quite indifferent about society now as I am perfectly happy with my husband and child so do not care if I never see a creature.'

Other ladies complained that their lives were ruled by a deluge of chits. These were little slips of paper that ladies were in the habit of writing to each other, to say that they had called or intended to call, or could not call upon them for some reason but would do so as soon as they were able. The ritual of leaving calling cards was observed with far more rigour in India than in England. When Peggy Pusinelli set off for India as the bride of a Gunner officer in 1939, she took with her a set of calling cards that, on the advice of old India hands, she had had printed. 'When you got there you walked around the cantonment and dropped your card off at people's homes if they weren't there. Then you'd probably meet them: they'd call on you or invite you to call on them. You had to call on the colonel's wife and the adjutant's wife, but you had to wait your turn: you had to wait until they asked you to call on them as they were senior wives. Good Lord yes, you couldn't get out of step by calling on them, you absolutely had to keep your place in the hierarchy . . . Of course all that went by the board when the war came.'

The business of calling, cards and chits could seem tedious at times, particularly as it meant that one always had to dress formally every morning with hair properly coiffured on the off-chance that a caller might appear, for it would never do to be found déshabillé. But it did at least provide a focus for women who, if their children were not at home, found that time weighed heavily on their hands. 'It is nearly impossible to give people at home the slightest idea of the monotonousness of a lady's life [in India],' wrote one lady visitor to the country in the 1850s. By the 1930s the same complaint was still being heard.

Daphne Hill enjoyed her privileged existence as an army daughter in Rawalpindi, North West India, where she and her sister and another pair of girls of a similar age were known by the collective sobriquet of the 'Pindi Poppets' by their numerous admirers among the subaltern fraternity. It was a time when the army was engaged in a fierce campaign against the tribesmen of Waziristan, and every fortnight a new lot of officers came down to Rawalpindi on leave with money to spend. As she admits, 'Even I got worn out, dancing and poodlefaking [flirting] . . . I'd wear a different evening dress every night – it was like being a debutante.' She sometimes rode for miles across the hills to attend functions in other stations, wearing jodhpurs under her evening dress which would be hitched up round her waist. She spent many a happy day playing tennis and drinking cocktails at the club, the centre of the social scene in most army stations. Nonetheless, she was deeply conscious that theirs was a rarified and somewhat purposeless existence: 'There was not a great deal for the women to do except be social.'

In the days of carriages and horses, a staple of the social scene in India was the nightly drive out to the racecourse or along the main road of cantonments, which could take on the appearance of a fashion parade in the larger stations. One newcomer to India noted that the nightly scene on Calcutta racecourse was, in some respects, 'very like home. Gentlemen on splendid Arabs are bending beside carriages in which recline languid ladies with the newest possible Paris bonnets on; pretty pale children go out for their airing in fairy equipages; graceful girls ride by, with the very same hats you saw a month or two ago in Rotten-row [Hyde Park]. Half shutting my eyes, I often fancied myself in the Park again; only here all the children are lying back sound asleep, exhausted with the heat. All the ladies look pale and weary, and the gentlemen tired and melancholy.'

Frances Wells, arriving in Calcutta in 1854, forgot her customary disapproval of frivolity long enough to enjoy 'a delightful drive' on the course, 'which was unusually gay owing to a regatta going on. The ladies here are excessively smart and pink is the predominating colour for bonnets: I am almost the only person with pink in my cheeks, and I notice that ladies' pallor is very much in proportion to the number of children they have with them: for all down to the babies are taken out on the Course, to "eat the air" as the natives express it.'

Keeping up with fashion was somewhat easier in Calcutta, where shiploads of new passengers arrived daily, wearing the latest London styles, and where the city was packed with tailors and emporia full of material. It took many months for innovations in fashion to reach the more remote stations. Getting the requisite materials and a tailor sufficiently well versed in European clothing was even harder. Those who had clothes sent out from England frequently found that by the time the boxes arrived (often having been lost several times en route) the longed-for items they contained were barely worth the wait. 'Many anxious expectants of Paris millinery, after patiently waiting a whole year for the appearance of the bonnet which is to electrify the station, and writing unweariedly to every postmaster on the road for information, finds the missing box has been peacefully reposing in some out-of-the-way receiving-house, and the contents are of course faded and old-fashioned; or having perhaps been fished up out of some river on the road, the finery that was to have totally eclipsed and struck envy into the heart of every other lady in the place, is reduced to an indistinguishable mass.'

In the face of such obstacles, and of the ravages wrought by an unforgiving climate, frequent bouts of illness and the exhausting business of childbearing, it is hard not to feel sorry for those ladies whose fresh-faced charms faded so rapidly in the East. Emily Eden encountered some of these unfortunates at a ball in Delhi and commented acidly: 'It did not look well for the beauty of Delhi, that the painted ladies of one regiment, who are generally called "the little corpses" (and very hard it is too upon most corpses) were much the prettiest people there, and were besieged with partners.' She was equally disparaging about the wives at another military station, Kurnaul, mocking their outmoded apparel. One appeared in a turban, 'made I think of stamped tin moulded into two fans', while Mrs Z was 'simply attired in a plain coloured gown made of a very few yards of sarcenet'. By the twentieth century the shorter journey times to India and within it have somewhat ironed out such discrepancies. Copies of *Tatler* and *Vogue*, posted by helpful relatives at home, were presented to *durzis* (tailors) who would be able to produce passable imitations within a few days.

In the debilitating heat, keeping up appearances in society was no easy matter. Aside from the vexing question of how to keep one's wardrobe refreshed and up-to-date so as not to appear too often in the same dresses (a real difficulty in regimental society and in small garrisons where the same people attended every social function), there was the problem of maintaining one's figure, complexion and hair. Some women lost alarming amounts of weight, while others, struck by torpor and lassitude, grew stout and matronly. More distressingly a number of women found that their hair fell out (usually as a result of illness). Emily Eden came across one army wife who had been unable to procure a wig in her remote station and so was reduced to covering her baldness rather ineffectually with a brown silk cushion fastened on top of her head. Another woman who had had the forethought to pack two lovely plaits of (false) hair when she travelled to India to guard against the possible ravages of fever on her tresses was mortified when the bag containing them was stolen when the ship docked at Suez on the journey out. 'What use will my beautiful false hair be to those nasty Arabs?' she complained crossly. 'They can't wear it, and will just offer it for sale to the next set of passengers.'

In stations where there were only a handful of women, married or otherwise, even the least fashionable and attractive females could expect to find themselves assailed with social invitations and besieged with partners at dances. Not all women wished to avail themselves of the social opportunities on offer. Frances Wells thought it scandalous for married women to dance and avoided any social function where such an iniquitous activity might take place. Others happily threw themselves into the social scene, attending every dance and polo match and enthusiastically participating in the amateur dramatic scene that sprung up in larger garrisons.

For soldiers' wives who, unlike the ladies, did not have the luxury of delegating all their childcare and household work to a small army of servants, nor a carriage in which to take the air on the course, the social opportunities were rather different. There was, of course, the canteen, where Paddy Burn made her fortune with her tin baby filled with rum. There were also dances for the soldiers and their families, and all-ranks balls to which the whole regiment was invited.

Another popular entertainment among all ranks was picnicking, a pastime that was enthusiastically exported from Georgian and Victorian England across the empire. Mrs Ilbert, arriving in Quebec in 1807, was pleased to learn that even in winter, 'There are frequently very pleasant excursions, made by parties into the country, they are Pic Nic parties where each person takes something towards the Entertainment, they drive to some house a few miles from Quebec, carry a Fidler with them & when they have finished their repast, they rise & dance until they agree upon separating, when the curricles [carriages] are ordered & the parties jovially return to their habitations, some get overturned but no accidents are ever met with but they only fall on a bed of snow, have a roll or two, to the great amusement of the Spectators, get up, shake themselves & resume their seats.' In Burma too, Major Sainsbury reported that when the fiercest heat of the summer was over, 'the death rate dropped and morale lifted. Picnics took place along the river Irawadi [sic], open air concerts were held and a relaxed atmosphere prevailed.'

Climate greatly influenced the liveliness or otherwise of the social scene in many postings. As she was nearing Quebec Mrs Ilbert heard that another convoy, heading in the other direction, included among its passengers the Governor of Quebec's wife and her family who were returning to England until spring as she found winter in Canada 'so dreadfully dull!!' The reason, as Mrs Ilbert discovered on her arrival, was that the difficulty of traversing the Atlantic in the winter meant that throughout the season there were few newcomers to invigorate the population. 'When the last ship sails, the inhabitants of Quebec set about being as sociable as possible and frequently they never see the face of a stranger until May, & the moment one appears in the Town, the news spreads like wild fire, & the poor unfortunate being excites as much attention & curiosity as if he were laden with all the affairs of Europe – After having daily (almost hourly) seen the same set of faces, for nearly 6 months together, think what a delightful refreshment gazing at a new Countenance must afford.' The absence of fresh faces had its compensations, as she admitted. 'There is a dreadful lack of beauty in Quebec – you will have no difficulty in believing this when I tell you I am one of the first rate belles, you see I have gained an eminence by travelling which in England I should not have attained in an hundred years.'

Some women found it difficult to adapt to the regimented, masculine-dominated way of army life. Iris Portal, used to the cultured, comparatively cosmopolitan society of Government House, Nagpur, found some elements of her new life with the army a rude shock. As well as being disappointed by the primitive little bungalow in Poona that was her first married home, she found the prescribed pursuits of an officer's wife stultifyingly dull. In a cavalry regiment these consisted chiefly of watching their husbands playing polo 'every single bloomin' afternoon' and endless conversations about how much to pay the servants. As a new bride in the 1920s, she did not easily adapt to living in a community that 'did not really cater for women, but it did teach one to be self-reliant. It was the custom for unmarried officers (the majority in those days) to visit the bungalows of the married for drinks on Sunday before lunch and sometimes before dinner on weekdays. I noticed very few came to us and as I knew Squire to be popular, I was anxious. "Bertie", I asked one friendly youth, "why don't more people come and see us?" He was embarrassed. "Well," he finally managed to blurt out, "It has got about that you read poetry". "Bother them all", I thought. "I have never read it aloud." ' Four decades on, another new bride, Melissa Cordingly, encountered similar prejudices. 'I always remember being surprised and thinking that the men in the army didn't seem to, other than army interests, have other interests, like artistic or creative interests. And I then realised that they all did, but they didn't actually speak about them much because in those days it was a bit sissy to.'

In overseas postings there was the vexed question of how much or whether one could mix with the natives. In Canada, pre-Revolutionary America and Australia, army communities mixed freely with the local white population. In India, Burma, China and the West Indies, however, socialising with indigenous locals was a more complicated matter. In India in particular, the position of women in society and the caste system made it difficult for Englishwomen to meet their Indian counterparts, should they wish to (which many of them avowedly did not: mixing informally with people with dark skins and non-Christian faiths was not the social norm, as evidenced by the furore that surrounded Bonny Byrne's relationship with her Nawab, even before the Mutiny). Once again, it was on the march and on campaign that rules relaxed and opportunities for meeting Indians occurred.

Fanny Duberly received an invitation from the Rao (ruler) of Burj when she accompanied her husband's regiment on campaign through India in 1858. As the only white woman with the column, she was an object of curiosity to the locals as much as they were to her. To her delight, she was invited into the ladies' apartments to meet the ranees (the rao's wives). 'I never saw such a profusion of jewellery in my life,' she marvelled. 'The forehead of each was hidden by a circular ornament of precious stones, and even their eyelids were fringed with diamonds. The ladies examined my watch and bracelets very minutely . . . ' Frances Wells was similarly thrilled to be invited to the palace of the Rajah of Burdwarn, a magnificent marble edifice with walls inlaid with mirrors. After being served a sumptuous banquet by his French cook, she was shown to his dressing room where 'I counted 24 pairs of slippers under his table and there were heaps and heaps of shawls worked with gold and sewn with pearls. I coveted some of these extremely.' Although she was disappointed at being unable to meet his wife, it was some compensation to be shown his menagerie where he 'had kept all the beasts in a starving state for our amusement'.

A century later, Bette Viner was lucky enough to be invited to visit the harem of a local Amir when she was living in Aden in the mid-1960s with her brigadier husband. Leaving their male driver some distance off, she and two female friends, one British and one American, climbed several flights of steps to the top two floors of the five-storey building where the harem was located. At the top they were greeted by a tiny, frail girl painted in henna, the Amir's wife, who ushered them in and sat down facing them on some cushions. From a vast tea kettle she produced cups of strong tea infused with cardomon seeds, served with dry cake. More women began drawing closer, but with very few words of common language between them conversation was difficult, and the encounter grew stilted. It was then that Mrs Viner's American friend Olga came to the rescue.

'She shot to her feet saying "Gee, I reckon they like to dance." She executed a few gay little steps in the middle of a large Persian rug and fortunately they got the message almost at once. One of the women ducked under an old brass bedstead at the far end of the room and produced an old gramophone with an enormous horn, also some Arabian and Hungarian (Heaven knows how they came to be there) records. Olga jived energetically and was rewarded with a belly dance from an immensely fat servant. I was called upon to perform a short ballet sequence and a young concubine retaliated with a passage from a sinuously seductive looking tribal dance. Our British lady friend flatly refused to make a fool of herself as a solo turn but did condescend to lead a conga round the harem. Everyone joined in except the Amir's wife who remained faithful to her tea kettle, but she smiled happily on us all. The women quickly found out how it was done and shouted and laughed and turned the music up louder and louder. When it was finally time to go the Amir's wife gave us each a gourd of local honey. Our Arab driver, waiting at a distance of about 100 yards, was grinning from ear to ear when he saw us and I realised with horror that the noise we had made must have burst through the slits in the walls in the harem and resounded across the desert. I hoped the Amir would not be angry and was consequently relieved, when I met him a few days later, and he told me that his family had enjoyed our visit very much indeed . . . '

Socialising with the local community could be a complicated business, even for those living closer to home. For families in Northern Ireland, particularly during the 1970s and 1980s, the political climate and security restrictions made it hard to mix with local people. Marion Weston, living in Lisburn in the late 1980s found it difficult to explain to her children that 'if they met an Irish friend that was fine, but if they then asked them to go to the cinema with them, they couldn't. I had an absolute stand up row with Roger [her teenage son] over that, because he wanted to go and simply couldn't understand why he couldn't. But of course if they went their voices immediately gave them away. And how can you tell a child not to say anything?' The danger was that, if their English voices were heard, they might have been kidnapped. How real this risk was it was not possible to say, but it was certainly perceived as a serious enough threat that Army children could not be allowed to mix freely in Irish society. The Army worked hard to compensate for such limitations, organising an endless round of activities and parties for army children, and as a result the Westons' children found that life in Northern Ireland resembled a holiday camp. Another bonus was that they lived 'beyond the wire', outside the peri- meters of the army camp, which lent their existence an air of normality.

For those living behind the barbed wire fences, with dogs patrolling and spotlights shining by night, even the simplest outing was attended by restrictions. Chrissie Collis, who lived in Omagh from 1975 to 1977 with her then husband, an army helicopter pilot, recalls, 'There were bombs going off all over the place, with monotonous regularity. We were surrounded by barbed wire and guarded by tracker dogs . . . whenever you went in and out of camp your car was searched for bombs. The sentries would use mirrors on long metal poles to look under the car and search inside it. You couldn't park in town centres, you weren't allowed to for security reasons [British cars were obvious bomb targets]. You had to park outside town and then walk in, and walk back again carrying all your shopping: quite a performance with two small boys [both under the age of two]. Shopping trips could take a long time.' But for Chrissie the vibrant social life of Omagh compensated for such drawbacks. 'It was very sociable, inside and outside the camp.' As well as regular dinner parties within the army community, to which the men came armed with their personal weapons and were frequently summoned away for duty by a telephone call, there were visits to and from local people from the Protestant community. 'They were very brave because frequently they lived in large, rambling, crumbling houses and frequently the husbands and wives were serving part time in the UDR which made them targets for the IRA, and entertaining the army put them at further risk. One local family we used to entertain, and vice versa, had their house burned to the ground. The IRA always knew who was visiting who.'

Deborah Richards found the army social life in Antrim 'incredibly tedious', because 'it was the same old people again and again and the local "chain gang" who had to be entertained – the mayor and so on. Much more fun were the incredibly nice local families who used to invite us for things and were incredibly grateful we were there.'

If fraternising with locals was fraught with complications, so too was mixing with people of different ranks within the army community. In India in the 1930s, Daphne Hill and her friends would sometimes get invited to dances at the Sergeants' Mess: 'But that wasn't such fun as, although they were very nice, it was very stilted. They wouldn't talk to you. It was the class thing. And you couldn't date a soldier – if, as an officer's daughter, you had fallen in love with a soldier, either he would be posted away or you would, to put a stop to it. It wasn't done.' When Dorothy Cook's husband became an officer she had to make new friends befitting his rank: officers' wives were not expected to mix too freely with soldiers' wives. Dorothy resented the application of hierarchy to every aspect of their lives and concluded, 'The army is the most snobbish of all careers . . . It is hardly ever the men, they are probably more broadminded than their wives. But some wives are truly hard to understand. It seldom occurs with the women of quality, they are naturally kind and helpful, but the ones who really "got my goat" had nothing to boast about in their own upbringing and background.'

Sometimes it could be the women themselves who were reluctant to move up the social ladder. The history of the Gloucestershire Regiment relates the tale of Bet Buffet, who ruled the ranks of the soldiers' wives at the end of the eighteenth century, and who was 'a true daughter of the Regiment, and privileged to call everyone, from the Colonel down-ward, by their Christian names'. When her husband, a sergeant major, was promoted to ensign (an officer's rank) as reward for his good conduct, the younger officers went over to his quarters to congratulate him. Ensign Buffet received them, and on being asked where Mrs Buffet was replied with some embarrassment that he did not know. Lieutenant Browne went off to find her and came upon her sitting on a three-legged stool by the fire in the communal kitchen, smoking a clay pipe and wearing a soldier's jacket thrown over her shoulders and a battered straw hat, back to front.

> 'Why Bet – Mrs Buffet I mean, how is it you aren't receiving your husband's brother officers in the parlour?' asked Lieutenant Browne.
>
> 'And is that all you're troubling about, Johnny?'
>
> 'Of course it is. We want to see you doing your duty at your husband's side on such a great occasion.'
>
> 'I know my duty, Johnny, as well as ere a soldier in the Regiment, but duty o' the like you say will cheat me out of my pipe of baccy and my chimbley corner, and I'll tell you what, old cock, the King may make my Jack a Gentleman if he likes, but I'm blessed if either he, nor the Sultan of the Ingees, can make Bet Buffet a lady! So now, Johnny my boy, you may trot; you've got my answer.'

This kind of self-imposed segregation can still remain a problem today. 'Soldiers' wives will never come to our houses,' explained one officer's wife regretfully, 'and they don't want their children mixing with ours.' Some younger officers' wives, though, believe that such barriers are slowly crumbling. 'I've got more in common with a soldier's wife who's running her own business than an officer's wife who's never worked,' declared one.

The limitations of army society is a theme that frequently recurs among army wives, from the eighteenth century to today. Although they might move house frequently, because the regiment moves together their social circle remains the same (although officers are posted outside the regiment they return to it regularly). Friends, or enemies, made in the first few days of their married life are likely to remain with them for the next twenty years. Moreover the cheek-by-jowl arrangement of army 'patches' (married quarters), and the fact that, abroad, most of their social life is conducted within the regiment or garrison community, produces, say some wives, a society so inward-looking as to be 'almost incestuous' as one described it, breeding gossip, scandal and intrigue. It was this that deterred Samantha Roberts from living in married quarters. 'It's always the same people, same conversations, everyone knows if you've had an argument. It's so unhealthy. It's like *EastEnders*.'

Yet for all the hierarchy and formality, the gossip and occasional back-biting, most army wives insist that their time spent with the army has been the happiest of their lives. For some, it is the unusual experiences that army life provides that compensate for the discomforts and drawbacks of their unstable lifestyle. How many civilian women could dance the conga in a harem, enjoy the hospitality of headhunters in Borneo, or eat a three-course dinner off silver service in an underground bunker in Northern Ireland? Other wives have found fulfilment in the close friendships that military life can foster. Frequently thrown together with their fellow women when their husbands are sent away for long periods, from the 'grass widows' of India to the 'abandoned' wives who wave their husbands off to Northern Ireland, Kosovo or Iraq, army women have responded by forming close bonds.

Wives whose husbands are serving in conflict zones today pay tribute to the support they receive from each other in the absence of their men. When, in October 2004, days before they were due to return home, soldiers from the Black Watch were redeployed on a hazardous mission into Iraq's notorious 'triangle of death' near Baghdad, their families were both disappointed and desperately worried. Within days the regiment had taken casualties: one man died in a traffic accident, three soldiers were killed by a suicide bomber and a fourth by a roadside bomb a few days later. The news devastated the bereaved relatives and increased the feelings of fear and dread among the other families. United by their anxiety, and by the regiment's strong family ethos, the wives leant on each other for support. One woman, pregnant with her second child, was profoundly grateful for the friendship of her fellow wives when the time came for her to give birth. One babysat for her toddler while two others drove her to hospital and assisted during her labour.

On the other hand, a gunner officer's wife found such sisterly behaviour noticeably lacking when her husband was allowed to come back from the Iraq war early to be by her side for their baby's birth after a difficult pregnancy. She found herself the target of bitter comments from women whose husbands remained out there and thought that she had indulged in special pleading.

But the predominant feeling is that the friendship of fellow wives is not only rewarding but vital in times of adversity. 'The wonderful thing about army life is that you make such terrific friends', is the sentiment repeated again and again by wives both past and present. Such friendships were tested to the utmost when women were caught up in the thick of war, thrown together for lengthy periods, struggling to survive – and, in the peculiarly taxing conditions of a siege, unable to escape.

IO

Under Siege

Never probably, indeed, has the noble character of Englishwomen shone
with more real brightness than during this memorable siege. Far from
being in our way, they were ever a source of comfort and help to us;
ready to tend the sick, to soothe and comfort the dying, and to
cheer and sustain the living by all those numberless offices of
love and affection which woman only understands.

Martin Gubbins, survivor of the siege of Lucknow, 1857

While wartime may always have brought violence close to the army
wife and her family, there was a particular horror attached to living
through a full-blown siege. The defenders had to contend not only with
the threat of attack, but isolation and claustrophobia, as well as severe shortages of food, clothing and medicines. The longer the siege continued the
more acute these deficiencies became and the greater the toll on the health
of the besieged men, women and children.

The popular imagination may see sieges as a feature of medieval
warfare, complete with battering rams, catapults and boiling oil poured over
battlements – but every age sees their equivalents as military technology
develops. In a momentous twentieth-century siege, of the island of Malta
in the Second World War, the weapons were bombs and bullets, delivered
in the most intense aerial bombardment the world had ever seen. From
June 1940, first Italian then German aircraft pounded the island. At the
end of 1941, after Hitler demanded that Malta be 'neutralised', the

bombardment intensified with hundreds of German bombers pounding the island daily, while U-boats cut supply routes. Civilians and soldiers alike suffered terrible shortages of food and materials, yet against tremendous odds they held out. In April 1942, when the islanders had suffered 117 days of continuous attack, their formidable courage was recognised by the awarding of the George Cross to the whole island – a unique tribute. The siege was effectively lifted at the end of 1942.

Whatever the armament, besieger and besieged are always in a battle of attrition. The British army has been on both sides of the barricades, with different outcomes, many times during its history. Gibraltar endured the longest siege: nearly four grim years, from June 1779 to February 1783. Like Malta in later years, it is still celebrated for the fortitude shown by the British garrison – and their wives. This same grit and determination were to the fore in the siege of Cadiz (1810–12) during the Peninsular War, most remarkably in the attack on the outlying fort of Matagorda. Here, in 1810, a small garrison held out against a ferocious bombardment in appalling conditions, again shared by soldiers and their families alike. And as much as in greater engagements, one individual, in this case an army wife, showed outstanding heroism and self-sacrifice.

Not all sieges are part of a planned military strategy. The sieges of Lucknow and Cawnpore erupted from the tumult of the Indian Mutiny of 1857–8, where elements of the local population rose up against the colonial power. There were other beleaguered towns during this terrible time, but these two demonstrate both extraordinary suffering and extraordinary resistance on the part of the men, women and children involved.

When the siege of Gibraltar began in the summer of 1779 Mrs Miriam Green, the wife of the Chief Engineer, Colonel William Green, was taken by surprise – like the rest of the population of the garrison from the Governor downwards. Gibraltar had been in British hands for seventy-five years, and relations between the garrison and its Spanish neighbours had always seemed amicable. British soldiers regularly rode out into the countryside where they were usually warmly received, not least by the young Spanish maidens. The Governor of Gibraltar, General John Eliott, and Don Joaquín Mendoza, the governor of San Roque, the Spanish settlement that overlooked Gibraltar, frequently entertained each other.

Spain had declared war on Britain on 16 June but, with poor communications, the news was not to reach Gibraltar until 6 July. When, on 19 June, therefore, General Eliott and his staff paid a visit to Mendoza, they were in happy ignorance. It was noticed, though, that Mendoza was rather less hospitable than normal. Mrs Green, whose husband had attended, recorded later in her journal, 'He [Mendoza] Did not receive this visit, as He ought to have done, but Seem'd uneasy, the whole time they Staid – which was not very long – as He did not even ask them to Partake of any Refreshment ...,...' The following day English officers were prevented from crossing through into Spain to go riding, as was their normal practice, and all those who were already on the Spanish side of the line were bundled unceremoniously back into Gibraltar. When, on 21 June, the mail failed to arrive from San Roque, it became apparent that all communication between mainland Spain and Gibraltar had been cut off. The siege had begun.

On the morning of 26 June, the Spanish were observed setting up a military camp on the common of San Roque. Although the message that Britain and Spain were now at war had still not been received from London, the reality was already apparent. Mrs Green, having recovered no doubt from the first shock, was now almost more affronted than afraid, noting crisply that, 'As it is not to be doubt'd, but the Intention of the Spainards [sic], is to attack this Garrison – I shall therefore from this time, call them – *The Enemy* – when ever I have occasion to speak of them.'

This enmity had in fact long been simmering: whatever outward appearances, the British presence in Gibraltar (which had begun in 1704) had been a source of intense irritation to Spain, which had been seeking an opportunity to pick a quarrel that would provide the pretext for an attack. In 1779, with Britain pouring resources into the increasingly problematic campaign against her rebellious subjects in the American colonies, Spain saw her chance. France had already declared war on Britain in February 1778. So Britain now faced a trio of hostile powers who made it their business to open up conflict on as many fronts as possible.

Gibraltar stands at the tip of an isthmus, its famous rock rising up into the sky, with a narrow neck of land at its north side. On the east the rock juts up abruptly from the water, while the west side slopes gently into the sea. It constitutes an almost ideal defensive position. Siege was therefore the most logical form of attack. Indeed, it was such an obvious strategy that Gibraltar had already been besieged thirteen times in its history. This siege, the fourteenth, became known as the Great Siege. The Spanish strategy was to cut off supplies to the garrison by blockading it by sea: the waters between Gibraltar and the North African coast, which were usually plied by merchant ships of every nationality, would be patrolled by hostile vessels. The Spanish planned to bombard the besieged population with heavy artillery from a camp on the other side of the isthmus, thus terrifying and starving the British into submission without the need for a frontal assault.

Although the British had not seriously anticipated this eventuality from their Spanish friends, they had long taken precautions, companies of engineers working hard to fortify Gibraltar's defences. At this time there was an engineer corps of 122 officers and men, commanded by Colonel Green; the main army presence comprised 5,832 officers and men under General Eliott, with Lieutenant General Robert Boyd second in command. As well as the garrison there was the civilian population of around 4,000, composed mainly of British, Jews and Moors, among them merchants and traders, milliners and bakers and, as Governor Eliott darkly observed, 'many suspicious characters'.

For Mrs Miriam Green, living with her husband and five-year-old daughter Charlotte in a comfortable house with a pretty garden, life in Gibraltar had been congenial enough. And in the early stages of the siege, it retained a degree of normality – though not helped, according to Mrs Green, by the local naval commander, Admiral Duff. She deplored his apparent disinclination to send out his ships either to intercept enemy vessels or to make the run for supplies themselves. Whenever a ship did manage to break through the blockade with stores from the Barbary coast or elsewhere it was an occasion for great rejoicing. As well as the occasional merchant ship or privateer bearing supplies, packet ships carrying mail managed to pass through the blockade with reasonable regularity, so Mrs Green and her fellow besieged were not entirely cut off from the outside world. More often, however, British ships were chased away or captured by the Spaniards, to the intense frustration of the watching inhabitants and members of the garrison who could observe all activity in the harbour from the Rock. Even when the Spanish ships left the bay empty, Admiral Duff failed to bring in waiting ships.

There was an element of the theatrical about the siege in the first couple of months. 'It now became quite fashionable,' Mrs Green remarked in August 1779, 'to get all the News, each one could Collect, & by way of Gaining all that anybody was using spy Glasses from Morning to Night . . . it was realy Laughable enough, to see, with what a Jealous Eye; each Aid de Camp looked at the other, fearing *He* should be the first to communicate his *Ideas.*'

By September 1779 the Spaniards, although busily engaged in building siege batteries, had still not fired a hostile shot. The British used the lull to practise artillery and improve their defences, but eventually Governor Eliott grew tired of waiting, and decided that the British would make the first strike. On 12 September the new bride of Lieutenant Skinner was allotted the honour of lighting the touch paper of the cannon and thus firing the first shot, which landed just short of the Spanish lines beyond Gibraltar. As Mrs Green reported: 'We kept up a very heavy Cannonading for an hour; Most off the Garrison got upon the Hill –I never heard such a noise in my life . . . It is not easy to discribe the hurry that this Days business Involved any body In – as it was supposed The Enemy would Soon Answer our Salutes, I have already Mentioned, that many of the Shop Keepers were removing Their Goods & c great quantitys were already gone; & This Day made them truely Anxious to remove what was still left – for This business, every Person had full imployment Porters running here, & there . . . ' She sent off her valuables to a store house out of the line of fire, but determined to remain in her house.

The Spaniards still refrained from firing on the besieged garrison, apparently determined that victory would be won by means of starvation. And indeed, as the blockade went on, so the situation worsened. Winter brought stormier seas and dwindling supplies of fruit, vegetables and meat.

Continuingly incensed by Admiral Duff's inertia, and after watching a Swedish ship loaded with supplies for Gibraltar being captured by a Spanish vessel, Mrs Green confided to her journal: 'We were deprived of Many Articals this Garrison stood in great need off, particularly Coals, as the owners were Certain there was a Large Quantity on board; about this time; Mr Holliday, the principle Baker in this Garrison, refused to Bake – owing to the Want of Wood – He had at this time, 55 Sacks of Flour left – the Govr took them all away except two, which He allowed him to keep for his Family.'

Shortly after Christmas, when it seemed that both garrison and inhabitants were in real danger of starving through the lack of firewood and flour, a miracle seemingly occurred. Just a few days after the bakers had ceased baking, a vast supply of wood was washed ashore and eagerly gathered up by soldiers and inhabitants. The price of food now began to soar and the predicament of those who could not afford to buy meat or other expensive foodstuffs grew worse. Captain Drinkwater, who published a history of the siege a few years after it ended, noted that officers and soldiers received only a bare pittance from the victualling office on which it was nigh impossible to support their families. 'A soldier, with his wife and three children, would inevitably have been starved to death, had not the generous contribution of his corps relieved his family: one woman actually died through want; and many were so enfeebled that it was not without great attention they recovered: thistles, dandelion, wild leeks & c were for sometime the daily nourishment of numbers.'

By January 1780 the situation had become so desperate that General Eliott proposed sending home 'all useless mouths amongst which many women and children, who upon their arrival in England will need some assistance till they are in a way of getting their bread'. The rule he imposed (although how effectually it was enforced is unclear) was that wives and children who had not got a year's provisions of flour and biscuit each must leave Gibraltar. Many did indeed leave that month, unmolested by the Spaniards (though not all refugee-bearing ships were so fortunate). Others later wished they had done so while they had the chance. Catherine Upton, an ensign's wife who kept her own journal of the siege, described the sufferings of the poorer families: 'I cannot now recollect the distress of a poor woman, without feeling a pang at my heart which gives me a sensible uneasiness. She sat weeping at my door with two children, the one about seven years old, the other an infant which she suckled: after the former had repeatedly asked her for bread, she laid down her youngest child, and gave her breast to her other son, saying, Suck me to death at once!'

On 14 January deliverance came again. An English store ship appeared on the horizon. A sloop of war was sent out to escort it into the harbour and relief turned to exultation when the ship's officers relayed the news that they were part of a large British convoy that was approaching Gibraltar. The next day, the convoy, commanded by Admiral Rodney, bore down to the south-east of Cape St Vincent (on the south-westerly tip of Portugal) where it met a fleet of Spanish men of war. The encounter resulted in a resounding victory for the British. The Spanish fleet was almost destroyed, and its admiral captured and brought into Gibraltar Bay as a prisoner. As well as much needed supplies, the fleet was carrying a thousand-strong regiment of Highlanders who had originally been intended to reinforce the garrison at Minorca. Governor Eliott persuaded their commander to remain in Gibraltar where their manpower was urgently needed to shore up the strength of the garrison.

As winter wore on, food supplies dwindled and the spectre of disease began to stalk the besieged garrison. In the previous November smallpox had broken out in a household in the town. By the end of February 1780 several children had died, but Governor Eliott would not listen to pleas that the populace be inoculated to prevent the disease from spreading further. Mrs Green, like many other mothers fearful for their children, was greatly distressed by this refusal. 'All Means are try'd to obtain Leave to Innoculate, but as Yet to no purpose,' she wrote on 25 February 1780. By Easter Day, a month later, smallpox was 'raging greatly. No Innoculations Yet!' And the following Monday 'Children Dieing every Day'. Even when the disease spread to the soldiers, the Governor remained obdurate, insisting 'He Could not answer it to his conscience!' to inoculate, leaving Mrs Green and her fellow mothers angry and frustrated. 'What the Govs Meaning is, I know not. I think He should make a point of getting this Cruel Disorder over as Soon as possible,' she wrote angrily.

In May, Mrs Green's daughter Charlotte began to sicken with a violent fever. Mrs Green's worst fears were confirmed when the doctor diagnosed smallpox. However, once the spots had erupted, Charlotte's condition began to improve. Her violent fever abated, 'she grew more cool & composed – She is keep in the Air – and Drinks Cold Drink – chiefly Toast & Water'. Within a week of being diagnosed she was convalescing and within a fortnight had fully recovered. But just as she was out of danger, the Greens' maid succumbed to the disease and within a fortnight was dead. Mrs Green was too upset to write very much in her journal, confining herself to lamenting once more the Governor's negligence

Although to Mrs Green the Governor's attitude was inexplicable and disgraceful, there were many who shared his distrust of vaccination at that time. The practice of variolation, injecting smallpox pus into a healthy person to trigger immunity to the variola virus that caused the disease, had been introduced in Britain in 1717. It produced a mild dose of the disease, which would give immunity from future infection. But sometimes the recipient would pass the disease on to others and an epidemic would occur, creating much suspicion of the practice. Some members of the clergy were also deeply distrustful of variolation, believing it to be immoral.

Mrs Green, however, continued to believe that the Governor's attitude derived not from legitimate concerns but negligence, or even more Machiavellian motives. In her journal entry for 6 June 1780 she reported a disturbing rumour that was gaining currency in the garrison: 'It can not be wonder'd that the Lower Degrees of People should be much hurt at all these bad times – their Provisions so bad – Nothing to be got to assist them, or their poor familys and the losing so many fine Children, has been a heavy Stroke upon them – but We hear – that a great Person in the Garrison says – He thinks it, a fortunate Circumstance to those Soldiers who have Large familys to Lose three or four Children.'

Could the Governor, or one of his senior advisers, really have believed such a thing? It seems unlikely, but Governor Eliott was frequently accused (not least by Mrs Green) of not doing enough to help the 'lower degrees'. In May 1780, when the price of meat had risen again, he declined to intervene to fix its price, even though it was now beyond the pockets of poorer families. The price of food, and the morale of the besieged garrison, fluctuated wildly according to the success (or failure) of British ships in penetrating the blockade. After Admiral Rodney's gallant mission in January, no further convoys arrived, but many merchant ships, both British and foreign, managed to run the blockade, although as they tended to sell their cargo to the highest bidder this brought little relief to the poor.

As well as smallpox, the lack of fresh food was causing scurvy to spread among hungry families. By November 1780 the only beef available was 'quite Rotten, & stinking' according to Mrs Green, and scurvy was rampant. By the end of the siege 500 soldiers had died of scurvy, while only 333 were killed by enemy fire. As their wives and children generally received less adequate rations, it is likely that they suffered more acutely and their death rate may have been even higher. Although few men had, until now, deserted, not least because it was extremely difficult to get off the Rock without falling on to the boulders below, now the rate of desertions began to increase with more men prepared to risk a painful death rather than slow starvation.

At the end of September 1780 a ship sailed for Britain bearing letters from Mrs Green to her family, and several passengers who had decided to go home. Mrs Green, her eyeglass trained upon the sea as usual, was vexed to see it being seized by the Spanish and taken into the nearby port of Algeciras.

One of the passengers on the vessel was a Mrs Gladstones, a field officer's wife, and her five children who had been invalided back to Britain because of her fragile health. The spectators on the Rock observed through their eyeglasses the enemy removing Mrs Gladstones and her children from the ship. 'Evry body is greatly concern'd for Her,' wrote Mrs Green anxiously. 'She took a letter from our Govr Disiring if she should be taken, That the Spainards, would forward Her & Family to Farro or to Lisbon.' The following day two more outgoing ships were taken into Algeciras. On board these ships were several officers who had resigned and sold their commissions and were returning back to Britain and civilian life. A delegation of Spanish officers then came over under flag of truce for a parley with their British counterparts. It was agreed that all the women prisoners would be returned to Gibraltar, except for Mrs Gladstones and family. They would be allowed to remain at Algeciras while a special request was made to the government in Madrid for permission to let her proceed to Britain. Mrs Green was pleased to hear that Admiral Barcelo had been 'exceedingly polite' to Mrs Gladstones.

Despite such courtly behaviour, the Spanish continued with their siegeworks, and the lack of supplies continued to bite. In January 1781 the English residents of the Barbary territory, across the water from Gibraltar, were expelled, closing off a useful source of supply to the garrison since many merchant ships had embarked from there. Three more months went by with food prices remaining high and the plight of the poor becoming steadily worse. Some soldiers' families carved out gardens from the rock and sowed them with vegetable seeds. After a spell of wet weather they were rewarded with an abundant harvest.

Then, on the morning of 12 April 1781, a convoy of 100 ships commanded by Admiral Darby broke through the blockade of Spanish gunboats, arrived in the harbour and triumphantly hoisted the British flag. The famished inhabitants gazed with joy upon the huge quantity of stores that began emerging from the ships' holds. But just as the rejoicing began a deafening bombardment suddenly started. The Spanish batteries, for so long silent, opened fire on the harbour, fortifications, military buildings and town. Buildings burst into flame, chunks of masonry came tumbling down and terrified inhabitants ran for the underground bomb shelters

In the confusion of the bombardment, with roofs and buildings collapsing all around, Catherine Upton was running with her two children and would have headed right into danger's path had she not been apprehended by an officer of the 58th Regiment. They cowered for several hours under a covered way as 26-pound shots flew overhead. Some hours later she emerged and picked her way through the rubble to Montague's Bastion, one of the bomb-proofs, where the soldiers told her: '"Never fear madam, if the d——d Dons fire to eternity they will never take the old rock nor the good souls that are upon it". I admired their courage,' she wrote, 'but could not eat any dinner with them agreeable to their kind invitation.'

Although she could not bring herself to eat with the soldiers she had no choice about sleeping among them, for the intensity of the bombardment made it impossible to leave the shelter when night fell. She spent a rest-less night, mortified by the 'disagreeableness of lying near an hundred private soldiers', separated from them as she was by merely a curtain, just as soldiers' wives and daughters were in barracks. After several uncom-fortable nights in Montague's Bastion she moved to another bomb-proof shelter, the King's Bastion. Here, on enquiring as to the cause of its 'dis-agreeable' smell, she was informed that a man had just been killed there by a cannon ball that came through a hole over the door.

A few days later the women and children were moved out of the town and sent to the south of the Rock where they were housed in tents. The town was right in the line of enemy fire and within the first few days of bombardment massive devastation had been wreaked upon the houses and inhabitants, among them many soldiers' families. A contemporary chronicler of the siege painted a bleak picture of their fate: 'A husband is called upon for duty, the service demands his immediate presence, nor dare he stay to take his farewell, By imprinting an affectionate kiss . . . On his return (O sensibility) what a ravaging scene is presented to his view! . . . [His] wife . . . is alas! no more – His dear beloved children that prattled with a thousand innocent and engaging smiles, and lisped forth their duteous accents . . . are now reduced to a lifeless lump of clay. Will not his heart break forth in exclamation, "Oh! My beloved wife – my charming Harry, my amiable Polly; not suffered to kiss those lips while warm, not to press you to a bosom to which you was ever dear." '

Catherine Upton was so eager to get out of the smelly, overcrowded refuge of the King's Bastion that she left the town in the middle of a bombardment: 'My husband carried little Charlotte, while my son Jack ran by my side.' The tent in which they were now housed was not comfort-able, but at least she had some privacy. They were still far from safe from bombardment by the Spanish gunboats that lay off the Rock. On 23 April Mrs Upton and her children had a close escape when a woman in a tent just below theirs was cut in two by a shot as she was drawing on her stockings. Often the gunboats struck at night, and Mrs Upton found herself continually dragging her bewildered children out of their beds to take shelter behind rocks. On 23 May the gunboats were so close to their position that she could hear the Spanish shout, 'Take care, English!' before they fired. Once again she grabbed her children and took shelter behind a rock, but another woman, Mrs Tourale, 'a handsome and agreeable lady, was blown almost to atoms! Nothing was found of her but one arm.'

It was clear that there was no part of the Rock that was safe, and many families now decided that they could no longer show solidarity with their husbands and fathers. They had to get out. On 27 May a convoy of ships sailed for England, passing through the blockade (the Spanish being generally more concerned about ships getting into Gibraltar than out of it). Among their passengers were Mrs Upton and her children.

Mrs Green stayed, despite her failing health. She had now become so weak that she had to be carried to the bomb shelter. Even so, she felt it her duty to remain and support her husband who, as Chief Engineer, carried a heavy responsibility for the defence of the Rock, a burden that often took a heavy toll on him. 'It has been the Utmost desire & attentions of my whole Mind,' she explained, 'to pay evry possible Regard to his Health; the more So; as his Complaints, always fall, upon his Nerves – & occasions, many unpleasing consequences.' She remained in her house, even when shells burst in the air above it. Meanwhile the soldiers' wives, lacking the means to return to England, continued to take their chances in the tents. Mrs Green described the sort of fate that they could expect. In the early hours of 12 June, 'an unlucky accident happened in a Tent belonging to a soldier of the 56th. His wife a very Good young Woman, & a young child of three months, were blown out off the Tent by a Shell . . . They were thrown into a Deep Gully & the Child Tore to pieces; & the Woman much burnt and otherwise wounded.'

The following month, her health shattered, Mrs Green finally left the Rock, sailing to England in a convoy with her young daughter. She died the following year, having never recovered from a chill she caught while sheltering in the bomb-proofs. By the time she left, the level of bombardment was starting to diminish. In September the tempo increased again but in November, in a bold action that took their enemy by surprise, a detachment of British soldiers destroyed most of the Spanish siegeworks. When 1782 dawned, both sides remained grimly determined to succeed in their aim: the Spaniards and their French allies to seize the fortress, the British to hold on to it. The British surrender to the American rebels at Yorktown in October 1781 had served only to stiffen resolve that Gibraltar could not be lost. Both sides devoted much energy to technological innovations by which they hoped to achieve victory. The British worked on producing red-hot shot to fire upon the enemy, while the Spaniards spent several months building floating batteries with which they could surround Gibraltar and pound their enemy into submission.

On 13 September the French and Spaniards launched their grand attack from their fleet of floating batteries, but the garrison retaliated with a shower of red-hot balls that turned the batteries into floating infernos. The Spanish sailors and soldiers frantically tried to save themselves by jumping into the water but many were burned alive, although British sailors rescued several from the water. The following month another convoy broke through, shoring up Gibraltar's supplies once again. Worn down by the garrison's dogged resistance, the French and Spaniards sued for peace in January 1783. When peace was finally declared on 2 February 1783 some of the gaunt, exhausted soldiers were too worn out to cheer, but their stalwart defence of Gibraltar made them heroes at home and turned Gibraltar into a something of a talisman for Britain. The victory went at least some way to restoring battered British pride after the humiliation of losing America (and the island of Minorca, whose garrison of 'old men' had also been besieged by the Spanish but were unable to hold out beyond six months and had to surrender in February 1782). General Eliott was eventually knighted in recognition of his role in defending the fortress, while the regiments who served during the siege won the right to bear the battle honour of Gibraltar on their colours and badges.

The efforts of the wives and daughters who remained to support their men through the years of starvation and bombardment were not publicly recognised, but many men were cheered immeasurably by their company in the darkest moments of a siege.

Thirty years after the hostilities at Gibraltar, Spain and Britain were once more engaged in conflict, but this time as allies – against France, their common foe. A British force held Cadiz, which had become the deposed Spanish government's seat of power, while a French army under Marshal Victor besieged it. The siege began in February 1810 and was not lifted until 1812. One of Cadiz's outlying forts, at Matagorda, was occupied by a detachment of British artillery and a company of the 94th (Scots Brigade) Regiment.

The defences at Matagorda were woefully weak. There were no trenches and few bomb-proof shelters, so several of the families had to live in flimsy huts. In one such dwelling lived Mrs Reston, wife of a sergeant in the 94th, and her four-year-old son. The French blockade prevented supplies coming in, while sporadic shot and shell kept them sheltering in the bomb-proofs or huts much of the time. The commander at Cadiz could do little to help as he too was under siege. On 21 April the French began to concentrate their fire on Matagorda, pouring fire and shell from forty-eight guns and mortars on to the little fort, only about a hundred yards square, whose garrison of 140 soldiers and sailors began to fall rapidly.

One night, Mrs Reston, who had been asleep in her hut, was awakened by a 24-pound shot striking the wall just beside her head. She quickly snatched up her child and took him down to the bomb-proof, then volunteered her services to help the wounded men whose numbers were multiplying by the hour. Tirelessly she tore up her own and her husband's clothes for use as bandages and helped to dress the men's wounds. The injured soldiers were gasping with thirst but there was no water to be had in the shelter. A well lay a few yards away in the centre of the battery but presented a ready target for enemy shot. The surgeon ordered a young drummer boy, probably no more that fourteen, to go and draw a bucket of water. The lad lingered, trembling with fear, as incoming shot continued to fall. Again the surgeon told him to go. Now Mrs Reston stepped in. 'The poor thing's frightened,' she told him, 'and no wonder at it: give it to me and I'll go for it.' So saying, she grabbed the bucket and, amid heavy artillery fire, crossed the battery to the well. As she let down the bucket to fill it the rope was shot out of her hand and cut. Still she did not abandon her task. With the help of a sailor she retrieved the bucket, brought it back filled with water to the wounded men, and continued to tend them. Colonel Napier, who devotes a short paragraph to her action in his history of the Peninsular War, found it difficult to decide whether 'it were most feminine or heroic'. The fact that Mrs Reston (or Retson as he calls her) managed to combine raw courage with being compassionate and maternal made her the perfect icon of female courage.

She must have been tough and capable as well as feminine, for she also took on many of the soldiers' duties. Joseph Donaldson, who was also at Cadiz, related how, in the pauses in the bombardment, 'She carried sand bags for the repair of the battery, handed out ammunition and supplied the men at the guns with wine and water; and when the other two women (who had been in hysterics in one of the bomb-proofs from the time the action had commenced) were leaving the battery, she refused to go.' After thirty hours of bombardment the British commander at Cadiz was able to send some boats across the water to evacuate the survivors. By now nearly half the garrison had been killed, but Mrs Reston, and her husband and child, had survived. Although the shot and shell were still pouring heavily down on the fort she made two separate journeys across the battery to collect her family's possessions. She then made a third trip to rescue her child from the bomb-proof where she had left him until the last possible moment. Years later Donaldson could still picture her 'while shot and shell were flying thick around her, bending her body over it [the child] to shield it from danger by the exposure of her own person'.

To Donaldson's indignation, Mrs Reston received no reward for her intrepid conduct. She had applied to the commander-in-chief of the army for some kind of payment in recognition of her services, but was rejected. When her husband died she was left destitute and ended up in Glasgow's poorhouse, an unjust end for a woman who had shown such humanity and courage. Like most soldiers' wives of that era, she lacked the ability or the inclination to write her memoirs and had no influential supporters to champion her cause when she was in need.

Enduring blockade and bombardment in a time of war was one thing. Being catapulted from a peaceful existence into a state of siege – in which nightmarish horror and savagery became part of life – was another matter entirely. Those who found themselves in such a plight in India in the mid-nineteenth century were utterly unprepared for the change of circumstances. As at Gibraltar, they were stunned that people whom they had thought of as complaisant and accommodating should suddenly strike against them. Here, however, the attack was not so much a stratagem of war but a revolt: the Indian Mutiny that began in May 1857.

The outbreak of the Mutiny, otherwise known as the First War of (Indian) Independence, seized British India with shock. When the first reports began circulating many simply refused to believe that they were true, or that anything of that kind could happen in *their* station or regiment. Although rumblings had been apparent for some time among discontented sepoys (Indian infantrymen) and in the bazaars, few of the ruling political class or the military hierarchy suspected that a widespread uprising would ensue.

Had they kept their ears to the ground, they might have noticed that fears were growing that the British were trying to destroy India's native religions and convert its people wholesale to Christianity. These fears had been stirred up by the activities of Christian missionaries, and by a rumour that arose concerning a new kind of cartridge. These cartridges, it was alleged, contained pig and cow fat, defiling Muslim and Hindu alike. Some seditious rumblings were heard, although many commanding officers were inclined to dismiss them as nothing but grousing by 'over-excitable' natives. Others reacted strongly and by doing so helped to fan the flames.

Colonel Carmichael Smyth of the 3rd Bengal Light Cavalry, stationed at Meerut, arrested all the soldiers who refused to use the new cartridges and had them court-martialled and sentenced to ten years' hard labour. On 9 May 1857 they were publicly humiliated by being stripped of their uniforms, shackled and led away. The following night, taunted by prostitutes from the local bazaar, a band of their fellow sepoys set out to liberate the prisoners, accompanied by a mob from the town. By now they had whipped themselves into a frenzy of hatred for the British and, returning to the bazaar, proceeded to murder several off-duty soldiers before rampaging onwards to the cantonments where they burned the bungalows and murdered every European they found: men, women and children.

Some had lucky escapes. Mrs Craigie, wife of a popular captain of the 3rd Bengal Light Cavalry (his was the only squadron in that regiment not to mutiny), was spared by the troops because of their loyalty to her husband. Her neighbour Charlotte Chambers, a beautiful and well-liked captain's wife, twenty-three years old and excitedly anticipating the imminent arrival of her first baby, received no such compassion. The mob set fire to her bungalow and when she rushed screaming from the house she was seized and hacked to death. In a final act of barbarity, her unborn baby was cut from her womb and laid on her chest. Another captain's wife, Louisa MacDonald, very nearly escaped the fate that befell her husband who was one of the first officers to be shot. Her loyal servants bundled her out of her house disguised in Indian clothes. Mrs MacDonald spoke fluent Hindustani, but when a band of rebels stopped and questioned her, in her nervousness she answered in English. She too was hacked to death. Her body was later identified by her glorious auburn hair. The MacDonalds' three children were saved by the same loyal servants, who hid them under a cartload of dried grass, and smuggled them out of Meerut into the jungle. The eldest child, five-year-old Emily, remembered the terror of the journey during which they were stopped and their cart searched several times. Emily was fearful that her ten-month-old brother would betray them by crying, but incredibly he kept quiet and the children reached safety and survived the Mutiny.

Even when news of the insurrection spread, many Europeans were slow to realise the implications. Officers afraid of provoking mutiny by displaying distrust in their men failed to take the precautions that might have saved them and their families. In Cawnpore in the province of Oudh the local commander Major General Sir Hugh Wheeler sent a dispatch on 18 May, when hundreds had already been slain at Meerut and Delhi, assuring the Governor General of India: 'All well at Cawnpore. Quiet, but excitement continues among the people . . . The plague is, in truth, stayed.' Most Europeans were comforted by the knowledge that the local maharajah, a jovial and hospitable man known to all as the Nana Sahib, seemed to be thoroughly pro-British. Yet a week later, on 26 May, Sir Hugh's optimism that all would remain well had faltered sufficiently for him to order all the women and children into an entrenchment he had prepared, but which turned out to be sadly indefensible during the siege that followed.

When the members of the garrison first trooped into the entrenchment there was an almost festive atmosphere. Ladies chattered excitedly while the gentlemen assembled in readiness for orders and children played gaily. But amid the bustle there were many who had misgivings about the sanctuary into which they had been bidden. Several of the officers were unhappy to note that the walls were pitifully low, only four feet high at most, and the trenches behind them absurdly shallow. There were too few buildings to shelter more than a fraction of the thousand fugitives who were crammed into the entrenchment (of whom over a third were women and children).

Forty miles from Cawnpore was Lucknow, the chief city of the province of Oudh, which had been annexed by the British only the previous year. The Lucknow garrison included 900 British troops of the 32nd (The Cornwall) Regiment, a source of great comfort to the European population. It seemed inconceivable to most of its members that an uprising could take hold here, but others, such as Frances Wells, were less confident. When Dr Wells was posted to Lucknow as doctor to the 74th Native Infantry she accompanied him with some reluctance as she had heard that Oudh was a den of iniquity. Her suspicions seemed justified when, on the night of 6 April, catastrophe struck. Frances and her husband were awakened by the screaming of their terrified female servants. Her heart hammering, Frances leapt out of bed and rushed outside to see their thatched roof consumed with flames.

'I never shall forget the horror I experienced,' she wrote to her father. 'I rushed back [and] tore my children out of bed and in my *nightgown* carried them over to the Dashwoods house but had I not met one of the officers who relieved me of the children I think I should have fainted by the way. At 12 o'clock the whole of the roof fell in and now there is nothing left of our nice house but the walls . . . I never knew such terror before and I hope I never may again . . . Our house was fired by a number of Sepoys: there is a very mutinous spirit in the native army now: three regiments have mutinied in the last month and our regt has been showing signs of it lately, but this is the first decided outbreak . . . It is a terrible loss to us and will of course compel us to remain in India longer than we intended.'

Although Frances was in no doubt that the fire was the first eruption of a general mutiny, few in the station shared her view. Most put the attack down to the tactlessness and arrogance of her husband. Dr Wells had a few days earlier been seen by a native hospital worker drinking from a medicine bottle, thereby causing all Hindu patients who partook of that medicine to lose caste. In the febrile atmosphere of the time Dr Wells's thoughtless mistake was seized upon and revenge demanded.

Sir Henry Lawrence, the Chief Commissioner of Lucknow, was no alarmist, but had taken precautions such as fortifying the grand Residency compound that lay on raised ground above the city. On 16 May, two weeks after the Meerut rising, Sir Henry called the women and children of the 32nd (The Cornwall) Regiment into the compound and over the following days other families followed. At first some were unconvinced that this was necessary. Some even blamed Sir Henry for provoking the mutineers (a mutinous regiment had been disarmed earlier that month elsewhere in Oudh). Others thought the measures inadequate. Georgina Harris, wife of an army chaplain, thought that a firmer hand was called for. 'You can only rule these Asiatics by fear,' she advised. 'If they are not afraid, they snap their fingers at you.'

For the first few days after they arrived at the Residency the ladies' liberty was scarcely curtailed: like the initial stage of the Gibraltar siege, life seemed to go on little changed. They continued to go out for drives in the evenings, returning to the Residency at night while the officers and men remained in the cantonments. Some were reluctant to leave their husbands. Mrs Bruere, wife of an officer in the 13th Bengal Native Infantry, ignored Sir Henry Lawrence's order summoning all women and children into the Residency on 26 May and stayed in her bungalow with her husband and children. She was still there on 30 May when the long-brewing storm finally broke in Lucknow and a force of sepoy mutineers began firing on the Officers' Mess of the 71st Bengal Native Infantry. A number of officers were shot and others hacked to death. The mutineers then moved on to the cantonments where they started setting fire to bungalows.

Meanwhile Mrs Bruere and her husband were in bed, oblivious to the mayhem that was about to overtake them. Suddenly a native soldier came rushing into the room and begged her to flee because the mutineers were approaching. Hastily awakening her five sleepy children, including a small baby, she gathered them up and, escorted by three loyal sepoys, fled into the servants' quarters where they hid. However, their refuge was soon discovered and they had to flee and take sanctuary in a deep ditch, clambering and sliding down its sides till they reached the bottom. After the trials of the night, when daybreak came she made her way up to the Residency where she was greeted with resounding disapproval for having disobeyed Sir Henry's orders. A few days later her baby, who had been clad only in a nightdress on the night of their escape, died from dysentery and exposure.

The inhabitants of the Residency (there were eight other houses besides the main building within the 33-acre compound) offered what hospitality they could to the incomers. Colina Brydon, wife of Dr William Brydon, attached to the 71st Bengal Native Infantry, was billeted in the main Residency building. Georgina Harris was given a room to share with her nephew's wife, Emmie Barwell, in the house of Dr Fayrer and his wife. Frances Wells was appalled to find herself bundled into the Residency, 'crammed like sheep in a pen, 8 in a room and the heat is awful: the vaults are filled with the wives and children of soldiers; and the noise is beyond description . . . The poor children are all ill from the heat and confinement and to-day measles has broken out among us. I have a tiny cupboard to myself and am considered very fortunate but if this lasts long I am sure I shall die: the crossness of the children, the loss of all rest at night, the heat, the fear, the misery and above all the separation from my husband are killing me . . . '

There was now no question of anyone being allowed to leave the Residency compound. The siege had without doubt begun in earnest and Sir Henry could only pray that the stores of meat and grain he had laid in would suffice until they were relieved. His precautions were based on the siege lasting for four months. He was not too far out: in fact the siege of Lucknow went on for nearly six.

The crucial difference from the Gibraltar siege was that the Rock was not cut off from relief supplies: friendly ships did manage to break the blockade and bring vital provisions, even if insufficient for the whole population. In Lucknow and Cawnpore no such succour was forthcoming – there were no ships at hand to bring deliverance by sea. Instead the enemy pressed closely around the besieged garrisons: no fresh supplies of food, water or clothing could get through to those trapped behind their walls.

At Cawnpore it became apparent within the first few days that the provisions hastily assembled in the entrenchment were hopelessly inadequate for the thousand souls assembled there. Just as worrying, with the summer sun blazing down on the unsheltered entrenchment – temperatures reached up to 138°F (58°C) – the only source of water was a single well which quickly became the target of the enemy guns, so that drawing water became a perilous if not suicidal mission, only to be undertaken under cover of darkness. Throughout the scorching days the men, women and children wilting under that remorseless sun had to make do with a few sips of water, and none could be spared for washing.

With every passing day the conditions at Cawnpore became more squalid; food became ever scarcer, and clothing too began to wear out. Many of the children were soon running around naked and the ladies, who had entered the entrenchment wearing fashionable dresses with skirts made up of cascading frills, were left with only the body of the skirt, the frills having been surrendered for use as bandages. They also gave up the boxes worn under their dresses, their parasols, anything they possessed, in a futile attempt to strengthen the barricades. By the end of the siege they appeared, as Amy Horne, one of the few survivors of the siege, recalled, 'like so many ghosts, tattered, emaciated, and begrimed!' Towards the end they were reduced to hacking the flesh off a wounded horse and turning it into soup to supplement their daily ration that had now been reduced to a tiny handful of horse fodder (the only food that remained) served with a little rum.

In Lucknow, thanks to the foresight of Sir Henry Lawrence and to the fact that many of the women had managed to pack a few supplies to bring with them, the food situation was slightly better, at least to begin with. But one of the most pressing problems facing the mothers of small children and babies was finding a ready source of milk. Frances Wells, whose own milk had dried up in the shock of the fire, was anxious about feeding her baby son Georgie, born just under a year after her second baby had died. Sadly, she did not have to worry about him for long. As she informed her father, after the siege was over, 'My darling Georgie died on the 13th of July [a month short of his first birthday] of water on the brain: poor little angel I have grieved for him bitterly, but quite see now that he was taken away in mercy for he must have starved: I had no food suitable for him and no milk, and it would have been harder to see him (as I saw other children) pine away to a skeleton and then die. I sometimes feel as if my heart would break when I think of him my sweet darling and he looked so lovely when he was dead: he was just laid upon a box all day and notwithstanding terror I read the service over him myself: and in the evening we sewed him up in the cloth and when it was quite dark Walter carried him down to the churchyard, dug a little grave and laid him in: and that is how my little pet angel was buried. I hoped to have seen his little grave before I left Lucknow, but there was always so much firing at the church yard I could never venture . . . '

Some were better off than others. Julia Inglis's husband, the Commanding Officer of the 32nd, had laid in a stock of sealed provisions, arrowroot, sugar and fodder for the family's goats, who kept their three little boys amply supplied with milk throughout the siege. Mrs Dashwood, in whose house Frances Wells had taken shelter the night of the fire, had two little boys, Ally aged two and Herbert, ten months. As she was expecting a third child she had employed a wet nurse for Herbert, a surly woman who was continually threatening to run away and leave the baby with no source of milk.

Mrs Harris, the chaplain's wife, had no children and devoted much of her time to assisting women like Mrs Dashwood, and Mrs Fayrer, wife of the doctor in whose house they were lodging, helping to nurse their children. But often there was little she, or their mothers, could do, as the diminished diet took its toll on vulnerable little frames. Mrs Harris's attempts to wean Herbert Dashwood, lest his wet nurse carry out her threat to desert, were unsuccessful. 'I feed him with thin arrowroot and sage mixed with a little milk, but he dislikes the change very much, and I fear it does not agree with him, for he has had diarrhoea, and now it has turned to dysentery.' Diarrhoea, always the enemy of infants in India, now reached epidemic proportions and often proved fatal. By the middle of August both Bobbie Fayrer and Herbert Dashwood were sinking fast. Mrs Harris watched the steady decline of the latter with anguish. 'It makes one's heart ache to look at his little suffering face. He is so weak he scarcely ever cries, and when he does it is such a little feeble wail it is pitiable to hear.' On 19 August his sufferings came to an end. He was eleven months old.

Mrs Harris committed the sad news to her journal: 'Dear little Herbert D died at halfpast three this morning. Yesterday he seemed so much better that Mrs D was quite happy about him; but fever came on in the night . . . . . I called up Dr Partridge who ordered a warm bath; and we sent the "dye" [servant] to prepare some water, but before she came up with it the little spirit had fled. One could not grieve; he looked so sweet and happy; the painful look of suffering quite gone, and a lovely smile on his dear little baby face. We closed his pretty blue eyes, and crossed his little hands over his breast, and there he lay by his mother's side till daylight; then she washed the little body herself, and put him in a white night-gown, and I tied a lace handkerchief round his face, as she had no caps. Charlie D [her brother-in-law; her husband had been killed earlier in the siege] came over to see her, and we left her quiet with him and the dead baby till eleven, when I was obliged to go in and ask her to part with it. She let me take it away, and I sewed the little sweet one up myself in a clean white cloth, and James carried it over to the hospital to wait there for the evening burials. Poor little Ally is so ill, it prevents Mrs D thinking so much of the loss of Herbert as she else would. She is so anxious, poor thing, about her last remaining treasure. He has fever and dysentery, and his life seems hanging on a thread.'

Twelve days later, Mrs Dashwood had another treasure to comfort her. In a room where moments earlier a shell had exploded, she gave birth to a baby, Arthur, who was the very image of his dead father. Severely weakened by illness and trauma, she had great difficulty in caring for him until she managed to engage as a nurse a Mrs Rider, whose soldier husband had been killed only days earlier. Mrs Rider nursed little Arthur (who, when aged seventy-nine, was still known as 'the Lucknow baby') throughout the rest of the siege and his mother attributed his survival largely to the devotion of this remarkable woman. Mrs Dashwood herself was no less remarkable. Within the space of a few weeks she lost her husband, her baby son and, later, her brother-in-law and gave birth to another baby who, together with his brother, she brought safely through the siege – all before her twenty-first birthday.

Colina Brydon lived only a few yards away from where the Dashwoods and the Harrises were struggling to keep their frail little charges alive. She too worried about the effects of the attenuated diet on her two young children, Mary Anne aged two and baby Herbert (Bertie), born the previous October. Their four elder children were safely back in Britain. Colina was a brave, resourceful woman and, as a doctor's wife, probably more medically knowledgeable than most other mothers. Her journal, which she began a few days before the siege, is dominated by her constant anxiety about her children, and her morale soars and plunges according to the state of their health. William, her husband, was constantly busy, visiting patients in the makeshift hospital and in the other houses, regularly exposing himself to enemy fire. Colina took her turn keeping watch for enemy movement at night, caring for the sick, manning the bastion and making tea, as well as watching over her two ailing children with increasing fear.

As the nights grew hotter the children became fretful and succumbed more readily to fever, while Bertie suffered terribly from teething troubles. As she watched infants all around her grow steadily more emaciated, fade and die, Colina could only pray that her own would, by some miracle, be spared. 'Baby still ailing and so thin,' she wrote anxiously on 25 July. 'M.A. [Mary Anne] drooping sadly, quite lost her appetite and lying about on a plaid all day . . . Poor M.A. constantly says "baby so tired"! *Obliged to give her small dose of quinine, she came & asked for them so must feel to do her good* [her italics]'. Colina too was suffering with feverish pains and diarrhoea, but stoically dosed herself up with brandy and laudanum and carried on. When Major Anderson's wife died leaving two small children she offered to take them on (in fact another woman had already agreed to take care of them) and continued to help her fellow women whenever she could, making baby clothes for newborns and comforting grieving mothers.

By the middle of the Lucknow siege scarcely a day went by without a child's death being recorded by one of the lady diarists.

In Gibraltar, disease found a ready foothold among those malnourished and ill-clad against bitter winter weather. In the tropical heat of India, conditions were even more conducive to pestilence – though for a while at least the Lucknow garrison benefited from living in well-appointed European houses. Throughout the siege, people were able to wash themselves and their clothes. The soap soon ran out, but then they could boil their linen to clean it. Even so, many of them suffered from lice and boils, uncomfortable and humiliating for women who prided themselves on being elegant and immaculate. For Frances Wells, the lice infestation was one of the hardest things to bear: 'It was dreadful and I used to cry about it so.' Within days of the siege beginning the Residency was assailed by outbreaks of diarrhoea, gastric fever, smallpox and cholera, which quickly spread through the crowded houses. As supplies of fresh food dwindled, scurvy became rife, particularly among the children. The prevalence of diarrhoea and cholera put tremendous pressure on a drainage system designed to cope with only a few households and soon the drains became filled with effluent, with flies congregating and spreading disease further.

In Cawnpore, in the melting heat of June, the besieged residents' clothes quickly became tattered and reeking. Ladies' once glossy ringlets clung limply to their heads, and the bodies of men, women and children became steadily more begrimed. Lacking adequate shelter from the sun, many died of heatstroke, others from diarrhoea and dysentery, while others lost their reason and began babbling incoherently. Young children faded fast and small babies wasted away in days.

As well as having to contend with disease and deprivation, the garrisons under siege were also subjected to terrifying bombardment as the enemy sought to batter their morale and defences. There was no lengthy lull as in the Gibraltar siege when the Spanish bided their time and the residents could build up their fortifications. In Cawnpore, the weak position of the garrison encouraged the besieging rebels to strike early. Nana Sahib, far from being the stalwart friend of the British, now placed himself at the head of the mutineers. Beneath his jovial demeanour he had long been nursing a bitter grievance towards the British who had, as he saw it, deprived him of his inheritance via a rule they introduced disbarring the adopted sons of Indian noblemen from claiming their lands and title. Furthermore, the pension they had promised him failed to match his expectations. He now saw his chance to avenge himself and reclaim his inheritance. On 6 June 1857, a week after the Cawnpore garrison had entered their entrenchment, he sent a message to General Wheeler, courteously informing him that the firing was about to begin. The men and women in the entrenchment could only watch helplessly as rebel forces began training their siege guns towards them and fortifying batteries from where they could man heavy guns raided from the magazine that Wheeler, from some oversight or misplaced confidence, had failed to empty.

On Sunday 7 June the firing began. All day a heavy bombardment of bullets and shell rained down on the exposed garrison. Rebels took up positions on buildings overlooking the entrenchment, some from only three hundred yards away. Cowering in the trenches, women and children trembled as the shells roared and whined over their heads, exploding with terrible effect on the few buildings within the entrenchment. One shell burst in a trench killing seven women, another fell on the thatched roof of the makeshift hospital, burning alive many of the patients inside. In the following days other buildings were blown down by the shells, collapsing upon their unfortunate inhabitants. One woman was killed while in the throes of labour when a ceiling collapsed on her. Mrs White, a private's wife, was walking through the entrenchment one day at her husband's side and with a baby twin in each arm when a shot injured one of the twins, killed Private White, and broke both his wife's elbows. She died a few days later, as did her babies.

The soldiers tried desperately to fight back, outmanned and outgunned though they were. But as their numbers steadily declined under the onslaught of bombardment, heatstroke and disease, it soon became apparent to Sir Hugh Wheeler that their position was hopeless. He had, since entering the entrenchment, smuggled several messages out to Sir Henry Lawrence in Lucknow, asking for a relief force to be sent to aid them. But Lawrence was in no position to help.

On 25 June, after three weeks of siege, a message was received from the Nana promising the garrison safe passage to Allahabad if they agreed to lay down their arms. General Wheeler was deeply reluctant to agree to what was, in effect, surrender. Yet with supplies of food, water and ammunition almost at an end, and with the fate of helpless women and children in his hands, there seemed little choice, abhorrent as the idea of surrendering to 'natives' was to British pride.

On 26 June the bedraggled remnants of the garrison hoisted a flag of truce and the roar of the cannon and the whistling of bullets ceased. Amy Horne bitterly recalled the joy that suffused the survivors as they savoured their liberty and began to walk about the entrenchment holding themselves erect, no longer forced to crawl on all fours or throw themselves to the ground to take cover from the shells. 'The soldiers were singing and dancing, and they tried to get up a little fun for the children. It was the first time since we entered the entrenchment that the little ones were allowed their liberty, and they soon made up for lost time. A cask was converted into a drum and belaboured with a stick; one man whistled a jig, while the others started to dance. The children, though very much broken down and emaciated, yet gathered round the dancers and tried to show their appreciation of the entertainment got up for them.'

The following day they staggered out of the entrenchment: a pitiful, ragged procession, most of them barefoot, some of them reeling with sickness or dementia, the wounded and sick carried and supported. Waiting for them were some soldiers from the rebel army, together with a number of elephants on which they would be conveyed to the boats that were waiting to take them to safety, or so they were told. Eventually everyone was mounted and the procession set off for the landing place. They were further perturbed when they arrived to find the boats in the middle of the river rather than next to the bank, forcing them to wade through the water and clamber up the sides of the boats, a difficult ordeal for the sick and wounded.

It was two hours before all were embarked and the signal to commence was given. Instead of moving off, the boatmen jumped into the water and made for the shore, but not before they had set light to the thatched roofs of the boats. In a few moments the boats began blazing furiously. Those passengers too feeble to move burned to death where they were. Other passengers leapt into the water but were immediately assailed by a hail of bullets from sepoys who had suddenly appeared on the river banks. British soldiers and officers attempted to protect the women and children but their cause was hopeless. The sepoys waded into the river with swords drawn and began cutting down those who were still alive. The river was red with blood, smoke billowed from the burning boats and the guns on the banks, children screamed for their mothers and women were hacked to death as they tried desperately to shield their babies. Only one boat managed to escape with eight survivors on board, four of whom made it to safety. A handful of other women, including Amy Horne, were rescued and concealed for the rest of the Mutiny by native protectors, some being forced to convert to Islam in order to survive.

When the initial massacre was over, the surviving men were at once rounded up on the riverbank and shot, together with any boys over the age of fourteen. The 125 surviving women and children, many of them wounded and bleeding, were marched from the river, under the guard of some of the Nana's troops, and led with their dazed, traumatised children to an old orphanage where they were incarcerated for three days. Then on 1 July they were moved to a small, poky little bungalow, known as the Bibigarh, 'the woman's house', where a British officer's Indian mistress had once lived. Here they were joined by a further eighty women and children who had been captured and imprisoned by the Nana and his troops earlier on in the Mutiny. They were crammed into two squalid little rooms, each measuring about sixteen feet square. Most could not even lie down to sleep. In the heat and filth dysentery and cholera broke out, causing twenty-five deaths in one week. Starving infants cried piteously for food, but only once was milk provided and meat never appeared.

Finally, on 15 July, one of the Nana's senior womenfolk, who had been supervising the captive women, appeared and announced the news that they had scarcely dared to hope for. The British were coming. A 2,000-strong force under Sir Henry Havelock was making its way towards Cawnpore to take on the Nana's army which, though 5,000 strong, was equipped with inferior guns, and its morale was drooping. The bleak despair of the huddled masses in the Bibigarh at once gave way to bright hope. Their prayers had been answered. All their efforts to keep themselves and their children alive were to be rewarded. But it was not to be.

Struck by panic, or enraged at the resurgence of the seemingly crushed British, the Nana ordered that the remaining women and children in the Bibigarh be slaughtered. On the night of 15 July the killing began. Even the Nana's rebel troops blenched at such orders so a couple of local butchers and two other men 'of low caste' were recruited. Armed with swords, they entered the rooms where the terrified women were still desperately trying to shield their children with their own bodies, and began to hack away. A few women, mainly soldiers' wives, tried to fight. One woman struck a blow on one of the butchers, but she was seized by the other men and her throat was cut, though not before she had been forced to watch her daughter hung from a hook by her chin. Many of the women tried to protect their necks with their arms but the butchers merely hacked off their arms, leaving them to bleed to death. Mothers kept pulling their children close to them and pushing them back into the corners of the building, but in the sweltering heat and the crush of bodies, many suffocated under their dying mothers' skirts. The terrible shrieks and groans emanating from the bungalow went on all night. When dawn came the sweepers were ordered to collect the bodies and throw them into a deep well. Some were not quite dead, but were either finished off or hurled into the well alive, soon to suffocate under the weight of the bodies thrown on top of them. An onlooker saw a number of children aged between five and seven who had miraculously survived the massacre, and began running round the well to try and escape from the sweepers until finally they too were caught and thrown into it, still screaming.

The next day, when Havelock's force arrived in Cawnpore, hoping to save the hostages, they found instead the bloodstained walls of the empty Bibigarh and the strewn detritus of those last horrific hours of the victims. Here a lock of hair, there a bloody bonnet, dresses, books, shoes all lay scattered about, drenched with blood. The well, with its shameful contents, was discovered and one soldier who gazed into the mangled mass of limbs wrote afterwards, 'I have looked upon death in every form, but I could not look down that well again.' These gruesome discoveries provoked such an eruption of disgust and fury among the troops that 'Remember Cawnpore' became a battle cry, the Bibigarh a sort of terrible shrine. The thought of the cruelties inflicted on helpless women and children incited them into acts of bloody retribution. Terrible excesses were carried out in the name of justice, with captured rebels being blown from the mouth of cannon, hanged by the dozen at the roadside, and given no quarter in battle. As one young officer put it, after hearing the news of Cawnpore, 'I felt as if my heart was stone and my brain fire.' Havelock's force defeated the Nana's army, though the Nana himself escaped and was never brought to justice.

It took a long time for the terrible news of Cawnpore to filter through to Lucknow. Totally encircled by the besieging forces, Lucknow was almost entirely cut off from the outside world. Only a few messages got in and out, thanks mainly to a brave Indian courier named Ungud who again and again risked death to sneak in and out of the besieged residency bearing messages to and from General Havelock's force. When he first arrived in the Residency, towards the end of July, he brought the welcome news that Havelock had defeated the Nana Sahib at Cawnpore. He also told them of the massacre, but at first was simply not believed. It was not until several weeks later that mounting evidence of the massacre forced the garrison at Lucknow to confront the terrible truth, and with it the knowledge that this fate would await them unless they held out till they were relieved, whenever that might be.

Fifty-seven wives and sixty-two children of men of the 32nd (Cornwall Regiment) had been left at the regimental depot at Cawnpore when their men were sent to Lucknow. These soldiers were tormented with worry for the safety of their families and frustration at being unable to go to their aid. When news of the massacre was broken to them some went almost mad with grief. News of other killings had already been received early on in the siege with mounting horror. At Sitapur, a station near Lucknow, the Europeans were all massacred barring a few survivors who managed to flee into the jungle. Some even got through to the besieged garrison at Lucknow. Mrs Harris went to visit them a few days after their arrival. 'One of them is expecting to be confined immediately. It is wonderful how little that class of people seem to feel things that would kill a lady,' she observed airily. Mrs Harris, though a compassionate and good-natured woman, thought women of 'that class' had coarser sensibilities than ladies like herself and did not 'feel' the deaths of their husbands, children and friends as acutely. That she was mistaken is illustrated by the fact that one of the women she visited, a sergeant-major's wife, upon hearing of her husband's death, was utterly inconsolable and refused all medical attention for a bayonet wound she had suffered. Consequently gangrene set in and she died. Perhaps, like others before her, Mrs

Harris mistook the stoicism and courage of the soldiers' wives for lack of sentiment. As the siege wore on women of all different classes found that they had to contain their emotion if they were to be useful to their children, husbands and companions. Colina Brydon confessed that after nearly four months of siege 'feelings seem deadened'.

At Cawnpore the garrison had only a week between seeking refuge and the first hail of bullets, but at Lucknow a whole month elapsed before the enemy began to fire upon the Residency. An abortive sortie by the garrison on 30 June, in which they were heavily outnumbered and lost 300 British casualties as well as several guns, emboldened the enemy to turn their guns on the Residency. A roundshot struck the house of the financial commissioner Martin Gubbins, where Colina Brydon had taken up residence, bringing down the chimney. The following day saw the first civilian casualty of the siege. The nineteen-year-old daughter of Colonel Palmer of the 48th Bengal Native Infantry was hit by a nine-pound roundshot that smashed through a door of the Residency and struck her leg, nearly severing it. The leg was amputated but she died early the next morning, screaming with pain. From then on the enemy kept up an intense fire that did not abate until the end of the siege. No house was safe and every day brought the news that some friend or acquaintance had been carried off by shell or shot. Sir Henry Lawrence was one of the first to be hit. A shell burst in his room and severed his leg. He lingered in agony for two days. Before dying he conferred command on Colonel Inglis of the 32nd (Cornwall Regiment), ordering him, 'Never surrender! If the small body of men under your command is unable to hold out until the arrival of reinforcements, the women and children must be blown up. The men must fire their way out.'

Colina Brydon's husband Dr William Brydon was severely wounded early in the siege, when a shot came through the window as he sat down to dinner and hit him in the back. Over the next two months he was completely incapacitated, depriving the garrison of a much-needed doctor (there were twelve doctors to care for nearly a thousand people). It placed a terrible burden on Colina who had to nurse him, care for two sickly children, and carry out domestic duties as well as take her turn on the night watch, when she was often far from well. She never allowed herself to sink into self-pity and had little time for those who did. When the majority of the servants fled, the ladies, who had been used to relying on an army of staff for all their domestic needs, suddenly found themselves having to become acquainted with such alien skills as making tea, washing clothes and cooking food and making clothes, often from dead soldiers' jackets. Some found it hard to adapt to their new domestic role. 'Many in distress about cooking and food,' remarked Colina, adding crisply: 'How we see real character now.'

Throughout the Lucknow siege the morale of the garrison was kept alive by the hope that they would soon be rescued by a relief force. After many false dawns Jessie Brown, a corporal's wife, who had been lying delirious for many days in the rat-infested cellar of the Residency building, had a vision that the relief was on its way. At first her prophecy was treated with scepticism, but soon the sound of bagpipes was heard in the distance. It was 25 September, the eighty-eighth day of the siege, when a force led by Sir James Outram and General Henry Havelock and including men of the 78th Ross-shire Highlanders, broke through the besieging force and, after sustaining heavy casualties, entered the Residency compound to ecstatic rejoicing. 'The big, rough-bearded soldiers were seizing the little children out of our arms, kissing them with tears rolling down their cheeks. And thanking God they had come in time to save them from the fate of those at Cawnpore . . . Everyone's tongue seemed going at once with so much to ask and to tell,' wrote Mrs Harris.

In fact, the incoming force brought hope, but not relief. Havelock and Outram's force, less than 2,000 strong, was too small to attack the enemy and break the siege, but large enough to constitute a terrible strain on the diminished resources of the garrison. They also brought confirmation of the Cawnpore massacre, plunging into despair all those who had still held out hope for friends and family they had left there.

The garrison limped on throughout September and October, enlivened only by the opportunities for looting as the British troops (and their loyal sepoy allies) gradually pushed out into the city, enveloping more buildings into their defensive cordon. Many of these buildings contained valuable goods from the royal palaces of Oudh. The children meanwhile, though weak, often adapted more readily than their parents to life under siege, playing marbles with spent musket balls. They became so accustomed to the noise of guns and shells bursting that they ceased to be frightened by them.

On 17 November a second relief force, commanded by the Crimean veteran General Sir Colin Campbell, arrived in Lucknow and succeeded in fighting its way through to the Residency. Two days later the evacuation of non-combatants began. Two-thirds of the original garrison had now died. A quarter of the children who had come into the Residency and over half the fighting men were buried, mostly in mass graves. Colina Brydon admitted to feeling anxious at leaving the compound that had for so long been her world, especially as they had to travel through areas where rebel troops were still at large.

Some families travelled in carriages, while others had to walk. Colina was helped by a servant who carried her youngest child, Bertie, while Mary Anne was carried by a Sikh orderly. They marched through the country-side, sometimes covering as much as thirty-eight miles a day, a strange procession of dhoolies (litters), camels, elephants, bullocks and carts, loaded with sick and wounded women and children, until finally they reached Cawnpore where they halted for some days. They were glad to move on a few days later, having observed the melancholy sight of General Wheeler's abandoned entrenchment where many of their friends had perished.

From Cawnpore they went on to Allahabad where they were finally able to change out of their old clothes; many were given new clothing, boots and other essentials from a relief fund set up in London to aid victims of the Mutiny. Colina Brydon's stoicism was fast evaporating: 'I am quite tired of chummery with people . . . we have never been alone since the 25th of last May and now have only half a tent.'

After the Mutiny, Colina Brydon and Georgina Harris both stayed in India. Frances Wells and her husband returned to Bristol with their surviving son. Julia Inglis, and Mrs Bruere whose husband was killed midway through the siege but who still had her four remaining children, travelled back to England on a steamer that was packed with surviving Lucknow families. By some cruel twist of fate those families who had endured so much were to face one further trial. As they sat on the warm deck one evening, a loud, grating sound interrupted their conversation and the ship began to shake violently. It had struck a reef off the coast of Ceylon. Hastily the passengers were loaded into lifeboats from where they watched the stricken ship sink. All were rescued and resumed their journey, shaken but alive.

Many of the Lucknow survivors published memoirs of the siege, some of them proudly including the laudatory order issues by Sir James Outram, commending the gallantry of the 'devoted band of heroes' who had managed to defend the vulnerable garrison. Others, like Martin Gubbins, paid tribute to the ladies. Private Henry Metcalfe saved his warmest praise for those 'tender and solicitous' women who had worked in the hospitals, risking death from infection – and bombardment as the buildings were frequently hit. Two sisters, the Miss Birches, were continually in the hospital and 'consequently almost worshipped by the soldiers'. Sadly, one of them died when a fragment of exploded shell struck her.

After the depressing stream of terrible news from India, of British troops routed and defeated by an enemy who was considered racially inferior, the sickening catalogue of brutalities committed against women and children including tales of babies being bayoneted and hung from hooks, the British public both in India and at home were glad to grasp this tale of heroism and victory against the odds, as Lucknow was portrayed, despite the heavy losses.

Whatever besieged communities have to endure, at least they are not subject to the direct control of the enemy. While they can hold out, there is some hope of eventual relief. Once, however, they fall into enemy hands, that small freedom is lost to them – as the Cawnpore victims most dreadfully found out. Whether captured by enemies or fleeing from them, many British army women and their children found themselves severed from society as they knew it, and left adrift, to fend for themselves without the protection of their men or the guidance of authority.

11

Captives and Fugitives

There was nothing to relieve the monotony. The room contained no
other furniture and had no window. A man with a rifle stood in the
doorway all the time and behind him the women and children sat
cross-legged on the floor staring in amazement at the first white
woman they'd ever seen. The only way I could escape
their curious brown eyes was to turn my face to
the wall. I became very depressed.

Molly Ellis, captive in Afghanistan, 1923

When armies fought protracted, mobile campaigns, marching long
distances through hostile terrain, there was always potential for
stragglers to fall into enemy hands. Women and children, travelling at the
rear, were often at risk of being taken prisoner – a risk that spurred women
on to pick themselves up and stumble onwards straight after giving birth,
or to drag their exhausted children on through bogs and over mountains.

During the Peninsular War large numbers of women on both sides
were taken prisoner. Officers' wives were generally treated courteously,
but soldiers' wives could not always expect such chivalry. Mrs Pullen, who
had been reunited with her husband and missing daughter after the evacuation from Corunna, experienced more than her fair share of troubles
on that retreat. Not only did she lose touch with both her children (she
never saw her son again), she was also badly treated when captured by
some French soldiers. She and some other women took shelter in a barn

one night, hoping to catch up with the main army the next morning. That night, according to Rifleman Harris, some French soldiers came into the barn and, finding the women there, proceeded to treat them 'in a very unceremonious manner'. After this the French gave them some food and packed them off back to the British column. Shortly after their return to England Mrs Pullen gave birth to a baby, a result, she believed, of that encounter in the barn.

At least Mrs Pullen's captivity, though brutal, was brief. Some men, and women, spent many months or even years in French prisons. Officers could be exchanged or paroled fairly rapidly, but ordinary soldiers could stay rotting in French or British jails for years, unless they were lucky enough to constitute an exchange for a senior enemy officer. For a general to be handed over, for example, as many as sixty soldiers would have to be exchanged. For women the arrangements seem to have been more ad hoc. Often their captors found it expedient to dispatch them back to their own lines as soon as possible. Some of the women who scrambled over the cliffs to gather up the treasure thrown down on the retreat to Corunna were captured by the French. They were sent on their way quickly, but not until they had been relieved of the money for which they had risked life and limb. In November 1812, while marching to the Spanish fortress of Ciudad Rodrigo near the Portuguese border, the army's baggage train was outflanked by the French cavalry who plundered the baggage and carried off a number of prisoners, including several women. They were returned to the British the next day while the male prisoners were retained.

Children too were considered a nuisance. Sergeant Costello of the 95th Rifles tells of an occasion when the French seized several donkeys, believing them to be carrying useful baggage. In fact many of their panniers contained soldiers' children. When their mothers realised that they were missing, panic ensued. 'One Irish woman, in particular, I remember seeing, whose grief seemed inconsolable for the loss she had sustained in that of her child. In a few days, however, the French, desiring to be as little encumbered as ourselves with children, sent them back with a flag of truce.'

Some women captured by the enemy were missed more than others. Captain Grattan relates the tale of Mrs Howley, whose husband served in the 88th Connaught Rangers, and who was greatly respected for her hard work and good humour. The regiment had been engaged in sharp fighting on 25 September 1811 when their division was surprised by a French attack. The 88th, together with several staff officers and men from other regiments, were withdrawing to their encampment at the nearby village of

Fuente Guinaldo when they were cut off and attacked by a detachment of French troops. 'Lieutenant King of the 11th Dragoons lost one arm by a sabre cut; Prior, of the same regiment, had all his front teeth knocked out by a musket shot, and Mrs Howley, the black cymbalman's wife, of the 88th, was captured by a lancer. The fate of the officers I have mentioned was deplored, but the loss of Mrs Howley was a source of grief to the entire division. The officers so maimed might be replaced by others, but perhaps in the entire army such another woman, take her for all and all, as Mrs Howley could not be found.' Such an accolade was rare indeed, especially for a soldier's wife, but then William Grattan was an unusually amiable and unprejudiced officer. (The Connaught Rangers, like other regiments, had several black soldiers in its ranks at this period.)

The seasoned campaigners of the Peninsular War were perhaps better equipped than most to cope with the rigours of an uncertain captivity. For women who had followed the army in peacetime, anticipating a settled existence, only to find themselves unexpectedly caught up in conflict and taken into captivity by an enemy uninterested in observing the normal conventions of war, the experience could be far more alarming. Women who married into the army of the East India Company, or into India-based regiments, were seldom embroiled in action, usually remaining in cantonments while their men went off to fight elsewhere. But when the fighting was over the men would send for their wives (or return to cantonments) and settle into domesticity once again.

In December 1838 the Governor General of India, Lord Auckland, sent a 16,000-strong force, grandly named the Army of the Indus, into Afghanistan. The army's purpose was to evict the incumbent ruler of Afghanistan, Dost Mohammed who, it was feared, was not sufficiently pro-British, and might allow Afghanistan to become a Russian satellite through which the Russians could invade India. The British therefore decided to install their own candidate, Shah Shujah, who had been deposed as Afghanistan's ruler thirty years earlier, on its throne. Convinced by what later transpired to be faulty intelligence that the Afghans would readily accept the new regime, the British were disquieted to find little enthusiasm for Shah Shujah. Morale was soon restored when the army successfully stormed the fort of Ghazni: Florentia Sale's husband Robert ('Fighting Bob'), now a major general, was knighted for his part in the victory. By August 1839 the army was in Kabul. Dost Mohammed, abandoned by his supporters, fled to the mountains of the Hindu Kush.

It soon became apparent that the British would have to stay not months, but years, to enforce Shah Shujah's reign. Some were perturbed by the fact that the few routes back to India involved perilously long marches through dangerous passes. Were these to become impassable, the army would be stranded. Despite such misgivings, many of the British officers were pleased with their new surroundings. Kabul, wrote one young lieutenant, 'is well built and handsome, and is one mass of bazaars . . . The shop windows are open to the sun, and the immense display of merchandise, fruits, game, armour and cutlery defies description.' Soon the British community was happily engaged in such pursuits as hunting, horse-racing, amateur theatricals and ice-skating. Lady Sale, who joined her husband at the end of 1839 together with her daughter Alexandra, was delighted to find that such English plants as sweet peas and geraniums flourished in her kitchen garden.

But by the end of 1841 the British situation was distinctly less comfortable. Although the political envoy, Sir William MacNaghten, who had accompanied the army (and lobbied for the intervention in Afghanistan), was writing cheerily that there was 'perfect tranquility' in the country, the reverse was true. Anti-British feeling was rife and although Dost Mohammed had surrendered to the British, his son, Akbar Khan, was still at large and commanded great loyalty among the tribes. Major General Sale had taken a force to clear the passes between Afghanistan and India, which had been occupied by hostile tribes. He held the fort of Jalalabad north west of Kabul, where Lady Sale intended to join him as soon as she could. But in November the British Resident in Kabul was hacked to death by a mob, the army's treasury attacked and looted and young Lieutenant Sturt, who had married the Sales' daughter Alexandra, was stabbed and badly wounded by an Afghan assassin. The army's frail, gout-ridden commander, Major General William Elphinstone, failed to act to quell the disturbances and the situation deteriorated further, with Afghan tribesmen hovering menacingly around the British cantonments and seizing the forts containing the army's supplies.

One half-hearted attempt to drive them off ended in a humiliating retreat back into cantonments. Lady Sale, observing these developments from a lookout point where she had to duck the occasional bullet, seethed at such incompetence.

With supplies of food, especially meat, running low, Sir William MacNaghten reluctantly decided to seek terms from the Afghans but, during negotiations with Akbar Khan, he was suddenly seized and dragged off, together with two officers (another officer, Captain Trevor, was killed in the ensuing melee). Hours later MacNaghten's body parts were paraded through the bazaars of Kabul, while his trunk was hung from a meat hook alongside that of Captain Trevor. Lady Sale was deputed to break the news of their deaths to their widows. 'Over such scenes I draw a veil. It was a painful meeting to us all,' was her only comment in her journal.

Despite Akbar Khan's treachery, the decision was taken to continue negotiating with him for a peaceful withdrawal. Accordingly, after a 'dismal' Christmas Day, plans proceeded apace for evacuating the cantonments and proceeding to India, via the snowy passes of the North West. The British-installed ruler Shah Shujah was to be abandoned. Finally, on the morning of 6 January 1842, the evacuation began, despite warnings from friendly Afghans that Akbar Khan's promises of a safe withdrawal were worthless. The 4,500 troops were already showing signs of malnutrition, having been on half rations since the uprising. The 12,000 camp followers had subsisted on only a small handful of wheat or barley per day. Progress was slow as the troops, camels, women and children trudged through the foot-deep snow.

Lady Sale and her daughter took their place at the head of the column with the widowed Lady MacNaghten and a dozen or so other British wives with around twenty children between them. Some of the women had given birth only days before and were too weak even to stand. Others were within days of their own confinements and barely able to walk, let alone withstand the rigours of a long march across countryside that Lady Sale described as a 'swamp encrusted with ice'. Within a few hours, watching horsemen had already begun to swoop down and harass the straggling column of camp followers, robbing and murdering them, while Afghan children amused themselves by stabbing wounded grenadiers as they lay dying. Some camp followers rushed up to the front, much to Lady Sale's disapproval, throwing the whole column into abject confusion.

By four o'clock the army had gone no further than five miles from the city and had left in its wake a pitiful trail of corpses whose blood was seeping into the snow. By now almost all the baggage had been carried off, and several artillery pieces had been abandoned. The prospects of the column reaching India in safety were looking increasingly remote and even the stoical Lady Sale had presentiments of disaster: ' . . . we have commenced our retreat so badly, that we may reasonably have our doubts regarding the finale'.

When the next day dawned many of the camp followers and troops lay stiffly in the snow, frozen to death. Again the column was attacked and baggage and guns carried off. After a few hours a halt was called and men, women and children settled down to sleep in the snow. As the sun rose over the bedraggled column on the third day of the retreat, Lady Sale surveyed the scene with bitter despair. 'Many frozen corpses lay on the ground. The Sipahees [sepoys] burnt their caps, accoutrements, and clothes to keep themselves warm.' Baggage lay strewn across the ground, including a cask of spirits, which was hastily seized and consumed by some British soldiers. Even Lady Sale succumbed to a tumbler of sherry, 'which at any other time would have made me very unlady-like,' she confided primly, 'but now merely warmed me, and appeared to have no more strength in it than water'.

Now Akbar Khan appeared in the camp and demanded a further subsidy to protect the troops. He also required that three of the most competent officers be surrendered to him as hostages until such time as Jalalabad, held by Sale, should be evacuated. Once again his demands were meekly accepted and the army moved off again, minus the three hostages. Lady Sale and her daughter and son-in-law rode ahead with some of the Afghan chieftains but had gone scarcely half a mile when heavy firing again rent the air. Lieutenant Sturt was shot in the abdomen; bleeding heavily, he had to be propped up on a pony. Alexandra Sturt's pony was shot in the ear and neck and Lady Sale noted matter-of-factly that she herself 'had fortunately only one ball in my arm; three others passed through my poshteen [fur pelisse] near the shoulder without doing me any injury'. She is said to have sharply reprimanded her daughter for ducking from the bullets, telling her to sit up straight and not let the Afghans see that she was afraid.

The other British women, mostly riding at the rear of the column, fared even worse than those at the front. 'Many camels were killed. On one camel were, in one kajava [pannier], Mrs Boyd and her youngest boy Hugh; and in the other Mrs Mainwaring and her infant, scarcely three months old, and Mrs Anderson's eldest child. This camel was shot. Mrs Boyd got a horse to ride; and her child was put on another behind a man, who being shortly after unfortunately killed, the child was carried off by the Afghans. Mrs Mainwaring, less fortunate, took her own baby in her arms. Mary Anderson was carried off in the confusion. Meeting with a pony laden with treasure, Mrs Mainwaring endeavored to mount and sit on the boxes, but they upset; and in the hurry pony and treasure were left behind, and the unfortunate lady pursued her way on foot.' Mrs Mainwaring, a merry, popular young woman whose husband was at Jalalabad with Sale's force, plodded on, earned the admiration of Lady Sale for her perseverance. 'Mrs Mainwaring's sufferings were very great; and she deserves much credit for having preserved her child through these dreadful scenes. She not only had to walk a considerable distance with her child in her arms through the deep snow, but had also to pick her way over the bodies of the dead, dying, and wounded, both men and cattle, and constantly to cross the streams of water, wet up to the knees, pushed and shoved about by men and animals, the enemy keeping up a sharp fire, and several persons being killed close to her. She, however, got safe to camp with her child, but had no opportunity to change her clothes; and I know from experience that it was many days ere my wet habit became thawed, and can fully appreciate her discomforts . . . Mrs Bourke, little Seymour Stoker and his mother, and Mrs Cunningham, all soldiers' wives, and the child of a man of the 13th, have been carried off.' Of the sufferings of the camp followers she makes no comment.

As the increasingly ragged column entered the jaws of the narrow Kabul–Khoord pass, the Ghilzai tribesmen, hovering on the rocky hill-sides above, began pouring a deadly stream of bullets on to the helpless hordes trapped below. By now many were stumbling, suffering from snow blindness, while others were crippled with frostbite and weak with hunger and exhaustion. Around 500 soldiers and 2,500 camp followers had perished. A halt was called in the pass to allow stragglers to catch up. Lieutenant Sturt had his wound dressed, although his mother-in-law could see that there was little hope of his recovering. The doctor, she noted, also 'kindly cut the ball out of my wrist, and dressed both my wounds'.

They lay down for another night in the snow, Lady Sale, her daughter and dying son-in-law huddled under a flimsy tent together with nearly thirty others. Sepoys and camp followers desperately tried to get in under the cover and by the next morning the tent was surrounded by stiff, frozen corpses. Lieutenant Sturt was dead, leaving his wife and mother-in-law with 'the sorrowful satisfaction of giving him Christian burial'. A message now came from Akbar Khan, asking Elphinstone to give up the married women and children to him as hostages for their own safety. Again, Elphinstone acquiesced. On 9 January Lady Sale, her freshly widowed daughter and a handful of other women and children, together with a few of the married men, were handed over to the dubious protection of Akbar Khan. So began nearly ten months of captivity.

There is little doubt that their situation as hostages saved their lives. Out of a total of 16,000 troops and camp followers, only one European, an army doctor named William Brydon (the same Dr Brydon who went on to marry Colina and survive the siege of Lucknow), reached Jalalabad where Major General Sale was still holding the city. Dr Brydon arrived on 13 January, 'The Last Man', as he soon became known, to have survived the terrible retreat. (There were in fact other, non-European, survivors.) Over the next few days the remainders of the army and its followers were massacred or died from cold, hunger and exhaustion.

Meanwhile Lady Sale and her fellow hostages were taken to a fort. Here Mrs Boyd was reunited with her son who had been feared lost, and young Seymour Stoker was found safe and well. Poor Mrs Anderson and her husband had their hopes of finding their young daughter Mary cruelly dashed. She, it later transpired, had been carried back to Kabul and offered for sale as a slave (they were not reunited with her until May). The other members of the party included Mrs Trevor and her seven children, Lieutenant and Mrs Waller and their child, Alexandra Sturt, Mrs Smith and Mrs Burnes (two soldiers' wives) and a few wounded men. Two days later they were marched to another fort, passing heaps of mangled, naked bodies of camp followers and soldiers.

On 13 January, the same day that Dr Brydon managed to reach Jalalabad, the hostages arrived at a place called Jugdaluk, where they found General Elphinstone and two other senior officers who had also been taken hostage. Over the next few months Lady Sale and her party were marched back and forth across Afghanistan by Akbar Khan. In the main they were well treated. Their captors even gave up their own tents to the women and children. Sometimes they marched up to twenty-four miles a day, along rocky mountain paths. On the first day the horses had to pick their way through the bodies of dead soldiers and camp followers. 'The sight was dreadful,' wrote Lady Sale, 'the smell of the blood sickening; and the corpses lay so thick it was impossible to look from them, as it required care to guide my horse so as not to treat upon the bodies.' In other places they came across fugitives from the column living in caves, reduced to cannibalism to survive.

On 19 January the prisoners were for the first time given water to wash with. As none had a change of clothes they could only wash their faces but as this was a luxury they had been denied for the past two weeks they delighted in it. However, as Lady Sale recorded, 'It was rather a painful process, as the cold and glare of the sun on the snow had three times peeled my face, from which the skin came off in strips.' The food they were given was basic but probably the best that their captors could produce in such barren land. Lady Sale was deeply unimpressed. 'God sends meat but the devil sends cooks,' she quipped.

As their captivity endured some of the women who had been pregnant when the column left Kabul gave birth. The fecund Mrs Trevor added an eighth child to her family. Mrs Waller and Mrs Boyd also had babies and on 24 July Lady Sale noted in her journal in her usual sparing manner, 'Mrs Sturt presented me with a granddaughter – another female captive,' having omitted to mention her daughter's pregnancy. Throughout her captivity Lady Sale was permitted to correspond with her husband, although their letters were carefully perused by her captors, and his letters to her were sometimes withheld for weeks. She carefully avoided pleading with her husband for deliverance, knowing that he would come when he was able.

As the months passed by they were dragged from one fort to another, to avoid rival chiefs who wanted to seize the captives and demand the ransom themselves. They were assailed by earthquakes, fever and lice, but worst was the uncertainty about their fate. Sometimes they were subjected to disturbing news, such as the (false) rumour that Jalalabad had fallen. Another rumour had it that they would be sold as slaves.

Lady Sale had weathered more than her share of trials during her life. She had lost five children and seen her son-in-law perish. She had little respect for Afghans, her captors especially, but she was nothing if not a pragmatist and was ready to co-operate with them if it would help to improve their lot. When she believed that they were being unfairly treated, she did not hesitate to remonstrate with her captors. 'As no one would fight for the ladies,' she sniffed disapprovingly, obviously referring to the men of the party, 'I determined to be *yaghi* [rebellious] myself.' Impressed (or perhaps cowed) by her forthrightness, her captors dutifully complied and gave them better quarters. Her robust approach earned her the sobriquet of the 'Petticoat Grenadier' from her fellow hostages.

Stoical though she undoubtedly was, seldom complaining even when racked with fever or with pain from her wound, Lady Sale cannot have been the easiest of companions. Tall and imposing with a habit of speaking her mind, she was also inclined to be selfish. She was fortunate enough to receive regular parcels from her husband in Jalalabad, so was well supplied with clothes, shoes and other necessities such as needles. Yet she refused to lend her needles to the other women who wanted to make their own clothes, to the disgust of Captain MacKenzie, one of the male hostages. He was also appalled by the snobbish attitude of some of the ladies who 'gave themselves great airs towards Mrs Riley', a soldier's wife. The kindly Mrs Mainwaring, on the other hand, did not hesitate to distribute her own possessions among the other ladies.

Throughout their captivity, as the hostages were marched across Afghanistan, Akbar Khan and his cohorts negotiated with the British the terms for their release. Several hostages, including the frail old General Elphinstone and a young child of Mrs Burnes', died in captivity. When one male hostage protested at the continuous moves one of Akbar's cohorts snarled that 'as long as there is an Afghan prisoner in India or a Feringhee [foreign] soldier in Afghanistan, so long will we retain you, men, women and children. When you can ride, you *shall* ride; when you cannot, you *shall* walk; when you cannot walk, you *shall* be dragged, and when you cannot be dragged, *your throats shall be cut.*'

Eventually in September 1842 the hostages, by now imprisoned near Kabul, began hearing rumours that they would soon be freed. A force commanded by General Pollock had got through the Khyber Pass in April 1842 and relieved Sale's garrison at Jalalabad. It was awarded the epithet of the Illustrious Garrison for holding out so resolutely. Both Pollock and General Nott, who was at Kandahar with his own force, were told that they must retreat from Afghanistan but that they could, if they chose, go via Kabul (although this lay in the opposite direction) and relieve the hostages. Consequently the two generals began leading their armies towards Kabul.

Although news of their approach raised the spirits of the hostages immeasurably, it also brought dangers of its own. There was a chance that their captors might panic and send them further west, or even have them killed. Lady Sale robustly professed herself unperturbed by such considerations: 'Now is the time to strike the blow,' she wrote in her journal, 'but I much dread dilly-dallying just because a handful of us are in Akbar's power. What are *our* lives when compared with the honour of our country? Not that I am at all inclined to have my throat cut,' she hastily added, 'on the contrary, I hope that I shall live to see the British flag once more triumphant in Afghanistan; and then I have no objection to the Ameer Dost Mohammed Khan being reinstated: only let us first show them that we can conquer them, and humble their treacherous chiefs in the dust.'

As the British forces neared Kabul their jailers grew jittery and the hostages were forced to move more frequently. They were warned that any who failed to keep up on the marches would be put to death. Lady Sale, undaunted, wrote to her husband to inform him 'of our resolution to hold out till we receive assistance, even should we be reduced to eating the rats and mice'. Such brave, patriotic sentiments would have played well back in England, where many of her letters had ended up after Sale had passed them on to the Governor General of India. Several had been published in the press and provoked controversy as some thought her too sympathetic to Akbar Khan. In fact she was merely truthful enough to admit that Akbar Khan had treated the hostages as well as he was able. She was also outspoken about the folly of the intervention in Afghanistan: 'I have been a soldier's wife too long to sit down tamely whilst our honour is tarnished in the sight and opinion of savages,' she wrote tartly.

Finally, on 19 September, after nearly ten months of captivity, Lady Sale was at last reunited with her husband, who led the force that liberated the hostages (their captors had by now departed to fight the British). Even she could not help but succumb to the emotion of the moment. 'It is impossible to express our feelings on Sale's approach. To my daughter and myself happiness so long delayed, as to be almost unexpected, was actually painful and accompanied to a choking sensation which could not obtain the relief of tears. When we arrived where the infantry were posted, they cheered all the captives as they passed them; and the men of the 13th pressed forward to welcome us individually.' As the soldiers broke out in cheers, Lady Sale's last vestiges of restraint melted away. 'My highly wrought feelings found the desired relief; and I could scarcely speak to thank the soldiers for their sympathy, whilst the long withheld tears now found their course.' Sale too was overcome. When one of his junior officers congratulated him on his wife and daughter's rescue 'the gallant old man turned towards me and tried to answer, but his feelings were too strong; he made a hideous series of grimaces, dug his spurs into his horse and galloped off as hard as he could'.

The liberated hostages were brought into Kabul where the inhabitants were trembling with trepidation for what vengeance would be wreaked upon them. They did not have long to wait. The splendid Great Bazaar, the centre of Kabul's commerce, was destroyed in a series of explosions. The bazaar was singled out for this display of retribution because it was here that the dismembered body parts of Sir William MacNaghten had been gleefully paraded, but inevitably many innocent citizens were killed or injured and their homes destroyed. Then, their mission accomplished, the British marched back to India. Thus ended the First Afghan War, a disaster for Britain that had achieved none of its objectives and resulted in the loss of more than 16,000 lives. Dost Mohammed was restored to the throne and his reign, characterised by stability and fairness, lasted for twenty years. Lord Auckland's political career never recovered from the debacle. As for the Sales, General Sale was mortally wounded in 1844 in the Sikh War at the battle of Mudki, as usual in the thick of the fighting. Lady Sale, whose journals had been published to much acclaim, retired to Simla where she regaled her acquaintances with tales of the bloody retreat. She eventually died in South Africa, whence she had gone for her health, in 1853. Her tombstone bore the epitaph: 'Underneath this stone reposes all that could die of Lady Sale.'

It was to be more than thirty years before the British dared again to intervene militarily in Afghanistan. A further two Afghan wars were fought, in 1878 and 1919, both ending in British victories. But hostilities continued on the Afghan-Indian border, as the tribes who lived in the hills of the North West Frontier made raids into British India to capture money, livestock or women. If a particularly heinous crime was committed British troops would be sent on punitive raids into tribal territory.

Victims of the raids were mostly Indian villagers, but towards the end of 1920 an officer of the Indian Medical Service, Colonel Foulkes, and his wife, were found murdered in their bungalow in the middle of the cantonment at the frontier post of Kohat. Mrs Foulkes had been shot in the chest, then dragged out of the bungalow and across several fields before being dumped and left to bleed to death. Amazingly she managed to crawl back across the fields to the bungalow, where her petrified twelve-year-old daughter, who had been cowering under a bed, raised the alarm, but Mrs Foulkes died shortly afterwards from her wounds. The culprits remained at large. Then an Indian army medical officer was killed and his wife abducted from Kohat. After 'undergoing horrible indignities' as one newspaper delicately put it, she was eventually returned to her bungalow. The Kohat cantonments were hastily surrounded by barbed wire to prevent a similar occurrence, but months later this was torn down again for fear of creating an impression of vulnerability.

So in April 1923, the cantonments were once again open and accessible when a band of four Afridi tribesmen, led by the brothers Ajab and Shahzada Khan, broke into the house of a Major Ellis of the Border Regiment. They unleashed a series of events that were to become part of North West Frontier legend. Ellen Mary Ellis, Major Ellis's forty-six-year-old wife, had long had a premonition that something terrible would happen to her while she lived in India. Despite her misgivings she threw herself into the duties of an officer's wife, working hard among the soldiers' families, and was much liked. Their seventeen-year-old-daughter, Molly, had travelled out to India six months earlier and happily immersed herself in the whirl of dances, riding, tennis and hockey that constituted social life for officers' families. Small in stature (she was five foot and weighed only six stone) and delicately pretty, she was, as one contemporary newspaper report described her 'a fine type of English girl'. But her sheltered upbringing in Devon and Cheltenham and the cloistered society of cantonments and the club had done little to prepare her for the ordeal she was about to face.

On the night of 13 April Molly and her mother had gone to sleep in twin beds in the same room to keep each other company, while Major Ellis was away in the frontier fortress of Razmak. At around 1.45 a.m. Molly was awakened by sounds of a struggle and the frantic screams of her mother. Through the darkness she could dimly make out the shapes of several figures and saw the glint of a dagger. Molly called out to her mother not to struggle. But Mrs Ellis did not heed her warning. Molly heard a sharp intake of breath and then her mother fell silent. Although she could not know for sure, she suspected then that her mother's throat had been cut. Molly herself was unable to struggle as her hands and legs were held in a tight grip. She later chastised herself for failing to put up a fight and for causing her mother's death. If she had not woken up, she felt 'they might have taken Mum away & left me asleep; but my one comfort about that is, that I know Mummy would *never* have gone with them & would have been the same, the darling had such a fighting spirit & of course would not give in to such brutes. I'm afraid I was such a coward, I was too frightened to do anything but give in as I did, & I don't know what people must think of me for doing it.' In fact, nearly seventy years after the Mutiny, public opinion had softened somewhat, and instead of being expected to die defiantly rather than let a 'native' touch her, Molly was admired for preserving her life.

The men then bore her out of the house, and half carried, half dragged her over the road and across the sports fields opposite the bungalow. Despite the commotion, an officer sleeping in the next-door room (the bungalows were semi-detached), heard nothing. It was only when the dogs barked, well after the party had left the house, that he awoke and, going to investigate, made the gruesome discovery of Mrs Ellis's body. He raised the alarm but by then Molly and her captives were well away. Alternately walking and running, the party plunged into some scrub, over a stream and across a main road until they reached the foothills north of Kohat where, after climbing a steep, rocky hill, they finally came to a halt. The sun was now rising and her captors did not want to risk travelling by daylight. Molly

On the march: soldiers' wives in the Peninsula shared the hardships of their men. When no transport was available, they had to carry their possessions, their children and sometimes even their husbands.

Doing the laundry: even when they were carrying out domestic duties, soldiers' wives risked being captured, wounded or killed by enemy fire.

An evening in camp, circa 1760: in this idyllic scene an infantryman puts a protective arm around his family while his fellow soldiers relax around them. In reality, the domestic and martial worlds did not always co-exist so harmoniously.

March of the Guards, 1745: William Hogarth's painting outraged George II because it depicted his Guards as a rabble of drunkards and womanisers. It also depicts the conflicting loyalties that soldiers faced as they marched to war. The drummer to the left seems to be trying to drown out the pleas of his wife and children, while the man at the centre is being beseeched to stay by his pregnant wife or sweetheart.

Home from the wars, 1856: a soldier is embraced by his wife and mother whose relief at his safe return is evident. Of those who did come home, many were broken down in health because of the appalling conditions.

An evening funeral during the Crimean War. An army chaplain conducts a service for a fallen soldier at a graveyard, across the straits from Constantinople. Grieving women, probably soldiers' wives, stand in the background.

The massacre at Cawnpore: this brutal slaying of men, women and children was one of the da[rkest]
episodes of the Indian Mutiny of 1857 and led to terrible acts of retribution against the 'rebels'

Florentia Sale: the perfect army wife, unflappable, resilient and loyal, Lady Sale spent more than nine months as a hostage in Afghanistan in 1842. Nicknamed the 'Petticoat Grenadier' for her courageous behaviour, she was not popular with all her fellow captives.

Lady Harriet Acland, who bravely went to the aid of her wounded husband. Her devotion won the admiration of both British and American commanders in the American Revolutionary War.

The Marquess of Granby aiding a sick soldier: appointed commander of the British forces in Germany in 1759, he was famously compassionate towards his soldiers and granted gratuities to many of them, enabling them to open public houses on their retirement. Many soldiers were not so fortunate. They and their families often faced penury when they returned from the wars.

The Duchess of Richmond's ball, on the eve of Waterloo: the Duke of Wellington and many of his officers attended this famous ball, at which Wellington received news of Napoleon's advance. The men had to bid farewell to wives and sweethearts and march off, some still in their dancing slippers, to encounter the French army at Quatre Bras.

was wearing only thin pyjamas and had bare feet when she was seized. After some miles one of the men had given her a thin cotton coat and some scraps of cloth to tie around her feet, but after walking and running nearly ten miles they were sore and aching. Her abductors brought her some raisins and fruit and, after eating these, the bewildered girl curled up under a rock and tried to rest. Here they stayed until the sun set in the evening and it was safe to set off again.

Back in Kohat, the British authorities were in a frenzy of activity. Major Ellis was contacted and the news of his wife's murder and his daughter's kidnapping broken to him. The pressing urgency was to find out who was holding Molly and retrieve her before she could be taken over the border into Afghanistan, from where it would be much harder to rescue her, the British having no jurisdiction in that country. The finger of suspicion began to point towards Ajab Khan and his brother Shahzada. The brothers, members of the warlike Bosti Khel tribe (a sub-tribe of the Afridis, themselves a sub-tribe of the Pathans), had been implicated in the recent theft of some rifles from a police station. The British had raided a village in the hills, seized back the rifles and, even more damagingly, clothing belonging to the murdered Colonel and Mrs Foulkes. Worse still, although the brothers themselves had been away at the time, their comrades had attempted to conceal themselves and their rifles by dressing up as women to deter the British from searching them. The ruse failed and the gang was taunted by the women of the tribe for their cowardice. Humiliated and angry, Ajab swore that he would perform such a deed of vengeance against the British as had never been heard of before.

Meanwhile Molly, shivering in the hills above Kohat, had decided that her best chance of staying alive lay in co-operating with her captors. So, tired and cold as she was, she exerted every fibre in her body to keep up with the men as, once again they set off, up and down hills and through long winding valleys. For the next four days this pattern of travelling by night and resting by day continued. They reached altitudes of 7,000 feet travelling up to nineteen miles a night. Occasionally, when she could walk no more, one of the men would carry her for a short way, slung across his shoulders, but this was not comfortable and she preferred to walk. Once or twice the group came across curious villagers and after these encounters they took circuitous routes to avoid villages. Molly was given milk and unleavened bread to eat. Once one of the men shot a partridge of which she was given the lion's share.

'I must say the brutes were as kind to me as they knew how to be except on one occasion,' she told a friend in a letter afterwards. That occasion was when, on the third day of her trek, she realised that she was trudging in almost bare feet through snow. 'Already exhausted, I nearly wept with frustration. For every step I took on the steep slope, I slipped back two. At last, as I slithered to the bottom for the umpteenth time, I stopped and refused to go on. Immediately one of the men drew his dagger and holding it across my throat pointed upwards. I just shrugged my shoulders. I was past caring. I'd rather be dead than walk another step. I suppose it was obvious I wasn't simply being awkward because the next moment the man put his dagger away, picked me up and carried me to the top.' Suffering intensely from cold, fatigue and hunger, she was relieved when, on the morning of the 18 April, they came to a village where she was told she could rest and eat.

Meanwhile three separate rescue missions were being dispatched into the Tirah, the area where the British suspected, rightly, that Molly had been taken. Firstly, a force of loyal Afridis was sent into the hills to comb the villages and valleys for any sign of Molly and her kidnappers. Secondly, Kuli Khan, the assistant political agent of the nearby Kurrum valley, departed for the hills to try to locate and negotiate with Molly's abductors. Thirdly, Mrs Lilian Starr, a British nurse from Peshawar, who had seen her own husband murdered by tribesmen six years earlier, was approached by the Chief Commissioner of the North West Frontier Province, Sir John Maffey. He asked her if she would go into the hills, unarmed, with a small party of men to try and secure Molly's release. Without hesitation, she agreed.

Up in the Tirah Valley, Molly had no idea of the frantic attempts to track her down. When they arrived in the village she had been taken into a small room at the top of the house and told to lie on a bed. Food was brought and some women washed her hands and feet. 'At first,' she recalled, 'I was just thankful to rest. After a few hours, however, I realised this imprisonment was worse than the walk.' Trapped in her little room, under the scrutiny of the curious villagers, Molly was unable to sleep and her mind turned to her mother. 'I think I knew in my heart of hearts she was dead but I tried not to believe it. I heard them mention Kabul, the capital of Afghanistan, several times and I was terrified. I was afraid they were going to take me away again.'

Unlike Florentia Sale, Molly had no fellow hostages from whom she could draw comfort. She was surrounded by people whose language she could not speak and who were desperate enough to kill if things did not go their way. In the account she wrote of her captivity a short while after her release, she drops few hints of the terrible despair she felt at times, but the letters she wrote in captivity tell a different story. On the third day of her incarceration her captors produced paper and a pen and told her to write to the District Commissioner at Kohat, stating the terms of her release. With no language in common it was difficult to make out their demands, but Molly did her best. Her note begins in a courageous tone, but towards the end her genuine fear that her captors could turn on her at any moment is all too evident.

20th April 1923 at 1pm

Dear Colonel Bruce

I am alive and fairly well, but very weak from living on bread and potatoes. I am in a village NW of the Samana, My captors tell me that the DC at Peshawar has offered a ransom for me. Is it true? If so, they are after it. They also want three or four men you took in connection with those rifles the other day. What can you do for me? If anything, will you comply with their terms at Hangu, as it is the nearest place from here. Could you give the bearer of this chit some warm clothes for me, coat, shoes, and breeches − a skirt is no use to me, the way I shall have to travel. Please do something. I can't stand it much longer. My fondest love to dad and Mum. How is the latter? They will kill me on the slightest pretext. Take care of yourself. I can't say more now.

Yours sincerely,
Molly Ellis

PS These are the names of the four men they want, as near as I can get them: −

Alam Khan   Sher Khan
Alliyar Khan   Thaa Shah

PS would you send an answer by the bearer of this? It would be such a relief to hear something. Remember they stick at nothing. I can't speak the language, so it is awful.

Molly suspected, rightly as it turned out, that her letter would not reach its intended recipient, at least not for several days. In fact it got as far as Khanki Bazaar, a village eight miles from where she was being kept, and was waiting there when Lilian Starr arrived there the next day, hoping to hear news of Molly. A second letter, written by Molly to Colonel Bruce, begged him to accede to the kidnappers' demands: 'They are very threatening and won't let me go till they have these things and money. They are frightening me more than ever and I am afraid I shall never get out of this . . . My love to Dad and Mum again. I fear the worst for Mum. Did they kill her?' The letters confirmed that Molly was alive and well, but that there was little time to lose in securing her release as the situation could change in moments.

With the arrival in Khanki Bazaar of Kuli Khan, the political agent (who managed to get a letter to Molly, sending with it a riding habit for her to wear in place of her thin pyjamas), negotiations for Molly's release began in earnest. The Khan brothers finally consented to bring Molly down to Khanki Bazaar so that she could receive the medical attention of Lilian Starr. At 10 p.m. on 21 April Molly was awakened and told to get ready for a night march. Dazed and tired, she set off once more. Her captors managed to communicate to her that a white woman was waiting for her, but she did not believe them. Unable to keep up with the men's swift pace, she was carried much of the way until finally, in the early hours of 22 April, they arrived at Khanki Bazaar where, to her joy, she found Lilian Starr awaiting her.

Still the ordeal was not over, as the negotiations were far from resolved. Ajab and his gang held out for generous terms, confident that they held the winning card in the shape of Molly. The tide began to turn when the first of the rescue parties sent into the mountains by Maffey began to attack the houses of the villagers who had hidden the gang. Now the locals began to put pressure on the kidnappers to remove themselves and the danger of Molly being spirited over the border into Afghanistan, only a few days' march away, became acute. Then the volatile Shahzada foolishly provoked the local mullah, who cursed Shahzada and immediately withdrew his protection from the gang. They were now without allies and their position weak. Accordingly they were forced to accept less generous terms for Molly's release. While negotiations proceeded Lilian Starr held a medical clinic for the locals.

On the 22nd Molly was cheered to receive a letter from her father, written just three days after she was seized. 'My own beloved darling baby,' he wrote, ' . . . Keep on being my own brave darling child & I shall have you in my arms at the very earliest possible moment & you shall never be out of my sight again as long as you are in this country . . . My heart is torn out with anxiety but today they have brought in news of you which gives me some hope at any rate.'

He was careful not to mention her mother's death, but Molly had by now had her worst fears confirmed by Lilian Starr. In a second letter her father confessed to 'the awful anxiety I am enduring . . . but I am living in hope that very soon after this gets to you I myself will be with you. God bless you my angel child & keep you from any further harm.' Molly had written to him the day before, reiterating her captors' demands. Aware of the tension in the atmosphere and feeling that she was living on a knife-edge, she poured out her fears that 'they will stick at nothing & will kill me on the slightest pretext as I fear they did Mum'. She ended by urging him to 'do something quickly'. Now, with Lilian Starr at hand and her prospects looking considerably brighter, Molly found new courage. Conscious that her father, widowed, alone and desperately anxious, was perhaps in even greater need than she of comfort and reassurance, she now wrote in a much braver tone. 'Darling,' she told him, 'you are all I have got now & all I have lived for the last 9 days . . . Darling don't give away to despair, remember we have each other. I am quite safe & in kind hands, so don't worry I will be with you soon. I will be your own brave baby & I won't ever leave you again unless I can help it. Tons of hugs & kisses, ever your loving Mollkin.'

The following day, Molly was taken to a fort twenty miles away where she had an emotional reunion with her father. The next day they drove down to Kohat where she stayed at Government House to escape the mass of well-wishers who wanted to see her. Molly had recovered sufficiently to be able to play tennis the next day and ride her beloved pony Brandy. The story of her kidnap had by now reached newspapers in London and even Los Angeles. There were questions in the House of Commons as to how such an outrage had been allowed to occur, and calls came for the government to take over the enclave of tribal territory bordering British India and impose law and order.

As soon as news of the rescue arrived in Britain it was announced in the House of Commons and Molly immediately became a heroine in the press. She was reported to have emerged from captivity emaciated and hobbling on lacerated feet, whereas in fact she was healthy if exhausted. As Lilian Starr was able to reassure Major Ellis, Molly had '*not* been bruised, damaged or violated in any way'. The gang escaped into Afghanistan but were killed the following year in an ambush by the Afghan army. After some months in Britain Major Ellis decided to return to army life and Molly took on the role of surrogate wife to her father, acting as his companion. Shortly after her ordeal she had said of India, 'I hate the country and the natives.' But a few years on she had recovered sufficiently to go back with her father. Here she met her husband, Major Wade, some fourteen years her senior, who had travelled from China to meet the heroine of whom he had heard so much. So Molly too became an army wife and, like her mother was revered for her kindness towards soldiers' families. In 1986 she revisited Kohat, now part of Pakistan, where she was fêted and honoured. The legend of 'Ajab and Ellis' continues to be told and sung about to this day in the Afridi heartland (one version of the story even has it that Molly fell in love with Ajab, but as she consistently described her abductors as 'brutes' this seems unlikely).

Less than twenty years after Molly's ordeal, thousands of other British women across Asia learned what it was to live as captives of an enemy who disregarded the normal rules on the treatment of prisoners, and kept them isolated from the world, not for days but for years on end. When war came to the Far East in 1942, 20,000 British civilians were herded into internment camps by the Japanese. In some camps conditions were so dire, with lack of sanitation, overcrowding and malnutrition all contributing to the spread of disease, that mortality rates were 30 per cent or higher. Women and children were usually imprisoned separately from their men, and so spent an agonising three years often not knowing whether their husbands and fathers were dead or alive. For some women it was the presence of their children that stiffened their resolve to survive, while others were buoyed up by the companionship of their fellow women – although many did not make it to liberation day.

Ruth Russell-Roberts, a beautiful former model for the society couturier Norman Hartnell, had lived in Singapore since the late 1930s. The very epitome of glamour, Ruth was a keen skier, a motor-racing devotee and a gifted musician. She had met her husband, Denis, then an officer in the British Army, in India in 1932 and they married two years later. When Denis's regiment left India for England, he exchanged into an Indian Army regiment, the 11th Sikhs, and moved with them to Singapore. Ruth was visiting England in 1939 when war broke out. After much string-pulling, she managed to get on board an aircraft that arrived in Singapore just before Christmas that year. Here, she and Denis resumed their gilded existence, seemingly safe from the horrors of war to which their families and friends back in Britain were being subjected. In January 1941 Ruth gave birth to a daughter, Lynette. Shortly afterwards, Denis was posted north to Ipoh in Malaya with the 5th Battalion of the 11th Sikhs which formed part of the 22nd Indian Infantry Brigade. To keep herself busy, Ruth began working for the RAF Headquarters casualties section.

Within months there were signs that the war, that had once seemed so remote from the tranquillity of Singapore, was creeping ever closer. On 7 December 1941 the first air raid on Singapore took place. In the same twenty-four hours Pearl Harbor was attacked and the Philippines bombed. That month the Japanese invaded Hong Kong and Malaya and began storming through the jungle of the Malay Peninsula, far faster than the British had imagined was possible. The British forces, lacking sufficient ammunition or air support, were forced to conduct a difficult fighting withdrawal. As the invasion progressed, the women and children of white Malaya began to pour into Singapore, the 'impregnable fortress' that, its inhabitants were assured, could never fall. Even when the bombing began there was no mass evacuation of women and children, as had taken place in London.

Ruth, like many British women working for the services, felt that it was her duty to remain in her post. Besides, she could not leave until she had news of Denis, still in Malaya and engaged in bitter fighting. But by mid-January 1942, with the bombing worsening (although the shops still stocked the latest London fashions and Raffles Hotel was still full at cocktail hour), the evacuation of 'useless mouths' began. Ruth was torn between her duty to her daughter and her husband. In the end she made the agonising decision to send Lynette back to safety in England in the care of a friend, while she remained in Singapore, planning to follow later. She saw Lynette off on the *Duchess of Bedford* while air raid sirens screamed as Japanese bombers flew above. She prayed that the ship would make it safely back to England past the enemy submarines. Ruth's reunion with Denis came a few days later when he turned up in Singapore, having retreated down the Malay Peninsula keeping just a few steps ahead of the Japanese. They spent a romantic few days together before the long-delayed evacuation of white non-combatants finally took place, on 11 February (although the Governor was still insisting 'Singapore Must Stand'). Now it was Denis's turn to wave from the dockside as he watched Ruth's ship, the *Mata Hari*, disappearing into the distance.

As the *Mata Hari* and the other vessels in the evacuation fleet chugged out to sea, heading for Australia via Java, Ruth leaned over the rail to watch Singapore, where she had been so happy, recede towards the horizon. The whole island seemed to be aflame as bombed oil installations blazed fiercely, the din of battle was audible and even the water itself seemed to be on fire. The little cargo ship held 480 passengers, several hundred more than it was designed to accommodate, and as it threaded its way through the Indonesian archipelago, Japanese bombers overhead frequently forced them to cram below decks as the sea erupted around them with exploding bombs. In the midst of this drama Ruth met a nurse called Christine Cleveley whom she had known in Singapore and whose friendship was to sustain her in the years ahead. As they headed into the Banka Straits the *Mata Hari's* luck began to run out. A Japanese fleet lurked in the waters ahead of them and, after frantically trying to dodge the enemy ships for many hours, the *Mata Hari's* captain was eventually forced to surrender to a Japanese destroyer on 15 February, the same day that Fortress Singapore finally fell.

Japanese launches drew alongside the *Mata Hari* and the frightened passengers were conveyed to the shore of tropical Banka Island. Carrying her luggage, which included a silver fox fur, several items of jewellery and a purse containing a hundred Singapore dollars, Ruth marched with her companions through sweaty jungle. Under the curious gaze of the accompanying Japanese soldiers, they walked until they arrived at Muntok, the island's main town, where they were brusquely shown into a dilapidated, filthy former coolie barracks. This was the first of many internment camps in which Ruth and her fellow women and their children were to spend the next three years as the Japanese moved them from one camp to the next. After sixty days Ruth and Christine were moved from Muntok to a camp in Palembang, across the Banka Straits in Sumatra. Here they joined 350 other women and children, British, Dutch and Australian, all crammed into fifteen small houses. Numbers quickly swelled as more Dutch women were rounded up and brought into the camp.

The Japanese guards treated the women and children contemptuously, slapping their faces if they stepped out of line. Rations were meagre and consisted almost solely of rice. The camp was surrounded by wire and completely cut off from the outside world. Unlike the men's camps, where clandestine radios were usually constructed allowing the prisoners to keep up with the course of the war, the women knew nothing of life beyond the wire. Red Cross parcels sent to the internees were never distributed (they were found after the war stacked in neat piles in warehouses), while letters took years to get through. It was not until late 1944 that Ruth heard the news she had longed for: the *Duchess of Bedford* had made it to England and Lynette, now three, was safe and well.

In May 1942, through great ingenuity and at considerable risk, Ruth managed to smuggle a letter out of camp that, seven months later, reached Denis, now a prisoner in the notorious Changi jail in Singapore. 'I am safe and well,' she wrote. 'I lost everything except my life, but no matter.' She told him how she was working hard, scrubbing, cooking and cleaning, although she had had to be taken off wood-chopping fatigue as it had become too much for her. She gave him advice as to how to avoid beri-beri (the disease, rife in interment camps, that caused the body to swell terribly as a result of vitamin deficiency). She ended with the words: 'I live solely on the thought of being reunited with you and Lynette. Look after yourself, darling, don't worry about me, I can take it. Ruth.'

In fact, Ruth's weak state was already giving cause for anxiety among her friends. Concerned by the swollen belly she was developing as a result of her rice-based diet (although like the other women, her limbs were grow-ing steadily more skeletal), Ruth had taken to jogging round the camp perimeter in an effort to regain her svelte figure. This exertion exacted a terrible toll on her slight frame, already weakened by malnutrition, and she became steadily thinner and frailer. In vain Christine Cleveley tried to persuade her to desist, but it was not until two years had gone by that Ruth was forced to give it up and by then the damage to her constitution had been done. As Denis later acknowledged, 'Ruth's life in India and the Far East had hardly trained her to become self-sufficient. So Christine took her in hand, and taught her to knit and to cook, and she even cut her hair. In return Ruth gave her friendship, gaiety and affection . . . The two of them shared a relationship which endured to the end.' When they were not work-ing on their vegetable patches, cooking or husking rice, the women tried to keep their morale up by playing cards, acting in sketches, and even singing in a choir. The friendships between women that so enhanced life in ordi-nary circumstances now became a lifeline as they supported each other.

Those who liberated the camps in Sumatra and Java found that women had, on the whole, adapted better to captivity than the men, having had fewer problems with squabbling and thieving. They had been subjected to similar levels of starvation and neglect by their guards, although they were treated less brutally than the men, but their survival rates were considerably better.

After two more moves of camp, by October 1944 the women were back on Banka Island. Many had died from fever and malnutrition. The survivors were weak from their near starvation diet, combined with the effects of the strenuous labour required to grow the quantity of vegetables that the Japanese camp guards demanded they produce. But in the surroundings of their new camp, cleaner and more airy than the last, their situation began to look brighter. Ruth had sold her precious jewellery for extra food, retaining only her emerald, diamond and ruby eternity ring, Denis's wedding present to her, from which she could not bear to part. Her silver fox fur, which would have fetched a high price, had long since been stolen.

Just before Christmas 1944, a malaria-like fever hit the camp and one by one the women succumbed to it. At first it seemed that Ruth had escaped, but then she and Christine both went down with it and lay side by side in the camp hospital, sweating and delirious. Christine recovered but Ruth, frail and thin, remained desperately ill. Her friends hoped that if they managed to procure some proper food it might aid her recovery. So, at last, Ruth's wedding ring was sacrificed for food. A brave Dutch woman risked punishment to buy the food from a trader beyond the wire and, on her return, brought not only the food but, miraculously, a letter from Denis, over a year old. By now too weak to read it herself, Ruth listened as Christine read it to her. She smiled happily and nodded. A few minutes later she turned over on to her side and died.

Denis did not learn of her death until some months after VJ Day (Victory over Japan Day, 15 August 1945). The surviving women prisoners from Java and Sumatra were gradually flown back to Singapore to await reunions with their husbands and families. Many of the women went straight to Singapore's Alexandra Hospital. It was here that Denis went. As he stood waiting he saw a line of women walk into the hospital. 'How ill and weary they looked, how unkempt, how thin. I felt a lump come into my throat and for the very first time a little stab of pain, of dread of what might be. Then I saw Christine [whom he had met before the war] and she saw me. She was overcome and found it difficult to say anything. She squeezed my hand and whispered in my ear, "I'm so sorry, Denis". It was just like that.'

As the success of the Japanese invasion of South East Asia had taken the world, and the British in particular, so much by surprise, there were many other army wives who found themselves in the wrong place at the wrong time in 1942. As the flag of the Rising Sun was hoisted over Malaya, Burma, Hong Kong and the Philippines, thousands of civilians who had failed to escape in time were herded into internment camps. There, for nearly four years, they would face a daily struggle for survival. Angela Templer, a gunner officer's wife, was living in Hong Kong in 1940 when it was decided to evacuate women and children to ensure that they were well out of the way should the fighting reach the colony. Unfortunately, the destination they chose was the Philippines, which was to become the scene of some of the bloodiest fighting and cruellest atrocities of the war. Angela's husband Bob stayed in Hong Kong. He was later awarded the DSO for his gallant actions in the Battle of Hong Kong in December 1941, but was taken prisoner when Hong Kong fell.

Angela, her three children (all under the age of nine) and their English nanny settled comfortably in a hill station in the Philippines and for almost a year, although they missed Bob, life was pleasant and comfortable. Then in December 1941 they heard the news that the Japanese had landed in Manila and their cosy security dissolved. To safeguard their possessions, especially jewellery, Angela and the other wives busied themselves making buttons into which they stitched their rings. The buttons were then sewn on to the children's pyjamas. 'I never could wash the children's pyjamas without practically sitting and looking at the line all the time to see the buttons were all right,' she recalled later.

For the first few months of the Japanese occupation, life continued much as normal for the Templer family. An internment camp was opened at Santo Tomas University in Manila. But it was not until March 1942 that Angela and her family had to give up their house and move into the camp, in a small room into which were crammed sixteen people, including eight children of three and under. The nights were noisy and restless but food, if a little unpalatable, at least was still in good supply. Soon, however, the rations began to diminish.

The Santo Tomas camp contained 3,500 internees, American, British, Dutch and Polish, businessmen and army families, prostitutes and criminals. Although, unlike many camps, it contained both sexes, they were segregated within it. The Americans, who accounted for about 70 per cent of the camp population, took the lead in the organisation of the camp, setting up committees, including a sanitation committee and a camp sewing department. But for all their hard work, as the months went by conditions for the internees deteriorated rapidly. Meat stews were replaced by 'mush': rice mixed with corn meal and boiled relentlessly into a sloppy porridge. Amazingly, with Nanny's help, Angela managed to keep her three children free from the more serious diseases such as TB, 'starch stomach' (the distended abdomen that resulted from a diet of almost pure rice), beri beri, and other problems that flourished in the camp, brought on by vitamin deficiency. Children often adapted more readily than adults to camp life. 'I think they really enjoyed some of it and when we got back and stayed with my mother they said "Aren't there any children in England?" They were used to going round in a marvellous mob. They thought it was awfully dull. And I don't think their teeth all fell out which I was expecting. No milk, no proper fresh vegetables, no eggs, no butter, no cheese, all the things you suppose a child must have that I think it was extraordinary. It jolly well teaches you what you can do without.'

In 1943 it was announced that some internees could move to another camp at Los Banos in the hills, forty miles south of Manila. Angela and Nanny decided that the countryside would be a healthier environment, so they and about 800 other internees were moved to the new camp. Here they lived for the next two years, in long barrack-style bamboo huts, getting progressively more emaciated; many died as the Japanese camp authorities cut the rations, first to half then to quarter. 'At the end we had about half a tumbler of rice a day and that's not very much among one, two, three, four people and three children. But before that people tried to run schools for the children and then everybody got too tired. You know, my normal weight is nine stone something or other and when I came out of the camp at the end I was seven stone four. Everything sticks through: your bones stick through and you don't feel like doing anything very energetic and you certainly don't feel like teaching school.'

In January 1945 it seemed as if their liberation day had finally arrived. The internees woke up one morning to find the Japanese guards had gone, leaving behind their stores of rice, which were quickly raided and distributed. Local people came into the camp to sell fruit and vegetables and the internees soon began to walk normally again rather than shuffling and dragging their emaciated frames around. The guards' radio was found and the internees listened with jubilation to reports that General MacArthur and his force had landed at Lingayen Gulf on the main Philippine island on 9 January (he had begun his liberation of the Philippine islands in October 1944).

Then, after just a week, the guards reappeared, furious that their rice had been stolen, and an even stricter regime was imposed. The internees were told to stay away from the wire on pain of death, and given unhusked rice as their ration, forcing them to spend hours every day banging it with shoes, baseball bats and hammers to unhusk it. Morale in the camp hit a new low and the death toll rose again. One man, maddened by hunger ate his pants. A pig, the camp's last, was killed, and shared out between 2,100 people. Some women's faces swelled up so much they could not see properly. Tortured by thoughts of food, they wrote out recipes of their fantasy meals. Liberation had to come soon or it would be too late for many of them. The camp ran out of coffins and a bathroom had to be converted into a psychotic ward as internees began to go insane with hunger.

Then, on the morning of 23 February 1945, as the pale yellow light of dawn began seeping through the windows of their huts, the internees awoke to the sounds of shouting. Angela ran outside to see the sky filled with parachutes, 'hundreds of little umbrellas coming down, hundreds and hundreds. And of course you didn't know if they were American, Japanese or what they were and so I went back into the little room and got the three children and said "I think we'd better get under the bed" thinking it would be vaguely safe. So I stuffed them under the bed and then all sorts of firing broke out right there because they were Americans who were dropping and they came right in and killed all the Japanese. Filipino guerillas who had been sitting round all night waiting as they knew this was going to happen came in and so it was bang, bang, bang and you hadn't the slightest idea who was doing what or why. Then it gradually stopped and we crept out from under the bed and in the passage was standing an American GI with a walki-talki [sic] radio. Well of course we didn't even know such things existed. We were all shrunk and thin little people and he looked simply gigantic as he was standing there with this thing and he said "come along now we are going to take you out – you've got ten minutes".'

Angela and Nanny picked up the children and hurried down to the camp football field, at the edge of a large lake, Lake Luzon. Here a fleet of American amtracs (amphibious craft) was waiting to take the internees to safety. Angela, Nanny and the three children were piled into an amtrac and began speeding across the lake. It was a nerve-wracking experience. 'We were all crouched down inside them and there were machine gunners up on the sides. There were Jap snipers firing from the shore and Hazel, my little girl, was sitting down below one of the machine gunners and of course his hot shells [empty cases] were coming down below and she said, "I'm dead, I'm dead, I'm sure I'm dead". Poor little thing she was terribly scared. However we pulled out to the middle of the lake and away we went and landed the other end . . .'

The rescue operation was carried out by the 672nd Amphibious Tractor battalion and the 188th Glider Infantry, belonging to XIV corps of the US army. It was, as XIV's report of the action later described it, 'an operation brilliantly conceived and meticulously executed'. The stakes were high because the Americans knew that the retreating Japanese had, elsewhere in the Philippines, burnt alive 150 American prisoners of war rather than let them be liberated, and 100,000 Philippine civilians were massacred. As the fighting moved closer, the peril of the 2,417 Los Banos internees increased. Just four hours' march from the camp on the San Juan River were 4,000 Japanese troops. The internees had to be rescued before this force could reach the camp. With precision timing, just as the parachutists of B Company of the 188th Glider Infantry descended on Los Banos, the other companies of the regiment attacked the Japanese force at San Juan River to prevent them moving on the camp. At the same time the amtracs of 672nd Amphibious Tractor battalion landed on the shore of the Laguna de Bay ready to receive the internees. As soon as they were on board the amtracs sped across the twenty-mile-long lake, under attack from some Japanese infantry who were in the area. When the escapees reached the other side they were driven in trucks, still well within the artillery range of the Japanese, to the town of Muntinlupa, where they were housed in a prison as their temporary accommodation. There were only two casualties among the relieving force and three internees slightly wounded. All the Japanese camp guards were killed.

That first night the freed internees were given a semolina-like cream to eat, in small quantities so as not to overfeed their shrunken stomachs. 'Coming to the evening my children had disappeared just like that,' Angela remembered. 'The place was full of American GIs who had fought up from New Guinea and hadn't seen a white child for months and they just took them off so I thought that's fine somebody else can look after them for a change. In the evening they came back loaded with sweets and chocolates and they said "Mum, you can have this we don't know what it is but it's not at all nice". Of course they had never had or couldn't remember what chocolate and sweets were and they said there are chocolate biscuits too – horrible! . . . . That night I woke up in the middle of the night and always before if you woke up at night the great thing was not to think how hungry you were because you just got more hungry and more frustrated and rattled. That night I woke up and thought I'm rather hungry and I think I'll have a chocolate biscuit. Much the best chocolate biscuit I've ever had. It was absolutely delicious.'

After a month, Angela and her family were taken by hospital ship to the United States and then on to Britain. It was another six months before her husband was released from his POW camp in Hong Kong. They were eventually reunited in England at the end of 1945. The following year Angela received the US Asiatic Pacific medal inscribed with her name. She had survived three years of boredom, disease, starvation and danger and succeeded, with Nanny's help, in keeping her three small children in health and even happiness throughout this time. As her husband proudly remarked, 'Medals have been awarded for much less.'

On the other side of the world from where Angela Templer and Ruth Russell-Roberts struggled to survive in captivity, another army wife also found herself pitched into terrible peril, although she did at least have the comfort of having her husband at her side throughout her ordeal. Barbara Egerton, whose husband Philip was a captain in 2nd Battalion, the Royal Irish Fusiliers, had been living on Malta since January 1939 when, in August 1942, Philip was posted home and the family was told to start packing. The Egertons and their young daughter Anne, aged six, had lived through the siege of Malta since it began in June 1940. The families of the five infantry battalions posted on the island at the outbreak of war had suffered alongside the Maltese civilians. By the time the siege was finally lifted at the end of 1942 many of them had been sent back to England in an evacuation so perilous that they might have wished that they were back in Malta.

Although many service families had left the island in the autumn of 1940, Barbara had decided to remain by Philip's side. She and Anne had become used to running for the air raid shelters several times a day and to living with gnawing hunger. During the last eight months the shortages had been particularly severe. Even so, Barbara was astounded when they were weighed before boarding the plane to find that when she stood on the scales with her fur coat on and suitcase in hand, she weighed only seven stone (she was five foot five inches). Philip was down from his usual twelve stone to ten.

Difficult as the situation in Malta had become, Barbara knew that their journey back to Britain would be fraught with risk. After a bumpy flight from Malta to Cairo, where they stayed for two weeks, the Egertons travelled to Suez, where they embarked on a ship bound for Durban. As Barbara stepped from the gangway on to the deck she dropped her handbag and a mirror fell out on to the deck where it smashed into pieces.

'Some hours later we sailed. It was the beginning of our adventure by sea. I remembered the broken mirror, remembered it was Friday, remembered also that there were five parsons aboard. Surely we must have bad luck ere long.'

In fact their journey down to the Cape was uneventful. At Durban they changed ships on to the 20,000-tonne *Duchess of Atholl*, a Canadian liner converted into a troopship. After a brief stopover in Cape Town the ship headed out to sea and up the West African coast. The most perilous part of the journey now lay ahead. The ship's captain warned that submarine attacks were possible and it was vitally important that nobody drop any litter overboard as ships could be tracked for miles by trails of refuse. Lifebelts had to be carried at all times and lifeboat drill was a twice-daily routine.

At 6.30 a.m. on 10 October the Egertons were lying in their beds, Philip and Barbara awake, Anne asleep, when a terrific jarring shook the ship. 'I put up my hand to switch on the light, there was no response. Total darkness as it was still blackout hour. "We seem to have hit something," said Phil. I could but agree. We both knew what we suspected. "Better get up and dress." I got out of bed and tried to dress quickly but a curious numbness seemed to blind my limbs and make my fingers like wool. Phil dressed too, we were very silent. By now we could hear a scream or two as people realised what had happened, doors opened and shut and then all was deadly quiet. I had at last dressed but had forgotten the most important part of female dress in my hurry, my bra, and was to bitterly regret it for the next week. A tap at the door and Smith [a ship's officer] looked in, "No need for alarm. Torpedo, Sir. I will leave this lamp in the corridor, no electricity.". He was gone. A master of that British art of understatement.'

The family made their way up to the deck and towards the lifeboats. There was, Barbara recalled, no panic. 'All very calm and very orderly. We might have been on our way to breakfast instead of taking to the boats. I shook with emotion and trusted that if anyone noticed it I should pass as being cold. Anne clutched "Charlie" [her teddy] as I carried her in my arms . . . we stood by our allotted boats awaiting orders.'

As they stood waiting another huge shudder ran through the ship and it swayed drunkenly. It had been hit by a second torpedo. The command came to lower the boats. 'Anne was the first to go, and she climbed into the boat assisted by a sailor. "Charlie" was under her arm, she went forward and sat down, I followed her, then three other women, a baby (9 months) and a six-year-old girl. Then came the men of the party. The sea surged and the waves heaved. The drop from the boat deck of a 20,000-tonne liner is no small distance and now it looked immense. "Hold on tight to Anne, darling, shut your eyes and keep still", Phil's voice said and at that moment the boat began to slide down on the davits. I felt horribly afraid, but soon a violently rocking motion occupied my senses. We were on the sea. We were safely down. The sheer side of the *Duchess* rose steeply above us and the decks were lined by army and RAF personnel. Wild cheers broke out as they saw us safely afloat, our oarsmen started to pull away from the ship. No mean task on that heavy sea. "Come on Cambridge, come on Oxford", shouted the troops, "Remember me to Mother" called a lone voice, other less suitable remarks were shouted and then more and more cheers broke out as further boat loads drew away. Our oarsmen were having a very stiff time keeping the boat away from the ship and preventing her getting swamped by the huge waves . . . Then I became appallingly sick and my reputation as being a "Good sailor" rapidly faded, and for four hours I cared but little what happened to me. Everyone suffered in some degree and the apologies at first so noticeable soon were absent as the sound of retching rent the air.'

Four hours after boarding the boats they watched as the ship was hit by a third torpedo. As she swayed in the water the captain and remaining crew swung over the side on a rope and into a boat. Five crew members had already died in the engine room when the first torpedo had hit. The *Duchess* began to list badly, smoke pouring from her funnels. 'Then she rolled sharply on her side, and very slowly and painfully slid under the waves. The sea boiled and hissed around her and at once wreckage came to the surface. Hundreds of oranges bobbed about, part of the cargo, spars, and furniture and not far off surfaced the enemy, with crew lined up on deck, the Hun submarine. She hung around like some large dark hound. We waited for the boats to be searched and feared we might get a burst of fire. The men in our boats wearing caps took them off and hid the badges, moments passed and to our relief the submarine dived and we were alone.'

The ship had been hit 200 miles east of Ascension Island. The radio operator had managed to send off an SOS message after the first torpedo, but no answer had been received. As the morning wore on any hope of a rescue grew increasingly slender and Barbara began to fear that they might drift indefinitely until death released them. There were fifty in the lifeboat, including three children and four women. The boat had a leak and the water swished around their legs. 'The sun beat down; we soon became very sunburnt and the children were the worst sufferers but we could do nothing for them. Shifts were taken at the oars by the men while we women were relegated to the stern and part of the sail were [sic] erected lengthwise to give us a bit of privacy; it was behind this screen that the necessities of life were performed – a pretty tricky job balancing on a small bucket with the boat rocking like a cork. However, needs must and we soon lost any sense of shame when we requested that the bucket be passed aft to the Harem!

'We were indeed lucky to be in a boat and not on a raft. So the day wore on, rations of very dry biscuits were issued with chocolate and Horlicks milk tablets, all very difficult to swallow and usually made one very sick. A small portion of water was dealt out. Some of us had salved oranges as they bobbed past, and in spite of their salty flavour we were glad to have them for the children. I think that the most pathetic sight was to see the baby of the party suffering great discomfort from the lack of proper food; it cried and then howled and its mother tried to comfort it with bits of biscuits, but as the child was barely a year old it couldn't eat food like that . . . Darkness fell and the children were settled as well as could be arranged for the night, a last meal of chocolate and biscuits were handed out topped up with a sip of water.'

All night the boat tossed and pitched in stormy seas while its passengers baled out frantically. At 2 a.m. it was hit by a large wave and it seemed as though it would sink, but after gasping through a sheet of salt water it righted itself. When daylight dawned they began rowing again. There was little conversation. Everyone was exhausted and dispirited as their prospects seemed bleak. Then, at 8 a.m., the shout went up: 'There's smoke over there, look.' Then a plane flew low over the lifeboats. To their joy the passengers recognised the Stars and Stripes on its fuselage. 'We cheered, we stood up and waved, I tried to cheer too but no sound came. Back came the plane the pilot waving and then he was gone. Conversation broke out. Some sang, some whistled, we were souls reborn. Breakfast was eaten with zest. We had the hope of life again. The nightmare was clearing.' In the midst of the excitement Anne's faithful teddy Charlie was dropped into the water at the bottom of the boat and had to be pinned to the mast to dry, like a small bedraggled figurehead.

The rowers were now pulling hard in the direction of the smoke and after some time drew up alongside the armed merchant cruiser, HMS *Corinthian*. The exhausted passengers hauled themselves up a ladder (the children were lifted up in a basket) and Barbara was offered tea. *Corinthian* had, it transpired, picked up their distress signal and had sped to their aid, rescuing all 830 passengers and crew in the lifeboats. The children were fed, the babies, who had no change of clothes, taken down to the sick bay and bathed while a party of burly sailors were busily cutting out and sewing tiny vests from rolls of lint. Most of the passengers were suffering from sunburn and a doctor treated Barbara's legs, which were badly swollen from exposure in salt water for thirty hours. They had to sleep on deck as the *Corinthian* had room for only 100 passengers and was now carrying over 900. Four days later they sailed into Freetown in the colony of Sierra Leone, a major supply base for Allied ships. As they drew into harbour an American soldier stepped in front of Barbara. ' "Say Mom, I want to take a snap of you and the kids to send back home, kinda remind them that there's a war on." He put his cine camera to his eye and I suppose "back home" later received a weird picture of an English woman and several children who had been very recently torpedoed and then thoroughly soaked in a tropical downpour.'

Their new ship was packed with survivors from seventy-two other ships that had been torpedoed off the coast of South Africa over the last month. Barbara had to spend the early part of the voyage lying in the sick bay as her swollen legs had become septic. Finally, on 1 November, they docked at Glasgow and, after a long and miserable train ride in blackout conditions and with no food and water, they arrived in London.

The feelings of helplessness, boredom and fear that were the lot of many prisoners, the terror of flight for those trying to escape – and the uncertainty for both as to when or if their ordeal would come to an end – were experienced by women and children who usually had no expectation of coming into contact with danger. In earlier centuries, however, other women faced almost constant peril as they exposed them-selves to life on the front line, even going on to the battlefield itself, in order to be near their men in the darkest moments of war.

12

At the Front and Under Fire

The shot and shell came hissing every two minutes. I could not but
feel a high degree of excitement, and I think it was not unnatural.
We were standing on the brow of a hill, backed by our magnificent
troops, and fronting the enemy; the doomed city beneath our feet,
and the pale moon above: it was indeed a moment worth a
hundred years of every-day existence. I have often prayed
that I might '*wear* out my life, and not rust it out', and it
may be that my dreams and aspirations will be realised.

Fanny Duberly, *The Crimea*

As both Florentia Sale and the revered Mrs Howley discovered in
Afghanistan and the Peninsula respectively, women who left the
confines of camp and quarters to accompany troops on the line of march
shared their perils as well as their rations. If they were surprised by the
enemy there was often little opportunity for the women and children to
take cover, and they found themselves in the line of fire. Some women
actually followed their husbands on to the field, but in the main wives
(particularly those with children) tried to keep clear of the fighting; and
commanders and husbands generally preferred it that way. Occasionally,
however, even women with no yearning for battlefield heroism, who

dutifully kept to their place in the rear, could be caught up in ferocious battles in which many of them were killed, wounded or captured.

In their campaigns in North America in the 1750s and the 1770s, the British frequently found themselves fighting in densely wooded hinterland. Both the Indians (fighting for the French) and, later, the American colonists used this terrain to their advantage, launching ambushes and surprise attacks against the British from the cover of the forest, after which they would melt away into the trees again. Major General Edward Braddock was one of the first British commanders to fall foul of this type of guerrilla warfare, when he marched through the thick woods around the River Monongahela to Fort Duquesne in 1755 to try to capture it from the French. Braddock's force of 1,300 men included 400 Virginia militia, one of whom, Colonel George Washington, was to reappear a decade later, this time as an enemy of the British. It also included, despite all Braddock's efforts to reduce their numbers, around fifty women, some of whom had children with them.

The going was slow at first as the pioneers had to cut their way through the uncharted forests with axes. Unfamiliar noises emanated from the dark woods. The women began to huddle together and clasp their children's hands tightly. As the journey went on, their fears mounted and they began to abandon their vulnerable position at the unguarded rear of the column, creeping forward to seek the protection of the armed men. Braddock eventually placed an officer over them to stop this. Deeper and deeper the column plunged into the forest, over hills and through streams, dragging heavy guns up steep mountains and down again through valleys. As the column snaked its way along the narrow roads, its very length increasing its vulnerability to attack from either side, both the scarlet-clad British soldiers and their blue-uniformed American allies began to feel the pace. Dysentery, hunger and exhaustion took their toll. But Braddock pressed on at an impressive pace and on 9 July 1755 the column safely crossed the River Monongahela (the obvious moment for an enemy to ambush them), bringing them within eight miles of their objective, Fort Duquesne. An air of optimism swept through the column, but within moments it was replaced by confusion when the scouting party suddenly came hurtling back, shouting that the enemy were less than 200 yards away. Seconds later the woods around the column suddenly erupted with the terrifying sound of Indian war whoops shortly followed by the rattle of muskets.

The bewildered British and American soldiers looked to see where this deadly fire was coming from. But almost all that could be seen were the puffs of smoke from the enemy muskets and brief glimpses of the fear-some Indian warriors of whose barbarity they had heard such terrifying accounts. For up to four hours (accounts vary) the battle continued. According to some sources, the Virginia militiamen wanted to pursue their enemy into the woods but Braddock, perhaps fearing that once among the trees they might desert, ordered them to stand and fight where they were. Women and children cowered in abject terror as the deadly stream of fire poured down on them. Braddock and Washington both had horses shot from under them.

Finally, after some hours, during which the wounded and dead mounted in piles on the ground, Braddock gave the order to retreat (or, according to some sources, could not prevent his panicked men from doing so). Just as the retreat began he was mortally shot and had to be carried from the battlefield. Now the invisible enemy at last began to show themselves. The 900-strong force, two-thirds of them Indian warriors, the rest French soldiers from Fort Duquesne, descended on the survivors who were desperately trying to struggle out of the trap. The French soldiers looked on in horror as their Indian allies began seizing and scalping the fleeing British soldiers. Nor did the women and children, who had spent the attack cowering among the baggage wagons or trying to cling to their husbands and fathers, escape the onslaught. Some had already been killed in the firefight, but several of those who had survived were now brought down as they tried to flee the killing ground. One witness noted that, in the stampede for safety, 'every one trying who should be the first, the Enemy pursued us, butchering as they came, as far as the other side of the River [Monongahela]; in crossing it they shot many in the water, both men and women, scalping and cutting them in a most Barbarous manner'. Another observer saw that 'in going Over the River there was an Indian Shot one of our wimen and began to scalp her. Her husband being a little before her shot the Indian dead.' A French officer who visited the scene of the battle two days afterwards observed, 'The bodies of a great number of men kill'd & those of eight Women or Girls entirely strip'd, lie promiscuously with dead horses for more than half a League.' The *Boston Times* reported on 18 August 1755 that 'out of 54 Women [with Braddock's column] only 4 returned'.

Not all were killed on the battlefield. Some were taken prisoner and tortured before being killed. Among them, legend has it, was Braddock's mistress whom he had taken on the expedition. This unfortunate woman was repeatedly raped, tortured to death and then eaten, a terrible fate that was to haunt the many British women with the army in America for years to come. In fact, historians have found it hard to confirm that Braddock had a mistress with him on the march. But if she was present and taken prisoner her fate could well have been as gruesome as the story suggests. In the recriminations that followed such a humiliating defeat at the hands of an inferior force, especially one that employed savages, the dead Braddock came in for excoriating condemnation for mindlessly adhering to European tactics. (In fact Braddock had employed Indian guides, although he had not always listened to their advice.) Equally loud were the cries for vengeance.

When William Pitt became Secretary of State in 1756 he was determined to avenge the Monongahela defeat. To this end the rival fort-building programme continued in the north of America. The British and American campaign received another setback when a key fort, Fort William Henry, fell to a French besieging force in August 1757. However, while the French won a victory, their reputation was severely damaged by its bloody aftermath. The fort's British commander, Lieutenant Colonel Monro, initially determined to hold out. But finding himself severely outgunned and outnumbered, he was forced to seek terms from the French. The French commander, General Montcalm, readily agreed to an honourable surrender which would allow the British and American garrison to march out with the full honours of war.

Even as the surrender was being formalised by French and British officers, Montcalm's Indian allies, who comprised a quarter of his 8,000-strong force, began violating its terms. Many of the Indians had been lured to the French campaign by the prospect of booty, brandy and scalps (Montcalm's aide-de-camp had been chilled by the sight of some Indians instructing their children in how best to prepare a human body for cooking). Now it seemed to them that the French were denying them their rewards by allowing the surrendering garrison to march away unmolested and with most of their property. Ignoring the orders and pleas of the French, the warriors descended on the British and American column as it assembled for the march out, stripping men of their clothing, swords, muskets, drums and fifes. They then began killing men, women and children. Witnesses recalled seeing Indians 'tearing the Children from their Mothers' Bosoms and their mothers from their husbands, then Singling out the men and Carrying them in the woods and killing a great many'. As men, women and children ran desperately in the direction of British-held Fort Edward, sixteen miles away, the Indians pursued, slaying and scalping those they caught. Out of 2,300 members of the garrison, only 600 made it to Fort Edward, among them ten out of the eighty women who had been at Fort William Henry. The other 1,700 had, it was presumed, been slaughtered in a massacre of horrifying proportions. News of the massacre quickly reached New York. Newspapers carried gruesome accounts of how 'the throats of most, if not all the women, were cut, their bellies ript open, their bowels torn out and thrown upon the faces of their dead and dying bodies: and, it is said, that all their women were murdered in one way or another'.

In fact, it later transpired that the massacre, while horrifying and barbaric, was not on the scale at first thought. A few days after the killing, five hundred soldiers, wives and other non-combatants were delivered to Fort Edward by the French who had taken them into their protection. Other members of the garrison, who had been taken prisoner by the Indians, were later released in return for ransoms. By the end of 1757 over three hundred of the Fort William Henry garrison were still missing. Although modern estimates put the number of those killed or permanently missing at 184 (of which probably ten were non-combatants), the early reports suggesting a slaughter of up to 1,700 stuck in the psyche of both British and Americans. The legend of the massacre of Fort William Henry was immortalised in James Fenimore Cooper's classic, *The Last of the Mohicans,* a fictionalised account of the siege and massacre, while 'Remember Fort William Henry' became a battle cry in coming conflicts.

Despite such atrocities, few women were deterred from accompanying their men to America and Canada. Some of them, too, became caught up in the fighting in the Revolutionary War. During the action leading to the occupation of Philadelphia at the end of 1777 a grenadier's wife was killed in the thick of the fight, while in a two-hour skirmish at Fort Ann in July 1777 a woman 'who kept close by her husband's side during the engagement' was mortally wounded.

By the time of the Peninsular War, generals were still having difficulty controlling the women, not only to stop them from disrupting marches but to prevent them from running on to the field before the action was over. Some women simply refused to be told. Captain George Landmann was heading into battle at Rolica, Portugal, in 1808, when he overtook a woman dressed in a cotton riding habit and straw bonnet, carrying a parasol and a large hand basket, also making determinedly for the thick of battle. 'The unexpected sight of a respectably-dressed woman in such a situation greatly perplexed me; for the musket-shot were showering about pretty thickly, and making the dust fly on most parts of the road. Moreover, at this place, several men killed, and others mortally wounded, all perfectly stripped, were lying scattered across the road. So that, in order to advance, she was absolutely compelled to step over some of them. At first I thought that the lady was unconscious of her danger, or was so bewildered at the surrounding confusion, in which she might have been accidentally involved, that she did not know she was then going towards the enemy. I, therefore, could not resist saying to her, *en passant*, that she had much better go back for a short time, as this was a very unfit place for a lady to be in, and was evidently a very dangerous one. Upon this, she drew herself up, and with a very haughty air, and, seemingly a perfect contempt of the danger of her situation, evidently proceeding from extreme agitation, she replied, "Mind your own affairs, Sir, – I have a husband before me." I obeyed.' A little later in the battle Landmann and some fellow officers again saw the woman, hastening towards the advance guard. They never managed to discover her identity.

Other ladies did more to endear themselves to their husbands' brother officers. Susanna Dalbiac, the 'delicate and beautiful' wife of Colonel Charles Dalbiac of the 4th Queen's Own Dragoons (later Hussars), followed her husband out to Spain in 1810 when she heard that he was ill with fever, leaving their young daughter to be cared for by relatives. Susanna was the daughter of an army officer but she did not seem robust enough for the arduous life of campaigning. Nonetheless, she stuck by her husband's side, enduring the privations and dangers of campaign 'with the fortitude and patience of her sex' as George Bell gallantly put it.

The night before the battle of Salamanca in July 1812 Susanna was sleeping on the ground beside her husband. For several days the two armies, the British under Wellington and the French under Marmont, had been marching almost parallel with each other across the plain of Salamanca. The nights were freezing and the soldiers, lacking tents, were driven to digging up coffins for firewood. Wellington himself declared that he had never been colder in his life. Mrs Dalbiac was at least able to share her husband's tent, but this did not protect her when a sudden thunderstorm erupted. The horses of the 5th (Princess Charlotte of Wales's) Dragoon Guards became frightened and broke loose, stampeding headlong down the hill to where the Dalbiacs lay. Colonel Dalbiac had just enough time to carry his wife under a gun, which saved them both from being trampled to death – the fate of several soldiers.

The following day the armies resumed their game of dare, marching within view of each other, but both refraining from attacking, until Wellington, who had been watching the French all morning, suddenly perceived that they were vulnerable as their column had become dangerously strung out. 'By God, that will do!' he exclaimed and, spurring on his horse, ordered his troops to attack. First the infantry surged forward, led by the 3rd Division under Wellington's brother-in-law Major General Edward Pakenham. Then came the cavalry, with the heavy dragoons, including Dalbiac's 4th Dragoons, under Major General Le Marchant. As the dragoons thundered up the hill towards the French, observers could see in their midst the extraordinary sight of a lady, hanging grimly on to her horse's reins, galloping beside her husband. As George Bell, who also fought at Salamanca (one of Wellington's greatest victories), wrote admiringly, 'There was no man present that day fighting the battle of his country that did not fight with more than double enthusiasm seeing that fair lady in such danger on the battlefield.'

The cavalry charge managed to shatter one French division and damage another, but the French fought back tenaciously, pouring cannon fire on to the advancing English. Le Marchant was shot through the spine, while other men fell all around. Yet Susanna Dalbiac rode on, her pale features set 'with a noble firmness', as one hyperbolic account later described. 'Leaden bullets in their deadly flight pierced her riding habit in many places. Miraculously she had escaped so far without hurt. A shell burst close to her husband's side and he reeled for a moment in his saddle. Then a stifled shriek burst from her lips. But her husband recovered his seat and rode on in calmness. The cavalry trumpets rang out an order, the horse broke into a rapid trot, she drew aside her horse, for she knew that a desperate charge was at that moment to be delivered.' Minutes later the cavalry returned from their charge and her husband rode straight towards her, gently lifted her from the saddle, and clasped her to him. 'As the regiment was dismissed from its ranks, all its remaining men gathered around the brave lady with demonstrations of deepest admiration and respect. They came from the breasts of men whose feelings were hardened through constant danger, but they knew that a woman had shared with them the risk of violent death.'

Another contemporary, Lieutenant Colonel William Tomkinson, while admiring her fortitude, believed that she actually remained about two miles from the battlefield while the fighting continued and did not venture on to the scene until nightfall when she set out to find her husband. 'She wandered some time alone on the hill where the action had taken place, amongst the killed and wounded. I cannot conceive a more unpleasant situation for a woman to be in, particularly at night.' Whatever the truth of her exploits, Susanna Dalbiac's presence was undoubtedly appreciated, not least by her husband.

At Quatre Bras and Waterloo too, many women managed to make their way on to the battlefield – a Welch Fusilier's wife, Jenny Jones, managed to stay on the field for the full three days without being sent away. Another devoted spouse, the pregnant wife of a private in the 27th (Inniskilling) Regiment (the regiment that suffered the highest number of fatalities in the battle), rushed on to the field to rescue her wounded husband. As she did so she was struck by a musket-ball and fell beside him on the ground. The two were taken together to a hospital at Antwerp. The soldier survived the amputation of both his arms, while his wife recovered from her wound and gave birth to a baby, to which the Duke of York became godfather, in recognition of the woman's heroic actions.

Several French women also took part in the battle of Waterloo. Harry Smith's brother Charles happened upon the body of a French officer 'of delicate mould and appearance' and, on closer examination, found it was that of a young, good-looking woman. 'What,' wondered Smith, 'were the circumstances of devotion, passion, or patriotism which led to such hero-ism, is, and ever will be, to me a mystery. Love, depend upon it.'

In the Crimean War there was less opportunity for wives to become caught up in the thick of battle, but several, like Margaret Kirwin, still came under fire in the course of their duties. Fanny Duberly frequently put herself in danger's way. When on 17 October 1854 the allies began their bombard-ment of Sebastopol's fortifications, she watched from her ship as immense clouds of smoke rose from the city and, later that evening, rode out to survey the damage to the town. Her journal records the mood of sunny optimism that at first prevailed in the British camp, but quickly began to evaporate as, two days after the massive bombardment began, Sebastopol had not fallen. 'We thought Sebastopol to stand, *perhaps*, a three days' siege – more likely a single day's; while some, more arrogant still, allowed it eight hours to resist the fury of the allies!'

Then, on 25 October, the Russians made their move. Hoping to cut the allies off from their supply base at Balaclava (the allied camp lay between Balaclava and Sebastopol but much nearer the latter), the Russians launched an attack on the allied defences at dawn. The first Fanny knew of the action was when, at eight o'clock, feeling far from well and still in her cabin, she looked out of her window to see Henry's soldier servant standing on the beach with her horse, saddled and waiting for her. Then someone thrust a note into her hand. It was from Henry and read: ' "The battle of Balaklava has begun, and promises to be a hot one. I send you the horse. Lose no time, but come up as quickly as you can: do not wait for breakfast." Words full of meaning! I dressed in all haste, went ashore without delay, and, mounting my horse "Bob," started as fast as the narrow and crowded streets [of Balaclava] would permit. I was hardly clear of the town, before I met a commissariat officer, who told me that the Turks had abandoned all their batteries, and were running towards the town. He begged me to keep as much to the *left* as possible, and, of all things, to lose no time in getting amongst our own men, as the Russian force was pouring on us; adding, "For God's sake, ride fast, or you may not reach the camp alive." Captain Howard, whom I met a moment after, assured me that I might proceed; but added, "Lose no time." ' As she rode towards the camp, Turkish soldiers came running in the other direction, having abandoned their positions to the Russians.

As Fanny neared the British lines she saw the cavalry retiring from their position before Sebastopol, leaving just the 93rd Sutherland Highlanders and 42nd Black Watch between the Russians and Balaklava. Fanny galloped in front of the 93rd, heading for the cavalry camp and Henry's tent, just before the 93rd began to discharge a volley of shot at the advancing Russians. An astonished officer of the 93rd later told Fanny that the last thing he remembered before the fusillade began was the sight of her hurtling across their front. The 93rd, standing fast as the Russians advanced, was described by the *Times* journalist William Howard Russell, looking on from the Sapoune Heights above the valley, as a 'thin red streak tipped with a line of steel' (which became altered in repetition to the famous 'thin red line'). The fleeing Turks, pursued by Cossacks on horseback, were heading straight for the camp and Fanny hastily gave orders that Henry's tent and all their valuables be packed up to save them from the clutches of the Cossacks.

Fanny's biographer, E.E.P. Tisdall, speculates that Henry might not have been so keen to summon his wife to the battle had he known just what danger he was placing her in. Possibly, like many others buoyed up by the British performance at Alma, Henry was confident that the Russians would be defeated before they got anywhere near Balaclava. Fanny, however, was unafraid and conscious that she was watching an event of great significance – the battle, it was hoped, that would bring the Russians to their knees and end the war. Together she and Henry made their way to a vineyard on the slopes above the valley, from where they could see the two armies were drawn up. Nearby, on the Sapoune Heights, Lord Raglan and his staff surveyed the battle, as aides-de-camp galloped frantically up and down the slope relaying messages to and from the officers commanding the troops in the valley, and William Howard Russell scribbled in his notepad. The atmosphere must have been heavy with expectation as they waited for the next action to unfold. Having seen the 'thin red streak' of Highlanders repel the Russians with just three volleys, Fanny watched as the Heavy Brigade of the cavalry came charging up the hill to where the Russian cavalry stood massed, 3,000 strong. The front line of the Heavy Brigade consisted of only 300 troopers, but this small force plunged into the midst of the Russians who, after some confused fighting at close quarters, drew back. The Heavy Brigade had scored a success, but all the result that Fanny could see was a bloody patch of earth, strewn with men and horses lying prostrate.

No sooner had the Heavy Brigade retired than the Light Brigade under Lord Cardigan, Fanny's erstwhile supporter, took the field. The circumstances of the Charge of the Light Brigade are still in dispute to this day. At its root was the ambiguous order given by Lord Raglan and drafted by General Richard Airey, the Quartermaster General. This instructed the cavalry commander Lord Lucan to advance with the cavalry and recover the heights taken by the enemy, followed by another order, instructing him to 'advance rapidly to the front, follow the enemy & try to prevent the enemy carrying away the guns. Troop Horse Artillery may accompany. French cavalry is on your left. Immediate.'

An aide-de-camp, Captain Nolan (Fanny's lunching companion) handed the note to Lord Lucan who studied it in confusion. Where, he asked Nolan, should the cavalry attack? Nolan, somewhat impatiently gestured not to the British guns on the heights, but instead to a battery of twelve Russian cannon. Behind the cannon stood the regrouped Russian cavalry, over a mile away at the far end of the North valley that lay between the British and Russian positions. 'There, my lord, is your enemy;' he replied with a sneer, 'there are your guns.'

In disbelief Lucan informed Lord Cardigan, his hated brother-in-law, that he was to advance with the Light Brigade. Cardigan, though horrified by the suicidal nature of the mission, began to lead it forward. Just as they moved off Captain Nolan suddenly appeared in front of them, galloping wildly across Lord Cardigan's path. Was he trying to urge the cavalry on, or had he suddenly realised that they were heading in the wrong direction and was trying to deflect them from their ill-starred course? Nobody can know for at that moment a shot struck him in the chest and, shrieking with agony he galloped to the rear where he tumbled from his horse and died. The Light Brigade thundered onwards into the Valley of Death (as Tennyson mistakenly named it, confusing it with a valley closer to Sebastopol), heading straight into the fire of the Russian cannon. Fanny and Henry watched aghast.

'So sick at heart am I that I can barely write of it even now,' she confided later in her journal. 'It has become a matter of world history, deeply as at the time it was involved in mystery. I only know that I saw Captain Nolan galloping; that presently the Light Brigade, leaving their position, advanced by themselves, although in the face of the whole Russian force, and under a fire that seemed pouring from all sides, as though every bush was a musket, every stone in the hill side a gun. Faster and faster they rode. How we watched them! They are out of sight; but presently come a few horsemen, straggling, galloping back. "What can those *skirmishers* be doing? See, they form up together again. Good God! it is the Light Brigade!"'

The whole engagement had lasted only minutes. The advancing cavalry charged into the mass of cannon and men, to the Russians' disbelief. Then, from the smoke and screams, Lord Cardigan emerged and began retiring back down the valley picking his way through the bodies of dead and wounded. The remnants of the Light Brigade followed in Cardigan's wake. All were splattered in blood, their own or that of their fallen comrades. Many of the officers and men of Henry's regiment, the 8th Hussars, were among the 113 killed and 134 wounded out of the 673 men who rode down the valley. 'You have lost the Light Brigade!' Raglan expostulated when he saw Cardigan. For Fanny, it was the loss of her friends such as Captain Lockwood (an aide-de-camp to Cardigan) and Cornet George Clowes (taken prisoner) that was most affecting.

In retrospect, the Light Brigade's charge might not have been such a disaster as it has generally been depicted. It had in fact temporarily pushed the Russians away from the Vorontsoff Road, preventing them from cutting this crucial supply route for the British.

Fanny rode up to the cavalry camp that evening, where survivors of the charge were assembling, and captured the mood of devastation and numbness. 'My nerves began to shake . . . ' she wrote. 'Past the scene of the morning we rode slowly; round us were dead and dying horses, numberless . . . One poor cream colour, with a bullet through his flank, lay dying so patiently . . . and then the wounded soldiers crawling to the hills!' Of her friend Captain Nolan she mentions nothing, perhaps wishing to disassociate herself from the notoriety that was already beginning to attach itself to his name.

After the excitement and pathos of the day she was utterly exhausted and retired to her cabin where 'I slept, but even my closed eyelids were filled with the ruddy glare of blood.' Her maid, Mrs Finnegan, whose husband had not returned from the battle, was in an even more shaken state. She found out the following day that he had died. Fanny did her best to comfort the distraught woman and must have succeeded in some measure for, as she told her sister, the woman 'will not leave me for a moment. "Oh ma'am, it's my heart that's bad. You seem to give me strength."'

The terrible sights she had seen at Balaclava had shaken Fanny, as she freely admitted. But after a few more months of war she became hardened by the terrible conditions she observed and experienced. As winter set in she saw conditions worsen. In the lines freezing, hungry horses began to gnaw each other's tails for want of other food, and men dropped dead at their posts from cholera, dysentery and exposure. Many lost fingers, toes, even hands and feet, to frostbite. A surgeon described how soldiers pulled off their gloves, leaving their frostbitten fingers inside them. Fanny's family back in England tried to persuade her to return. She resisted their entreaties. 'I can't come home. It is impossible. I cannot leave Henry alone out here, where he may be ill or die any day – and I wouldn't if I could – as I believe I am his only comfort.'

Devoted as she was to her rather needy spouse, Fanny had her own more selfish reasons for wanting to stay as well. It was far better, in her eyes, to be at hand in case of terrible news than to have to wait helplessly to receive dreadful tidings at Constantinople or Malta, surrounded by other anxious women. Besides, despite the horror and sadness all around her, she felt more alive here in the Crimea than she had ever felt before. In a later letter she again referred to the mixture of motives, selfish and unselfish, that kept her at the front. 'I am not coming home,' she wrote to her sister and brother-in-law. 'I should suffocate. You may say that is all bosh, but I tell you it is the truth. Fancy coming from being the only *woman* [by which she means lady] back into all the artificial muslin rags, conventionalities and slanders after being out here as free as air. Besides, I wouldn't leave Henry, as I believe in my heart he would die – in short I won't leave him – I was very foolish to write the letter, [in which, in a fit of misery, she had expressed a wish to return to England] but was hipped [sic] and cold and hungry. After H had read your letter he said: "Pussy, if you go away from me I think I should die" – so he got his ears boxed for supposing I was going to leave, but as for being ordered home – I am not now (or very seldom) gentlewomanly after a Crimean winter.'

The Peninsular veteran George Bell, now a colonel, described the miserable winter conditions endured by the soldiers and their wives at the front. 'The men go down to the trenches wet, come back wet, go into hospital tents wet, die the same night, and are buried in their wet blankets next morning! Nine of my good men lay stretched and dead this morning outside one tent, rolled up in their blankets. Look into this tent and observe the household. You see it is all in rags about the skirting, and the floor is a thick paste baked nearly dry by the heat of the fevered patients. That bundle of a dirty, wet blanket rolled up contains a living creature, once a comely useful soldier's wife, now waiting for death to release her from such misery . . . That young woman, once perhaps the belle of her village, now in rags but in good health, is eating her dinner, the broth of a bit of salt fat pork, with broken brown biscuit pounded into it; a tin plate and iron spoon is all her fortune. I had ten or twelve women who stuck to the regiment throughout the winter. "What is that down the hill there?" "O, Sir, that is poor Mrs H–, sitting on her husband's grave; she is always there shivering in the cold." '

Fanny, who had been asked to visit a sick soldier's wife in camp in February 1855, was also appalled by the conditions in which she found her. She was 'lying on a bed on the wet ground; she had lain there, in cold and rain, wind and snow, for twelve days. By her side, in the wet mud, was a piece of ration biscuit, a piece of salt pork, some cheese and a pot with some rum! Nice fever diet! She, having failed to make herself popular among the other women during her health, was left by them when she was sick; and not a soul had offered to assist the poor helpless, half-delirious creature, except her husband, and a former mate of his . . .' The price of having no allies among other wives was heavy indeed.

When Sebastopol finally fell to the allies in September 1855 Fanny was one of the first to enter the evacuated city. Her description of Sebastopol in the aftermath of the year-long siege is one of the most vivid accounts that exist. Riding down to the docks of the deserted port, she relates how she and her companions were assailed by a smell 'so putrid, so nauseating, so terrible . . . For heaven's sake, ride faster, for the stench is intolerable . . . What is it? It cannot be – oh horror! – a heap, a piled-up heap of human bodies in every stage of putrid decomposition . . . I think the sight of that foul heap of green and black, glazed and shrivelled flesh, I never shall be able to forget. To think that each individual portion of that corruption was once perhaps the life and world of some loving woman's heart – that human living hands had touched, and living lips had pressed with clinging and tender affection, forms which in a week could become so loathsome, so putrescent!'

It was not until May 1856 that the 8th Hussars arrived back in Portsmouth. Fanny's initial excitement at being 'home', where the publication of her journals had made her a household name, quickly began to fade. At Dundalk in Ireland, where the 8th Hussars were now stationed, the incessant round of parties and race meetings grew tedious and costly. When the news came in September 1857 that they were to go to India to take part in the campaign against the Indian mutineers, Fanny was thrilled. Here was the chance to reprise her role as darling of the troops and to clear some of the Duberly debts with a well-paid sojourn abroad. Among the first possessions she packed was a sturdy journal to record her experiences.

When Fanny disembarked at Bombay on 19 December 1857, she found a shaken, bruised British India struggling to come to terms with the horror of the Mutiny. Those officers' wives who had chosen to remain in India were forbidden from joining their husbands in the camps and cantonments where they would normally have gone. Instead they were ordered, initially, to remain in the towns while the men went off in pursuit of the remaining rebels. Almost all had lost friends, husbands or children in violent and distressing circumstances. They could therefore be forgiven for finding Fanny, whose arrival in India was preceded by a reputation as an adventuress, a little too brazen for their taste, and they regarded her with suspicion. 'I cannot say that I found the manners of my fellow-countrywomen in India characterised by real politeness,' Fanny wrote. She was soon impatient to get back into the campaigning saddle, determined to accompany the column, once again defying all orders to the contrary.

Accordingly, when the 8th King's Royal Irish Hussars set off to confront the rebel armies in the plains of Rajputana in February 1858, galloping figurehead-like at the front of the column (the better to avoid the dust), rode Fanny Duberly. Her elegant figure was clad in one of the pale grey linen riding habits she favoured, her white veils streaming behind. Once more she was in the environment she loved, performing the part in which she excelled: elegant regimental mascot, brave forces' sweetheart and devoted wife. Over a period of eight months the column covered eighteen hundred miles and, barring a few days when she was physically unable to mount her horse, Fanny rode all this distance. Regularly in the saddle for seventeen hours at a time in temperatures of up to 119°F (48°C), she coped stoically with the dust, thirst and fatigue that felled many soldiers in the column, as well as other annoyances such as the white ants that gnawed their way through linen, wooden boxes, bridles and tent poles. Even when she was ready to drop from heat and exhaustion, Fanny summoned the reserves to continue. Not that she had much choice: once they had journeyed away from the army cantonments and loyal villages, the option of leaving the column and heading for the comforts of a shady bungalow simply did not exist.

Sometimes even Fanny, resilient though she was, found herself wondering whether it had really been such a good idea to accompany the column. In June, at the height of the hot season, she had to spend a week being carried on a dooley (stretcher) at the head of the column as a bad fever, coupled with an agonising abscess on her buttock, prevented her from sitting in the saddle. On one occasion, when she had to ride because no dooley was available, the pain was so excruciating that she fell from the saddle in a dead faint.

Although at times likes this she sometimes wished that she were elsewhere, her companions were apparently profoundly grateful that she was not. Her constant presence, whatever the dangers and the heat, was apparently an inspiration to the men. In an undated letter to Selina she reported how one day in the field, sick with pain and exhaustion she was 'sitting on a box having a good cry, [and] was startled to find a deputation of the non-commissioned officers of the regiment who came to express their sorrow that I was sick. They said many kind things, and said that many and many a man had been saved from giving way to sickness because he could not give in as long as I was seen daily riding at the front of the column . . . Well, I was much gratified of course.' In another letter to Selina she told with satisfaction of a note she received from an anonymous but evidently smitten officer: 'When I recall your face and figure I am astounded. You will eclipse every woman of modern times. You must give an enormous fillip to the men of your regiment when they see a delicate woman beating them clear out of the field.'

Who could not help preening themselves at such lavish accolades?

Spurred on perhaps by the heroic image she had acquired, Fanny was emboldened to move beyond her figurehead status to take an active role with the column. On more than one occasion she actually took part in a cavalry charge. When the column neared the town of Gwalior a mass of rebel cavalry could be seen in a valley below the fort. Fanny (who was still suffering agony from a boil on one buttock and a deep scar on the other from where her abscess had been), rode with Henry towards where a squadron of the 8th Hussars and the 14th Light Dragoons had taken up position. Suddenly the order came to charge. As she explained in a letter to Selina, she could not help but be caught up in the rush that ensued. 'As they started my little horse sprang away. I sung out to Henry – "I must go!" – "Go along then!" said he, eager for an excuse, and away we went at a rushing gallop right up to the fort.' As they thundered through the thick clouds of dust Fanny could hear and glimpse flashes of steel as they began to clash with the enemy. She was transported with excitement. 'The impulse to accompany the cavalry was irresistible, and I never shall forget the throbbing excitement of that gallop, when the horse beneath me, raging in fierce strength, mad with excitement, scarcely touched the ground.' She and Henry returned to camp exhausted but elated.

On another occasion, when the column attacked a rebel force in a surprise dawn raid near the town of Dum Dum in November 1858, Fanny (armed with only a lady's revolver and a small dagger) rode among the advance guard. As the enemy fled in confusion, leaving behind clothes, food, arms and even children, the British galloped in pursuit. Afterwards, as the mangled bodies of the dead and dying lay strewn on the bloodied earth, Fanny retired to the comparative comfort of her tent. Even she was shaken by some of the things she had seen that day including 'a man shot in the head, and who was bleeding profusely from his wound, [who] was tended by his daughter, apparently about twelve years old, who held up her hands imploring mercy and pity as we passed. Nor was I the only one who tried to reassure and comfort her.' Often, however, she reacted with bravado, remarking of one attack by the enemy: 'The firing struck us, who were accustomed to the rain of shot at Sebastopol, as remarkably slack . . . we fell asleep again and missed the assault.' Entering a city recently taken by the British she observed wild dogs and pigs 'tearing the limbs off the bodies and gorging themselves on their entrails', without being unduly perturbed.

Fanny's journal of her Indian campaign received a warm reception in England, but in India the critics were less kind. Perhaps the idea of an

Englishwoman seemingly glorying in strife and violence was unpalatable at a time when British India was still reeling from the brutality of the Mutiny. Again, many of Fanny's sentiments, her fiery independence and thirst for action were out of kilter with the social mores of her time. She was emphatically a man's woman and seldom troubled to hide her low opinion of most of her fellow females, and of conventional feminine behaviour. 'I love this life,' she wrote of the Rajputana march, 'I am *living,* seeing things and feeling them. 'Tis better than morning visiting and worsted work.' Already she had alienated Queen Victoria by such unfeminine sentiments. The Queen rejected Fanny's request to dedicate her journal to her, having apparently been appalled by the indelicacy and brashness of the writing and her impudent criticism of the military authorities. When the Queen welcomed the 8th Hussars back to Portsmouth at the end of the Crimean War, she declined to either shake Mrs Duberly by the hand or address a single word to her. Victoria would have been even more shocked if she had read Fanny's letters to her sister, in which her belief that she was the stronger half of the marriage was evident. Henry, she told Selina, was 'kind and patient and good, indolent, complaining, uninterested and bored. Bored – there is no more expressive word. I sometimes am afraid when I see how much stronger I am than he. I am sometimes still more afraid that my single strength will not suffice for both . . . ' Such views would have been anathema to Victoria, who espoused John Ruskin's maxim that 'A true wife, in her husband's house is his servant. It is in his heart that she is queen.'

Fanny, it was clear, was queen of both heart and hearth in the Duberly household and took little trouble to disguise the fact. Undoubtedly she loved her somewhat uninspiring husband, and her concern for his welfare was one of the factors that took her to India and the Crimea. But it was her thirst for excitement after a staid middle-class existence that drove her to seek out danger.

In the eighteenth century, long before Fanny went off to war with her hair oil and her pretty ribbons, other women from far humbler backgrounds and of more limited means than her, cut loose from their domestic ties and ventured into camp and battle disguised as soldiers, like the fallen Frenchwoman Charles Smith's brother found on the field of Waterloo. The most famous of these amazons is Christian Welsh (or Kit Welsh, Christian Davies or Mother Ross as she was variously known).

Christian was born in Dublin in 1667. Her father was a brewer and maltster, her mother managed the family farm. Their origins were humble but they were respectable people and Christian had a comfortable upbringing. She learned to read although she preferred more tomboyish activities and helping out on the farm, and, following her mother's example, she developed into an independent-minded young woman. On the death of her aunt she inherited a pub in Dublin and after a short while fell in love with and subsequently married one of her servants, a handsome, charming fellow named Richard Welsh. They had two sons and Christian was pregnant with a third child when Richard went out on an errand one day and never returned. For a year she believed him to be dead. Her third child was born, her second son died and she had begun to come to terms with the loss of her husband when a letter arrived. To her utter amazement she found that it was from Richard (the twelfth he said he had written but the first she had received). He, it transpired, was alive and serving as a soldier in Lord Orrery's Regiment of Foot, part of the British force sent to the continent to fight the French. In 1689 William III, straddling the thrones of England, Ireland, Scotland and Orange, and Admiral-General of the Dutch provinces, committed his kingdoms to the struggle against the the expansionist French whose king, Louis XIV, appeared bent on European domination.

Richard Welsh had, according to his letter, met an old schoolmate while on his errand and had gone for a drink with the man, who was now an army officer. After one bowl of punch too many Richard found himself on board a ship with his friend and before he knew what was happening the ship set sail. He woke up, hungover and in the Netherlands. Lacking any means to return home, Richard had had no option but to enlist as a soldier.

Finding out that her husband was, after all, alive but as far removed from her as if he were dead threw Christian into a violent fit of despair. But at length she pulled herself together and became determined to go in search of him. Consigning her elder child to the care of her mother, the baby to a nurse, and her pub and house to friends, she cut off her long hair and dressed herself in a suit of her husband's. Then, 'having had the precaution to quilt the waistcoat, to preserve my breasts from hurt, which were not large enough to betray my sex, and putting on the wig and hat I had prepared, I went out and bought me a silver-hilted sword . . . ' She then took herself off to a pub where recruiting sergeants were known to ply their trade and, having impressed the recruiter with her sprightly demeanour (he deemed her to be 'a clever brisk young fellow'), enlisted in a foot regiment under the name Christopher Welsh. Whatever medical checks were carried out must have been cursory for within days she was sailing for Flanders, her sex undetected, and drilling in preparation for battle.

Within weeks Christian had fought, been wounded and taken prisoner (and freed), all without her true identity being revealed. Although she carefully scrutinised the faces of every man in every regiment she came across, her husband was not among them. Christian indulged in a flirtation with a young Dutch girl over whom she fought a duel with a fellow soldier. This quarrel led to her leaving her regiment and enlisting in Hay's (Royal Scots) Dragoons. It was with the dragoons that she fought in 1695 at the siege of Namur. After this fortress town fell to the English and their allies the dragoons went into winter quarters for several months. In 1697, peace was signed and the troops disbanded. Along with thousands of her fellow soldiers, Christian boarded a ship bound for Ireland. On reaching Dublin, she found that none of her family recognised her in her new attire. As she did not have enough money to pay the nurse who had looked after her youngest child for the past four years, she decided not to make herself known. During the next four years she remained in Dublin and although she quickly found a job, she neither paid the nurse nor made any attempt to introduce herself to her family. Perhaps she had no inclination to return to a domestic role after her four happy years as a soldier, and her maternal love had diminished during her years of absence.

In 1702 war broke out again when a dispute arose over the succession to the Spanish throne. France supported the claim of the French king's grandson, and the Grand Alliance, comprising the British kingdoms, Austria and the Netherlands, opposed it because it would bring Spain, France and the Netherlands under Bourbon rule. Once again regiments were raised and Christian found that the news of war 'awakened my martial inclination'. So, stirred by the craving to return to military life (and perhaps still nursing hopes of finding her husband), she rejoined the Dragoons and was soon back in Flanders. Over the next two years she marched, fought and drank like any other soldier and enjoyed herself so fully that, by her own admittance, thoughts of her husband were banished from her mind. She was even accused of fathering a child. It was not until the winter of 1703 that she remembered the reason behind her quest, but after her enquiries yielded no news of Richard she resolved to forget all about him. 'To do this, I had recourse to wine and company, which had the effect I wished, and I spent the season pretty cheerfully,' she admitted.

In her memoirs, purportedly ghost-written for her by Daniel Defoe, she makes no allusions to how she coped with the practicalities of maintaining her deception. How, one wonders, when spending weeks on end in a trench at the siege of Namur, or sharing a tent and even a bed with several fellow soldiers, did she manage to conceal such occurrences as menstruation? What about urination? Surely her fellow soldiers would have remarked on the fact that she did not relieve herself standing up? One theory, put forward by an early biographer, was that she used a tube that was fastened with straps to her body. This method was certainly used by another female cross-dresser of that era who, when examined in court in 1721, confessed that she had made use of a 'leather-covered horn through which she urinated and [which she kept] fastened against her nude body'. Or perhaps her fellow men did not remark upon the fact that she chose to perform her ablutions in private. After all, there was no reason to be suspicious of a soldier who drank, sang, and womanised with the best of them.

In any case, her identity was still undetected when her regiment was ordered into battle at Schellenberg in 1704. The allied armies were commanded by John Churchill, created Duke of Marlborough two years previously. Marlborough, as well as being a skilled soldier and strategist, was a supremely efficient administrator, who ensured that not only were his soldiers fairly regularly paid (at the time it was not unusual for regiments to be several years in arrears of pay) but adequately fed too. The soldiers, accustomed to being ill-used by their commanders, affectionately nicknamed him 'Corporal John'. Discipline and morale in the army were high when, on 2 July 1704, the British and their allies attacked the French and Bavarians at Schellenberg, a long, low hill near the town of Donauworth in southern Germany. The hill, held by the French and Bavarians, was a strong defensive position, but Marlborough was undeterred and determined to take it before enemy reinforcements arrived. Christian's regiment was one of those handpicked by the Duke to be in the forefront of the attack. The 6,000-strong force of storm troops formed up at the base of the hill. They had had a hard march to reach Schellenberg and now faced a steep climb up 400 yards of open hill that lay before the enemy defences.

At 6 p.m. the signal came for the storming to begin and the troops rushed forward, quickly at first and then more slowly as the terrain became harder. As they reached the most exposed area of ground the enemy opened fire and a torrent of bullets and grenades tore into them. Scores of men tumbled to the ground including many officers, conspicuous in their lace-trimmed hats and coats. Still the attackers pushed forward up the steep slope. As Christian reported, they were 'twice repulsed, with very great loss; but this did not abate anything of our courage; our men, rather animated by this resistance, gave a third assault, at the time the prince of Baden arrived with the German troops [part of the allied army] of the right wing, who attacked on his side. The slaughter, which was very great, had lasted above an hour.' Then finally the allied troops overran the enemy's trenches and put them to flight.

Christian, however, did not take part in this third and glorious assault. 'In the second attack, I received a ball in my hip, which is so lodged between the bones that it can never be extracted; to this day the wound is open, and has almost deprived me of the use of my leg and thigh. Captain Young . . . desired me to get off but, upon my refusal, he ordered two of my comrades to take me up, and they set me at the foot of a tree, where I endeavoured to animate my brother soldiers, till I had the pleasure of seeing them get into the trenches and beat down their enemies . . . ' In only an hour the battle had been won. Christian was carried to the hospital and placed under the care of three surgeons, in which she was remarkably fortunate as there was generally about one doctor to every 600 soldiers. To her relief her secret was not revealed while she was in hospital.

Less than six weeks after Marlborough's victory at Schellenberg, the two sides clashed again. The battlefield of Blenheim covered an expanse of about four miles, and encompassed several villages, including those of Blindheim (or Blenheim as it later became known), Oberglau and nearby Hochstadt. During the battle Christian was again in the thick of the action as Marlborough, using all his tactical genius, outmanoeuvred the French and Bavarians at a cost of an estimated 30,000 men to the allies' losses of 10,000. It was the first time in living memory that the great French army had been so crushingly defeated. France had now been unseated from her position of unquestioned dominance in Europe, and the Austrian empire was now secure again, restoring the balance of power.

For Christian the aftermath of Blenheim was more significant than the battle itself. While observing the happy reunions of women whose husbands had returned from the battle (and the terrible grief of those whose men had not) she noticed among the couples a familiar face. It was her husband, the man she had spent the last eleven years pursuing. She managed to arrange a meeting with him at which, after a few moments, he realised with astonishment that the young soldier with whom he was talking was his long-lost wife.

Although overjoyed at finding her husband after her long quest, the reunion was soured for Christian by the fact that she had discovered him with another woman, to whom he had apparently promised marriage. In addition, Christian was reluctant to abandon her soldiering life. So she informed Richard that she would not live as his wife but as his brother soldier. By refusing to share his bed she was not only punishing him for his infidelity, but ensuring that she could not become pregnant (for, as she later explained, 'a great belly could not have been concealed'). Yet Christian continued to flirt with local women without a qualm.

For the next two years Christian and Richard fought and marched together across Flanders with not one of their fellow soldiers suspecting that their relationship was anything other than brotherly. The next major battle after Blenheim was fought at Ramillies in May 1706. Once again, Marlborough used bluffs and feints to trick the French into deploying their forces wrongly, and he was able to inflict another rout on the Bourbon army. As at Blenheim the battlefield was a wide expanse four miles across, but riddled with marshes, rivers and other obstacles. As their forward ranks fell the men behind had to step over their bodies and one soldier complained of getting his feet entangled in the entrails of one of his dead comrades. Marlborough himself narrowly avoided being taken prisoner. Christian came unscathed through the murderous battle and it was only after the French had began to leave the battlefield in defeat that a shell struck her on the back of the head, fracturing her skull. She was carried at once to a hospital in a nearby town where a surgeon performed a trepanation, the process of drilling a hole in the skull bone to relieve pressure. After the operation her clothing was removed in order to dress the wound properly. At last Christian's secret was uncovered, to her utter dismay: 'Though I suffered great torture by this wound, yet the discovery it caused of my sex, in the fixing of my dressing, by which the surgeons saw my breasts, and, by the largeness of my nipples, concluded I had given suck, was the greater grief to me.'

Christian had now been living as a man for twelve years. She had enjoyed swaggering across Flanders as part of a victorious army and revelled in the camaraderie of regimental life. Now she would be just another wife or camp follower, consigned with the baggage to the background when battle was joined. The senior officers were astounded when they heard the news that their 'pretty dragoon' was in fact a woman. Even more amazed was the soldier with whom she had shared a bed (as was customary) for many years, who protested that she could not be a woman as it was well known that she had fathered a child. Although she had to be dismissed from the service, the senior officers made sure that during her ten-week stay in hospital she continued to receive her pay. On her discharge they insisted that she must now go through another wedding to reaffirm her marriage to her husband. Moreover, they told her, she now had no reason to withhold his conjugal rights.

Devastated as she was at having her secret revealed and the 'blessed trade' of soldiering disbarred to her, Christian had little option but to channel her energy into being the most devoted of wives, cooking, washing, cleaning for her husband and earning money by keeping a sutlering tent. Not that she found the transition back to traditional woman-hood easy – she could not readily shake off the aggression and readiness for a fight that had made her such an effective soldier. As she modestly put it: 'I may safely say I had as little fear about me as any man in the army.' On one occasion, having brought food to her husband in the trench during a siege, she seized the weapon from one of his comrades and shot an enemy soldier, receiving in return a musket shot in the mouth. She spat the ball out into her hand, together with a tooth. Her lip was sewn up and she was rewarded with the valuable gift of five pistols by a senior commander. At another siege she tried to accompany her husband into battle, and claimed to have been with him when he tunnelled underground hunting for enemy mines.

Less controversially, she found she had a talent for foraging – ranging far afield in the Dutch countryside, often at night, seeking food and other valuables. Bales of hay, casks of wine and beer, vegetables, bread, chickens and sheep were all slung over the backs of her two mares, one of which she rode, the other she led. She enjoyed the freedom this new role gave her; otherwise she chafed at the restraints of being a wife again – and a mother too. She gave birth prematurely to the child conceived on her 'wedding' night, whose death after six months she mentions only in passing. She did, however, show a little more maternal care for the small daughter of a soldier whom she came across during a march on the eve of a battle, and looked after the girl until her father was found.

She continued in her privileged position as sutler, mascot and camp celebrity who could get away with speaking to officers in a manner that, had she been either a soldier or ordinary wife or camp follower, would probably have seen her punished or banished. Such small freedoms could not make up for the liberty she had lost by reverting to her true sex, but at least she had the compensation of being able to live with her beloved Richard again as husband and wife. By night she lay by her husband's side, by day she marched with him, foraged for him and fed him, delighting in surprising him and his fellow men with her ingenuity and courage, until his death.

Christian Welsh may be the most famous woman to have marched with the army in disguise, but she was far from the only one. A generation later Phoebe Hessel, who was born in 1713 (about the time that Christian was returning to civilian life), joined the army as a drummer boy. Her mother had died while following the army in Flanders and her father realised that the only way to keep her by his side, and earn some money, was for Phoebe to enlist as a drummer boy. Accordingly he cut her hair, taught her how to play the drum and fife, and she remained with the army.

As her formative years had been spent with the army it is unsurprising that Phoebe, aged fifteen or sixteen, fell in love, with Samuel Golding, a private in the regiment then called Kirke's Lambs. No sooner had they met than Golding's regiment was ordered to the graveyard posting of the West Indies. Fearing that she might never see him again Phoebe once again donned male attire and enlisted in a regiment of foot to follow him out there. She continued serving with the army for the next seventeen years until, at the battle of Fontenoy in 1745, she received a severe wound in the arm from a French bayonet. Like Christian Welsh, it was in hospital that her sex was revealed. She was discharged but given an invalid's pension. She and Golding then returned to England and lived happily until he died and she married a Brighton fisherman named Hessel. During her time in Brighton she met the Prince Regent who, hearing her amazing story, decided to pay her half a guinea a week from his own pocket that she might live in comfort as she deserved. She died, many years after her husband, aged 108.

Some other female warriors, however, who dressed as men and served for years beside their unsuspecting comrades, were not impelled by a desire to remain by the side of their husband or father. A round-faced, rosy-cheeked dyer's daughter from Worcester called Hannah Snell, or the Female Marine as she became known, claimed to have been recruited into the army in 1745, then enlisted in the Marines two years later, in male guise. She fought in India and was wounded at the siege of Pondicherry before returning to Britain and revealing her true sex. She made a living by appearing on stage in her Marine's uniform, before marrying a carpenter with whom she had two sons. In old age she became insane and died in the squalor and horror of Bedlam in 1792.

Miss Roberts, a bricklayer's daughter, enlisted in the 15th Light Dragoons as William Roberts in the late eighteenth century and served for twenty-one years in that regiment, fighting in Flanders, Egypt, France and Spain and receiving several wounds. She then served with the 37th North Hampshire Regiment before a stay in hospital revealed her true identity. She managed to remain with the army by marrying a private and followed him to the Peninsular War. She was taken prisoner and spent two years in a French jail until she was freed following the Battle of Waterloo in 1815. That year she applied to a church in Manchester for poor relief and her story emerged, leading to her being known as the Manchester Heroine.

A more hapless she-soldier was Mary-Anne Talbot who was born in 1778, the illegitimate daughter of a peer. Her mother died in childbirth and after several guardians she ended up, aged thirteen, in the charge of a Captain Essex Bowen of the 82nd Regiment, who seduced her. When his regiment sent to the West Indies he forced her to accompany him, dressed as a footboy under the name John Taylor. When the regiment was ordered back to Flanders she went too, enlisting as a drummer, and fought in several actions. She later worked on naval ships as a cabin boy and powder monkey. Her gender was revealed only after she had spent eighteen months as a French prisoner of war. On returning to England she found it hard to adapt to life as a woman and frequently donned male clothing, explaining, 'Having been used to male dress in the defence of my country I thought I was sufficiently entitled to wear the same whenever I thought proper.' She died aged thirty.

The reluctance of Christian, Mary-Anne and Phoebe to relinquish their male identity stemmed, it seemed, from the knowledge that by putting on petticoats once again they would consign themselves to a passive role. No longer would they be entitled to a share in the glory and the loot of warfare, although they would still have to endure many of the discomforts and dangers. Although it was love or necessity that drove them first to put on men's attire, they all retained their male identity long after the original reasons for doing so had disappeared.

As the army became more removed from civilian society in the mid-nineteenth century, with billeting being replaced by barracks, so to did the army community itself become more segregated and formalised. Many of the tasks that had hitherto been carried out by the wives were now taken over by army support services, removing the need for women to be allowed on campaign. Nonetheless, although the Crimean War was supposed to be the last to which women followed their men, many continued to accompany their husbands to the seat of war, although few got close to the front line, unless inadvertently.

Today, the debate continues as to whether women have a place in combat and on the front line. Whatever its eventual conclusion, there is little doubt that, while the stories of Susanna Dalbiac, Fanny Duberly and Christian Welch are clearly those of exceptional women, they illustrate that femininity is no bar to courage. Indeed, a woman's presence on a battlefield, far from creating divisions and undermining morale, can often provide support, comfort and inspiration to the men around her.

Such courage is never more necessary than when a woman has to face the hardest ordeal of all, harder than privation and peril: the reality that the man to whom she has devoted her life has not returned from battle, and that she may never see him again.

13

The End of the Line

She now ceased to speak, and rocked backwards and
forwards over the bleeding corpse; but her parched quivering lip,
and wild fixed look, showed the agonized workings of her mind.
I stood not an unmoved spectator of this scene, but I did not
interrupt it. I considered her sorrow too deep and sacred for
commonplace consolation.

Joseph Donaldson, observing a widow finding
her husband's body at Badajoz, 1812

Every army wife knows that her husband could be called upon for
active service, during which he runs the risk of being killed. This is
the situation to which she has effectively 'signed up' when she marries a
soldier. Today, the death of a serviceman never goes unmarked. Intelligence
is swift and usually reliable. Killed in open fighting or by covert suicide
bomb, each grim statistic is meticulously logged; no time is lost informing the bereaved. In earlier centuries there could be no such certainty for
families waiting at home for news of a soldier serving abroad. It could be
months – years – before they heard of his death in battle, or even from
heatstroke or disease in a peaceful garrison. Post was ponderously slow in
the days before steam: letters from India and the East could take six months
to get to Britain, if at all. Even when they did arrive, it was not always
easy to track down wives who had returned to their home parishes when
the regiment embarked.

Some women, hearing no news of their husbands for years on end, would assume they were dead and, as widows, marry again – only to find they had been mistaken.

Mrs Rachel Heap of Halifax, having heard nothing from her soldier husband in many years, assumed he must have been killed and married Samuel Lumb in 1802. She went on to have three children with him, only for Heap to suddenly reappear, alive and well. He agreed to sell Rachel to Lumb and she was delivered in a halter to Halifax Cross as his bride, though legally she was still married to Heap. When Heap died twenty-five years later Rachel and Samuel Lumb remarried, this time legally.

Sergeant Edward Costello of the 95th, the Rifle Brigade, told of a sergeant of his acquaintance, a 'fine, smart-looking fellow', who returned to England's shores in 1814 after ten years spent fighting abroad, eager to be reunited with his wife, from whom he had parted a few months after their wedding. As he had not heard from her throughout the decade he had been away he was afraid that she might have died, but with hope still aflame he tramped the streets of Portsmouth enquiring after her. Eventually he was directed to a small cottage. Knocking on the door, he was at first delighted to find it answered by a pretty girl of about ten who was quite clearly his daughter. But when he went inside he was perturbed to find several other children, and his wife who, on seeing him, fell into a fit of hysterics. Within a few minutes the other children's father, a carpenter, appeared and the two men squared up, their eyes boring in to each other, while the shrieking woman clung to the carpenter. At length the soldier threw a rope lightly around his wife's neck and proposed to the carpenter, "'Suppose we have a bargain in the matter? It's no use our skirmishing about in this manner any longer; and I have no doubt of your abilities,'" he added, pointing to the crowd of children. "'With Mary's consent, as she seems to prefer your manner of doing business, suppose you clinch the bargain with a sixpence, and take her to you altogether?'" The matter was thus settled and the soldier departed, but not before he had thrown a guinea into the lap of the oldest child, his only daughter. After drinking a draught of ale at a nearby pub he went off strutting down the street 'as if nothing whatever had annoyed him'.

Women who had accompanied the regiment abroad or on campaign, on the other hand, usually found out soon after the end of a battle whether their husbands had survived. If their men did not return from the battle-field, the women would begin questioning their comrades – but among the smoke and musket fire, the chaos of the charge or retreat, it was not easy for soldiers to see what was happening even two yards away from them. If there was no positive news, the only recourse for the women was to go on to the battlefield itself, to pick their way through the bloodied and mutilated corpses until they came to a familiar shape or uniform. Then they would study the face, perhaps disfigured by musket shot or slashed by sabre, to see if it was the one on which they had planted a goodbye kiss only hours earlier.

It might be that the man had only the appearance of death – the timely arrival of a wife could save him from being interred alive by the burial parties who went out on to the field shortly after the action was over. Women who alighted upon the prone bodies of their husbands, frantically embracing them as if trying to bring them back to life, were often acting less irrationally than one might suppose. Medical knowledge was not what it is today and mistakes could be made. As Sir Charles Napier, an illustrious and much-wounded veteran of the Peninsula (and India), once put it, 'When a fellow has no life they are sometimes, on a field of battle, overquick in burying him.' One commanding officer came across a party of soldiers conducting a funeral service over the grave of a man who had dropped dead only fifteen minutes earlier. Anxious that his burial might have been too prompt, he looked into the grave and saw the man stir. He was quickly disinterred and recovered from his near-death experience in a few days.

In any case, it was essential for a wife to get to her husband before the body-strippers removed all his clothing and valuables, often hastening his demise if he were not already dead. Stripping a man of his uniform and any distinguishing accoutrements made it harder to identify the body. Mrs Currie, who had so dazzled the officers at Sir Rowland Hill's dinner table in the Peninsula, was left uncertain of her husband's fate for several days after Waterloo. Her husband, by then a colonel, was conversing with Hill during the battle when a cannonball took his head clean off. Afterwards the (mainly local) marauders who poured on to the field stripped all the clothing from his body, which led to a long delay in identifying it.

Christian Welsh saved her husband's body from the attentions of battlefield vultures. After being reunited with Richard and living with him as a soldier's wife for a little over three years, she was widowed at the battle of Malplaquet in 1709. Her husband was among the 20,000 casualties lost by Marlborough in the most costly action of his career. It took several days to bury the dead, many of whom lay in the thick woods through which the allied troops had assaulted the French. Christian's husband was among those attackers and, knowing roughly where he should have been, she set out to find him. As she made her way through the wood, with shot and wood splinters flying all around, her small dog that accompanied her began to howl piteously. An English soldier, who happened to be standing nearby relieving himself, remarked with astonishing tactlessness, 'Poor creature, he would fain tell you that his master is dead.' Horror-struck, Christian could not at first believe him. How could this have happened? she asked. But the soldier could tell her nothing more. Hastily backtracking, he insisted he was not sure whether Richard was dead or badly wounded.

Hoping desperately to find him alive, Christian began to run through the wood towards the fighting. 'I was almost out of my wits; but though I feared the worst, my hopes of finding him alive supported me. I ran among the dead, and turned over near two hundred . . . before I found my husband's body, which a man, who was a stranger to me, though I was not unknown to him, was stripping. At my approach he went off, and left his booty, fearing the effects of the rage I was in at the sight of my dead husband; and I certainly had killed him, could I have laid my hands on him; for I was in so great a fury, that I bit out a great piece out of my right arm, tore my hair, threw myself on his corpse, and should have put a period to my life had I had any instrument of death. Here I lay some time before my tears flowed, which at length gushed forth in such abundance, that I believe the stream saved my life, at least my senses.'

After some time she laid her husband's body across her horse and, taking it to a suitable piece of ground, dug a grave and buried him. She claims that she would have thrown herself in after him had not she been stopped by her companions. She even tried to ride towards the French lines to wreak vengeance upon those who had killed her husband, but again she was held back. For a week she did not eat, and went frequently to her husband's grave to scrape away the earth with her bare hands that she might gaze again on the features of he 'whom I loved with greater tenderness than I did myself'. Eventually a colonel's wife succeeded in shaking Christian out of her morass of despair. After six weeks of being prostrate with grief she began to return to normal life.

The difficulty of establishing what had happened on the battlefield, and the natural reluctance of those who did know the terrible truth to be the bearer of such tidings, resulted in some women being plunged into unnecessary despair. Others went into raptures of relief that their husbands had been spared, only to have their spirits dashed some hours or days later when the truth emerged. In close-knit communities, rumour and counter-rumour flourished. News received by one wife, or by soldiers left behind in camp, would do the rounds long before any official confirmation of casualties was received and was often wildly inaccurate. John Shipp was twice knocked down by musket fire when storming the fort of Huttrass (in India) in May 1817. He was not badly wounded but his new bride, Ann, left behind in Cawnpore, fell victim to the well-intentioned but misdirected commiserations of her fellow wives. 'Several ladies of the regiment had called on my young wife,' wrote Shipp, 'for the purpose of breaking to her the news of my being killed . . . and nothing but a letter written in my own hand could have satisfied her that these reports of my death were unfounded.'

Another wife whose husband was also involved in the attack received similar premature condolences. Her letter to her husband (which reads as if it was dictated), which Shipp includes in his own journal, evokes the purgatory of uncertainty, fear and hope that soldiers' wives are condemned to inhabit until they receive definitive news:

My dear Pat,

I wish you would be after writing me a single line, to tell me if it is true that you were killed in the storming-party the other night. People tell so many lies that I never believe one of them; but I am mighty unasy [sic] about it, and should like to know the truth. If you are dead, honey, sure Sergeant Logan will be after reading it and letting me know. Och! If you're dead, dear Pat, let this console you, that I will never marry again; but perhaps you are not, and will only make redicule [sic] of me for opening my heart to you. I saw Dennis M'Guire, who told me it was all a lie, that you were not dead, and that if I wrote you you would let me know. Dear Paddy, you don't know, sure, how distressed I have been till I know; therefore, write, if you are live; if no, Corporal Hagan or Sergeant Logan will have the goodness to let me know. I shall look out for the post every hour, though I know I cannot expect under three days, but that's no matter. So no more from

Your affectionate wife, Molly Kaneaghan
Cawnpore.

PS Before I close this, pray don't forget to write to me as soon as you are able.

Fortunately for Mrs Kaneaghan, her husband responded promptly to her pleas, reassuring her that 'Whoever told you that I was kilt, it is a great big lie, without a morsel of truth. It's truth I got a ball in my side, but I assure you, if I had been kilt, you should have been informed by me; but I am worth a hundred dead men, and hope I shall live till it's my turn to die, and then you know, dear Molly, I cannot help it.'

My paternal grandmother, Ruth Venning, experienced the shock of a similar false alarm when she was living in Bannu on India's North West Frontier in 1941. My grandfather Ralph Venning was taking part in fierce fighting against the tribesmen in the mountainous region of Waziristan. Ralph had been away for several days when Ruth, bicycling through the camp one morning, was accosted by a young Indian soldier. 'Good morning, Memsahib,' he addressed her cheerfully. 'Your Sahib was killed today,' drawing the edge of his hand across his throat to illustrate just how he had met his death. It was not until some hours later that Ruth learnt that the young soldier had made a mistake – it was the previous inhabitant of her bungalow, an officer in the Frontier Constabulary, who had been shot and decapitated, not Ralph. In Aden, in 1965, Bette Viner coped with astonishing aplomb when, with nationalist terrorists targeting British forces and their families, she received a telephone call from a man speaking pidgin English. He informed her that Ziam (Brigadier) Viner had been beheaded and that his head was on display in the market place. Mrs Viner quickly telephoned his headquarters and was relieved to discover that her husband was in fact alive and well.

Even for women on the spot, discovering the truth about their husbands' fate was often difficult and traumatic. In the Peninsula, Juana Smith once saw her husband Harry's horse charging from the battlefield with his master's lifeless body hanging from a stirrup. With a shriek of anguish she rushed towards the galloping horse. It was only when she was nearly upon it that she realised that it was not Harry's horse but another officer's, and it was this poor man's body that was suspended. She later accompanied Harry to the Waterloo campaign and, the morning after the battle, unable to sleep until she knew he was safe, set out to find him. On the day that the battle had been fought, 18 June, she had been in Brussels, but an alarm reached the city that the French were approaching and in panic the inhabitants and many of those who had accompanied the army began packing their bags and fleeing the city. The baggage of the army (including wives and children) was ordered back to Antwerp, so Juana joined the exodus. Her journey was more fraught than most as her excitable mare ran away with her and she was thrown onto the road, eventually arriving in Antwerp covered from head to toe in mud. The following day came the news that, far from driving the allies from the field and descending on Brussels, the French had been defeated. But Juana could discover nothing about Harry (or 'Enrique' as she called him), and so determined to set off for Waterloo to find him. She and her servant left Antwerp at three o'clock the next morning and, riding hard, covered the twenty-five miles to Brussels in four hours. Here she saw met soldiers from the Rifle Brigade. It was then that her ordeal began in earnest.

'To my horror they told me that Brigade-Major Smith of the 95th [Rifle Brigade] was killed. It was now my turn to ask the 'Brass Mare' [her horse] to gallop, and in a state approaching desperation I urged her to the utmost speed for the field of battle to seek my husband's corpse. The road from Brussels to the field almost maddened me, with wounded men and horses, and corpses borne forward to Brussels for interment, expecting as I was every moment to see that of my husband, knowing how he was beloved by officers and soldiers. The road was nearly choked which was to lead me to the completion, as I hoped, of my life; to die on the body of the only thing I had on earth to love, and which I loved with a faithfulness which few can or ever did feel, and none ever exceeded. In my agony of woe, which of course increased as my expectations were not realized (it was now Tuesday), I approached the awful field of Sunday's carnage, in mad search of Enrique. I saw signs of newly dug graves, and then I imagined to myself, "O God, he has been buried, and I shall never again behold him!" How can I describe my suspense, the horror of my sensations, my growing despair, the scene of carnage around me?'

A few miles on, having examined several corpses but not found Harry's among them, Juana met an officer friend who told her that it was Brigade Major Smyth, not her own Major Smith, who had died. Indeed, he assured her, Enrique was alive, unwounded and at a village some miles from Waterloo. Having spent the past few hours convinced that her husband was dead, Juana could not at first accept that he was alive and well. As she recalled, 'This sudden transition from my depth of grief and maddening despair was enough to turn my brain, but Almighty God sustained me.' Hardly daring to believe the news until she saw Harry with her own eyes, she pressed onwards. After riding sixty miles in one day she was rewarded the following morning by the longed-for reunion. Even as she sank gratefully into his embrace she still found it hard to comprehend that he was alive, 'such a hold had my previous horror taken of my every thought and feeling'.

Soldiers themselves were understandably reluctant to be the bearers of tragic tidings. When Private William Wheeler was wounded at the battle of Nivelle in 1813 he was accosted by one anxious wife, Mrs Foster, asking for news of her husband. Wheeler could not bring himself to tell Mrs Foster the truth and merely shook his head in reply, but she was not fooled. 'Oh it is too true,' she cried. 'Your silence confirms what I have just been told, he is dead.' She then ran back to the battlefield to look for him. Wheeler turned to his companion, another wounded soldier, and confided that he had seen Mrs Foster's husband fall dead. His companion was markedly unsympathetic towards her plight, complaining: 'There is so many of these damned women running and blubbering about, enquiring after their husbands. Why the D__l don't they stop at home where they ought to be. This is no place for them. Come let us go in an get something to drink, not stop here to be pestered to death by a parcel of women.'

Rifleman Harris was confronted by a similar dilemma to Wheeler's when he witnessed the death of a fellow soldier, Joseph Cockayne, during the Battle of Rolica in 1808. He found himself put on the spot when the roll call was taken after the battle to establish who had survived and who had died.

> When the roll was called, some of the females came along the front of the line to inquire of the survivors whether they knew anything about their husbands. Amongst other names, I heard that of Cockayne called in a female voice. It was not replied to. The name struck me, and I observed the poor woman who had called it. She stood sobbing before us, apparently afraid to make further inquiries about her husband, No man had answered to his name, or had any account to give of his fate . . . I had observed him fall whilst drinking from his canteen, but as I looked at the poor sobbing creature before me, I felt unable to tell her of his death. At length Captain Leach observed her, and called out to the company:
>
> 'Does any man here know what has happened to Cockayne? If so, let him speak out at once.'
>
> Upon this order I immediately related what I had seen, and told the manner of his death. Mrs Cockayne appeared anxious to seek the spot where her husband fell, and asked me to accompany her over the field. Notwithstanding what I had told her, she trusted she might find him alive.
>
> 'Do you think you could find the place?' said Captain Leach,

upon being referred to. I told him I was sure I could, as I had remarked many objects whilst looking for cover during the skirmishing.

'Go then.' said the captain, 'and show the poor woman the spot, as she seems so desirous of finding the body.'

I accordingly made my way over the ground we had fought on. She followed sobbing. We soon reached the spot where her husband's body lay and I pointed it out to her. She now discovered that all her hopes were in vain. She embraced a stiffened corpse, then rose and contemplated his disfigured face for some minutes. She took a prayer-book from her pocket, and with hands clasped and tears streaming down her cheeks, she knelt down and repeated the service for the dead over the body. When she had finished she appeared a good deal comforted, and I took the opportunity of beckoning to a pioneer I saw near with some other men. Together we dug a hole, and quickly buried the body. Mrs Cockayne returned with me to the company to which her husband had been attached, and laid herself down upon the heath near us, amongst other females, who were in the same distressing circumstances. The sky was her canopy, and a turf her pillow, for we had no tents with us. Poor woman. I pitied her much, but if she had been a duchess she would have fared the same.

Indeed, death and grief are never respecters of rank. Officers were frequently in the forefront of action, leading their troops into battle or directing the army's movements from a strategic point that was often within range of the enemy's guns. Marlborough had several horses shot under him while commanding the army in Flanders. Wellington was wounded in the leg by a musket ball at the battle of Orthez in 1814, and at Waterloo all but one of his aides-de-camp were killed. According to Harry Smith, every staff officer had two or three horses shot beneath him – and one had four. Wellington's military secretary, FitzRoy Somerset (the young Lord Raglan) lost an arm, and Lord Uxbridge lost a leg to a cannonball as he rode beside Wellington. Several other officers were killed or seriously wounded around him including Sir William de Lancey, Wellington's Quartermaster General, who was hit by a ricocheting cannon ball. His wound seemed so severe that in the initial draft of the dispatch he wrote hours after the battle, Wellington reported that he had been killed. De Lancey himself was sure that he could not survive long and begged to be left to die in peace.

However, his comrades removed him to a barn at the edge of the battle-field and from there to a house in the village of Mont St Jean where he lay in agony from his wounds. His young bride Magdalene (they had been married just two and a half months earlier) was about to endure an emotional tumult even greater than that of Juana Smith – but with no happy outcome.

Magdalene had been staying with William in Brussels in the weeks before the battle. In the early hours of 16 June she had leant out of her window and watched the regiments march past on their way to the battle of Quatre Bras, solemn and melancholy, before they melted away into the distance. After saying a fond farewell to her husband, she and her maid departed for Antwerp. She later wrote an account of her time at Brussels and Waterloo and of how misdirected kindness by those seeking to soften the blow exacerbated her misery. Charles Dickens was so moved by her narrative that he commented, 'If I live for fifty years, I shall dream of it every now and then, from this hour to the day of my death, with the most frightful reality.'

Impatient for news but unwilling to expose herself to the rumours that would inevitably be swirling around Antwerp, Magdalene shut herself in her lodgings as soon as she arrived in the city. Even so, she could hear the thunder of cannon at Waterloo, more than thirty miles away. At midnight she had the news she longed for from her husband: he had survived the battle of Quatre Bras. The next day, news came that there was to be another great fight. The Battle of Waterloo began at 11 a.m. on 18 June; at 3 p.m. Sir William was struck by the cannonball. On the morning of Monday 19 June the list of killed and wounded arrived in Antwerp; Sir William's name was not among them – a staff officer quickly informed Magdalene that her husband must be safe and well. She was still almost feverish with joy at his deliverance when a few hours later an acquaintance, Lady Jane Hamilton, came to call on her.

To her surprise, Lady Hamilton did not seem to share in her happiness but grew increasingly agitated, until at last she confessed that it was she who had written out the list of killed and wounded and, 'with a most mistaken kindness' as Magdalene bitterly described it, had omitted several names including Sir William's, because she did not want their friends and families to receive news of their fate in so brutal a fashion. Her good inten-tions had the opposite result. The elation Magdalene had felt on learning of his wellbeing only compounded her misery now at hearing that he was seriously wounded. Utterly confused, she did not know what to believe, and begged her informant: "Lady H I can bear anything but suspense, let

me know the very worst. Tell me, is he killed? I see! You know it is so."
She then solemnly assured me he was only desperately wounded. I shook
my head and said "Ah it is very well to say so yes he must be wounded
first, you know you say!" And I walked round and around the room fast,
"Yes. Yes you say so, but I cannot believe what you say now." She was terrified for I could not shed a tear.'

Eventually Lady Hamilton convinced her that this time she was speaking the truth. Distraught, Magdalene resolved at once to go to her husband
so that she might see him before it was too late. Leaving Antwerp in her
carriage together with her maid and a kindly officer, Magdalene chafed at
their slow progress as they had to force their way through a crowd of
wagons, cars, horses, deserters and wounded men all trying to leave or enter
the city. At last, when they were nearly halfway to Brussels (twenty-five
miles from Antwerp), they met an officer who told them that their journey was in vain: Sir William had died. In despair, Magdalene returned slowly
to Antwerp where she spent a miserable night, hysterical with grief. The
following morning (20 June), yet another conflicting report reached her,
this time stating confidently that her husband was after all alive.

Yet again, her world was turned upside-down. Nearly maddened with
confusion and anxiety, she was at last convinced that this report was true
and set off once again for Brussels, furious that she had wasted yet more
precious time while her husband's life might be ebbing away. As they drew
near Brussels the smell of gunpowder became perceptible. The roads were
thronged with wounded and exhausted soldiers, their families and other
travellers, but once again a protector materialised, an officer who rode
before the carriage with sword drawn to clear a way through the crowds.
Nonetheless it took three and a half hours to travel the nine miles from
Brussels to Waterloo. At the same time, on another part of the road, Juana
Smith was riding hard, also bewildered by contradictory reports of her
husband's death.

As Magdalene's carriage neared the battlefield, the horses began to scream
at the stench of rotting flesh. Magdalene was only twenty-two. She had
had a happy, sheltered upbringing in an upper-class, intellectual Scottish
family. She had been presented at court, taken the waters at Bath, and was
at ease in society. She can have been ill-prepared for the terrible sights and
smells of the aftermath of a great battle, or for the duties of nursing a terribly wounded man. But she pressed onwards and, a short distance from the
house where her husband was lying, met General Scovell, an old friend of
Sir William's, who told her that her husband was still alive. When she finally

entered the room where Sir William lay (and where Wellington himself had visited him only hours earlier), she found him stronger than she expected. He held out his hand to her saying, "Come, Magdalene, this is a sad business, is it not?" I could not speak, but sat down by him and took his hand.' Now the agonies of the past few days served to strengthen her for, having been told of his death and then finding him alive meant that she was now ready 'to bear whatever might ensue without a murmur'.

Over the next six days Magdalene stayed by her husband's side in the humble cottage in Mont St Jean, tenderly nursing him as best she could. He was attended by two surgeons (including Wellington's personal physician, Dr John Hume) who regularly bled him and applied leeches and blisters. As the cannonball had not actually penetrated his body the surgeons were at first hopeful that he might survive, but his condition did not improve.

Magdalene stoically assisted the surgeons, even applying leeches, a difficult and unpleasant task for a young woman whose whole life had been one of delicacy and refinement. She seldom slept, 'for I grudged wasting any of such precious time', except for one night when Sir William begged her to lie down next to him and they slept side by side. All the time she tried hard not to let him see how desperately afraid she was. Her husband too did his best to appear cheerful, thanking her profusely for every small service she performed. Meanwhile, outside the windows of the small cottage, carriages rumbled back and forth for several days conveying the wounded from the battlefield to the hospitals in Brussels.

By the third day of her vigil it was clear that Sir William's condition was worsening, and on the fourth day the surgeons warned Magdalene that he would not last much longer. Although she had twice believed her husband to be dead, and was aware how serious his condition was, Magdalene was still stupefied with shock. Immediately she went in to her sleeping husband's room and sat down to watch him. 'My mouth was so parched that when I touched it, it felt as dry as the back of my hand – I thought I was to die first, – I then thought, what would he do for want of me, for the remaining few hours he had to live – This idea roused me and I began to recollect our helpless situation . . . ' When Sir William awoke she told him that he had not long to live, and that if he had any last wishes or words he must express them now. Tenderly he told her that 'He felt at peace with the world – he knew he was going to a better one, &c &c. He repeated most of what he had told me were his feelings before – that he had no sorrow but to part from his wife, and no regret but that of leaving her in misery – He seemed fatigued, and shutting his eyes desired me not to speak for a little.' Two days later he was still alive. While they waited for the surgeons to dress his wound, Magdalene took her husband's hand. 'He said he wished I would not look so unhappy – I wept – and he spoke to me with so much affection. He repeated every endearing expression – he bid me kiss him – he called me his dear Wife.' A few minutes later he 'gave a little gulp, as if something was in his throat – the Doctor said "Ah poor De Lancey, he is gone" – I pressed my lips to his and left the room.' She returned to spend some time with the body and 'envied him not a little that he was released – I was left to suffer.' Two days later she was standing beside his grave at a little cemetery just outside Brussels. She visited it once more before leaving Brussels, on 4 July 1815. As she noted in her memoir, 'that day, three months before, I was married'.

At least Magdalene had the consolation of seeing her husband decently buried. Charlotte Waldie heard of one officer's wife who did not arrive on the field of Waterloo until nearly a month after the battle. She was left to wander wildly across the field together with her sister-in-law hunting for the body, 'vainly demanding where the remains of him they loved reposed, and accusing Heaven for denying them the consolation of weeping over his grave'. Charlotte also observed sadly the frequent funeral cortèges that filed along the streets of Brussels in the days after the battle as soldiers died of their wounds. 'I could not help thinking,' she wrote, 'that, though no eye here was moistened with a tear, yet in some remote cottage or humble dwelling of my native country, the heart of the wife or the mother would be wrung with despair for the loss of him who was now borne unnoticed to a foreign grave.'

In the Crimea, too, many of the soldiers' wives preferred to go out on to the battlefield to ascertain their husbands' fate rather than trust the word of soldiers returning from the fight. Elizabeth Evans, who had travelled out with the 4th (King's Own) followed the men on to the battlefield of the Alma until she was ordered to the rear. When the fighting ceased she and her companions rushed on to the field past wounded horses screaming in agony, severed legs, piles of corpses humming with flies, and wounded men crying piteously. The heart of each woman stood still whenever she saw a body in the uniform of her husband's regiment. At length, Mrs Evans was satisfied that her husband was not among the dead, but one of her companions was granted no such mercy. She was found some hours after the battle keening beside her husband's dead body.

Mrs Longley, whose old employer Lord John Russell had helped her get to the Crimea, was relieved to see her husband return safely from the Alma, only to have her heart broken a month later at Balaclava. Mrs Longley had made her way up to the Sapoune Heights above the battlefield, taking her place alongside several other women who were observing the scene below them. Like the Duberlys in their vineyard, her eyes were trained on the Light Brigade to which her husband's regiment, the 17th Lancers, belonged. Pleased at first to see that the Light Brigade was not being used, her relief turned to trepidation as, in the valley below them, they saw it take the field and watched as the mass of men and horses began to gallop towards their doom, with the 17th Lancers in the front line. There was a boom of guns and roundshot, grape and rifle cut into the front ranks of the charging mass. Smoke obliterated their view. Then, as it cleared, they saw a whole section of Lancers and Light Dragoons go down. Mrs Longley and her fellow spectators stood looking on in horror.

When the charge was over and the remnants of the heroic brigade began straggling back up the valley, women rushed down to welcome back the survivors. Mrs Longley, meanwhile, began to thread her way through the bodies of wounded men, heading right for the very Russian guns that had just cut down the cream of the British cavalry. Her head bent in sorrow, she knew that her husband would not have escaped unscathed. Her only hope was that she might find him wounded. As she walked resolutely down the valley a bullet from a Russian marksman on the hills above struck her wrist. Even this searing pain did not deflect her from her task. Stifling the impulse to turn and run as she came across yet more horribly maimed men and horses, she pressed on. A comrade of her husband's saw her and came to join her in her task. They scoured the valley for Sergeant Longley's corpse until at last they found it. Together they wrapped the body in a greatcoat and, as Mrs Longley was adamant that her husband must have a coffin and a decent grave rather than being slung into one of the communal pits, they began to gather wood, under the gaze of Russian gunners who forbore from firing on them. When they had constructed the makeshift coffin they dug a grave and lowered the body of Sergeant Longley into it, before trudging back to the British lines.

Mrs Longley remained in the Crimea for the remainder of the war, working as a nurse, and afterwards travelled to India where her nursing skills were in much demand during the Mutiny. She received a medal for her nursing services from Queen Victoria.

Such women as Mrs Longley and Magdalene de Lancey epitomised the ideal of a devoted widow. Not all women managed to live up to that image. Captain Harry Ross-Lewin, who served in the Peninsula with the 32nd (The Cornwall) Regiment, recalled with wry amusement the reaction of a beautiful young woman whose officer husband had been killed at the battle of Salamanca.

Ross-Lewin happened to be sharing a billet with her and, along with other observers, was touched by the intensity of her grief for her husband. 'For some time the young widow remained perfectly motionless, and her eyes had settled into a vacant stare, but at length she began to exhibit symptoms of returning recollection, and made some signs to her countrywoman [whose husband had been severely wounded in the same battle]. "It is her husband's watch that she wants," said that lady. The watch was found fastened under her habit, and as soon as it was placed in her hands she kissed it repeatedly, and then laid it in her bosom. The worthy old miller whose house we occupied, melted at this touching spectacle; neither could any of his family, from the oldest to the youngest, restrain their tears. I myself, even though no stranger to scenes of woe, testified that my bosom had not yet become callous. The mules that were turning the mill wheels came to a full stop; and even the brown muleteer who crossed the yard participated in the very general sympathy that the misfortunes of these afflicted ladies excited, and blubbered outright. The first paroxysms of the fair mourner's grief were succeeded by violent hysterics, and then a flood of tears came to her relief. When I found that reason began to resume her empire over her mind, I sent in my name with an offer of my services. I had previously provided their servants with rations. And, on receiving a promise from the good family of the house that every attention should be paid to them during the night, I retired to my room.'

The next morning Ross-Lewin was surprised to note that the ladies' carriage had already departed. A few days later he walked into Salamanca and was stunned to see the young widow, who had seemed almost demented with sorrow, now 'leaning on a young commissary with two gold epaulettes, and evidently enjoying excellent spirits. She set off with this gallant on the following day for Rodrigo.' Her mourning had been brief indeed.

George Gleig, who recorded the tragedy of Duncan and Mary Stewart, the couple torn apart by the ballot, entertained a fairly low opinion of soldiers' wives in general. He especially felt that women who accompanied the army on campaign soon lost whatever delicacy and other feminine virtues they had once possessed, through being continually exposed to danger and hardship. 'The sort of life which they lead, after they have for any length of time followed an army in the field, sadly unsexes them (if I may be permitted to coin such a word for their benefit) . . . ' He claimed that he could recall only one instance of a widow displaying symptoms of real sorrow. When his regiment, the 85th (Bucks Volunteers) Light Infantry, took part in the siege of Bayonne in February 1814, one of the last actions of the Peninsular War, a young soldier named McDermot was killed in a brief skirmish with a French force making a sortie.

Sergeant McDermot was 'a fine young Irishman' with a handsome face and a manly figure. His wife, Nancy, had been a respectable lady's maid, whose family had tried hard to prevent her marrying a common soldier. Despite such opposition and the rough nature of campaigning life, Nancy was blissfully happy with her soldier. The two were accounted 'the most virtuous and the happiest couple in the regiment', while Nancy's 'unblemished character' set her apart from many of her fellow women. McDermot was a brave, almost reckless, soldier and in this action he had been laughing at his fellow soldiers for ducking as the cannonballs flew above, assuring them that 'every bullet has its billet', when a roundshot struck his head. The soldiers screamed, not only because of the terrible sight but because he was a popular soldier and a great favourite with all ranks.

And then, wrote Gleig, at once all thoughts turned to his poor young wife, 'so spotless, and so completely wrapped up in him. "O, who will tell Nance of this?" cried the soldiers, one and all; so true is it that virtue is respected, and a virtuous woman beloved, even by common soldiers. But there was no hiding it from Nancy. The news reached her, heaven knows how, long before we returned to our tents, and she was in the midst of us in a state which beggars all description, in five minutes after the event took place.' McDermot's body was brought into camp and shown to Nancy, but the poor woman was in such a state of shock and denial that she would not believe that the mangled carcass in front of her eyes was her husband. ''That, O that is not he!' cried she; 'that McDermot – my own handsome, beautiful McDermot! O no, no – take it away, or take me away, and bring me to him!" Unable to convince her of the truth, the soldiers gave up trying and took her back to the camp. The body was buried and a young fir tree planted over it.

It was some days before Nancy could come to terms with what had happened. When at last the horrible truth sunk in, 'the feeling of utter desolateness came over her; and instead of listening, as women in her situation generally listen, to the proposals of some new suitor, all her wishes pointed homewards'. The army was now in the south-west of France and it was comparatively easy to put Nancy on a ship back to Ireland. Because of her popularity a subscription was raised with every officer and man in the regiment contributing something, enabling Nancy to live out her days as a respectable widow in Cork without being obliged to remarry.

Many officers were of the opinion that few soldiers' wives suffered genuine grief when they were widowed. Captain Grattan, usually less prejudiced than most, confessed that he found the scenes of leave-taking between husbands and wives before battle singularly unmoving. 'The worst that could happen to them [the women] was the chance of being in a state of widowhood for a week' before another man stepped up to fill his shoes. Yet for every accusation of heartlessness on the part of soldiers' wives there is a story of a wife devastated by grief, like Nancy McDermot, or like the women observed by the commissariat officer John Edgecombe Daniell not long afterwards at the battle of Toulouse, the final battle of the Peninsular War.

Daniell noted that the baggage camp, in which the women were left while the fighting took place, was situated on this occasion rather too close to the battlefield. This meant that the women could not be prevented from coming up to the rear to inquire after their husbands in the midst of the fighting. Tragically, many among those killed in the regiment to which Daniell was attached were married men, so many of the beseeching women had their worst fears confirmed. One of the most affecting scenes witnessed by Daniell was that of a woman whose husband, an artillery-man, had just died of his wounds. His wife became so frantic that, 'she ran into the field exposing herself to the enemy's fire, until she was dragged off to the rear by a sergeant'.

In any case, for all the jibes about serial wives, remarriage after widowhood was far from uncommon even in the civilian world. With life expectancy far lower than today, many marriages would not endure beyond a handful of years. Even by the early nineteenth century the death rate among young adults was such that almost 30 per cent of all marriages were ended within the first fifteen years by the death of one spouse. For soldiers in wartime, life expectancy was lower still and it would have been surprising if their wives, devoted or otherwise, did not consider the future and how to provide for themselves and their children if they were to be widowed. It was equally natural for soldiers to view their companions' wives as potential partners if the worst was to befall their husbands.

Even Christian Welsh, whose grief on her husband's death had been so violent, was prepared to listen to a marriage proposal within weeks of burying him. One of her husband's former comrades, a soldier named Hugh Jones, had long shown his devotion to her. Touched by his kindness and alarmed by his threat to kill himself if she would not marry him, eleven weeks after the battle of Malplaquet Christian became Hugh Jones's bride. The swiftness of her transition from widow to bride caused one sergeant to remark cuttingly that 'The cow that lows most after her calf went soonest to bull.' But the marriage was over in less than a year when Jones was shot in the thigh. In spite of all Christian's nursing, his wound became gangrenous and he died.

Once again Christian was left on her own, with no entitlement to rations and no reason to stay with the army. By now, however, she had enough allies among the officers that she was allowed to remain and was given work as a cook that enabled her to live. But finally, after two years, a new Tory government in Britain decided to oust Marlborough and to press for peace, and in 1712 the army, which had spent most of the last twenty years fighting on the Continent, began to trickle back to England's shores. Back in London, Christian found herself almost penniless and forced to take lodgings in a brothel. She applied to the Duke of Marlborough for help. Both he and the Duchess helped her present a petition to Queen Anne, who gave her a grant of money in recognition of her soldiering services. Christian went on to marry a third time, another soldier named Davies, who squandered much of her money. She ended her days in Chelsea where, as a day pensioner at the Royal Hospital, she spent her time reliving old war stories with fellow veterans.

The authenticity of Christian's colourful story is sometimes called into question. It is hard not to suspect that she occasionally exaggerated, aggrandising her own prominence in battles or her bravery. Her existence is, however, verified by the admission roll of pensioners at the Royal Hospital, which records that Christian Davies, 'A fatt jolly woman received several wounds in the service in ye habitt of a man [was admitted] from 19th July 1717.' When she died in 1739 she was buried alongside other pensioners and three volleys of shots were fired over her grave.

The more usual difficulties of women widowed on campaign had long been recognised and the Duke of Marlborough, ever solicitous for the care of his troops, had turned his attention to the subject. A scheme for support-

ing officers' orphans already existed under which the child of a dead officer would be commissioned into his father's regiment and receive pay without actually undertaking any duties. This caused problems when regiments
ordered overseas were found to be full of 'officers' who were still in their
cradles, so an order was made limiting the number of orphan officers to
two per regiment. Marlborough encouraged regiments to start voluntary
schemes for the support of widows to which officers' subscribed. Ordinary
soldiers could not afford such schemes so Marlborough decreed after the
battle of Schellenberg (1704) that women widowed by the fighting should
be enrolled as nurses. This allowed them to receive some remuneration.
Those remaining after these posts had been filled were entitled to have
their passage back to England paid.

In the Peninsular War, of which Brown, Gleig and Grattan were writing, widows and orphans on the strength would normally continue to
receive rations for some time after the soldier's death. An order published
by Horse Guards in December 1811 stipulated that 'widows and orphans
of officers or soldiers are to be victualled until they can obtain a passage
home'. Remarriage was by no means mandatory, as the case of Nancy
McDermot demonstrated – she was able to return to Ireland, and the regiment's generosity ensured that she did not face destitution. Mrs Cockayne
also decided against remarriage (to the disappointment of Benjamin Harris,
who proposed to her a few days after helping her bury her husband). She
too sailed for home. Harris never married. But other women were daunted
by the prospect of the journey back to Britain, perhaps with several children in tow, and the uncertain future they faced when they got there.
Without any income they would have to throw themselves on the mercy
of their family or the authorities. Many preferred to remain with the army
and the easiest means of doing so was to become a soldier's wife once
more. Those who had children were particularly in need of the security
that a husband could provide. The soldiers they wed were often comrades
of their husbands, men whom they had come to know well over the past
months and years, who might have helped them with their children on a
long march, or drunk rum with them around the fire of an evening. Long
courtships were neither necessary nor possible in such circumstances.
Nonetheless there were women who remarried so swiftly and so frequently
that they were bound to attract some unfavourable comments.

Captain Browne was scandalised by the 'daring & enterprise of these
creatures' who, he claimed, 'had no hesitation in engaging themselves three
or four deep to future Husbands, & according to the activity in mischief,

of each, was the number of candidates for her hand, in case of disaster to her lawful Lord; & one of them has been heard to reply to a Soldier, who offered himself, as successor to her then Commanding Officer: "Nay, but thou'rt late, as I'm promised to John Edwards first, & to Edward Atkinson next, but when they two be killed off, I'll think of thee."' Another, much repeated, story tells of the widow who, weeping after she had buried her husband, was approached diffidently by a sergeant who proposed marriage. She at once burst into tears, at which he apologised for offending her by proposing so soon. 'No, it's not that!' she explained between sobs. Her tears were because she had already accepted the proposal of a mere corporal, unaware that a greater catch was about to be offered.

It was not always the prettiest or most charming women who were besieged with suitors upon being widowed. Soldiers in wartime had more practical considerations in mind. A woman who had proved her worth by always having a hot meal ready for her husband at the end of a hard day on the road, who was tough and sturdy enough to march for miles without complaining, or who earned a useful income by sutlering or working for officers, would be greatly sought after. (Equally, as Captain Browne alleged, the women who were most adept at 'mischief' such as plundering or body-stripping were often highly esteemed.)

Samuel Hutton married his wife only hours after her first husband was killed. Kate Keith, as she was then, was a 'pretty little Scotchwoman' who had accompanied her husband to the Seven Years War and made a good income from keeping a sutler's tent for the officers. When her husband was killed in action in Germany in 1761, suitors began to line up at once. As Hutton explained, 'In such a situation, the woman must not remain a widow, and with such qualifications, she was a prize to any man. Another comrade said to me, "I advise you to marry Kate Keith. If you won't, I will. But there's no time to be lost, for she'll have plenty of offers." I took a few hours to consider of it, and determined upon soliciting the hand of Kate Keith. I found that *plenty* had been before me; but my person and good conduct obtained me the preference; and the little black-eyed Scotchwoman accompanied me to the chaplain of the regiment the second day after her husband had fallen.' The marriage was a success. Kate soon bore him a son (the baby who arrived in the world to the accompaniment of cannon fire). In Hutton's words, 'I had passed gaily through a military life; and when united to an active young woman, accustomed to her share of hardships, I had found my happiness increase, but not my cares.'

William Wheeler met one serial widow after the battle of Toulouse. He had just escaped from his encounter with the distraught Mrs Foster when his churlish companion, a soldier named Marshal, urged him to make haste —

> 'Here comes Cousins' wife, snivelling as if she was a big girl going to school without her breakfast.'
>
> 'She has reason to snivel as you calls it,' said I, 'she is the most unfortunate creature in the army.'
>
> 'Unfortunate indeed,' said M[arshal], 'why I think she is devilish lucky in getting husbands, she has had a dozen this campaign.' M[arshal] was drunk and had rather stretched the number. This unfortunate woman was now a widow for the third time since the battle of Victoria [Vittoria].

The battle of Vittoria had been fought only five months earlier. Similarly John Green, a soldier in the 68th Foot (the Durham Light Infantry), recalled the frantic grief of Mrs Dunn, whose sergeant husband had both legs shot from under him at Salamanca and died a few minutes later. 'Her loss,' thought Green, 'certainly was great; but in less than a week she took up with a sergeant of the same company, whose name was Gilbert Hinds, with whom she has lived ever since. This poor woman was unlucky, for she had lost five husbands: Hinds is her sixth!'

Even in peacetime it was common for widows to remarry quickly, especially when a regiment was abroad. In India, where single white women were scarce, and death rates among soldiers high due to the combined evils, of heat, disease and drink, soldiers' widows could be assured of plenty of suitors. Although women continued receiving their husbands' pay for six months, when that time expired they had either to go home or remarry. Many chose the latter option. Sergeant Pearman, who was stationed in Ambala in 1849, noted that there were often as many as five weddings a day at Ambala and a large number of these involved either fourteen-year-old girls (children above the age of fourteen did not receive orphans' benefits) or widows. 'Some women in that country have several husbands before they are very old,' noted Pearman. 'I knew one that married her sixth husband in the regiment to which I belonged. She had been in several regiments. She came from the 75th Foot [later the Gordon Highlanders] to us.' Sergeant MacMullen also thought that for a woman to be widowed in India was less than catastrophic, as 'She is besieged by admirers while the tears which decency demands are still coursing one another down her cheeks.' MacMullen claimed to know one woman who had married three husbands within six months, and another who had married her fifth, having children by each husband.

Officers' wives also often preferred to stay in India where, as time went on, many of them had been born, rather than pack their belongings and make the lonely journey to England. It was a daunting prospect to start a new life in Cheltenham, Bath or wherever they had any family connections. There they would have to try to maintain the sort of lifestyle that their class demanded, but their widow's pension might not sustain. Rudyard Kipling, the great chronicler of British Indian social life, noted wryly that, should the summer heat take its toll on the men's health, their widows, who spent the summer in the hill stations, often had a replacement rather too readily at hand:

> *Jack's own Jill goes up hill*
> *To Murree and Chakrata,* [hill stations]
> *Jack remains to die on the plains,*
> *And Jill remarries soon after.*

Attractive, ambitious women could sometimes marry their way up the social ranks. Emily Eden met one girl who had begun life as a soldier's daughter but 'She was pretty, and by dint of killing off a husband, or two, she is now at nineteen the wife of a captain here. I should think she must look back with regret to her childish plebeian days. The husband interrupts her every time she opens her lips . . . '

Nor did widowers shrink from remarrying, sometimes with indecent haste, as a lady visitor to India in 1856 noted: 'Many wives have acknowledged that tender and good as their husbands wre, they knew that, should anything happen to them, a successor would be appointed within a year.'

Even those who had no intention of remarrying could sometimes be persuaded to do so. The history of the Royal Sappers and Miners records the tale of Mrs Brown, a sergeant's wife whose husband had been seconded to the employment of the Sultan of Morocco in 1776 to help him improve the fortifications of Fez. Some time after completing his work Sergeant Brown died and his wife sought an audience with the Sultan to obtain a pension and a means of returning home. The Sultan, however, was so taken with Mrs Brown's 'fair and comely appearance' that he proposed marriage, notwithstanding that she was Catholic and refused to convert to Islam. And so the 'poor, friendless Irish widow' became the Sultana of Morocco.

★

Today, no widow has to traipse over the battleground trying to discern the features of her loved one among the charred or mutilated bodies that lie on the ground. No army wife now faces the choice of remarriage or being left destitute or instantly homeless (although there has been one controversial recent case of an Iraq war widow being told to leave her quarter within three months, an order that was swiftly retracted when it became public knowledge.) Much has improved since the days of the Peninsula or the Crimea – today there are Casualty Visiting Officers, welfare provision and war widows' pensions. But the wife left at home for month after month, both longing for and dreading news from some far distant battle zone where her husband is engaged, undergoes much the same emotions as the women left behind in the camps and quarters of earlier centuries.

'They also serve who only stand and wait', wrote Milton, and in some ways, the waiting has only got more difficult, despite or perhaps because of the rapidity of communications and the availability of twenty-four-hour news and the drip-feed of information it brings to the families. Families of men in combat zones often become glued to the television, radio (and now the internet), hungry for information about what is happening, yet dreading any news that might heighten their anxiety. As one wife of a soldier serving in Iraq put it, 'You only have to hear the words 'near Basra' then your world stops.' There then follows an anxious wait of many hours, hoping against hope that the casualty reported is not their own husband or father. When it becomes clear that they have been spared, the relief is often followed swiftly by guilt, knowing that their deliverance is a tragic loss to another woman.

Since the start of the Iraq conflict, a review by the Ministry of Defence of all aspects of the operation, including the procedure for informing the families of casualties, found that the policy of providing only vague details of incidents involving British casualties until next of kin had been informed resulted in large numbers of families suffering concern. As a result, the Ministry decided to release more details as quickly as possible to spare families needless anguish.

When Britain's task force sailed to the Falkland Islands in 1982, the wives and families who waved the men off at Portsmouth and Southampton found themselves plunged into a front line of their own. The Falklands conflict was, in a sense, Britain's first modern media war. It was the first time that audiences back home received updates from the front several times a day and could watch dramatic footage of events only hours after they took place. Families found themselves glued to the radio and television bulletins as events unfolded with astonishing rapidity, although it took longer for news of casualties to reach the families involved. Sara Jones, whose husband Lieutenant Colonel 'H' Jones was commanding 2 PARA, remained in Aldershot with the other wives and families. She remembers living from one radio bulletin to the next. 'When they landed [at San Carlos Water] we knew that they'd landed because it came across the media and [I remember] lying awake all night waiting for the latest bits of news.' It was with intense relief that she finally heard that the landing had been unopposed. A week later came the battle for Goose Green.

When the first reports of the battle came through, the atmosphere in Aldershot was jubilant. Sara Jones recalls that 'There was great excitement as it had been fairly successful.' A note of caution was sounded by an officer friend who telephoned to tell her of the victory. 'He said "We must guard against undue optimism" which was a funny thing to say, because I think he already knew H was dead, but I don't think it had been properly confirmed . . . he obviously thought 'Oh dear, she's getting all excited and I think we've got some dire news to tell her." The next day her two sons, David aged sixteen and Rupert aged thirteen, were due to come home for half-term from boarding school. Still delighted by news of the victory, Sara went to fetch them from the train station. 'I remember picking them up and there were headlines all over the newspapers – 'H for hero' – and all that sort of business because at that stage they didn't know – I mean he was the CO [Commanding Officer] – but they didn't know that he was dead and I remember saying to David something about "It's all exciting" and he said "Oh, but there may be casualties". And this was a sixteen-year-old boy, really very sad.'

The boys were in the garden when a car drew up outside her house. Before 2 PARA had left for the Falklands, as the Commanding Officer's wife Sara had discussed with the Families Officer the procedure for informing the families of casualties. It was arranged that the Families Officer, together with the Colonel of the Regiment (a former commanding officer) and the padre would visit the bereaved family and that Sara too would go to give her support. So when she saw the car, and who was inside it, Sara assumed they were coming to collect her to break the news to some other unfortunate family: 'Little did I know that they were coming to knock at my door.'

The next few hours passed in a blur. Like many other women in such a situation, Sara at first was unable to believe what she was being told. 'I think you go into sort of shock mode – you think 'I'm sure they must have got this wrong' . . . I was lucky because [among] the other people I had in the house, curiously, was a very dear friend of mine . . . and my mother was there as well because it was half term. So it was quite good, the house was fairly full of people, which was as well because you don't need to sort of be on your own them . . . . It was funny, I probably did it all wrong. You just carry on, you just get on with it. The boys were due to go out to a barbecue [the evening after they heard the news] so I said you must go. I don't know if they wanted to, I'm sure they didn't in fact, but what else do you do except carry on?'

One difficulty that Sara had to contend with was becoming the subject of intense media interest. Because H was one of the war's first and, thanks both to his rank and his heroism, most high-profile casualties (he was awarded a posthumous VC), journalists were desperate to talk to his widow. 'The media always hit on one person and it was me. I had all the press camping outside the house. I had soldiers at the gate to stop people knocking on the door day and night . . . I don't know if it made it more difficult or whether the media interest helped. I suppose in a sort of way it gave one a lot to think about and to contend with rather than to sit there thinking "It's the end of my world, what do I do now?"'

Sara remained in her army quarter for ten months after H's death and could have stayed longer, but after the regiment had returned from the Falklands, she began to find it hard to watch other people resuming their lives all around her. 'I used to notice all the men going to work in the morning in their uniforms with their berets on and that was really difficult.' In the early days after H's death, however, she found that the close-knit regimental community was a lifeline, especially the presence of other wives. Sara had been an army wife for seventeen years and had made firm friends within the regiment as well as in H's original regiment, the Devon and Dorsets. Such friendships, together with the support of her family, now sustained her. 'There were 16 or 17 casualties in 2 PARA so there were a lot of families in the same boat.' The bedrock of support from people who could readily empathise with her situation helped immeasurably. 'You know, when you're left on your own as a widow it could be quite lonely but in the army, people feel "that could be me on my own" so they're very good to you.'

Although many of the bodies of those killed in the Falklands were repatriated to Britain at the end of the war, the Jones family preferred to let Colonel H remain buried at the 'serenely lovely spot' on the Falklands not far from where he fell in the islands' defence. Since then Sara has worked for the Falklands Families Association as its chairman and has remained in close touch with other Falklands widows and families. 'It's a common human emotion that it's nice to have someone else in the same boat. You feel "Thank God I'm not the only one."'

Two decades later Samantha Roberts, an army wife of less than two years' standing and living apart from the army community in the house that she and Steve had bought together in Shipley, West Yorkshire, had a very different experience. Unlike Sara Jones, she was alone in the house when the Casualty Visiting Officer arrived, bearing news that she had never seriously contemplated having to face. On a normal day she would have been at work, but some strange sixth sense persuaded her to stay at home that morning.

It [Iraq] was on the television 24/7 and I was up really late watching. I'd written him a letter, and it was a really from-the-heart letter. I'd written it and I couldn't sleep and I was up till 3 or 4 in the morning. I finally fell asleep, woke up about 7 o'clock, got up and I was supposed to be in work for about 10. I've got a friend that lives with me, and she also worked with me at the time, and I couldn't stop crying. And I said, 'I really don't want to go into work today, I think I might ask if I can have a holiday.' And she said, 'All right, fine. Anything in particular that's upsetting you?' I said, 'No, I just want to be at home, someone might need to get hold of me.' . . . She was shocked. She said, 'Well, who?' I said, 'I don't know I just really want to be at home.' I was weepy, couldn't be bothered to do anything. She left at ten o'clock and then at twenty past ten Captain Potts came.

I was sitting on the sofa, I was still in my pyjamas, and I heard the gate. Because when you sit there on the sofa you can actually see the gate. And this guy came in and I thought, 'Oh God, he's got a suit on, it's a Jehovah's Witness or something.' And then he knocked on the door, and I got up and as soon as I saw him I thought, 'Oh God he's from . . .' You can tell if someone's a soldier. He wasn't in uniform. I said, 'Can I help you?' And the door was locked – and I said, 'Can I help you?' like that and he took out his ID card and showed me and said, 'I need to come in and speak to you.' And then he came in and he said, 'I think we'd better sit down.' And I said, 'No, it's OK, what's the problem?' and he said, 'No, come and sit down.' It's a bloody long walk all the way down there to the sofa, and I said, 'Just tell me what's going on.' And then he said [that Steve had been shot and killed], and I said, 'I appreciate you coming, but I think you've made a mistake, because Steve was in a tank, and he wouldn't have been in a position where he could have been shot, I think you've got me mixed up with somebody else.' And I was adamant that he'd got . . . that he'd made a mistake . . . But he hadn't.'

It was 24 March 2003, the fourth day of the Iraq war.

The first few hours and days after Steve's death were a terrible blur. 'People say, 'I don't know how you coped.' And you just do, because there's nothing else you can do, you can't change a situation. You can't bring him back, because, Christ, if you could, you would, and so you just have to live it really.' Steve's regiment were quick to rally round when the news broke. Nonetheless, unlike Sara Jones, Samantha was glad to be living away from the army patch. 'I think that would have been a bit intense . . . I certainly wouldn't have liked to have been on the camp to have received that news . . . because you couldn't get away from it. Not that you could anyway in your mind, it's there, you're living it, but there would have been so many awful reminders.'

Steve had been away for less than three weeks when he died, not enough time for Samantha to come to terms with him being at war, let alone the possibility that he might not return. Before he left, Steve, like many soldiers leaving for war, was anxious to make preparations in case the worst happened, but Samantha was reluctant to confront the possibility. 'If anything that is my biggest regret and guilt that I have, was that I would not discuss it with him . . . I suppose you don't want to think it's possibility, really.'

When the terrible news finally sunk in, Samantha went into a state akin to shock. 'I was sick the day it happened, I just felt really ill and I just couldn't eat, I couldn't sleep . . . I could not go up to my bed, I slept on the sofa for the first week.'

Within hours of the news being broken to her, Samantha was surrounded by friends and family. She believes that having people around her twenty-four hours a day literally saved her life. 'God knows what I would have been like if they hadn't been there. I don't think I'd be here today. I think it's quite natural to have these thoughts of 'I really don't want to be here' and you go through your mind of how you would do it . . . I wasn't panicking about it, I just felt, 'I don't want to be here any more and I could do this, or take that' but those thoughts gradually become fewer and fewer, and I did not have a minute alone to actually do that anyway . . . But one thing that my best friend said to me [was] . . . 'You know you might not find him if you do it.' I said, 'I want to see him again, I want to speak to him.' And she said, 'Well you might not find him.' And I think that's when I thought to myself, 'Well, I could, you know, finish it, but what if I go somewhere different and I don't see him, that would be even worse."

The decision was made before the Iraq war that all bodies of servicemen killed there would be repatriated to Britain, but it was not until two weeks after Steve's death that his body finally arrived back at Brize Norton airport in Oxfordshire. 'It was like an eternity, all we wanted was for him to come back, to come home. I said, 'I really want to see him,' I think just to make sure it was him. That was probably the worst day of my life because it was a reality then . . . When I have to go down the road and actually go past Oxford, I can't bear it, I hate Oxford, I can't stand it. And whenever I see a signpost to Oxford, it's horrible. It's funny how certain things make you react. I hate that place more than anything.'

The ceremony at Brize Norton was 'incredibly dignified, and they just did everything they could to make things as comfortable for us as possible. It was a horrendously long wait. They landed at 12 and it was half past four before we could see him . . . That was a really awful day.' She then had to wait a further two weeks while a post mortem was done before Steve's body was released and his funeral could finally be held. 'He had two funerals. He had a military funeral, up here in Harrogate, and then we took him down to Cornwall and we had sort of a family funeral in his home town and he was cremated . . . I remember thinking, 'God, it's been a month, he's been gone a month.' It just seemed like forever.'

One difficulty for Samantha was adjusting to life as 'a widow' at the age of thirty-one. 'Someone came up to me and said, 'Oh, you're the *widow*,' and I was like 'I don't want to be a *widow*.' It's a horrible label and conjures up this old, big fat Italian woman in black.' Another problem was finding out how and why Steve died. His regiment, 2nd Royal Tank Regiment, had been called to control a riot, south-west of Basra, on 24 March 2003. A scuffle ensued and Steve, who had got out of his tank to try to calm the crowd, was shot in the chest. It later transpired that he was killed by friendly fire as one of his fellow soldiers tried to defend him from an Iraqi attacking him with rocks.

However, Samantha remembered that a week before he was killed he had told her (in one of two telephone calls he made from Kuwait) that he had had to give up his body armour as there was a shortage and priority had to be given to soldiers not in tanks. Samantha was anxious to find out whether he had been wearing his body armour when he died, but it took three months for her to receive an answer from the Ministry of Defence that confirmed he had been without it. She is quite sure that if she and Steve's family had not kept up a persistent campaign to get information, they would still be in the dark. Not only was he without his flak jacket because of the shortage of 'enhanced combat body armour' that would, according to the pathologist's report on his death, have saved his life had he been wearing it, but his weapon had jammed. 'It looks like the odds were stacked against him from the very start. He didn't stand a chance really.'

Infuriated by the apparent lack of candour and co-operation forthcoming from the Ministry of Defence surrounding Steve's death, Samantha pursued a vigorous campaign, calling the Defence Secretary to account for the equipment shortages that left some troops in Iraq, including Steve, without the protection they needed. 'Ivor Caplin [then Under-Secretary for Defence] said, 'We can't be held accountable for every little glitch' like that. He's saying Steve was a little glitch. Well he wasn't a little glitch to us. They can be so insensitive.' For all her grievances about the way that Steve was served by the Ministry of Defence, Samantha has no regrets that she did not persuade him to leave the army. 'When we got married he said, 'If you want me to leave I will.' But he was army through and through . . . He wouldn't have been the same person.'

As long as there are wars there will be women who, in a split second of violence, are turned into widows long before their time, and children made fatherless by conflicts far from home of which they have little understanding. Yet from Christian Davies in the early eighteenth century to Samantha Roberts in the twenty-first century, women have summoned up reserves of courage and strength that they might not have hitherto realised they possessed. Some have behaved with quiet dignity, others have reacted with intense, even violent, grief. Others still have moved on by remarrying and starting life afresh, some (such as the merry widow whose behaviour so scandalised Captain Ross-Lewin) more swiftly than others.

Some widows have used their position to try to help others. Sara Jones continues to work for the Falklands Families Association and the Commonwealth War Graves Commission. Samantha Roberts' tireless campaign to ensure that soldiers will not, in future, go into war without vital life-protecting equipment was rewarded. In October 2004, eighteen months after her husband's death, the Secretary of State for Defence wrote to inform her that the ministry had changed its policy on enhanced combat body armour. Within two years all servicemen will be given this armour as standard issue. Soldiers should never again be in the position in which her husband was placed, of having to give up their armour to another man. She has also co-founded an organisation to support army widows in the initial stages of their bereavement with practical and emotional support. Such work, she says, has helped her enormously to come to terms with her grief, by bringing something positive out of tragedy.

Whatever their initial reactions, all have had to learn to live with the 'lingering grief of the fallen soldiers' widows'. In Sara Jones's words, 'You just carry on, you just get on with it . . . what else do you do except carry on?

Postscript: Looking Ahead

Army spouses are a different breed from those of forty, even twenty, years ago – for one thing, with the advent of female soldiers, about 2 per cent of them are men. Wives as well as husbands of serving soldiers may have careers of their own: of those who responded to the Families' Continuous Attitudes Survey in 2004, which canvassed the views of military families on army life, 66 per cent had jobs.

Whatever their work commitments, few now see the role of the army wife as any kind of all-absorbing occupation. The army can no longer assume that every wife is willing to take on the panoply of duties that her predecessors assumed. As one officer said to me: 'If the CO comes into the mess nowadays and asks an officer if his wife can arrange the flowers on a particular day, he's likely to get the response, "Sorry, she can't, she's a barrister and she's in court that day", or "She's a surgeon and is needed at the hospital" – or she may be in the army herself.'

Nor are they as susceptible to the pressures that often influenced their predecessors' behaviour. The idea that they could jeopardise their husband's promotion prospects if they fail to toe the line is dying out (except, as some have commented, among a few 'hard-core' wives of the old-fashioned school). Tor Walker, whose husband rose to the very top of the army, happily admits that as a young wife, if she ever felt that this sort of emotional pressure was being applied, she refused on principle. But she willingly got involved in pastoral duties among the regiment's families when living in Northern Ireland, because although 'I could have said no . . . you're part of a big family and you want to help.' Many modern wives adopt a similar attitude. They will help when and where they can, but those who have careers and other commitments, or who simply do not feel cut out to dispense marital advice or emotional support, are increasingly willing to say so.

In other ways too army wives have begun to loosen the bonds that once tied them to the military establishment. A growing number are now reluctant to follow the drum from one army quarter to the next. Nearly 25 per cent of those who responded to the 2004 Families' Survey were living in their own homes, at arm's length from the military community in a physical as well as an emotional sense. Such considerations as getting a foothold on the property ladder, giving their children the option of attending local schools (without constant disruption) rather than boarding schools, and above all a yearning for stability, are in many cases taking precedence over the desire to be at their husband's side. As one wife explained: 'You have to choose between putting your husband first and putting your children first.' So the dilemma faced by army wives in former times still confronts their modern-day counterparts.

Another factor is the nature of the posting itself. The vast majority of accompanied tours are now within the United Kingdom, Northern Ireland or Germany (97 per cent of respondents to the Families' Survey were living in these three postings). Travelling across the globe to sample life in such exotic climes as Burma, India, Malaya or Aden is no longer a perk (or privation) that army wives can expect to experience. Even in the last decade one of the most popular foreign postings, Hong Kong, has gone. Only a handful of overseas garrisons such as Brunei, Gibraltar and Cyprus remain. Those who might have been prepared to trade stability for adventure are unlikely to be enticed by the prospect of a fourth stint in an unprepossessing part of Germany, in accommodation almost identical to that of their last three German postings, especially when they know that they might be living there alone for long periods when their husband is sent away.

Yet, much of the time, the choice of whether to stay or to go, whether to sacrifice togetherness for stability, is still not theirs to make. Operational tours, training exercises and short postings are mainly unaccompanied and wives, partners and families have no option but to sit at home and wait, whether that home is in mainland Britain or abroad. In the Families Surveys of 2004 and 2002 the issue of separation, both its length and frequency, was cited as one of the primary problems of army life. The former chairman of the Army Families' Federation, Lizzie Iron, wrote to the Under Secretary of State for Defence in early 2004 to highlight grave dissatisfaction among army families with the current high levels of separation, increased by the impact of the Iraq conflict, and their effect on family life. Families, she reported, were concerned that the army was (and is) being asked to do too much with too few troops and that they and their families were suffering as a result.

The Ministry of Defence is sensitive to charges that army families are paying the price for overstretch, and acknowledges the fact that 'stability of family life is of great importance for the welfare of soldiers'. The minister was therefore quick to agree that 'excessive separation, particularly when caused by soldiers being sent on repetitive tours' was damaging to the army, which was now considering introducing limits (although the suggestion that the limit would be set at 480 days' separation over a rolling three-year − 1,095-day − period can have brought scant comfort).

The latest plans for modernising the army, published in December 2004, did try to tackle the problem of reconciling family life with military requirements by giving families the chance of a more settled lifestyle. Accordingly, the new blueprint for the army's future structure heralded the end of the system by which infantry battalions move every two years. Instead, units will have 'home' bases, from where its members can be sent on expeditionary forays, while the families remain at home. This will enable soldiers' families to put down roots: children will be able to settle into local schools and spouses pursue careers without such regular disruption, and without having to face so frequently the choice between stability and togetherness.

These plans have been generally well received by families. There were, however, some less welcome aspects of the new structure, such as the news that nineteen famous regiments are to be amalgamated into 'super-regiments'. Many wives were saddened to learn that the regimental communities to which many had belonged for most of their adult lives, and which have supported them through the most difficult of times, were to lose their identity.

Of particular concern to families was the announcement that the infantry would be reduced by 1,500 men, at a time when the army already appears to be sorely overstretched on dangerous missions from Iraq to Afghanistan and beyond. Some fear that this loss will offset the gain of greater stability for army families that the reforms seem to offer. The Ministry of Defence insists that these reductions will not be an issue. But many are worried that, if the army is continually being asked to do more with less, resulting in repetitive tours for its soldiers, its families will have to spend more time without their fathers and husbands. Could the new home-based structure lead to a partial return to the old days, when the majority of soldiers (those whose wives drew 'not to go' in the ballot) spent long periods of their service away from their home, their country and their families, having to reintegrate themselves into family life, often with some difficulty, on their return?

In the 2004 Families Survey wives were asked if they ever put pressure on their spouses to leave the army; 76 per cent said that they had not, although more than 30 per cent of couples had discussed the possibility. If families begin to feel that they are not being listened to, that political decisions affecting the army's manpower and commitments are having an unacceptably damaging impact on their lives, and that the soldiers themselves are not being given sufficient support in return for the sacrifices they make, then it is easy to see how these figures might change, with potentially devastating effects on both retention and recruitment.

It will be some years before the impact of the new army structure becomes apparent. Certainly it seems likely that fewer and fewer women will 'follow the drum' so continuously as the wives of the past. There will be more Kitty Wellingtons, staying at home to watch, wait and pray for their husband's safe return, and fewer Florentia Sales or Biddy Skiddys, sticking 'like bricks' to the army wherever it was sent, sharing in its trials and triumphs.

And whether they opt to work and live outside the confines of military life, or they choose to immerse themselves in the regimental community, army wives will still face trials and challenges that set them a world apart from their civilian sisters. When their families are wrenched apart as they wave their husbands off to war, when they spend months praying for their safe return, while they manage the household, raise their children and give birth in their absence, when every knock on the door causes them to freeze with fear – they have more in common with army wives of historical times than with most of their non-military contemporaries.

That the majority of wives are still willing to accept the unique conditions of army life, and support their husbands in the career they have chosen, is testament to those qualities of loyalty, endurance and resourcefulness that army women have proved, over the centuries, that they possess in abundance.

It is also, perhaps, due to the fact that while service life often brings more than its fair share of danger and discomfort, it also brings excitement, adventure, and feelings of camaraderie and loyalty that are rarely matched in civilian communities. Many former army wives and children talk of being enriched by the unique lifestyle they have enjoyed. Their memories of their time with the army are full of parties and picnics, practical jokes, fun and frivolity. It is hoped that, in years to come, there will still be plenty of women who will echo the words of one who remarked wistfully of her thirty years as an army wife: 'It was a wonderful life.'

Endnotes

Chapter 1: Marriage and the Military

'But you, my dear girl . . .' Thackeray, *Vanity Fair*

'As a woman was created . . .' Turner, 1683

Around 50 per cent . . . General Sir Michael Walker, in correspondence with the author

'A walking bordello . . .' quoted in Holmes, *Wellington: the Iron Duke*

'Discourage Matrimony . . .' Wolfe, quoted in Kopperman, *The British High Command . . .*

'Is generally beloved by two sorts . . .' Victor Neuberg, *Gone for a Soldier*, London, 1989, quoted in Holmes, *Redcoat*

'When War is proclaimed . . .' quoted by Metcalfe, *Chronicle*, 1953

Children of 'squaddies' . . . Lizzie Iron, chairman of Army Families Federation, 1999–2004, author interview

'Therefore left her father's house . . .' Peter Henly, 1799, quoted in Roy Palmer

'We then shall lead . . .' *The Recruiting Officer*, George Farquhar, 1706, in Frey et al.

'If any 'prentices have severe . . .' *The Recruiting Officer*, George Farquhar, 1706

'My lad, you've only to 'list . . .' Edwin Mole, 1893, quoted in Roy Palmer, ibid

'It would be as wrong . . .' General Sir Michael Walker, in correspondence with the author

'Many Women in the Regts . . .' Wolfe, quoted in Kopperman *The British High Command . . .*

'Yesterday, a private gentleman . . .' Gibraltar Garrison Order Book, 2 December 1727 in Fortescue, *Following the Drum*

Only a small number . . . Major Cartan, *Regulations Affecting Non-Commissioned Officers' and Soldiers' Wives . . .* 1854, RAHT papers; Trustram

'Of a likely figure' Cowper

'*What is a man's life* . . .' Shipp, 1830

'*No woman is to be allowed in Barracks* . . .' Standing Orders of the 90th Infantry, quoted by Major TA Bowyer-Bower, *JSAHR*, Volume 33, 1955

'*The Hungry Army* . . .' Palmer

Limited enlistment was . . . Cartan, 1854 *Regulations*; Trustram

Several of his comrades took German wives . . . Corporal Todd

Substantial part of the British army . . . Trustram

'*Too lazy and good for nothing* . . .' RER Robinson, 1988

Jacintha Cherito . . . in Grattan, Oman (ed), 1902

'*Those who stayed on and behaved* . . .' Letter from President and Council to Deputy Governor *18 December, 1675*, quoted in Dennis Kincaid, *British Social Life in India*

'*Pale faded stuffs, by time grown faint* . . .' quoted in Dennis Kincaid

'*Now sail the chagrined fishing fleet* . . .' *Illustrated Weekly of India* in 1936, quoted in Dennis Kincaid

'*Induce by all means our Soldiers* . . .' quoted in Dennis Kincaid, ibid

'*She keeps house for him* . . .' Richard Burton quoted in Lawrence James, *Raj*, 1997

'*Ought, therefore, attentively to consider* . . .' Sergeant J MacMullen, 1846

'*He is a fortunate man* . . .' MacMullen, 1846

Marriage and Baptism records of 14th Foot . . . quoted in Major HAV Spencer, *Families of the 14th Regiment of Foot 1794–1831*, in *The White Rose* Volume 18, August 1976, No 3

'*A grizzled bombardier* . . .' Marianne Postans, quoted in Wilkinson, 1976

Average age of marriage . . . statistics taken from Stone, 1977

Courtship of Lieutenant Hudson and Maria Burnside: in Scott-Daniell, 1951

'*More than one senior officer's wife* . . .' Madeline and Rosalind Wallace-Dunlop, 1858

'*After moving around as a child* . . .' Lady (Tor) Walker, author interview

'*The husband being an object* . . .' Emily Eden, 1866

'*Is very poor herself* . . .' Emily Eden, 1866

Even the Iron Duke . . . Holmes, *Wellington*, 2002

'*Some had amassed money* . . .' Captain Grattan, 1902

'*A being more transcendingly lovely* . . .' John Kincaid, *Random Shots* . . . 1835

Lucy Twining and Esmond Venning . . .

'*How grey and dull everything is* . . .' Lucy to Esmond Venning, 16 March 1910, Venning [PC]

Chapter 2: To Stay or to Go

'*The distraction of the poor creatures . . .*' Rifleman Harris, in *Recollections . . .*
  1848, Hathaway (ed) 1995

By 1670 British explorers . . . Binns, 2002

Evacuation of Tangier garrison . . . Bowyer-Bower, *JSAHR*, Volume 33,
  1955; Cowper, Volume I, 1963

'*Nothing but vice . . .*' E Chappell, *The Tangier Papers of Samuel Pepys (N.RS)*,
  1935, Volume LXXIII, quoted in Paterson, Volume 1

'*That which adds to the number . . .*' *Edward Southwell to Nottingham, Secretary
  of State,* 29 August 1703, calendar of State papers, domestic, 1703–1704,
  quoted in Godfrey Davies, *Recruiting in the Reign of Queen Anne, JSAHR*,
  Volume 28, 1950

If vacancies occurred . . . Queen's Regulations, 1857

'*Which are indeed very numerous . . .*' Wier Papers, quoted in *The Organization
  of the British Army in the American Revolution*, 1926, in Kopperman *The
  British High Command . . .*

Colonel John Maunsell . . . quoted in Kopperman, *The British High
  Command . . .*

'*There is no part of the Expedition . . .*' quoted in Paterson

In 1800 the Duke of York . . . Williams, 1988

For companies of . . . Cartan, *Regulations . . .* 1854, RAHT papers; Trustram

In 1818 this travel allowance . . . An Act Enabling Wives and Families of
  Soldiers to return to their Homes, 1818, Amgueddfa, The Royal Welch
  Fusiliers Regimental Museum

'*When Mary unrolled the slip of paper . . .*' Gleig, 1825

'*O Sandy, you'll no leave me . . .*' Donaldson, 1845

'*In making the selection of women . . .*' Queen's Regulations, 1857

'*Provided they and their wives . . .*' 29th Regiment Standing Orders, 1863

'*Commanding Officers of Corps . . .*' Clinton, in Kopperman, *The British High
  Command . . .*

'*Should be carefully selected . . .*' quoted in Kopperman, *The British High
  Command . . .*

'*Not one woman must . . .*' Annual register 1798, appendix to Chronicle
  189, in Cowper

'*Most affectionate couple . . .*' Mrs Ilbert, 1807, RAHT papers MD 2627

Private John Pearman . . . Pearman, 1968

The Times reported on one wife . . . in Compton, *Colonel's Lady and Camp
  Follower . . .* 1970

Mrs Williams . . . Duberly, *Journal kept during the Russian War*, 1856

One soldier, John Wager . . . Compton, 1970

'The sorrow of separation . . .' *The Times*, in Compton, 1970

'Excepting the idea of dishonour . . .' Lord St Leonard quoted in the *Third Report of the Central Association in Aid of the Wives and families of Soldiers Ordered on active Service Read at the Anniversary Meeting of the General Committee in London, on the 7 March 1856,* RAHT papers

'Should be a place of hardship . . .' HH Milman quoted in AN Wilson, *The Victorians,* 2002

'No Person whatever enlisted . . .' Annual Mutiny Act quoted in Trustram, 1984

'Legalised seducers' . . . quoted in Trustram, 1984

'Any attempt to offer a maintenance . . .' Lord Panmure, quoted in *Third Report of the Central Association* . . . 7 March 1856. RAHT papers

'Camp, Sebastopol, Nov 30th 1855. My Dear Wife . . .' quoted in *Third Report of the Central Association* . . . 7 March 1856. RAHT Papers

'One of the most difficult times . . .' Marion Weston, author interview

'I used to say to my children . . .' Midge Lackie, author interview

Chapter 3: Travels and Travails

'Those who have not been at sea . . .' Sherwood, *The Life of Mrs Sherwood,* Sophia Kelly (ed), London, 1854

'Continual Destruction in ye foretop . . .' Private John Marshall Deane, A Journal of the Campaign in Flanders, 1846; quoted in RE Scouller, 1966; Rogers, 1963

In 1706 a force of 8,000 sailing . . . Barnett, 1970

In 1710 a Commissary of Musters . . . Scouller, 1966

Between 1776 and 1780 the death rate . . . Holmes, *Redcoat,* 2002

'A state-room!' Major Patterson, 1840

'A wave dashing through the little scuttle hole . . .' Mrs Ilbert, 1807, RAHT papers MD 2627

'Disclosing to the impious stare . . .' Major Patterson, 1840

'What promiscuous exchanges were made . . .' TH Edsall (ed), *Journal of Lieutenant John Charles Philip von Krafft of the regiment von Bose, 1776–1784,* Collection 15, New York Historical Society, quoted in Frey, 1981

'There was not even a screen . . .' MacMullen, 1846

'Sickening, foul repulsive breath . . .' Anton, 1841

'A dead calm . . .' Browne, Roger Norman Buckley (ed), 1987

'Some of the Sergeants had no legs . . .' Le Couteur, Donald E Graves (ed), 1993

'You will wonder . . .' Mrs Ilbert, 1807

'As big as drums . . .' Shipp, 1830

'Crazy floating prisons . . .' Major Patterson, 1840

'She chose a bad method . . .' Mrs Ilbert, 1807

A soldier named McCowen . . . WO 71/83 [National Archives]

'So mangled and bruised . . .' Cowper, Volume I, 1939

The Seahorse . . . Holmes, *Redcoat,* 2002; Bourke, *Shipwrecks,* 2000

The Arniston . . .' Bamfield, 1974

The Birkenhead . . . Sinking of the *Birkenhead* in Bevan, *Stand Fast;* Rogers, *Troopships,* 1963

The Three Sisters . . . Cowper, 1939

'I have seen stewards pouring . . .' Harriet Tytler [née Earle], Anthony Sattin (ed), OUP, 1986

'We have plenty of music . . .' Frances Wells, Wells papers [MS], CSAS Archive

'Many of the women . . .' in Kopperman, *The British High Command* . . .

'More sensible of it . . .' The journals of Col James Montresor, GD Scull (ed), Collections of the New York Historical Society XIV (1881), Kopperman, *The British High Command* . . .

'An awful risk . . .' Harriet Tytler, 1986

Wellington expressly forbade . . . RER Robinson, 1988

'The captain rode first . . .' Memoirs of Baron Lejeune, Volume II, trans. Mrs Arthur Bell, New York, 1897, quoted in Napier, Williams, Davies et al.

The water, still icy . . . Cowper, Volume I, 1939

'An act of glaring impropriety . . .' Mr Stoequeler, *Overland Trip,* article published in the *Asiatic Journal,* quoted in Dennis Kincaid, 1973

'Every tree and shrub . . .' Margaret Hannay, journal [MS], The Gurkha Museum

'Very delightful, indeed . . .' Wells papers

'One of the fellows . . .' Tytler, 1986

In 1853 the first railway line . . . Ferguson, *Empire* 2003

Chapter 4: A Home from Home

'Ten men, ten women . . .' Charles Dickens, *Household Words,* 19 April 1856 in Williams, 1988

A survey was carried out . . . Gaffney, *The Army Wives Study: the Report. Part 1,* 1986

In a statement in December 2003 . . . Chief of the General Staff's Message to the Army Implementing the Future Army Structure, 16 December 2003

Nearly a quarter according to a recent survey . . . Families' Continuous Attitude Survey by AFF Families Journal, sent out to a 10% random selection of Army spouses in November 2003, with response rate of 32%. Findings published in AFF Families Journal, June 2004

'Inns, livery stables, ale houses . . .' Mutiny Act, 1703, in Scouller, 1966

'Great number of women and children . . .' Cowper, 1939

In Montreal in 1764 . . . Scott–Daniell, 1951

In New York in 1711 one third . . . Sir John Fortescue, *The Last Post,* 1934, quoted in Scouller, 1966

Viscount Molesworth . . . in TA Bowyer-Bower in JSAHR, Volume 33, 1955

Even in 1786 . . . Laffin, 1966, 2004

No other arrangements were made . . . Cowper, 1939

In 1792 . . . Laffin, 1966, 2004

'Picture her making her entry . . .' Dickens, *Household Words,* Volume 9, 1851

In 1852 one officer . . . Bamfield, 1974

Convicts enjoyed . . . Barnett, 1970

Mortality Rates in the Foot Guards . . . Barnett, 1970

The Barrack Accommodation Committee . . . in Laffin, 1966

The War Office later bought . . . Laffin, 1966

'The result of this degradation . . .' Dickens, *Household Worlds 1856,* in Williams

'Starvation . . .' quoted in Laffin, 1966

'In reality . . .' Dorothy Cook, 1973

Melissa Cordingly . . . author interview

'Nail up, and pull down . . .' Patterson, 1840

'Were filled with brass elephants . . .' Leonora Starr, *The Colonel's Lady,* G Bell & Son, 1937, quoted in Pat Barr, *Dust in the Balance,* 1989

'Once you stepped inside . . .' Vere, Lady Birdwood, transcript of interview by Charles Allen for *Plain Tales from the Raj,* OIOC

'Cavalry Lines, Poona . . .' Iris Portal, Portal Papers [TS], CSAS Archive

'You have to give out . . .' Rosemary Montgomery letters, Montgomery Papers, CSAS Archive

'I must say on the whole . . .' Wells papers, CSAS Archive

'You would be quite astonished . . .' Hannay, journal [MS], Gurkha Museum

Dorothy Cook, who had begun . . . Dorothy Cook, 1973

'The tent was pitched on the river . . .' Ruth Barton, Barton Papers, CSAS Archive

Mary Anton had not . . . James Anton, *A Retrospect* . . . 1841

Lady Harriet Acland . . . Anbury, *Travels Through the Interior Parts of North America,* Vol I, 1789

'A Pandemonium full of . . .' Lady Alicia Blackwood, *A Narrative of a Residence on the Bosphorus Throughout the Crimean War,* 1881

The Naval and Military Gazette . . .' quoted in Compton, 1970

'With such uncombed, scurfy hair . . .' Fanny Duberly, letter to Selina Marx, 23 July 1854 quoted in Tisdall, 1963

'Looks more after her . . .' Colonel Edward Cooper Hodge, 28 April 1855, in *'Little Hodge',* Marquess of Anglesey (ed), 1971

'Not a very active officer' Hodge, 11 May 1855, in Marquess of Anglesey (ed), 1971

'Forrest had his wife . . .' Hodge, 10 June 1855, in Marquess of Anglesey (ed), 1971

'Sort of cattle pen . . .' Midge Lackie, author interview

'Never had a cross word . . .' Peggy Pusinelli, author interview

'Our comfortable house . . .' Fanny Pratt, letter, 9 May 1846, MacMillan and Miller (ed), 1997

'The ritual humiliation . . .' Penny Little in *The Sirmooree,* Number 29, Summer 2002

'A sort of thing of pride . . .' Marion Weston, author interview

Chapter 5: Mothers and Children

'Having children certainly increased . . .' Donaldson, 1845

Infant mortality . . . figures from Stone, 1977

'The cramped conditions . . .' Frey, 1981

Regimental schools . . . Bowyer-Bower, *JSAHR,* Volume 33, 1955

'The dreadful evils . . .' in Longford, *Wellington,* 1992

'She has grown ugly . . .' in Longford, *Wellington,* 1992

'Oh my baby! . . .' Sherwood, Kelly (ed), 1854

'Horrified, from the rain-spotted . . .' MM Kaye, *The Sun in the Morning,* 1990

'We are much disappointed . . .' Fanny Pratt, letter, 18 March 1844

'I have just received . . .' Fanny Pratt, letter, 15 August, 1844

'Have you made any . . .' Fanny Pratt, letter, 23 October 1844

'We shall fancy we see you . . .' Fanny Pratt, letter, 1845

'My darling children . . .' Fanny Pratt, letter, 17 May 1846

'I can honestly say . . .' Harriet Tytler [née Earle], Anthony Sattin (ed), OUP, 1986

'The more I see of . . .' Wells papers, CSAS Archive

'But this can't be helped . . .' Sherwood, Sophia Kelly (ed), London, 1854

'I trust that ladies . . .' F Corbyn, *Management and Diseases of Infants, under the Influence of the Climate of India,* Calcutta, 1828, cited in *Lancet, 16 (1828);* quoted in Fildes, 1988

'One of them was in the regiment . . .' Shipp, 1830

'For four days we had but little hope . . .' Wells papers, CSAS Archive

'What sorrow it is to lose a child . . .' Wells papers, CSAS Archive

'My husband brought me my Bible . . .' Harriet Tytler, Anthony Sattin (ed), OUP, 1986

'Just as fat and happy . . .' Fanny Pratt, letter, 8 June 1848

'We have had much anxiety . . .' Fanny Pratt, letter, 3 May 1849

'I feed him like a little bird . . .' Fanny Pratt, letter, 20 June 1849

'Our darling Chalmers breathed his last . . .' Fanny Pratt, letter, 7–10 August 1849

'I hastened to his side . . .' Sherwood, Sophia Kelly (ed), London, 1854

'The intrepidity which enabled them . . .' Greenhill–Gardyne, 1929

'My wife is dead.' quoted in Greenhill–Gardyne, 1929

'When I lifted up his clothes . . .' Wells papers, CSAS Archive

'When the poor thing gave a fearful . . .' Harriet Tytler, Anthony Sattin (ed), OUP, 1986

'Par excellence a soldier's wife . . .' Dictionary of National Biography

Three weeks afterwards she died . . . MacMullen, 1846

'Having no children of her own . . .' Sainsbury, 1931

'Divided her maternal attentions . . .' Shipp, 1830

Michael Golougher Case . . . General Court Martial Records, 8 August 1774–August 1775, WO 71 80

John Fisher Case . . . General Court Martial Record, 27 February 1778, WO 71/85

'The greatest hardship and distress . . .' General Order, 10 October 1808, quoted in Hibbert, *Corunna,* 1961

'There a group of British . . .' Fortescue, *History of the British Army, Volume IV,* 1906, quoted in Bryant, *The Years of Endurance,* 1942

'Some of these unhappy creatures . . .' Hamilton, 1847

'Endeavouring to drag along . . .' Rifleman Harris, 1848

'She presented a ghastly picture . . .' Rifleman Harris, 1848

'I think the light left my eyes . . .' Mrs McClelland, quoted in Scott-Daniell, 1951

'A soldier's wife had sought shelter . . .' Schaumann, Ludovici (translator, ed), 1924

On one occasion, on 27 February 1814 . . . Donaldson, 1845

A rifleman named Richard Pullen . . . Rifleman Harris, 1848

Charles Steevens of the 20th . . . Steevens, 1878

Donald McBane . . . Falkner, 2002

'Saluted by cannon . . .' Samuel Hutton, *'The life of an old soldier'* in *Derbyshire Biography*, quoted in Roy Palmer (ed), 1985

'In the midst of the snow storm . . .' Codrington, letter 15 January 1855, NAM 1978-08-90

Less than three months . . . Codrington, letter 8 April 1855, NAM 1978-08-90

Excavators at battlefield sites . . . Cohn, *Evidence of Children at Revolutionary War Sites*, Brooklyn Children's Museum, NAM 8312–23

'At last a bright idea . . .' Tytler, Anthony Sattin (ed), OUP, 1986

Chapter 6: On Parade

'The Wives of non-Commissioned . . .' 1859 Standing Orders of the 13th (Somerset) Light Infantry

'Without her earnings at the wash-tub . . .' in Trustram, 1984

'Useless sloths . . .' *United Services Gazette,* 25 July 1857, in Trustram, 1984

Wolfe later acknowledged . . . Scott-Daniell, 1951

'Killed and scalped . . .' Knox, *An Historical Journal of the Campaigns in north America for the Years 1757, 1758, 1759 and 1760,* quoted in Kopperman, *The British High Command* . . .

'Immediately to join the artillery . . .' Knox, quoted in Ward, 1971

'Some of them begged . . .' Anbury, 1789

'A sufficient number of Nurses . . .' Thomas Sullivan, in Kopperman, *The British High Command* . . .

'Lady Harriet, with her usual serenity . . .' Burgoyne in de Fonblanque, 1876

Jane McCrea . . . in Bicheno, 2003

'There is scarcely an instance . . .' Lamb, 1809

'The wretchedness of Lady Harriet . . .' Miss Warburton in de Fonblanque

'We must risk something . . .' Bell, 1956

Mrs Maibee, a sergeant's wife . . . Wheeler, Letters, 1808–1828, Liddell Hart (ed), 1951

'I was on my knees ironing . . .' Margaret Kirwin, in an interview with Major Michael Ferrar, *The Green Howards Gazette* in 1898, quoted in Roger Chapman (ed), 2004

'Look well at that, Mrs Evans . . .' in Cowper, 1939

Becky Box and Mrs Longley . . . in Compton, 1970

'I called my servants . . .' Mrs Webber-Harris, recollection, [TS], [PC]

'As a book on British gallantry . . .' Abbott and Tamplin, 1981

Mrs Buckley, a Colonel's wife . . . Buckley, 1913

Iris Portal once arrived . . . Portal papers, [TS], CSAS Archive

'Excessively boring, trivial . . .' Vere, Lady Birdwood, in Allen, *Plain Tales* . . . 1975

'I went and had public speaking lessons . . .' Lady Howlett, author interview

Chapter 7: Crime and Punishment

'The wives of non-commissioned officers . . .' Standing Orders of the 2nd Battalion the Durham Light Infantry, 1891

'Responsible for the conduct of their wives . . .' 29th Regiment Standing Orders, 1863

'Must suffer for his weakness . . .' Standing Orders of the 2nd Battalion the Durham Light Infantry, 1891

'A mighty pretty creature' Chappell, *The Tangier Papers of Samuel Pepys*, Vol LXXIII, 1935, p89, quoted in Paterson, *Pontius Pilate's Bodyguard*, Vol I, 2000

In 1859 for every . . . Myna Trustram, *'Distasteful and Derogatory? Examining Victorian Soldiers for Venereal Disease'*, in London Feminist History Group, *The Sexual Dynamics of History*, London, Pluto Press, 1983, quoted in Trustram, 1984

'Disorderly women' . . . Paterson, 2000

'If any Woman in the Regt has a Venerial Disorder . . .' New York Historical Society Series 6A, Volume 3 (Order Book 1, 12 February 1748–15 December 1755, and 4 May–12 September 1759], quoted in Kopperman, *The British High Command* . . .

'Any women suspected to be . . .' in Kopperman, *The British High Command* . . .

'As there are great complaints of Drunkenness . . .' Regimental Order, Gronenberg, 29 May 1759, in 'The Scots Grey' Magazine, 1966, Royal Dragoon Guards Museum

Some of these women were so paralytic . . .' MacMullen, 1846

Paddy Burns . . . Pearman, Anglesey (ed), 1968

'By the way of banishing care . . .' Nelly Carsons' story in Grattan, Oman (ed), 1902

'The most shocking spectacle . . .' in Hibbert, *Corunna*, 1961

'Obliged to apply for a passage . . .' Forrest, letter, NAM 1963–09–5–1

'Her tail was immediately turned up . . .' General Pulteney to the Duke of Cumberland, in Williams, 1988

'Swarm of beings . . .' Proposed Plan for bringing the Army under strict discipline with regard to marauding by Patrick Ferguson, November 1779, in The American Rebellion: Sir Henry Clinton's Narrative of His Campaigns 1775–1782, William B Willcox (ed), 1954, quoted in Frey, 1981

Mary Colethrate and Elizabeth Clarke case . . . General Court Martial, 27 June 1778, WO 71/83

'The source of the most infamous . . .' A British Orderly Book 1780–1781, ed AR Newsome (ed), in North Carolina Historical Review, 9 (January 1932) quoted in Frey, ibid

'Sickened when I saw them coolly step . . .' Charles Von Hodenberg, quoted in Fletcher, In Hell Before Daylight, 1984

'She said nothing . . .' Captain Browne

'Exercised schoolboy discipline . . .' Colonel Leslie's journal, Worcestershire Regiment Museum Trust

'Sax and thirty lashes a piece . . .' John Scott, Paris Revisited in 1815, quoted in Brett-James (ed), Wellington at War 1794–1815: A Selection of his Wartime Letters, 1961

'There was no order for punishing women! . . .' Wellington, in Letters of the Duke of Wellington to Mary, Marchioness of Salisbury 1850–2, John Murray 1927, JSAHR, Volume 7, 1928

'To be gagged and receive . . .' Williams, 1988

'In despairing accents . . .' Donaldson, 1845

William Cross, a soldier who left the ranks . . . Corporal Todd, Cormack and Jones (ed), 2001

'I never stripped a man . . .' quoted in Godfrey Davies in Recruiting in the Reign of Queen Anne, in JSAHR, Volume 28, 1950

'A man falls by your side . . .' Gleig, 1825

'Estimated them in proportion to their proficiency . . .' Bell, 1956

Case of Peggy McGuire . . . General Court Martial, 19 February 1781 WO 71/93

'Seeing him taken out of the Ranks . . .' in Loudoun Papers, Henry E Huntington Library, in Kopperman, The British High Command . . .

In 1776 an Irish troop . . . in George Penny, Traditions of Perth, 1836, quoted in Palmer, 1985

'Beating better manners . . .' in Fortescue, Following the Drum, 1931

'For proper reasons' in Fortescue, Following the Drum, 1931

'She was set upon a stone . . .' in Fortescue, *Following the Drum,* 1931

'Using abusive language . . .' Wives Punishment Book of 82nd Foot 1866–1890, Museum of the Queen's Lancashire Regiment

Chapter 8: Scandal and Strife

'The military ladies . . .' Julia Maitland, *Letters From Madras,* 1843, Alyson Price (ed), 2003

'By Cutting her throat . . .' Corporal Todd, Cormack and Jones (ed), 2001

'Awake, arouse Sir Billy . . .' quoted in Major Reginald Hargreaves MC, 'Good-Natured Billy', Army Quarterly, Volume 93, January 1967

'Sir William, he snug as a flea . . .' quoted in Hargreaves, 1967

Case of William Norrington . . . Record of General Court Martial, 28 July 1776, WO 71/82

Case of Alexander Frazer . . . Record of General Court Martial, 25 April 1763, WO 71/93

Case of John Lindon . . . Record of General Court Martial, 19 February 1781, WO 71/93

'Assisted much to keep up . . .' Edward Costello, 1852

'As her ill conduct . . .' William Surtees, 1833

Private James Cairns . . . Record of General Court Martial, 28 November 1776, WO 71/83

John Siborn . . . Loudon Papers 2826, in Kopperman, *The British High Command* . . .

'With her Cap of . . .' Corporal Todd, Cormack and Jones (ed), 2001

Lieutenant Kelly . . . Holmes, *Redcoat,* 2001

Sergeant Bishop's wife . . . John Spencer Cooper, 1869; 1996

'Would have made a magnificent model . . .' Schaumann, Ludovici (ed), London, 1924

'He got more by his heels . . .' Patterson, 1840

He suffered from piles . . . Thomas, 1974

'We take wonderful rides . . . Fanny Duberly, letter from Varna, August 1854, in Tisdall, 1963

'The grass in the plain . . .' Hodge, letter, 9 May 1855; Anglesey (ed), 1971

'An odd woman . . .' Forrest, letter, 8 May 1855; 6309/5/1–2 NAM

'Beware General X . . .' Villiers-Stuart, 1989

'A youth of rather fashionable . . .' Patterson, 1840

A corporal's wife, was evicted . . . Midge Lackie, author interview

'I thought, "What the hell . . . "' Sam Roberts, author interview

'Is it paternalistic . . .' Lizzie Iron, author interview

'Brian used to help the Families Officer . . .' Valerie Fagg, author interview

'Now I come back to air . . .' Emily Eden, 1866; 1983

Amelia Eliza Byrne, known as Bonny . . . PJO Taylor, 1993

'Sex was a subject . . .' Lieutenant Colonel Paddy Massey MC, quoted in Miles Clark, 1991

'Every facet of your life . . .' Vere, Lady Birdwood, in Charles Allen, 1975

'I always think those wives who are driven . . .' Emily Eden, 1866; 1983

'To be constantly alone . . .' Nan Warry, 1990

'Grass widows were considered . . .' in MM Kaye, *Golden Afternoon,* Penguin, 1997

'Had a good leave . . .' Nan Warry, 1990

'They did not know whether . . .' Nan Warry, 1990

'Place's Law . . .' in *Autobiography of Francis Place,* M Thale (ed), 1972, in Stone, 1977

'Who as a rule went about . . .' Schaumann, Ludovici (ed), London, 1924

'They were assailed by every . . .' Donaldson, 1845

'It had really got going . . .' Lady Howlett, author interview

'I saw bits of society . . .' Marion Weston, author interview

'What she ought not to be . . .' Gronow, 1892

Renshaw case . . . Hawkey, 1969

Emmett-Dunne case . . . Daily Mail, 5 July 1955; *Sunday People,* 10 July 1955; *News of the World,* 10 July 1955; *Empire News,* 31 July 1955

'Monsieur le Duc était de beaucoup le plus fort.' in Holmes, *Wellington,* 2002

Chapter 9: Social Functions

'Every day added something to their knowledge . . .' Austen, *Pride and Prejudice,* 1813

'We have seldom known a ball . . .' Brighton *Gazette,* 26 November 1840, in Donald Thomas, *Cardigan,* 1974; 2002

'All the Ladies of Loose Character . . .' Capel Letters *1814–1817,* Marquess of Anglesey (ed), in Longford, *Wellington,* 1992

'Hard to decide which . . .' Longford, *Wellington,* 1992

'Another day such as yesterday . . .' Colonel Sir Augustus Simon Frazer, letter, 30 May 1815; Sabine (ed), 1859

'Balls are going on here . . .' Capel Letters

'Duchess, you may give your ball . . .' in Longford, *Wellington,* 1992

'The numerous friends of Napoleon . . .' quoted in Baron Von Muffling, *A*

Sketch of the Battle of Waterloo (6th edition), London, 1870, in Longford, *Wellington*, 1992

'*And Belgium's capital . . .*' Byron, '*The Eve of Waterloo*'

'*Ah! Then and there . . .*' Byron, '*The Eve of Waterloo*'

'*Numbers were taking leave . . .*' Charlotte Waldie, 1817

'*A fine holland smock . . .*' Cowper, Volume I, 1939

'*Neither forgot the deference . . .*' R Blakeney, *A Boy in the Peninsula,* Murray, 1899, quoted in FCG Page, 1986

'*A fair and beautiful . . .*' Bell, 1956

'*So cruel, so unsportsmanlike . . .*' Duberly, 5 March 1855, *Journal kept during the Russian War,* 1856

'*The longer I live, the greater . . .*' Duberly, letter, in Tisdall, 1963

Ellen Palmer's visit to the Crimea . . . Rod Robinson, *The Travelling Heiress: Ellen Palmer's Crimean Excursion,* in The War Correspondent, Volume 20, no 3, October 2002

'*George is such a bore . . .*' Duberly, letter, in Compton, 1970

'*It is all very well . . .*' Codrington, letter, 7 August 1855, NAM 1978–08–90

'*As if they have dropped . . .*' Violet Cecil, in Hugh and Mirabel Cecil, *Imperial Marriage: An Edwardian War and Peace,* John Murray, 2002

'*About the same as [for] Cannes . . .*' Mabell Airlie in Hugh and Mirabel Cecil, 2002

'*You hear amazing stories . . .*' Mortimer Menpes, *War Impressions,* London, 1901, quoted in Brian Roberts, *Those Bloody Women,* John Murray, 1991

'*Watching from the "intrigante" . . .*' Mabell Airlie, 1992

'*I wish there was no such thing . . .*' Mrs Grule Money, Diary, 1889 [MS]

'*Quite overwhelmed with morning visitors . . .*' Wells papers, CSAS Archive

'*When you got there you walked . . .*' Peggy Pusinelli, author interivew

'*It is nearly impossible to give . . .*' Madeline and Rosalind Wallace-Dunlop, 1858

'*Even I got worn out . . .*' with Daphne Hill, author interview

'*Very like home. Gentlemen on . . .*' Madeline and Rosalind Wallace-Dunlop, 1858

'*A delightful drive . . .*' Wells papers, CSAS Archive

'*Many anxious expectants . . .*' Madeline and Rosalind Wallace-Dunlop, 1858

'*It did not look well . . .*' Emily Eden, 1866; 1983

'*What use will my beautiful false hair . . .*' Madeline and Rosalind Wallace-Dunlop 1858

'*There are frequently very pleasant excursions . . .*' Major Sainsbury, 1931

'*When the last ship sails . . .*' Mrs Ilbert, 1807, RAHT papers MD 2627

'*Did not really cater for women . . .*' Iris Portal, Portal Papers [TS], CSAS Archive

'*I always remember being surprised . . .*' Melissa Cordingly, author interview

'*I never saw such a profusion of jewellery . . .*' Wells papers, CSAS Archive

'*She shot to her feet saying . . .*' Bette Viner, Aden diary [TS], [PC]

'*If they met an Irish friend . . .*' Marion Weston, author interview

'*There were bombs going off . . .*' Chrissie Collis, author interview

'*It was the same old people . . .*' Deborah Richardson, author interview

'*But that wasn't such fun . . .*' Daphne Hill, author interview

'*The army is the most snobbish . . .*' Dorothy Cook, 1973

'*Why Bet – Mrs Buffet I mean . . .*' in Scott-Daniell, 1951

'*It's always the same people . . .*' Samantha Roberts, author interview

Chapter 10: Under Siege

'*Never probably, indeed, has the noble character . . .*' Martin Gubbins, An Account of the Mutinies in Oudh and the siege of the Lucknow Residency, 1858, quoted in Cunningham, 2003

'*He [Mendoza] Did not receive this visit . . .*' Mrs Green, Journal [MS]

'*A soldier, with his wife and three children . . .*' Captain Drinkwater, *A History of the Siege of Gibraltar*, 1785, quoted in Russell, 1965

'"*Never fear madam, if the d___d Dons . . .*"' Mrs Catherine Upton *The Siege of Gibraltar from 12 April to 27 May 1781*, London, 1781, quoted in Russell, 1965

'*A husband is called upon . . .*' Samuel Ancell, quoted in Russell, 1965

'*The poor thing's frightened . . .*' Donaldson, 1845

Charlotte Chambers' death . . . in various 'Mutiny' sources including Frances Wells' papers; Jane Robinson, 1997

Louisa MacDonald . . . obituary of Emily Hay (née MacDonald), from *Trinidad Sunday Guardian*, Sunday 8 July 1934, reproduced on www.rootsweb.com

'*All well at Cawnpore . . .*' Jane Robinson, 1997

Walls were pitifully low . . . Williams, Lieutenant Colonel G, Commissioner of Military Police, North West Provinces, *Review of the Evidence taken at Cawnpore regarding the revolt at that station in June and July 1857,* Allahabad, 31 December 1859, OIOC

'*I never shall forget the horror . . .*' Wells papers, CSAS Archive

'*You can only rule these Asiatics . . .*' Georgina Harris, 1858

'*Like so many ghosts . . .*' Amelia Horne, Narrative [MS], quoted in Jane Robinson, 1997

'The Lucknow baby . . .' Letter from Arthur Frederick Dashwood to *The Listener* magazine, 2 December 1930, DCLI Museum

'*Baby still ailing and so thin . . .*' Colina Brydon, diary [MS]

'*The soldiers were singing . . .*' Amelia Horne, Narrative [MS], quoted in Jane Robinson, 1997

'*I have looked upon death in every form . . .*' quoted in Jane Robinson, 1997

'*I felt as if my heart was stone . . .*' Lieutenant Arthur Lang, quoted in Lawrence James, 1997

'*Tender and solicitous . . .*' Metcalfe, 1953

Chapter 11: Captives and Fugitives

'*There was nothing to relieve the monotony . . .*' Molly Ellis, interview with *The Express*, 1978

'*In a very unceremonious manner . . .*' Rifleman Harris, 1848

'*One Irish woman, in particular . . .*' Costello, 1852

'*Lieutenant King of the 11th . . .*' Grattan, Oman (ed), 1902

Kabul '*is well-built and handsome . . .*' Lieutenant Rattray, quoted in MacCrory, 1966

'*Over such scenes I draw a veil . . .*' Lady Sale, *Journal*, 24 December 1841, published 1843

'*We have commenced our retreat . . .*' Lady Sale, *Journal*, 6 January 1842

'*Many frozen corpses . . .*' Lady Sale, *Journal*, 8 January 1842

'*Had fortunately only one ball . . .*' Lady Sale, *Journal*, 8 January 1842

'*Many camels were killed . . .*' Lady Sale, *Journal*, 8 January 1842

'*The sight was dreadful . . .*' Lady Sale, *Journal*, 11 January 1842

'*It was rather a painful process . . .*' Lady Sale, *Journal*, 19 January 1842

'*Mrs Sturt presented me . . .*' Lady Sale, *Journal*, 24 July 1842

'*As no one would fight for the ladies . . .*' Lady Sale, *Journal*, 24 May 1842

'*Gave themselves great airs . . .*' Colin MacKenzie, *Storms and Sunshine of a Soldier's Life*, 1886, quoted in MacCrory, 1966

'*As long as there is an Afghan . . .*' Lawrence, quoted in MacCrory, 1966

'*Now is the time to strike . . .*' Lady Sale, *Journal,* 10 May 1842

'*Of our resolution to hold out . . .*' Lady Sale, *Journal,* 13 September 1842

'*I have been a soldier's wife too long . . .*' Lady Sale, *Journal*, 21 August 1842

'*It is impossible to express . . .*' Lady Sale, *Journal*, 19 September 1842

'*The gallant old man . . .*' MacKenzie, quoted in MacCrory, 1966

'*Underneath this stone . . .*' in Meyer and Brysac, 2001

Molly Ellis . . . account of Molly Ellis's kidnap and rescue taken from private family papers, including statements she made, letters she wrote and received during and after her captivity, and press reports by kind permission of her son, Colonel Peter Wade and family

'*They might have taken Mum* . . .' Letter from Molly Ellis to her friend Barbara Edge, written 23 July 1923 (three months after her release)

'*I must say the brutes* . . .' Letter from Molly Ellis to Barbara Edge, 23 July 1923

'*At first* . . . *I was just thankful to rest* . . .' Molly Ellis, interview with *The Express*, 1978

'*Dear Colonel Bruce* . . .' letter from Molly Ellis to Colonel Bruce, 20 April 1923

'*They are very threatening* . . .' letter from Molly Ellis to Colonel Bruce, 21 April 1923

'*My own beloved darling* . . .' Major Ellis to Molly Ellis, 17 April 1923

'*The awful anxiety* . . .' Major Ellis to Molly Ellis, 19 April 1923

'*They will stick at nothing* . . .' Molly Ellis to Major Ellis, 21 April 1923

'*Darling* . . . *you are all I have got* . . .' Molly Ellis to Major Ellis, 22 April 1923

Questions in the House of Commons . . . questions put to the Earl of Winterton, Under-Secretary at the India Office, reported in contemporary newspapers

'Not *been bruised, damaged* . . .' Lilian Starr, quoted in letter from Sir John Maffey to Major Ellis (undated)

'*I hate the country* . . .' Letter from Molly Ellis to Barbara Edge, 23 July 1923

Ruth Russell-Roberts . . . account taken mainly from Denis Russell-Roberts, 1965; additional background from Warner and Sandilands, 1982

'*I never could wash the children's* . . .' Angela Templer, lecture, 1978, RAHT papers MD 1649/4; background to Angela Templer's story taken mainly from Lucas, 1975; and obituary of Brigadier CR Templer DSO in *Gunner Magazine,* May 1986

Barbara Egerton . . . Barbara Egerton, *Triangle for Home* [TS], [PC] by kind permission of Mrs Philippa Szymusik

Chapter 12: At the Front and Under Fire

'*The shot and shell came hissing* . . .' Duberly, *Journal,* Tuesday 10 October 1854

'. . . The Enemy pursued us, butchering . . .' quoted in Kopperman, *Braddock at the Monongahela*, 1977

'In going Over the River . . .' in Kopperman, *The British High Command* . . .

'The bodies of a great number . . .' in Kopperman, *The British High Command* . . .

'Out of 54 Women only 4 returned' . . . in Kopperman, *The British High Command* . . .

Montcalm's aide-de-camp . . . in Steele, *Betrayals*, 1990

'Tearing the Children from . . .' quoted in Steele, 1990

'The throats of most . . .' quoted in Steele, 1990

'Who kept close by . . .' in Frey, 1981

'The unexpected sight . . .' Landmann, 1854

'With the fortitude and patience . . .' Bell, 1956

'By God that will do . . .' Holmes, *Wellington*, 2002

'There was no man . . .' Bell, 1956

'Leaden bullets . . .' Major WJ Elliott, *The Illustrated Naval and Military Magazine*, 1890, at Imperial War Museum, *Women and War Exhibition*, October 2003, April 2004

'She wandered some time alone . . .' Tomkinson, *Diary*, 1894

Jenny Jones . . . gravestone inscription provided by Amgueddfa, The Royal Welch Fusiliers Regimental Museum; Palmer

Another devoted spouse . . . Waldie, 1817

'Of delicate mould and appearance . . .' Charles Smith, quoted in Harry Smith

'We thought Sebastopol . . .' Duberly, *Journal*, 19 October, 1854

Fanny Duberly's account of battle of Balaclava . . . Duberly, *Journal*, 25 October 1854

'Will not leave me for a moment . . .' Duberly, letter, 27 October 1854, in Tisdall

'Many lost fingers, toes, even hands and feet, to frostbite . . .' Massie, 2004

'I am not coming home . . .' Duberly, letter, 9 March 1855, in Tisdall

'The men go down . . .' Bell, 1956

'Lying on a bed on the wet ground . . .' Duberly, *Journal*, 24 February 1855

'So putrid, so nauseating . . .' 13 September 1855

'I cannot say that I found . . .' Duberly, *Campaigning Experiences*

'Sitting on a box having a good cry . . .' Duberly, letter, 1858, in Tisdall

'When I recall your face and figure . . .' Duberly, letter, 18 March 1858, in Tisdall

'I sung out to Henry . . .' Duberly, letter, 9 July 1858, in Tisdall

'The impulse to accompany . . .' Duberly, *Campaigning Experiences*

'A man, shot in the head . . .' Duberly, *Campaigning Experiences*

'The firing struck us . . .' Duberly, *Campaigning Experiences*

'I am living, *seeing things . . .'* Duberly, letter, in Tisdall

'Kind and patient . . .' Duberly, letter, 21 February 1858, in Tisdall

Christian Welsh . . . Defoe, 1740

'Leather-covered horn . . .' Suzanne J Stark, *Female Tars; Women Aboard Ship in the Age of Sail*, Constable, London, 1996, quoted in Stephens, 1997 Matthew Stephens, *Hannah Snell; The Secret Life of a Female Marine 1723–1792*, 1997, Ship Street Press, London

Phoebe Hessel . . . in Forty, 1997; archives of Royal Regiment of Fusiliers' (Northumberland), museum

Hannah Snell . . . Stephens, 1997

Manchester Heroine . . . the Hampshire Regimental Journal, June 1908, courtesy of Royal Hampshire Regiment Museum; Forty, 1997

Mary-Anne Talbot . . . 'The Intrepid Female or Surprising Life and adventures of Mary-Anne Talbot, otherwise John Taylor' in *Kirby's Wonderful and Scientific Museum, Vol II*, London 1804, quoted in Wheelwright, 1990

Chapter 13: The End of the Line

'She now ceased . . .' Donaldson, 1845

Mrs Rachel Heap of Halifax . . . in The *Guardian*, 1 January 1973, reviewing an issue of the *Journal of the Institute of Population Registration*, quoted in Palmer

' "Suppose we have a bargain . . . " ' Costello, 1852

'When a fellow has no life . . .' Charles Napier

One commanding officer . . . Fortescue, *Following the Drum*, 1931

'Poor creature . . .' Defoe, 1740

'Several ladies of the regiment . . .' Shipp, 1830

Ruth Venning . . . Chevenix Trench, 1985

Bette Viner . . . author correspondence with her son, Richard Viner

'To my horror they told me . . .' in Smith, 1910

'Oh it is too true . . .' Wheeler, Liddell Hart (ed), 1951

'When the roll was called . . .' Rifleman Harris, 1848

'If I live for fifty years . . .' Charles Dickens in Miller, 2000

Madgalene de Lancey . . . De Lancey in Miller, 2000

'Vainly demanding . . .' Waldie, 1864

Mrs Evans . . . Cowper, 1939

Mrs Longley . . . Compton, 1970

'For some time the young widow . . .' Ross-Lewin, 1904

'The most virtuous and the happiest . . .' Browne, 1987

'The worst that could happen . . .' Grattan, 1902

'She ran into the field . . .' Daniell, 1820

Even by the early nineteenth . . . Statistics on remarriage taken from EA
    Wrigley, *Population and History*, London, 1969, quoted in Stone, 1977

'The cow that lows most . . .' Defoe, 1740

'A fatt jolly . . .' Extract from Chelsea Admission Roll of 18 November
    1717, by kind permission of Royal Hospital Chelsea

'Widows and orphans to be . . .' Horse Guards order, 1811, quoted in Page,
    1986

Marlborough encouraged . . . Scouller, 1966

'Daring & enterprise . . .' Browne, 1987

'In such a situation . . .' Hutton in *Derbyshire Biography*, quoted in Roy
    Palmer (ed), 1985

'Here Comes Cousins' wife . . .' Wheeler, Liddell Hart (ed), 1951

'Her loss . . .' John Green, 1827

'Some women in that country . . .' Pearman

'She is besieged by admirers . . .' MacMullen, 1846

'She was pretty . . .' Eden, 1866, 1983

'Many wives have acknowledged . . .' Madeline and Rosalind Wallace-Dunlop
    1858

'You only have to hear the words . . .' quoted by Claire Bates, BBC World
    Magazine, bbc.co.uk, 22 April 2004

A review by the Ministry . . . *Operations in Iraq: Lessons for the Future*, Ministry
    of Defence, July 2003, www.mod.uk

Sara Jones . . . author interview

Samantha Roberts . . . author interview

Postscript

Families Continuous Attitudes Survey 2004 . . . survey sent out in November
    2003 to 10% random sample of army spouses, response rate of 32%.
    Results published in *AFF Families Journal* June 2004

Tor Walker . . . author interview

Families Continuous Attitudes Survey 2002 . . . survey sent out in March
    2002 to a 10% random sample of army spouses, response rate of 36%.

Results published in *AFJ (Army Families Journal)* November 2002

'Stability of family life . . .' Ministry of Defence website (www.army. mod.uk/soldierwelfare/familysupport/familyspgen/armyfamily/)

'Excessive separation . . .' Ivor Caplin MP, Under-Secretary of State for Defence, reply to letter from Lizzie Iron, chairman of Army Families Federation, 1999–2004. Correspondence published in *AFF Families Journal* March 2004

Future Army Structure, Ministry of Defence 2004

Bibliography

Abbreviations

NAM = National Army Museum

CSAS = Centre of South-Asian Studies Archive, University of Cambridge

RAHT = Royal Artillery Historical Trust

DCLI = Duke of Cornwall's Light Infantry

PC = Private Collection

MS = Manuscript

TS = Transcript

General Works

Abbott, PE and Tamplin, JMA, *British Gallantry Awards*, Nimrod Dix & Co, London 1981

Allen, Charles (ed), *Plain Tales from the Raj*, Futura, 1975; and transcripts of interviews, OIOC

Anderson, Fred, *The Crucible of War: The Seven Year's War and the Fate of Empire in North America, 1754–1766*, Vintage, 2000

Bamfield, Veronica, *On the Strength: The Story of the British Army Wife*, Charles Knight 1974

Bannatyne, Lieutenant Colonel Neil, *History of the Thirtieth Regiment now the First Battalion East Lancashire Regiment 1689–1881*, 1923

Barnett, Correlli, *Britain and Her Army 1570–1970*, Penguin Press, 1970

Barr, Pat, *Dust in the Balance: British Women in India 1905–1945*, Hamish Hamilton 1989

Barr, Pat and Desmond, Ray, *Simla: A hill station in British India*, Scolar Press, London 1978

Bayly, Christopher and Harper, Tim, *Forgotten Armies: the Fall of British Asia 1941–1945*, Penguin 2004

Bevan, David, *Stand Fast: the Sinking of the Troopship Birkenhead in 1852*, The Traditional Publishing, 1998

Bicheno, Hugh, *Rebels & Redcoats: the American Revolutionary War*, HarperCollins 2003

Binns, Stewart, *The British Empire in Colour*, Carlton Books 2002

Bourke, Edward J, *Shipwrecks of the Irish coast, 1105–1993*, 2000

Brett-James, Anthony, *Life in Wellington's Army*, 1972

Brooks, Chris, and Faulkner, Peter, *The White Man's Burdens: an Anthology of British Poetry of the Empire,* University of Exeter Press, 1996

Bryant, Arthur, *The Years of Endurance, 1793–1802*, Collins, London 1942

Bryant, Arthur, *Years of Victory, 1802–1812*, Collins, London, 1944

Bryant, Arthur, *English Saga, 1840–1940*, Collins, London 1946

Cassidy, Martin, *Marching With Wellington: With the Inniskillings in the Napoleonic Wars*, Leo Cooper 2003

Chapman, Roger, *Echoes from the Crimea*, Green Howards Museum, 2004

Chevenix Trench, Charles, *The Frontier Scouts*, Jonathan Cape, 1985

Cole, Howard, *The Story of Aldershot*, Gale and Polden, 1950

Compton, Piers, *Colonel's Lady and Camp Follower: the Story of Women in the Crimean War*, London 1970

Connolly, TWJ, *A History of the Royal Sappers and Miners*, 1857

Coogan, Tim Pat, *The IRA*, HarperCollins, 2000

Cowper, Colonel LI, *The King's Own, the Story of a Royal Regiment, Volumes 1 & 2*, University Press, Oxford, 1939

Cunliffe Marcus, *The Royal Irish Fusiliers 1793–1968*, University Press Oxford 1970

Dalton, Charles, *The Waterloo Roll Call, with Biographical Notes and Anecdotes*, London 1904

Davies, Godfrey, *Wellington and His Army*, London 1954

Emsley, Clive *Crime and Society in England, 1750–1900*, Longman, 1996

Enloe, Cynthia, *Does Khaki Become You? The Militarisation of Women's Lives*, Pluto Press, 1983

Falkner, James, *Great and Glorious Days: Marlborough's Battles 1704–09*, Spellmount, 2002

Farwell, Byron, *Queen Victoria's Little Wars*, Penguin 1973

Ferguson, Niall, *Empire: How Britain Made the Modern World*, Allen Lane (Penguin) 2003

Fildes, Valerie, *Wet Nursing*, Oxford 1988

Fletcher, Ian, *In Hell Before Daylight: the Siege and Storming of the Fortress of Badahoz, 16 March to 6 April 1812*, Spellmount 1984

Forty, George and Anne, *Women War Heroines*, Cassell, 1997

Forty, George and Anne, *They Also Served*, Midas 1979

Frey, Sylvia R, *The British Solider in America: A Social History of Military Life in the Revolutionary Period*, Austin, Texas, 1981

Fortescue, Sir John, *Following the Drum*, London 1931

Fortescue, *History of the British Army*, volumes VI and VII

Gavin, RJ, *Aden under British Rule*, Hurst, 1975

Greenhill-Gardyne, Lt.Colonel C, *The Life of a Regiment: The Gordon Highlanders, 1794–1898*, 2 volumes, Medici Society, London, 1929

Goldstein, Joshua S, *War and Gender: How Gender Shapes the War System and Vice Versa*, Cambridge University Press, 2001

Gurney, Lieutenant-Colonel Russell, *History of the Northamptonshire Regiment 1742–1934*, 1935

Harris, John, *The Indian Mutiny*, Wordsworth 2001

Hawkey, Arthur, *Last Post at Mhow*, Jarrolds, 1969

Hibbert, Christopher, *Corunna*, BT Batsford, London 1961

Hickman, Katie, *Daughters of Britannia*, HarperCollins, 1999

Holland, James, *Fortress Malta: An Island Under Siege 1940–43*, Orion 2004

Holmes, Richard, *Redcoat: The British Soldier in the Age of Horse and Musket*, HarperCollins 2001

James, Lawrence, *Raj: the making and unmaking of British India*, Little Brown, 1997

Kincaid, Dennis, *British Social Life in India, 1608-1937*, London, 1973

Kopperman, Paul E, *Braddock at the Monongahela*, University of Pittsburgh Press, 1977

Laffin, John, *Tommy Atkins: the Story of the English Soldier*, Cassell 1966, Sutton 2004

Latimer, Jon, *Burma: the Forgotten War*, Jon Murray, 2004

Leeke, Reverend William, *The History of Lord Seaton's Regiment, (the 52nd Light Infantry) at the Battle of Waterloo*, 2 Volumes, London 1866

Lucas, Celia, *Prisoners of Santo Tomas: Civilian Prisoners of the Japanese*, Leo Cooper 1975

MacCrory, Patrick, *Signal Catastrophe: The Retreat of 1842*, Hodder & Stoughton 1966

MacKenzie, Francis Griffiths (ed), *With Napoleon at Waterloo*, London 1911

Malcolmson RW, *Life and Labour in England 1700–1780* Hutchinson, 1981

Mason, Philip, *A Matter of Honour*, Jonathan Cape 1974

Massie, Alastair *The National Army Museum Book of The Crimean War: the Untold Stories*, Sidgwick & Jackson 2004

Meyer, Karl, *The Dust of Empire: the Race for Supremacy in the Asian Heartland*, Abacus 2004

Meyer, Karl and Brysac, Shareen, *Tournament of Shadows: The Great Game and the Race for Empire in Asia*, Abacus 1999; 2001

Moorhouse, Geoffrey, *India Britannica*, Harvill Press 1983

Napier, Colonel WFP *History of the War in the Peninsula and in the South of France, From the Year 1807 to the Year 1814*, Vol 5, London and New York: George Routledge and Sons 1878

Page, FCG, *Following the Drum: Women in Wellington's Wars*, Andre Deutsch 1986

Paget, Julian, *Last Post: Aden 1964–67*, Faber 1969

Palmer, Roy, (ed), *The Rambling Soldier*, Alan Sutton 1985

Paterson, Robert H, *Pontius Pilate's Bodyguard: A History of the First or the Royal Regiment of Foot, The Royal Scots (The Royal Regiment)*, Vols I & II, Edinburgh, 2000

Richards, DS, *The Savage Frontier: a History of the Anglo-Afghan Wars*, 1990 MacMillan

Roberts, Brian *Those Bloody Women*, John Murray 1991

Robertson, Ian C, *Wellingotn at War in the Peninsula 1808-1814*, Pen & Sword 2000

Robinson, Jane, *Angels of Albion: Women of the Indian Mutiny*, Viking, 1996; Penguin 1997

Robinson, RER *The Bloody Eleventh: A History of the Devonshire Regiment, Volume I: 1685–1815*, Exeter 1988

Rogers, HCB, *Troopships and their History*, Seeley, 1963

Royle, Trevor, *The Great Crimean War 1854–1856*, Abacus, 1999

Russell, Jack, *Gibraltar Besieged 1779–1783*, London 1965

Scouller, RE *The Armies of Queen Anne*, Oxford, Clarendon Press 1966

Scott-Daniell, David, *Cap of Honour: the Story of the Gloucestershire Regiment (the 28th/61st Foot) 1694–1950*, George G Harrap & Co, London 1951

Steele, Ian K, *Betrayals: Fort William Henry & the 'Massacre'*, OUP 1990

Stone, Lawrence, *The Family, Sex and Marriage in England 1500–1800*, Weidenfeld & Nicolson, 1977

Taylor, PJO *A Star Shall Fall, India 1857*, HarperCollins India (Indus), 1993

Tillotson, HM *With the Prince of Wales's Own 1958-1994*, Michael Russell, 1995

Trustram, Myna *Women of the Regiment: Marriage and the Victorian Army*, Cambridge University Press 1984

Turner, Sir James, *Pallas Armata, Military Essayes of the Ancient Grecian, Roman and Modern Art of War*, 1683

Usher, George, *Dictionary of British Military History*, Bloomsbury 2003

Van Creveld, Martin, *Men, Women & War: Do Women Belong in the Front Line?*, Cassell 2001

Vickery, Amanda, *The Gentleman's Daughter: Women's Lives in Georgian England*, Yale University Press, 1999

Walker, Helen, *A History of the Northumberland Fusiliers 1674–1902*

Ward, Marjorie, *The Blessed Trade*, Michael Joseph, London 1971

Warner, Lavinia and Sandilands, John, *Women Behind the Wire: a story of prisoners of the Japanese 1942–4*, Michael Joseph, London 1982

Wheelwright, Julie, *Amazons and Military Maids*, Pandora, London 1989

Wilkinson, Theon, *Two Monsoons*, Duckworth 1976

Williams, Noel St John, *Judy O'Grady & The Colonel's Lady: The Army Wife and Camp Follower Since 1660*, Brassey's Defence Publishers, London 1988

Wilson, AN, *The Victorians*, Hutchison 2002

Wood, Anthony, *Nineteenth Century Britain*, Longmans, Green and Co, 1960

Woodham-Smith, Cecil *The Reason Why*, London 1954

Yalom, Marilyn, *A History of the Wife*, HarperCollins 2001

Memoirs, Letters, Autobiographies, Biographies – Published

Albemarle, George Thomas, Earl of, *Fifty Years of My Life*, 1877 MacMillan, London

Anbury, Thomas, *With Burgoyne from Quebec: An account of the life at Quebec and of the Famous Battle at Saratoga*, Sydney Jackman (ed MacMillan, Canada, 1963). First Published as *Volume One of Travels Through the Interior Parts of North America, 1789*

Anton, James, *A Retrospect of Military Life*, W H Lizars, 1841

Bayley, Emily, Lady Clive, *The Golden Calm: An Gnelish Lady's Life in Moghul Delhi*, MM Kaye (ed), Webb & Bower, 1980

Bell, Major-General George, *Soldier's Glory: Rough Notes of an Old Soldier*, Stuart, Brian (ed), G Bell and Sons Ltd, London 1956

Blackwood, Lady Alicia, *A Narrative of Personal Experiences and Impressions During a Residence on the Bosphorous during the Crimean War*, 1881

Brett-James, *Wellington at War 1794–1815: A Selection of his Wartime Letters edited and introduced*, London 1961

Browne, Captain, *The Napoleonic War Journal of Captain Thomas Henry Browne 1807–1816*, Roger Norman Buckley, (ed) Bodley Head for the Army Records Society 1987

Buckley, Mrs (published anonymously), *Wayside Lamps*, Longmans, Green and Co 1913

Canning, Charlotte, *A Glimpse of the Burning Plain: Leaves from the Indian Journals of Charlotte Canning*, Charles Allen (ed), Michael Joseph 1986

Cecil, Hugh and Mirabel, *Imperial Marriage: an Edwardian War and Peace*, John Murray 2002

Clark, Miles, *High Endeavours: The Extraordinary Life and Adventures of Miles and Beryl Smeeton*, Greystone 1991

Cook, Dorothy VM, *I married a Soldier*, Dragon Books, 1973

Cooper, John Spencer *Rough Notes of Seven Campaigns in Portugal, Spain, France and America During the Years 1809–1815*, the Spellmount Library of Military History 1996 (First published 1869)

Costello, Edward, *The Adventures of a Soldier or Memoirs of Edward Costello, KSF, Formerly a Non-Commissioned Officer in the Rifle Brigade, and late Captain in the British Legion, Comprising Narratives of the Campaigns in the Peninsular under the Duke of Wellington and the Recent Civil Wars in Spain*, London 1852

Cunningham, John C, *The Last Man: the Life and Times of Surgeon Major William Brydon*, New Cherwell Press, 2003

Daniell, John Edgecombe, *Journal of an Officer in the Commissariat Department of the Army*, 1820

Defoe, Daniel, *Life and Adventures of Mrs Christian Davies* 1740, republished in *The Novels and Miscellaneous Works of Daniel Defoe vol VIII*, London 1840

De Fonblanque, Edward Barrington, *Political and Military Episodes in the Latter Half of the Eighteenth Century Derived from the Correspondence of The Right Hon John Burgoyne, General Statesman, Dramatist*, Macmillan and Co, 1876

De Lancey, Magdalene, *A Week at Waterloo*, 1906 in *Lady De Lancey at Waterloo*, David Miller, Spellmount, 2000

Donaldson, Joseph, *Recollections of the Eventful Life of a Soldier 1845*, Ian Fletcher (ed), Spellmount 2000

Duberly, Mrs Henry, *Journal kept during the Russian War*, 1856

Duberly, Mrs Henry, *Campaigning Experiences in Rajpootana and Central India during the Suppression of the Mutiny, 1857–8*, 1859

Dunscombe, Captain, *The Real Crimean War*, Major Colin Robins (ed), Withycut House, 2003

Eden, Emily, *Up the Country: Letters from India, 1866*; Virago 1983

Fitchett, WH (ed), *Wellington's Men: Some Autobiographies*, London 1956

Foreman Amanda, *Georgiana, Duchess of Devonshire*, HarperCollins 1998

Frazer, Colonel Sir Augustus, *Letters of Colonel Sir Augustus Simon Frazer,*

KCB, *In the Army under the Duke of Wellington, Written During the Peninsular and Waterloo Campaigns*, Major-General Edward Sabine of the Royal Artillery (ed), London 1859

Gleig, George Robert, *The Subaltern: A Chronicle of the Peninsular War, 1825*; Ian Robertson (ed), Leo Cooper, 2001

Grattan, Captain, *Adventures with the Connaught Ranges, 1809–1814*, Charles Oman (ed), London 1902; Greenhill Books 1989

Green, John, *The Vicissitudes of a Soldier's Life or a Series of Occurrences from 1806 to 1815*, Louth and London 1827

Gronow, *Reminiscences of Captain Gronow*, London 1892

Hamilton, Sergeant Anthony, *Hamilton's Campaign with Moore and Wellington During the Peninsular War*, Troy, New York 1847; London 1998

Harris, Benjamin, *The Recollections of Rifleman Harris, 1848*; Eileen Hathaway (ed), Shinglepicker 1995

Harris, Mrs Georgina, *A Lady's Diary of the Siege of Lucknow*, London 1858

Henly, Peter, *The Life of Peter Henly, otherwise Peter Robertson, of Wootton Bassett, in the County of Wilts. Containing an account of his Travels and adventures in America, the East and west Indies, & c. With the Extraordinary Circumstances which led him from a Profligate to a Pious Life. Written by Himself*, Calne, 1799. Quoted in Roy Palmer (ed), *The Rambling Soldier* Alan Sutton 1985

Hibbert, Christopher, *The Destruction of Lord Raglan*, Longmans Green, 1961

Hodge, *Little Hodge: being extracts from the letters and diaries of Colonel Edward Cooper Hodge written during the Crimean War*, Marquess of Anglesey (ed), 1971

Holmes, Richard, *Wellington: the Iron Duke*, HarperCollins 2002

Kaye MM, *The Sun in the Morning*, Viking 1990

Kaye MM, *Golden Afternoon*, Penguin 1997

Kaye MM, *Enchanted Evening*, Penguin 2000

Kincaid, Captain John, *Adventures in the Rifle Brigade*, London 1838

Kincaid, Captain John, *Random Shots from a Rifleman*, London 1835

Lamb, R (Roger), *An Original and Authentic Journal of occurrences During the Late American War, from its commencement to the year 1783*, Dublin 1809

Landmann, Colonel, *Recollections of my Military Life*, (2 vols 1854)

Le Couteur, Lieutenant John, *Merry Hearts Make Light Days: the War of 1812. Journal of Lieutenant John Le Couteur, 104th Foot*, Donald E Graves (ed), Carleton University Press, 1993

Leslie, Colonel, *Military Journal 1807–1832*

Longford, Elizabeth, *Wellington*, Weidenfeld and Nicolson, 1992

MacMullen, Sergeant J (published anonymously), *Camp and Barrack Room, or The British Army As It Is*, London 1846

Maitland, Julia (published anonymously), *Letters from Madras, During the Years 1836–1839*, 1843; Alyson Price (ed), Woodstock Books, 2003

Metcalfe, Private Henry, *The Chronicle of Private Henry Metcalfe, HM 32nd Regiment of Foot, and other particulars*, Sir Francis Tuker (ed), Cassell & Co 1953

Mole, Edwin, *A King's Hussar*, 1893, in Roy Palmer (op cit)

Napier, Sir W, *The Life and Opinions of General Sir Charles James Napier, GCB*, John Murray, 1857

Patterson Major J, *Camp and Quarters: Scenes and Impressions of Military Life* (2 vols) Saunders & Ottley, 1840

Pearman, John, *Sergeant Pearman's Memoirs, being chiefly an account of his service with the Third, King's Own, Light Dragoons in India*, the Marquess of Anglesey (ed) London 1968

Pratt, Fanny, *Exiles of Empire: Family Letters from India and Australia by Fanny and Annie Pratt 1843–1863*, Mona Macmillan and Catriona Miller (ed), Pentland Press 1997

Riedesel, Baroness, *Letters and Journals, relating to the War of the American Revolution*, New York, 1867

Robertson, FM Sir William Bt, *Private to Field Marshal*, Constable & Co Ltd 1921

Ross-Lewin, Harry, *With 'The Thirty-Second' in the Peninsular and Other Campaigns*, John Wardell (ed), Dublin, 1904

Russell-Roberts, Denis, *Spotlight on Singapore*, Times Press and Anthony Gibbs & Phillips, Great Britain, 1965

Sainsbury, Major H, *A Retrospect of Interesting Events in the 32nd Light Infantry, later, 1st Battn. Duke of Cornwall's Light Infantry*, 1931

Sale, Lady Florentia, *A Journal of the Disasters in Afghanistan: a Firsthand Account by One of the Few Survivors, 1843*; Tantallon Press, Tenessee, 2002)

Schaumann, August Ludolf Friedrich, *On the Road with Wellington The Diary of a War Commissary in the Peninsular Campaigns*, translated and edited by Anthony M Ludovici, London 1924

Sherer, Moyle *Recollections of the Peninsula*, Spellmount 1996 (first published 1824)

Sherwood, Mrs Mary, *The Life of Mrs Sherwood*, Sophia Kelly (ed), London 1854

Shipp, John, *Memoirs of the Extraordinary Military Career of John Shipp*, London 1830

Smith, Sir Harry, *The Autobiography of Sir Harry Smith*, GC Moore-Smith (ed), 1910

Steevens, Lieut Col Charles, *Reminiscences of My Military Life, From 1795 to 1818*, Lieut-Col Nathaniel Steevens (ed), Winchester 1878

Stephens, Matthew, Hannah Snell: *The Secret Life of a Female Marine 1723–1792*, Ship Street Press 1997

Surtees, William, *Twenty-Five Years in the Rifle Brigade by the Late William Surtees, Quartermaster*, Edinburgh and London, 1833

Terrot, Nurse Sarah Anne, *With Florence Nightingale at Scutari*, Robert G Richardson (ed), John Murray, 1977

Thomas Donald, *Cardigan: A Life of Lord Cardigan of Balaclava*, Cassell & Co 1974

Tisdall, EEP, *Mrs Duberly's Campaigns*, McNally, USA 1963

Todd, Corporal, *The Journal of Corporal William Todd 1745–1762*, transcribed 1775–76

Andrew Cormack and Alan Jones (ed), Army Records Society/Sutton Publishing 2001

Tomkinson, Lieut-Col, *Diary of a Cavalry Officer in the Peninsular War and Waterloo Campaign 1809–1815*, 1894 James Tomkinson (ed), London 1971

Tytler, *An Englishwoman in India, The Memoirs of Harriet Tytler 1828–1858*, Anthony Sattin (ed), OUP 1986

Villiers-Stuart, WC, Maxwell, RM, *Villiers-Stuart Goes To War, 1914–1924*, London 1989

Walker, General Sir Walter, *Fighting On*, New Millennium 1997

Wallace-Dunlop, Madeline and Rosalind (published anonymously, 'by Two Sisters'), *The Timely Retreat; or, A Year in Bengal Before the Mutinies*, London 1858

Waldie, Charlotte (later Eaton), *The days of battle; or Quatre Bras and Waterloo, by an Englishwoman resident at Brussels in June, 1815*, London 1864

Ward, Marjorie, *The Blessed Trade*, Michael Joseph, 1971

Warry, Nan, *In the Shade of the Mango Tree*, Square One Publications, 1990

Wheeler, Private William, *The Letters of Private Wheeler, 1808–1828*, B Liddell Hart (ed), Adlestrop, 1951

Woodberry, Lieutenant, *Campagnes de Portugal et d'Espagne, de France, de Belgique et de France (1813–1815)* Traduit de L'Anglais Par Georges Helié, Paris 1896

Memoirs, Journals and Letters – Unpublished

Barton, Ruth, Memoir of life in India, CSAS

Bayley, Mrs B, [MS] Memoir of ten years in India as an Army wife, Bayley Papers, CSAS

Brydon, Mrs Colina, *Diary*, [MS] [PC], by kind permission of Mr D Atkin-Berry and family

Codrington, Major General Sir William, Letters from the Crimea, NAM 1978–08–90

Egerton, Barbara, *Triangle for Home*, [TS], by kind permission of her daughter, Mrs Philippa Szymusik

Ellis, Molly [PC] (by kind permission of her son, Colonel Peter Wade)

Includes: letters written and received by Molly Ellis during and shortly after her captivity

Molly Ellis's signed statement

Contemporary newspaper reports

Lilian Starr's account of her rescue mission

Background to The Bosti Khal Outlaws and Kidnapping of Miss Molly Ellis 1923 *in History 53rd Sikhs (3rd Royal Frontier Force Regt), The 3rd Sikhs on the Frontier 1921/23*

Forrest, Major William, Letters from the Crimea, NAM 6309/5/1–2

Green, Mrs Miriam, *Diary of Siege of Gibraltar*, 1779–1781, [MS], by kind permission of Royal Engineers Museum

Hannay, Margaret, *Journal* [MS], by kind permission of The Gurkha Museum

Ilbert, Mrs Courtenay, *Voyage to Quebec*, [MS], RAHT Papers, MD 2627

Llewellyn, Lt Richard, *winter Sketches from the Crimea 1854–1855*, [MS] DCLI

Macleod, Mrs C C, *Leaves from the Diary of an Officer's Wife*, 1922, RAHT Papers MD1150/15

Mill, Maria, *A Personal Journal of the Mutiny in India in 1857*, Mill Papers, CSAS

Monckton, Rosa, *Letters home from India*, Monckton Papers, CSAS

Money, Mrs Grule, *Diary of travels around India*, 1889 [MS], by kind permission of The Gurkha Museum

Montgomery, Rosemary, Letters home from India, Montgomery Papers, CSAS

Murison, Margaret, Memoir, printed 1969, Murison Papers, CSAS

Portal, Iris, *Song at Seventy* (Typescript Memoir), Portal Papers, CSAS

Rose, Lance Corporal AW, *The Diary of 2874, His Experiences in the South African War*, DCLI Museum, 1901

Templer, Angela M, *Account of her Internment in Santo Tomas University and*

Los Banos Camps by the Japanese, March 1942 to February 1945, from a Lecture to the Conservative Association, Crediton, February 1978 RAHT papers MD 1649/4

Templer, Brigadier CR DSO, *Article about a 'friend' who received the USA Asiatic Pacific Campaign Medal*, private papers of Brigadier CR Templer DSO, RAHT, MD 1649/4

Venning, Lucy and Esmond, Letters, [PC]

Viner, Bette, *Diary* [TS] [PC], by kind permission of her son Richard Viner

Walker, Beryl, *Following the Drum*, memoir of last days in India, MS [PC]

Webber Harris, Mrs Elizabeth, *Recollection*, by kind permission of the Man family [PC]

Wells, Frances Janet, *Letters home from India*, Berners Papers, CSAS archive, Cambridge

Articles – Newspapers and Peridocals

AFF Families Journal (various issues, 2000–2004)

Bowyer-Bower, Major TA, *The Presence of Women and Children in Tangiers*, JSAHR, Vol 33 1955

Cohn, Michael, *Evidence of Children at Revolutionary War Sites*, paper published by Brooklyn Children's Museum NAM 8312–23

Dashwood, Arthur, letter to *The Listener* magazine, 2 December 1930

Davies, Godfrey, *Recruiting in the Reign of Queen Anne*, JSAHR, Vol 28 1950

Dickens, Charles (ed), *Chips: Soldiers' Wives* in *Household Words*, Volume 9, Leipzig 1851

Hargreaves, Major Reginald MC, *'Good-Natured Billy'*, Army Quarterly, Vol 93 January 1967

Kirwin, Margaret, interview in *Ours, The Greens Howards' Gazette*, Volume IV, no 43, October 1896

Kopperman, Paul E, The British High Command and Soldiers' Wives in America, 1755–1783, JSAHR, Spring 1982

Little, Penny, in *The Sirmooree*, Number 29, Summer 2002

Obituary of Brigadier Bob Templer, *Gunner Magazine*, May 1986

Spencer, Major HAV, Families of the 14th Regiment of Foot 1794-1831, *The White Rose* (regimental Journal of the Prince of Wales's Own Regiment of Yorkshire) Volume 18, August 1976 No 3

Soldiers' Wives, Chips, *Household Words*, Volume 9, Charles Dickens (ed), Leipzig 1851

Ubique, The Monthly magazine of the 23rd Field Brigade RA, January 1925
The War Correspondent, Journal of the Crimean War Research Society, Vol
   20 no 3 October 2002

Emmett-Dunne Case reports
Daily Mail 5 July 1955
Sunday People, 10 July 1955
News of the World, 10 July 1955
Empire News, 31 July 1955

Reports, Publications and Official Documents
An Act Enabling Wives and Families of Soldiers to return to their Homes,
   1818, courtesy of Amgueddfa, the Royal Welch Fusiliers Regimental
   Museum
Artillery Records Volume II – Regimental Intelligence, RAHT
Certificate to be delivered to the Wife or Widow of a Solider when sent
   to her home; under the Royal Warrant of the 1st July 1848, RAHT
Chief of the General Staff's Message to the Army Implementing the Future
   Army Structure, 16 December 2003
Extract from Chelsea Admission Roll of 18th November 1717, by kind
   permission of Royal Hospital Chelsea
Families' Continuous Attitude Survey by AFF Families Journal, sent out to
   a 10% random selection of Army spouses in November 2003, with response
   rate of 32%. Findings published in AFF Families Journal June 2004
Families' Concerns 2002 (report by AFF)
Changing Attitudes Survey 2000–2001 (report by AFF and SSAFA Forces
   Help)
The Gaffney Report: *The Army Wives Study: the Report. Part 1: the Findings*,
   by Colonel and Mrs Gaffney, Ministry of Defence, June 1986
Handbook of the 5th Annual Conference of the Federation of Army Wives,
   UKLF, 1987
Health Memoranda for the Wives and Children of British Soldiers in India,
   Government Central Press, Simla 1921, RAHT, Papers MD3156/6
Madras Artillery Records, Proceedings Special Board of Artillery officers'
   correspondence, Vol 2, RAHT Papers
Ministry of Defence website
Operations in Iraq: Lessons for the Future, Ministry of Defence July 2003,
   www.mod.uk

Report on General Meeting, July 30th 1858, *The Soldiers' Daughters' Home in Hampstead for the Maintenance, Clothing and education of the Daughters of Soldiers, Orphans or Not*, RAHT Papers

Regulations Affecting Non-Commissioned Officers' and Soldiers' wives, Considered with Reference to the Army Ordered to Turkey, by Major Cartan, London 1854, RAHT Papers

Review by Lieutenant Colonel G Williams, Commissioner of Military Police, North west Provinces, of the evidence taken at Cawnpore regarding the revolt at that station in June and July 1857, Allahabad 31 December 1859

Queen's Regulations and Orders for the Army, 1844, 1857

Regimental Orders of Royal North British Dragoons, Gronenberg, 29 May 1759

Return showing the Number of Married Women belonging to each of the Regiments ordered on Foreign Service, specifying the Number permitted to Reside with their Husbands in Barracks, and the Number of Soldiers' Children', Parliamentary Paper, NAM 8211–16–4

Review of the Evidence taken at Cawnpore regarding the revolt at that station in June and July 1857, by Lieutenant Colonel G Williams, Commissioner of Military Police, North West Provinces, Allahabad 31 December 1859, OIOC

Standing Orders of:

29th Regiment, 1852, Worcestershire Regiment Museum Trust

29th Regiment, 1863, Worcestershire Regiment Museum Trust

29th Regiment, 1862, Worcestershire Regiment Museum Trust

36th (the Herefordshire) Regiment, 1829, Worcestershire Regiment Museum Trust

1st Battalion, the Worcestershire Regiment, 1890, Worcestershire Regiment Museum Trust.

68th Light Infantry, 1875, Durham Light Infantry Museum

106th Light Infantry, Durham Light Infantry Museum

2nd Battalion the Durham Light Infantry, 1907, Durham Light Infantry Museum

2nd Battalion the Durham Light Infantry, 1891, Durham Light Infantry Museum

13th Light Infantry 1831, Somerset Military Museum Trust

13th or Prince Albert's Light Infantry, 1845, Somerset Military Museum Trust

13th Light Infantry, 1859, Somerset Military Museum Trust

Third Report of the Central Association in Aid of the Wives and Families of Soldiers

Ordered on Active Service, 7th March, 1856, RAHT Papers

Two pamphlets concerning pensions and annuities for the widows of Royal Artillery officers, RAHT Papers

Wives Punishment Book of 82nd Foot, 1866–1890, Museum of the Queen's Lancashire Regiment

Wives Punishment Book of 78th Highlanders 1880, Museum of the Queen's Own Highlanders, Inverness

Court Records of General Courts Martial (held at National Archives):

Fisher Case, 27th February 1778, WO 71/85

Frazer Case, 25th April 1763, WO 71/93

Golougher Case, 8th August 1774 – August 1775, WO 71 80

Lindon Case, 19th February 1781, WO 71/93

McCowen Case, 15th and 16th June 1778, WO 71/83

McGuire Case, February 19th 1781 WO 71/93

Norrington Case, 28th July 1776, WO 71/82

Interviews:

Rose and Tommy Atkins

Chrissie Collis

Melissa Cordingly

Dona Dales

Valerie Fagg

Daphne Hill

Elizabeth Howlett

Sara Jones

Lizzie Iron

Midge Lackie

Peggy Pusinelli

Deborah Richards

Marion Rickman

Samantha Roberts

Cecilia Ross-Hurst

Amanda Taylor

Tor Walker

Marion Weston

Fiction

William Thackeray, *Vanity Fair: A Novel without a Hero*, London 1848

Jane Austen, *Pride and Prejudice*, London 1813

Thomas Hardy, *Far From the Madding Crowd*, London 1874

Picture Credits

Plate section one

p. 1 (bottom) – Courtesy of the Director, National Army Museum, London

p. 2 (top) – Courtesy of the Director, National Army Museum, London

p. 4 – Courtesy of the Director, National Army Museum, London

p. 5 (bottom) – Courtesy of the Director, National Army Museum, London

p. 6 (bottom) – Worcestershire Regiment Museum

Plate section two

p. 1 (top) – Courtesy of the Director, National Army Museum, London

p. 1 (bottom) – Courtesy of the Director, National Army Museum, London

p. 2 (top) – Courtesy of the Director, National Army Museum, London

p. 2 (bottom) – Courtesy of the Director, National Army Museum, London

p. 3 (top) – Home, c. 1856 (oil on panel), Paton, Sir Joseph Noel (1821–1901)/Private Collection, The Fine Art Society, London, UK/www.bridgeman.co.uk

p. 3 (bottom) – Courtesy of the Director, National Army Museum, London

pp. 4–5 – Courtesy of the Director, National Army Museum, London

p. 6 – National Portrait Gallery, London

p. 7 (top) – Lady Harriet Acland during the American War of Independence by Robert Pollard, Killerton House (The National Trust)

p. 7 (bottom) – Courtesy of the Director, National Army Museum, London

p. 8 – Before Waterloo (oil on canvas) (see also 65297), O'Neil, Henry Nelson (1817–80)/Mallett & Son Antiques Ltd, London, UK/www.bridgeman.co.uk

Index